Magazine and Feature Writing

Hiley H. Ward
Temple University

Mayfield Publishing Company
Mountain View, California
London • Toronto

To Joan Bastel

Library of Congress Cataloging-in-Publication Data

Ward, Hiley H.
    Magazine and feature writing / Hiley H. Ward.
        p.   cm.
    Includes index.
    ISBN 1-55934-086-X
    1. Feature writing.   2. Journalism — Authorship.   I. Title.
PN4784.F37W37   1992
808'.02 — dc20   92-15674
                                                              CIP

Manufactured in the United States of America
10 9 8 7 6 5 4 3 2

Mayfield Publishing Company
1240 Villa Street
Mountain View, California 94041

Sponsoring editor, Lansing Hays; production editor, Sharon Montooth; manuscript editor, Joan Pendleton; text designer, Jean Mailander; cover designer, Terry Wright. The text was set in 10½ × 12 Janson by TypeLink, Inc. and printed on 50# Finch Opaque by Malloy Lithographing.

Magazine and Feature Writing

Preface

This book is a comprehensive, practical and positive approach to writing newspaper features and magazine articles. The emphasis is on writing and learning to publish from the outset. Why write, if not to publish? Throughout this text, the published work of students and professionals is used to illustrate how to plan, organize and write all manner of articles. With initiative, planning, common sense and hard work, students can see their class assignments published.

I have been teaching nonfiction writing classes to undergraduates and graduates for 18 years and have never found a textbook that adequately covered both trends and current, practical issues as well as the basic writing skills necessary to write excellent magazine and feature articles. I hope study and discussion of this variety of subjects will open more opportunities for students to publish.

Chapter 1 acquaints students with the places they might publish their work and the trends that affect those markets. Chapters 2 through 5 cover pertinent writing-related skills such as querying, researching, anecdote-writing and interviewing. Chapters 6 through 13 put students to work on the major types of articles and genres found in feature writing: there is emphasis on the profile, how-to, in-depth and investigative article as well as coverage of columns, genre writing and business and trade writing. Finally, Chapters 14 and 15 round out the book with complete chapters on ethics and legal issues.

The book draws constantly on the interviews, remarks and reports of leading editors and writers from all journalistic backgrounds: you will find that helpful comments come from editors at small specialty publications as well as from people at *Esquire* and *Vanity Fair*. Throughout, I have attempted to cover topics extensively and to present a diversity of expert opinions that not only are informative but also will lead to classroom discussion. In discussion questions and project suggestions following each chapter, students are encouraged to put their reading to work.

This book declines to categorize magazine and feature article writing as expository, argumentative or narrative, or as informative, descriptive or personal. In fact, most articles are a blend of information, description, subjective material, advocacy and storytelling. Much of article writing is an integration of techniques, not a separation of disciplines. I hope that the student writer or new graduate trying to publish newspaper features and magazine articles sees the task as organic, as creating a unified, well-crafted whole.

Acknowledgments

Without mentioning them one by one, I would like to acknowledge with appreciation the editors and writers whose names and advice are sprinkled throughout this book. Information was gathered directly from the persons mentioned, unless indicated otherwise. Readers will undoubtedly notice here and there the names of editors who no longer hold the titles given in this book. High mobility is part of the publishing scene, and no textbook can keep up with changing assignments and positions. Suffice it to say that in most cases the persons quoted gave the remarks while in the positions mentioned.

I am grateful to my wife, Joan Bastel, managing editor of the Doylestown (Pa.) *Intelligencer*, and to Joan Pendleton, manuscript editor, both of whom gave the manuscript a judicious reading. I am appreciative too of the American Society of Magazine Editors and the American Society of Journalists and Authors, many of whose members are represented in these pages.

I would also like to thank those reviewers who have taken the time from their busy schedules to offer their counsel regarding the content of this book: Brenda Payton, San Francisco State University; Abe Peck, Northwestern University; and David Sumner, Ball State University.

Contents

Writing to Publish

If you're reading this book, you've probably decided on a journalism career. In other words, you don't want just to write, you want to publish what you write as well. Even though your main job might be writing hard news, you will still need to know how to write newspaper features and magazine articles. Most professional writers — working for newspapers, magazines, even public relations firms and corporations — need these skills. Besides, there can be extra dollars in turning out extra feature and magazine pieces.

This book's focus will be on the approaches to take, the methods to use and the development of style in order to publish magazine and newspaper feature articles. This chapter starts by making distinctions between features and hard news and between magazine and newspaper features. Then comes a broad look at the markets and trends in publishing today.

FEATURES VS. HARD NEWS

Newspaper feature articles and magazine articles normally differ from standard news articles. Traditionally, the hard or breaking news report in newspapers has the most important information at the top, characterized by the five W's—who, what, when, where, why, plus how, with information given in descending order of importance. Sometimes, as you know, all of the five W's are packed into the lead paragraph, or at least the most important facts come first.

Although some feature stories look like hard news stories, a feature story for newspapers often has a softer, "walk-in" approach. Certainly, all features—and magazine articles—as well as news stories should let you know very quickly what is going on and what the article is about.

Ways that feature and magazine articles may differ from hard news include:

- *An emphasis on anecdotes and case histories*, telling stories and describing episodes in someone's life.
- *Detailed description of setting and place.*
- *A narrative, story-telling style.*
- *A softer lead*, perhaps a description, anecdote or story that doesn't long delay letting the reader know what the article is about.
- *A wider time frame*, because features and magazine articles are usually written not for the next daily edition but for a later time.
- *An in-depth approach*, allowed partly because of having (1) more time to develop sources and search out information and (2) more space than is allowed for normal news articles.
- *A sense of unity*, usually achieved by developing an overriding theme that holds the material together.
- *A different sense of organization*. Features and magazine articles often develop complete sections before moving on to the next phase. You will more likely have "chunks" of writing tied together (more about this later) rather than a descending, linear development of information.
- *A people orientation*. The reader gets to know character traits and sees people in action.

MAGAZINE ARTICLES VS. NEWSPAPER FEATURES

Although a distinction between hard newswriting and feature/magazine writing can be made, newspaper features and magazine articles are very much alike. If you mixed up a batch of newspaper features and magazine articles and drew them out of a box at random, it could be hard to tell which ones appeared where, especially if you read the text alone and can't see pictures or layout. (Newspaper features are traditionally printed in narrow columns; magazine articles have wider columns, perhaps full page width, and use pictures and display elements, stretching over a group of pages.)

Point of View

On the other hand, whether a story will be published in a newspaper or magazine frequently determines the point of view from which it can be told. Feature articles in newspapers are usually more objective and are "told" or presented through the third-person point of view — "he," "she" or "it." For example, "John Jones climbed to the podium. His lips quivered. He was going to change his speech and say what he wanted to say all along. . . ."

In contrast, magazine articles — especially in the slick national magazines — are often written in the first person, using the word "I." For example, in a magazine, you might read: "I climbed to the podium. I felt my lips quivering. I was going to change my speech and say what I wanted to say all along."

The use of "I" signals a more leisurely and intimate approach than does the more matter-of-fact third person used in newspapers. Using "I" provides the reader with the sense that a friend — or a personal authority — is talking. We talk further about point of view and the more elusive subject of "voice" later.

Writers

News and news feature articles are likely to be written by full-time staff reporters working on many things at once, facing hourly and daily deadlines. Even staffers who write exclusively features work on short deadlines.

Magazine writers may take considerably more time to produce an article. They are likely to be free-lancers, not on staff, although a free-lance writer may hold down another job. Indeed, middle-rank magazine and newspaper feature editors form a sizable group of free-lancers, writing for publications other than their own.

The newspaper feature writer may be a jack-of-all-trades, while the successful magazine free-lance writer frequently develops specialties and writes primarily about those.

The extra time a magazine writer has to prepare an article permits more extended research, but deadlines still remain. A magazine writer also must take into account the lapse of time before the article appears. Although a newspaper might want an article on a 110-year-old man, magazines probably won't risk his surviving until the article can appear. The magazine might want the writer to take a wider look — how people live to be 100, for instance; and if the writer focuses on a 110-year-old, the idea still works whether he is alive or not when the article appears.

SELLING: THE NAME OF THE GAME

Even when you're still a student and just beginning a writing career, write for publication and get paid. Getting published gives you a track record that can lead to important contacts for future articles and also strengthens a résumé for full-time job applications.

Knowing the Markets

If you want to publish nonfiction, you must target your articles to the right magazine or paper. You need to study the publication before you write, primarily to understand the audience. You need to know just who the reader will be; what has been published already; what the taboos are; what standard lengths are for articles in that publication. You need to determine the predominant emphasis — whether fashion or racing cars; the style — whether prosaic, clipped, literary, poetical or hard news; the usual point of view and voice; art and photo use; humor or lack of humor, and so on.

What you propose to write might be far off target if you don't take a close look at the proposed outlet for your article before you even write your query letter. (See Chapter 2 for more on getting started.)

Targeting a Newspaper

Your news feature may be aimed at the local newspaper you have been reading for years. Or you might decide to write a sectional or regional feature on a local industry or politician for a national newspaper (such as *USA Today*, the Washington *Post*, the New York *Times*).

If you're going to be a regular, but non-staff, writer — sometimes called a stringer — you'll need to get on an approved list at the newspaper. For a large newspaper, write to the national desk of the newspaper. Send a résumé and any relevant clippings of articles you produced locally. Present three or four of your best ideas. Remember, the large national newspapers and the news magazines cover big metropolitan areas by using moonlighting reporters from major newspapers in those areas. You have a better chance of being a stringer if you come from a small, out-of-the-way community.

"Hub" newspapers also offer possibilities. These newspapers in the state capital or the biggest city in the state are usually unionized; contracts require that most of the articles be written by staffers, but the papers do have sections on travel, lifestyle, people, sports and food as well as a Sunday magazine. These may be open to free-lancers.

Articles for local papers don't always have to deal exclusively with local situations, but ideally there should be local people in them. If you write about skiing areas up north, talk to people from the paper's circulation area who are staying in the region's lodges. That makes your article more appropriate for local consumption. Suppose you're going to a popular resort in the Caribbean and want to write about it. Find other visitors or transplants from your area and describe what they are doing. Tell the story through local eyes.

You may want to talk to a newspaper editor directly, because mail inquiries to newspapers can get shuffled aside. If you want to discuss a possible feature by phone or in person, call ahead and find out what time of day or week is most convenient. Try to have an idea you feel an editor can't refuse and also a backup idea, in the event the editor does refuse. If both ideas are rejected, don't cut off the conversation without asking for the editor's suggestions about stories you could write.

Make sure you know whom to contact. The *Editor & Publisher Yearbook* lists all newspapers in the United States and Canada, with names to contact. For the dailies, the yearbook lists every editor of any rank and with any speciality. You would probably want to contact the features editor or Sunday magazine editor. *Editor & Publisher* (11 W. 19th St., New York, NY 10011) also puts out an annual *Syndicate Directory* with listings for syndicates and services that produce and buy articles for distributing to media clients. An article sold to a syndicate might appear in a number — even hundreds — of newspapers.

Targeting a Magazine

Writing for magazines requires more research into your target publication. Chances are that you have heard of the magazine but have not seen it regularly. You need intimate, firsthand, up-to-date knowledge.

The topic you select could determine the magazine or genre of magazines you write for. If you write about guns, you need to find a gun magazine; if it's dieting, then a food, women's or general magazine; tennis, a tennis or sports magazine; and so on. But which particular publication?

Wander into a store that has an extensive magazine rack. See what is being published. Flip through the pages of magazines that cover your area of interest. Get the name of the editor.

Another way to find a good place to publish your story is to consult the listings in the directories. Perhaps the best for all practical purposes is *Writer's Market*, a Writer's Digest book, published by F&W Publications, 1507 Dana Ave., Cincinnati, OH 45207. Here magazines are listed and described by categories, which include Animal, Aviation, Business, Entertainment, Food, Games, History, Hobbies, Humor, Juvenile, Men's, Religious, Retirement, Sports, Teen and Young Adult, Travel, Women's, and so on. If you don't find a category of magazines to match your subject, check the index. Perhaps your idea on "20 Ways to Display Your Gun Collection" will work for *Gun World*, which *Writer's Market* describes this way:

GUN WORLD:

34249 Camino Capistrano, Box HH, Capistrano Beach CA 92624. Editorial Director: Jack Lewis. 50% freelance written. For ages that "range from mid-teens to mid-60s; many professional types who are interested in relaxation of hunting and shooting." Monthly. Circ. 136,000. Buys 80-100 unsolicited mss/year. Pays on acceptance. Publishes ms an average of 6 months after acceptance. Buys first rights. Byline given. Submit seasonal material 4 months in advance. Reports in 6 weeks. Computer printout submissions acceptable; prefers letter-quality to dot-matrix. Copy of editorial requirements for SASE.

continued

continued

Nonfiction and Photos: General subject matter consists of "well-rounded articles—not by amateurs—on shooting techniques, with anecdotes; hunting stories with tips and knowledge integrated. No poems or fiction. We like broad humor in our articles, so long as it does not reflect upon firearms safety. Most arms magazines are pretty deadly and we feel shooting can be fun. Too much material aimed at pro-gun people. Most of this is staff-written and most shooters don't have to be told of their rights under the Constitution. We want articles on new developments; off-track inventions, novel military uses of arms; police armament and training techniques; do-it-yourself projects in this field." Buys informational, how-to, personal experience and nostalgia articles. Pays up to $300, sometimes more. Purchases photos with mss and captions required. Wants 5 × 7 b&w photos. Sometimes pays the expenses of writers on assignment.

Tips: "The most frequent mistake made by writers in completing an article for us is surface writing with no real knowledge of the subject. To break in, offer an anecdote having to do with proposed copy."[1]

If you don't think your article will work for *Gun World*, you can consider *American Handgunner, The American Shotgunner, Firepower, Gun Digest, Shotgun Sports, S.W.A.T., Special Weapons and Tactics*, plus a host of hunting and game magazines under the sports subhead: "Hunting and Fishing."

Other publication directories to consult include *The National Directory of Magazines*, the Library of Congress *Union List of Serials, Gale Directory of Publications* and *Ayer Directory of Publications*. The *Magazine Industry Market Place* is a good source of names and phone numbers, but it is not published every year. *The Writer's Handbook* (published by Writer, Inc.) combines articles and listings.

A new, little-known directory, the *All-in-One Directory*, published by the Gebbie Press, with Amalia Gebbie as editor and publisher, offers listings for daily and weekly newspapers, general and consumer magazines and business papers; for the trade press, black press and Hispanic press; for farm publications; and for news syndicates. It includes editors' names, addresses, phones, circulation and a statement of purpose of the publication.

To become familiar with a magazine, editors recommend you look over a year of copies. You may need to visit a library to find back copies, but it would be worth your while. Reading through a year's worth of issues means you're not likely to submit an article proposal that would be of little interest to a magazine's readers. Looking back over a number of issues also tells you if your idea has been used.

1. Glenda Tennant Neff, editor, 1991 *Writer's Market* (Cincinnati: F&W Publications, 1990), p. 548.

If you want to be absolutely up-to-date on the needs of a magazine, call the magazine. Ask who is editor as of that day, or who is the feature articles editor, or who heads a special section for which you want to write. Make sure you address your queries to the correct editor — to the extent that's possible. Ask for the latest guidelines spelling out current needs. Many publications are happy to provide these, sometimes along with free copies of the magazine.

UNDERSTANDING TRENDS

Although newspapers and magazines appear constant from week to week, subtle changes take place. An editor moves on, and a new design or format emerges; the audience shifts (in age or lifestyle); a merger occurs. What the magazine needs from writers also changes. Writers have to pay attention to the style, design and substance of a publication and to how those might change in the future.

Newspaper Magazines and City Magazines

The feature sections of newspapers are eliminating stereotyped categories. Fewer papers have exclusively women's sections. Today these sections have names such as Emphasis, Accent or Living; the features and columns are aimed at a wide audience. This new type of feature section emphasizes service to readers; and the "how-to" — how to do something, how to fix something — is as likely to be found in a newspaper as in a magazine. Other traditional sections, such as food and real estate, supported by advertising, continue.

A good place to break into feature writing on a major newspaper is in the neighborhood sections. Papers such as the Philadelphia *Inquirer* print neighborhood tabloids twice a week; the features and sports vary with each suburb. These sections, inserted into the main paper, offer good outlets for beginners. One university student sold articles she wrote in her first reporting class to one of the *Inquirer* neighborhood sections.

Some Sunday editions of newspapers include magazine inserts. The San Francisco *Chronicle* and *Examiner*, now jointly owned, publish a combined Sunday paper with a variety of magazine sections. The *Chronicle* has its imprint on *This World*, a tabloid dealing with issues and people at large; *Sunday Punch*, a broadsheet insert section with editorials, columns, humor and lighter pieces; a *Review* section on books and the arts; *Datebook*, dealing mostly with TV and films. The *Examiner* inserts a smaller, slickly designed *Image* magazine billed as the "Magazine of Northern California." Newspapers are rethinking their Sunday magazines because nationally syndicated Sunday newspaper magazines, such as *Parade* and *USA Weekend*, are increasingly competing for the advertising dollar.

As a result, the content in some newspaper magazines is softening. Some of the change can be attributed to the influence of television and the lighter, short-formula approach of the national *USA Today*. Service articles have become important, and the threat of libel suits and lack of reader interest in lengthy pieces frequently mitigate against an in-depth investigative effort.

A few newspapers see in-depth articles as necessary to the future of their magazines. Diane Carman says the *Plain Dealer Magazine*, which she edits in Cleveland, "will continue to move in the direction of more in-depth, sophisticated journalism or it will fold. There is no in-between."

Because it doesn't have a daily newspaper to fall back on, the city magazine may be more likely to use in-depth and/or investigative articles (although they are often staff-written) than is a Sunday newspaper magazine. Monthly deadlines and inability to publish every day perhaps also contribute to the longer look.

Among those city magazine editors using more in-depth pieces than they did five years ago is James D. Selk, editor and publisher of *Madison* (Wis.) magazine: "We are using more in-depth/investigative stories because they are more interesting and attract more readers. Also, they are more fun to do." He says he tries to run one in-depth story in each issue, along with one personality profile, an entertainment guide and a restaurant guide.

Among newspapers, Melissa Hovette, editor of the *Dallas Life* magazine of the Dallas *Morning News*, found her publication using more in-depth pieces "because I felt there was a gap in our paper for that sort of material; however, we constantly work at maintaining a solid mix of stories, and every magazine includes a home and design feature, a food page and a 'new products and services' spread. Readers consistently respond favorably to some of our most demanding pieces."

Alan Borsuk, who edits *Wisconsin*, the Milwaukee *Journal* magazine, says his general interest magazine "looks for a wide range of stories that will interest a wide range of people. Our focus is very strongly on the state of Wisconsin." He expects circulation to be "fairly steady" in the future and adds, "I expect we'll continue to be committed to putting out a punchy Sunday magazine."

City and regional magazines are often aimed at the more affluent, the middle class and up. Hillel Levin, editor of *Chicago* magazine, says his audience is "upscale, college-educated, culturally oriented; average age is 44 and growing younger." When he was editor of *Philadelphia* magazine, Ron Javers said he aimed to "cover the town, all aspects, for the intelligent reader."

Despite access to top writers on their newspaper staffs, the big-city newspaper magazines use a mix of staff and free-lance writers. The prestigious *New York Times Magazine* uses half staffers and half free-lancers, the magazine's editor James Lloyd Greenfield told a session of the American Society of Journalists and Authors just before his retirement in 1990.

One newer regional magazine, *Midwest Living*, a glossy bimonthly produced by the publishers of *Better Homes and Gardens*, is slanted toward strictly a Midwest audience, with articles on places to visit, regional recipes, garden advice. The premiere issue profiled 15 little-known Midwest state parks, contained a guide to weekending in Cincinnati and described a tour of houses in St. Louis' Lafayette Square.

Mark Powelson, editor and associate publisher of San Francisco's *Focus* magazine, serving the 11-county Bay region, notes "the audience is older, upscale, 48 and up, highly educated. We do what most city magazines do — an editorial mix: ready service, arts, entertainment, fashion, food; but we also do some occasional reportage." He notes a trend toward sophisticated design. "Illustrations are definitely coming back." His magazine also includes short fiction: "A new generation of magazines is developing, influenced by *Vanity Fair* [an upscale, sophisticated magazine revived recently]. People are more design-oriented." The "post-modern movement," Powelson says, has brought a design consciousness to everything, from color schemes on radios to self-conscious landscape design.

American Express started to buy city magazines in its effort to develop magazines in the top 20 markets in the country, but the recession of the early 1990s slowed its effort. In 1990, American Express acquired Southwest Media Corporation, which publishes *D.* magazine for the Dallas–Fort Worth area. The company had already taken over *New York Woman*, *L.A. Style* and *Atlanta*. American Express also launched *Connections* for college students and *Departures* for the affluent reader. Using its database of 34.1 million American Express cardholders, American Express can formulate circulation lists along lines of specialized interests.

Los Angeles, one of the more prosperous as well as populous areas, saw the advent of yet another city-area magazine in the fall of 1990 — *Buzz, The Talk of Los Angeles*, which its developer, Eden Collingsworth, said would emphasize business, science and the arts and which would compete against *Los Angeles*, *Exposure*, *L.A. Style* and the regional *California* (formerly *New West*) and free publications such as *In Beverly Hills*, *Angeles* and *L.A. West*.

However, the 15-year-old *California* found the competition — and the recession — too much and ceased publication. *Buzz* itself suspended publication after a few months but promised to emerge again as a bimonthly. *Exposure* also shut down. Also perishing at the start of the 1990s were *Washington Dossier*, a District of Columbia monthly dealing with political figures and socialites, and its competition *Regardie*.

A *Folio* magazine writer wondered if the local newspaper magazine, with its backing and support as a part of the newspaper, was better able to withstand the wiles of a sagging economy and an advertising dip than were city and regional magazines. Yet both newspaper and city or regional magazines are losing advertising. In the *Folio* article, Tony Silber cites a *Media Industry Newsletter* report revealing that 28 out of 45 city and regional magazines had ad page decreases from 1989 to 1990. Fifteen of these had drops of 10 percent or more.[2]

Who's going to win out, local newspaper supplements or the city and regional magazines? It depends whom you talk to. Silber quotes, on the one

2. Tony Silber, "Are Sunday Supplements Bad News for Regionals?" *Folio*, July 1, 1991, p. 52.

hand, Fred Mann, editor of the Philadelphia *Inquirer*'s *Inquirer Magazine*, who believes independent local Sunday magazines have a future despite recent setbacks. Said Mann: "It's a whole different ball game if you do it right. The formula is to stand out. Local Sunday magazines have huge circulations and don't have to sell themselves on the newsstand, so they don't have to put out stories on the best cheesecakes. You can play off the news. What the newspaper magazine is doing is giving readers an added bonus."

But Silber adds a quote from Ron Javers, who at the time was editor of *Philadelphia* magazine. According to Javers, "Those Sunday supplements are awful things. They're where they put the reporters who write real long and real dumb. They're like the isolation wards of newspapers."[3]

The *Inquirer*'s Fred Mann was less optimistic when addressing a fraternity of his colleagues. In *Style*, a journal of the American Association of Sunday and Feature Editors, he reported that from 1988 to 1991 attendance at the annual Sunday Magazine Editors Association meeting he was addressing dropped from 75 to 40. He cited as reasons for a "more somber tone than usual," the demise of five newspaper magazines in the previous six months (the first half of 1991) — magazines at the New York *Daily News*, Louisville *Courier Journal*, Portland *Oregonian*, Omaha *World-Herald* and *Newsday*. "Often, the intrusion of mass-market magazines (*Parade*, *USA Weekend*) has greatly weakened the local magazines' advertising base," he complained. "Virtually all editors at the April conference acknowledged that their jobs today require some emergency room physician skills to keep their patients alive. Constant meetings with advertising, marketing and senior editors — all to sell the magazine and ensure its existence — take up more time and energy than anything else these days."[4]

A new book, *Regional Interest Magazines of the United States*, edited by Sam Riley and Gary Selnow, offers listings and background information for metropolitan and regional magazines.

Syndicated Newspaper Magazines

Although *Family Weekly*, *USA Weekend*, *Parade* and other Sunday magazines produced for national distribution appear in Sunday newspapers as a special section or insert, they are independent of the particular newspaper. "We do not compete with newspapers; we add our own voice," says Fran Carpenter, senior articles editor of *Parade*, which boasts 65 million readers in 33 million homes. "We are as diverse as the 65 million. We are national. We really keep in mind the human side of the story, what real people are talking about."

To write for *Parade*, says Carpenter, "Start with an idea, which is where most fall short." A subject such as "Violence in Film and TV" is too general and academic, she says. "Who are you to write about it?" You might be on

3. Silber, p. 53.

4. Fred Mann, "In Sickness and in Health," *Style*, summer 1991, pp. 6, 7.

target "if you have a more direct angle, such as you belong to a group in the Midwest that is doing something about it. Show us you're the best person to do it." She did use such an article from a woman who had organized her community against violence, "a woman who made a difference."

"Writing is a business; ask who wants to read it," says Carpenter. She remembered advice from a former *Reader's Digest* editor to the effect, "Take the incidental and make it universal." Adds Carpenter: "Appeal to everyone and touch everyone." A general article approach won't make *Parade*. A universal approach, on the other hand, finds the common denominator in people and human nature and predicaments; it taps into personal experience understood by all. It starts with a specific subject and finds universality.

Magazines

Keeping track of national magazine trends allows you to see what readers want and gives you ideas for articles. You can keep up on magazines by reading the Media Business section weekdays in the New York *Times*; *MagazineWeek*, "The Newsweekly of Magazine Publishing" (432 Park Ave. S., New York, NY 10016); and *Folio*, "The Magazine for Magazine Management" (6 River Bend, P.O. Box 4949, Stamford, CT 06907-0949). Media and press sections in the newsmagazines also track developments.

Baby Boomers   One trend is the awareness magazines have shown of the aging of the population. The "baby boomers" (76.5 million born in the postwar period between 1946 and 1964) form a significant part of the magazine audience. Even *Modern Maturity* is preparing for the day when this group becomes its audience.

In 1989 the Magazine Publishing Congress dedicated a workshop to "The Aging of America: How It Will Change Magazine Content." Speakers noted not only the buying power of baby boomers but also the large aging generation ahead of the baby boomers—a generation that also has an active agenda and needs.

The impact of the baby boomers on magazines was cited by Landon Y. Jones, when he was managing editor of *Money* (he's now with *People*), in a speech before the American Society of Magazine Editors. He noted that many of *Money*'s 1.8 million readers are baby boomers. "And it is to this audience that *Money* is directing its redesign."

One of the latest baby-boomer trends that magazines must cater to, according to Jones, is "informational grazing. They sample the media for information, picking up a little of what they are interested in from TV here, a little more from a newspaper, a catalog here, a direct-mail pitch there, perhaps something else from a friend. What they are looking for is a tool to help them organize and understand the loose information rattling around like so much spare change in their lives." So *Money*, he says, will be using more charts and graphs in its articles, subheads, boxes, checklists, "and just about anything we can think of to serve as entry points to a reader who is just flipping through."

Jones is author of a book on baby boomers, *Great Expectations: America and the Baby Boom Generation*.

As they age baby boomers are showing signs of becoming more inner-directed, a concern which could be reflected in magazine content. A marketing survey released in fall 1991 suggested that factors and values other than consumer concern with goods were at work in readership preferences. A marketing survey of consumer viewpoints by the social research firm Yankelovich Clancy Shulman, presented to the annual American Magazine Conference, found that readers were less concerned with health and physical fitness and that their idea of status was less tangible, having "more to do with being in control of one's life than with having expensive possessions, and that their concern about the environment, which had been intensifying since the mid-1980's, has fallen off somewhat."[5]

The baby boomers' own baby boom has created a demand for new magazines aimed at parents. Local magazines for parents have risen in some 70 cities. In some areas, these new magazines are pitted against each other. In the Philadelphia area, for instance, three parent publications are slugging it out: *Parents Express*, *SKiP* and *MetroKids*. The publications, dependent on ad revenue, are given away at libraries, day-care centers and supermarkets.

Stereotypes and Discrimination   Stereotypes are breaking down. Forty percent of the models for *Elle* are black, for instance. Myrna Blyth, editor-in-chief of *Ladies' Home Journal*, told a workshop on "American Popular Magazines and Issues of Race" in 1990, "When we use a group picture, a black is always included. . . . We are extremely sensitive about showing [stereotypes] — if teenage violence is the subject, then we absolutely do not show a black."

Yet segregation continues in the magazine offices. At the same workshop, Joel Dreyfuss, senior editor at *Fortune*, said, "Magazines are the most backward and most segregated section in media. Most major newspapers have black editors, managers, particularly in large urban areas, but not so in the magazine business. I still hear in 1990 the same arguments that we can't find competent blacks.

"Magazines have always tended to be more elite, using Ivy League hiring. But now, as many of the elite schools are changing, magazines are not reflecting it. In broadcasting, the FCC got tough in the 70s to desegregate."

When Dreyfuss, a black, started in the newspaper business, "I got hired because nobody wanted to get a white reporter hurt. Magazines have no great compelling reason to have black folk, although there are some visionary editors looking at demographics, that there will be a majority of people of color by 2020; it's not a white America, yet magazines perpetuate that image. It [integration in the magazine business] will not come out of altruism; do-good

5. Deirdre Carmody, "Magazine Publishers Get Some Answers," New York *Times*, Oct. 7, 1991, p. D10.

efforts peter out. It will come out of politics and from a critical economic mass. The black middle class of 10 million is one of the most identifiable groups in America. Yet I rarely read a magazine without being insulted."

At the same workshop, Daniel Okrent, founding editor of *New England Monthly*, noted that TV, with its better salaries, was proving more attractive to blacks, and that the TV audience more closely reflected the reality of society. Stephanie Stokes Oliver, editor of *Essence*, said that black students needed to be tapped earlier for magazine internships.

Yet specialized minority magazines continue to emerge. For blacks, the issue-oriented *Emerge*, started up in 1989, and *Reconstruction*, an intellectual publication, was founded by a black Harvard professor in 1990. Asian Americans, a fast-growing minority in the country, have two new magazines: *AsiaAm* and *Rice*.

The Affluent   One trend in the late 1980s, which may turn out to have been a flash in the pan, is the catering of magazines to the affluent. So many magazines were either started or redesigned to appeal to the upper-income bracket that the proverbial shakeout is now expected. According to the New York *Times*, "Wealthy readers have never been more popular. . . . They have been wooed by magazines ranging from an American version of *Elle*, the French monthly, to *New York Woman* [it died in 1991] to Condé Nast's *Traveler*. . . . But now publishers who have been flooding the market with these slick magazines are making what appears to be a not-so-startling discovery: Their target audience may have fatter pocketbooks, but there is still only so much that it can or will read."[6]

Aiming upward at a more affluent audience are travel magazines, most notably in the air travel industry. One company, the East/West Network, publishes seven airline magazines, replacing slim staid efforts by the airlines with slick publications having laminated covers and full, sophisticated color throughout. With increased frequent flying by women, the magazines "are now better balanced in both editorial and advertising content," says Fred R. Smith, executive vice president and chief editor of East/West Network. The magazines are no longer specifically edited for men, but for "the upscale consumer who happens to be flying. Fragrance, art, antiques and consumer products are the fastest growing advertising category."

Other Trends   The interest in fashion soared in the late 1980s. Besides the splash of the French *Elle*, new entries on the American scene included *In Fashion*, Condé Nast's *Details* (for men) and *Allure*, originally launched as an in-depth publication in 1991 but retooled to look like other traditional fashion magazines. The former *House & Garden*, now called *HG*, once featuring rooms without people, has, as one New York *Times* commentator observed,

6. Geraldine Fabrikant, "Wooing the Wealthy Reader," New York *Times*, Oct. 14, 1987, p. D1.

"exploded into a zippy mix of fashionably dressed models in quirky environments, of 'society lady' decorators in their designer duds, of a playwright petting dogs on his unmade bed."[7]

New campus magazines are decidedly upscale, among them *Campus USA* of the Collegiate Marketing & Communications Company in Rockville, Maryland. The American Collegiate Network, Santa Monica, launched a slick news tabloid, *U*. Many of the articles are reprints of articles appearing on campus (Address: 3110 Main St., Santa Monica, CA 90405). *Key DC* seeks to reach 190,000 college students in the Washington, D.C., area. *Newsweek on Campus*, resembling the parent *Newsweek*, did not find a separate life of its own and folded in 1988.

The leading children's magazines, many now owned by the Children's Better Health Institute in Indianapolis, reflect a concern for the child's well-being and health, with attention to diet. These magazines (see Chapter 12), like today's books for children, reflect a greater concern for the real world and real problems. *Sassy*, the magazine for teen-age girls, 14 to 19, is dealing realistically with sex and relationships (some recent titles: "Losing Your Virginity," "The Truth About Boys' Bodies," "Teen-age Stripper," "My Friend Died of AIDS," and an article that profiled two homosexual couples). Magazines for younger children have fewer fairy tales and animal fantasies and are likely to deal with child abuse, divorce and family unemployment, among other issues. In spring 1992, the owner of *Sassy*, Dale Lang, launched a magazine for male teens, *Dirt*, after trial issues in fall 1991. According to *Time*, quoting one of the *Dirt* editors, the magazine would be for "L.A. hip-hoppers, guys from the New York club scene or boys in Alabama who are into heavy metal."[8]

Art magazines for the coffee table form a multibillion-dollar industry. They include *Artforum*, *Art in America*, *Flash Art*, *Art & Antiques*. Magazines on collectibles were new in the late 1980s. With the popularity of *Victoria*, there are now "at least six new magazines with the name *Victoria* in the title," magazine research Samir Husni reported to the American Society of Magazine Editors.

Specialization   You name it and you can find a magazine for it. One of the newest is a bimonthly for the polo set, the *National Polo Advertiser*. Every sport, every hobby has its logo on a cover. Examples include *Juggler's World*, *The Leather Craftsman*, *Miniature Collector*, *Needlepoint News*, *Pipe Smoker*, *Postcard Collector*, *Sew News*, *Teddy Bear Review*, *Quiltworld*, *World Coin News* and *Laughtrack*, a magazine for distribution on the comedy club circuit.

But specialized magazines are always changing, especially in reference to the newer industries. At the beginning of 1992 some 181 computer magazines existed. However, out of the 20 cataloged by Standard Rate and Data Service

---

7. Susan Heller Anderson, "HG Magazine Is Not What It Used to Be," New York *Times*, June 8, 1988, p. C21.

8. Emily Mitchell, "Talk About Dishing Up Dirt!" *Time*, Oct. 21, 1991, p. 92.

in 1972, only one still exists. Observed James B. Kobak, head of James B. Kobak & Co., a consulting firm specializing in print media, computer publications ballooned to a total of 244 from 1984 through July 1991; but, he noted, at the same time 144 computer magazines folded.[9]

New technology such as desktop publishing has made starting magazines easier and cheaper. Harry Hochman and his daughter Suzanne launched a magazine company, Grass Roots, in New York in 1985 on only $45,000. Six years later they had a seven-magazine operation, with $30 million in revenues annually. Their specialized titles serve mostly women: *Quick and Easy Crochet*, *Creative Quilting*, *Decorating Digest*, *Cookbook Digest*, *Word Wise*, *I Love Cats* and *Real People*.

Offbeat magazines continue to have a place. *Spy* spoofs the rich and powerful. *Utne* (loosely, Norwegian for "far out") *Reader* served as a kind of alternative to *Reader's Digest*, as *Time* described it.[10] In 1990, three years after its start, *Utne Reader* reached 204,000. Editors glean articles from offbeat and marginal magazines on the left and right.

A front-page feature in the New York *Times* in March 1992 called attention to the development of new publications for homosexuals. *Puhleeze!*, a humor magazine, was to debut in May, and *Out*, which regarded itself as "a gay and lesbian *Mirabella* or *Esquire* with a little bit of gay and lesbian *Cosmo* thrown in," was due in June. Other new magazines aimed at the gay and lesbian community in the past few years include *Genre* and *NYQ*.[11]

Men's Magazines   The beginning of the 1990s saw a glimmer of new interest in men's magazines, yet the revival was shaky because men are not regarded as dependable readers of magazines. In 1990 the new *Men's Life* lasted only one issue. *Manhattan Inc.* merged with *M Magazine* to form *M Inc.* Other relatively new publications include *Details*, *Men's Health* and *Smart* (merging with *Men*). Jann Wenner, who started *Rolling Stone* in the 1960s, fathered the new *Men's Journal* in March 1992 to pursue subjects such as scuba diving, skiing, backpacking, tennis and travel. In April 1992 Straight Arrow Publications launched *Men's Journal*, featuring travel and adventure topics.

A newsstand trend, according to magazine researcher Husni, was a "proliferation" of survival-type magazines dealing with hunting, fishing and military operations, reflecting, he said, "the new conservatism and demise of sex magazines on the newstand."

The combined circulation of three men's magazines—*Esquire*, *GQ* and *M Inc.*—total 1.6 million. *Playboy*, however, has 3.4 million. Yet six women's magazines have more than 4 million circulation each, with women's magazines in all totaling 48 million circulation. Some 15 or so women's magazines have circulations over 1 million (see Table 1-1).

---

9. James B. Kobak, "The Life Cycle of Business Magazines," *Folio*, January 1992, p. 68.

10. "What Tune Does the *Utne* Play?" *Time*, Dec. 3, 1990, p. 94.

11. Deirdre Carmody, "New Gay Press Is Emerging, Claiming Place in Mainstream," New York *Times*, March 2, 1992, p. 1.

Table 1-1 The 100 Leading Audit Bureau of Circulations Magazines, Second Half of 1991 (average paid combined circulation per issue). Source: Magazine Publishers of America.

Rank	Magazine	Combined Circulation	% Change From June-Dec 1990
1	Modern Maturity	22,450,003	0.1
2	NRTA/AARP Bulletin	22,270,390	0.8
3	Reader's Digest	16,269,637	0.0
4	TV Guide	15,053,018	−3.5
5	National Geographic Magazine	9,763,406	−4.2
6	Better Homes and Gardens	8,002,794	−0.1
7	Good Housekeeping	5,188,919	0.7
8	McCall's	5,066,849	0.9
9	Ladies' Home Journal	5,065,135	1.3
10	Family Circle	5,065,131	−6.8
	Total for Top 10	114,195,282	−0.9
11	Woman's Day	4,619,505	−3.8
12	Time — The Weekly Newsmagazine	4,073,530	−0.5
13	Redbook	3,860,294	−1.2
14	National Enquirer	3,758,964	−1.2
15	Playboy	3,547,165	1.7
16	People Weekly	3,380,832	5.4
17	Sports Illustrated	3,297,493	2.4
18	Newsweek	3,224,770	0.4
19	Prevention	3,204,583	6.0
20	Star	3,102,026	−9.6
21	The American Legion Magazine	2,935,379	−0.7
22	AAA World	2,800,733	8.8
23	Cosmopolitan	2,741,802	5.4
24	Southern Living	2,361,076	0.9
25	U.S. News & World Report	2,237,009	−3.2
	Total for Top 25	163,340,443	−0.5
26	Smithsonian	2,140,349	−4.2
27	Glamour	2,081,212	−3.5
28	V.F.W. Magazine	2,063,354	2.5
29	NEA Today	2,034,846	2.8

Rank	Magazine	Combined Circulation	% Change From Jun-Dec 1990
30	Motorland	2,022,412	3.3
31	Field & Stream	2,002,732	−0.7
32	Money	1,933,864	1.0
33	Home & Away	1,881,346	0.2
34	Seventeen	1,851,665	4.5
35	Country Living	1,839,065	2.0
36	Popular Science	1,837,026	1.6
37	Ebony	1,834,011	1.3
38	Life	1,815,916	−1.6
39	First For Women	1,764,430	−33.4
40	Parents Magazine	1,752,474	0.5
41	Discovery	1,677,022	2.0
42	Popular Mechanics	1,639,033	−0.7
43	Adventure Road	1,523,853	2.0
44	Outdoor Life	1,502,818	−0.6
45	Sunset, The Magazine of Western Living	1,491,509	5.8
46	Soap Opera Digest	1,447,483	0.0
47	The Elks Magazine	1,442,326	−2.1
48	Golf Digest	1,421,797	4.7
49	Penthouse	1,390,919	−13.8
50	New Woman	1,350,392	0.7
	Total For Top 50	207,082,297	−0.8
51	Boys' Life	1,299,061	−4.3
52	The American Rifleman	1,296,027	−6.0
53	Woman's World	1,279,280	−15.0
54	US	1,271,055	−4.2
55	Bon Appetit	1,255,006	−10.2
56	Vogue	1,252,566	3.0
57	Globe	1,237,822	6.7
58	Rolling Stone	1,229,525	0.0

continued

Table 1-1, continued

Rank	Magazine	Combined Circulation	% Change From Jun-Dec 1990
59	Mademoiselle	1,206,175	2.4
60	Self	1,201,375	9.1
61	The American Hunter	1,178,462	− 3.9
62	Sesame Street Magazine	1,162,236	− 7.0
63	'Teen	1,161,734	− 1.1
64	Discover	1,124,115	0.2
65	Kiplinger's Personal Finance Magazine	1,121,072	− 1.6
66	Golf Magazine	1,116,786	2.6
67	Travel & Leisure	1,100,398	− 1.5
68	The Workbasket	1,095,119	− 9.9
69	Country Home	1,091,976	6.1
70	The Family Handyman	1,076,905	− 19.1
71	Home Mechanix	1,043,896	− 14.1
72	Car and Driver	1,024,964	6.8
73	YM	1,018,865	1.0
74	Michigan Living	1,010,956	− 1.6
75	Weight Watchers Magazine	1,001,484	− 1.8
	Total for Top 75	235,939,157	− 1.1
76	Scouting	998,003	1.8
77	Vanity Fair	991,178	25.5
78	Cooking Light	960,131	3.9
79	Jet	955,751	− 1.3
80	House Beautiful	954,455	− 3.1
81	Home	948,925	0.7
82	Elle	897,234	7.3
83	Consumers Digest	888,735	1.7
84	Business Week (North America)	887,150	− 0.3
85	Working Woman	883,060	− 1.3
86	Sport	880,221	− 4.9
87	Gourmet	871,950	− 3.1
88	PC Magazine	870,052	10.7

Rank	Magazine	Combined Circulation	% Change From Jun-Dec 1990
89	Victoria	868,627	7.8
90	Essence	868,504	2.1
91	Nation's Business	859,340	− 0.1
92	Hot Rod	853,127	− 2.7
93	Motor Trend	852,888	− 4.5
94	Organic Gardening	851,287	− 17.7
95	Popular Photography	851,039	− 6.6
96	American Health–Fitness of Body and Mind	847,246	5.1
97	Endless Vacation	840,981	5.3
98	The American Legion Auxiliary National News	837,204	1.3
99	Workbench	820,082	− 5.0
100	Food & Wine	809,826	− 1.0
	Total Combined Circulation for Top 100	258,086,153	− 0.9

*Includes general and farm magazines of the Audit Bureau of Circulations.
Groups and comics not included.

The American Society of Magazine Editors sponsored a panel with editors of three men's magazines in December 1990. "Our men want more editorial content," said Jane Lane, editor-in-chief of *M Inc.*, not "just putting a newspaper between covers." She added that "what men want may not be terribly different from what women want. Information, entertainment, news, style are elements we all want. I am not convinced men should be treated differently."

Fashion is high on the list of men's interests, the panelists indicated. "Fashion belongs in a magazine," said Art Cooper, editor-in-chief, *GQ*. "I believe men are more vain than women. Men who look to see their reflections in a window on Fifth Avenue are thought to be *GQ* readers." Cooper also noted that one-third of *GQ* readers are women, and 70 percent of subscribers to *GQ* are given subscriptions by women.

Terry McDonell, editor-in-chief of *Esquire*, said 35 percent of newsstand sales of *Esquire* are to women. "The literary tradition of *Esquire* brought women readers," said McDonell. Editor Lane said her husband looked at fashion in the women's magazines. Panel moderator, Ellen Levine, at that time editor-in-chief, *Woman's Day* (now at *Redbook*), noted: "A lot of men read women's magazines but are not counted." The consensus seemed to be that at least among sophisticated readers, men and women liked much of the same editorial content, which could mean a reshaping of men's and women's magazines to more universal themes.

Women's Magazines   Women's magazines continue to be potential markets for new writers. The trend here also is upscale and service- ("how-to")-oriented, with an emphasis on a greater range of topics. Australian magnate Rupert Murdoch entered the field by purchasing *New Woman* magazine (later sold to K-III Holdings, along with *Seventeen* and six other Murdoch publications). Another Australian firm, John Fairfax Ltd., which launched *Sassy*, also purchased the feminist *Ms.* magazine. But in six months control of *Ms.* passed to a group of its executives, then to Citicorp Venture Capital Partners and the State Bank of New South Wales. In order to regroup and cut losses, the magazine suspended publication from November 1989 to June 1990. *Ms.* then passed to Dale W. Lang, who brought it into the 1990s with an enlarged format and without ads. The *Ms.* image of the woman reader has gone from the woman of the 1960s with glasses and headband to include a "model" type with earrings and blow-dried hair.

Condé Nast's fitness magazine for women, *Self*, once featuring athletic models, now sports celebrities in outdoor shots; it is aimed at the working woman. *American Woman*, mostly concerned with dating problems of young women and with some attention to the young mother, was brought to life in 1991 by the GCR Publishing Group.

Older women have *Lear's*, created in 1985 by Frances Lear from $30 million of her $112 million divorce settlement from TV producer Norman Lear. A typical ad for the magazine, which has reached 350,000 circulation, begins:

> Wherever your pursuit of happiness is about to take you — find inspiration in the pages of *Lear's*, the magazine for the woman who wasn't born yesterday.
>   *Lear's* celebrates women who have the courage to risk change and the drive to accomplish something of lasting value.
>   In our pages, you'll meet American beauties with the grace of experience in their faces.[12] *Time* reports *Lear's* readers are at the average age of 51, with annual household income of $91,000.[13]

The age span in women's magazines can be great. The new *First for Women*, a 146-page slick magazine selling 8 million of its premiere copy for only 25 cents in early 1989, features a twentyish woman on the cover but includes articles on an elderly couple groping with the wife's Alzheimer's disease.

When Murdoch launched the prototype for his new magazine for women, he did not put a woman of any age on the cover. He called it *Mirabella*

12. Ad in *New York Times Book Review*, Jan. 15, 1989, p. 35.

13. Martha Smilgis, "Profile: A Maturing Woman Unleashed," *Time*, May 15, 1989, p. 70.

after Grace Mirabella, hired as editor after an abrupt separation from a long-time editorship of *Vogue*. The preliminary cover had only the logo, *Mirabella*, and a partial blowup of a pair of lips. The first issue in June 1989, selling for only $1, featured part of a face through a misty lens — an eye, part of a nose and part of a mouth. The point was, of course, not to pinpoint a woman of any certain age. The sophisticated variety magazine, with an emphasis on fashion, settled down to targeting the 30- to 40-year-old woman. *Mirabella*, however, ended 1990 with a loss of $16 million for the year. Martha Stewart brought her name to a magazine in 1990 — *Martha Stewart Living*, a bimonthly emphasizing how-to articles for 40-year-old homemakers and others.

The "seven sisters" still rule the women's field — *Woman's Day, Good Housekeeping, Family Circle, Ladies' Home Journal, McCall's, Better Homes and Gardens* and *Redbook*. Of these, *Woman's Day* earns the greatest profit. The New York-based magazine tries to keep in touch with middle America by requiring its editors to live in New Jersey or some place close to "Little League baseball." Each editor receives selected out-of-town newspapers to monitor for ideas. *Woman's Day* continues to crowd its covers with food and clothing items.

Ellen Levine, who left *Woman's Day* as editor-in-chief to take the same position as head of *Redbook*, outlined the future of *Redbook* before a session of the American Society of Magazine Editors in 1992. "What is so different about *Redbook* now?" she asked. The articles are shorter, she said, there is "visual sophistication," better paper and "a redesign to make the magazine more accessible." There would be more sections, "but what is [really] different is the point of view. Who is she [the *Redbook* reader]?" Levine said the formula in women's magazines has been, "her baby comes first; husband second; job third. She comes last. *Redbook* plans to put her first. *Redbook* visits her where she lives emotionally."

The women's magazines usually sought a balance, a juggling of topics, but Levine was asked at the session if *Redbook* was going from "juggling" to being "juicy." "We want to speak about what other 'sisters' might not," Levine said. And she illustrated her point with current topics in *Redbook*: "Married men and masturbation habits," "Why I date your husband," "I'd kill for my daughter," "Is married sex safe — do you know where your husband has been?" "Are you overdosing on antibiotics?" At the end of the magazine each month would appear a "happy ending" column with an upbeat incident from real life.

Eclecticism   One of the most popular and successful new editors is Tina Brown of *Vanity Fair*, probably one of the highest paid magazine editors. *Vanity Fair*'s rates are at the top at $2 a word, sometimes $25,000 for an article. (She left *Vanity Fair* in July 1992 to edit the *New Yorker*.)

Brown appears to be on top of trends. She took *Vanity Fair*'s circulation from 220,538 to 692,537 in five years. She developed a mix that "would fly in the face of specialized magazines," she explained. "There was no real attempt to do a general interest magazine. If the previous generation was a 'me' generation, then we are in a 'media' generation. In all this glut we wanted to take a point of view, an attitude. You don't have to read 500 magazines to know what is going on. We wanted to cut a path through all of this stimulus." She said she has no fixed agendas and could produce 70 different *Vanity Fairs* a month, as testimony to the variety that the magazine seeks. "We have a sense of what people are talking about and a desire to bring the world alive." The celebrity-conscious magazine was printing mostly profiles in 1992, with the January issue's subjects ranging from the cover story, an article on actor Kevin Costner, to feminist Gloria Steinem, to a politician, Nebraska's Senator Bob Kerrey.

Brown says her magazine seeks to be eclectic, all things to many people, but that it is not a catchall. It has a "unified" look. She wants "clean and strong" design. "We want very little exciting typography. It would give us a migraine headache. We were mistaken at first, trying to do it [the magazine] by design." Excitement should be in the text, not design, she said. "The last thing I want to do is to look at whirling type." She strives for a "continuous, seamless" approach that is "anti-formula." "Nothing is constant except it has to work together as a unit."

Another preacher of the unified gospel of eclecticism is Edward Kosner, editor and publisher of the very successful *New York* magazine. "No other magazine is as eclectic as we are," he says. "It's an eclecticism within each issue and from issue to issue. I'm always happy if people say they found at least one article they liked." The New York City–oriented *New York* will have an issue on fashion one week, and in other weeks a service guide to the city, a family saga, an in-depth look at a candidate, a spread on interior design. One article discussed how much of Manhattan Japanese entrepreneurs owned, and *New York* included a map that pinpointed each property. Like Tina Brown at *Vanity Fair*, Kosner believes his magazine is a clear path through a world of stimulus.

The philosophy of eclecticism should encourage free-lance writers; a variety of subjects means many opportunities for getting published. On the other hand, writers need to do more than casually browse through a magazine checking topics; they need to determine the tone and overall mystique that the eclecticists would say are so essential to the magazine.

New Concepts   Changes and new developments in the magazine world encompass concepts and distribution as well as new magazines and new focuses. Whittle Communications has created large-size, glossy, single-topic "magazines" for doctors' offices. An issue of *Special Report*, for instance, features only short mystery stories or only sports stories. The publication sells space to only one advertiser in a category.

Doctors are offered the magazine free but must suspend most of their other subscriptions. Christopher Whittle, a former publisher of *Esquire* and founder of the Whittle firm, found in his research that 10 percent of all magazine reading was done in doctors' offices. In arguing for the single advertiser stretched over an issue, he noted that one-shot ad retention is low. "Ninety-three percent cannot recall a commercial 15 minutes after and the reader can only remember 2 percent of ads in magazines," he told members of the American Society of Magazine Editors. "A paid magazine is not necessarily better. The fact people paid for it does not mean it is read. It must have greater appeal than what's on the cover. Tried and true ways of running magazines may not be the best way."

Whittle has a veterinarian magazine solely sponsored by Purina and a travel agents' magazine sponsored only by American Airlines. Some observers worry about the separation of editorial and advertising when one company "controls" the product through its one-ad-throughout policy.[14]

McGraw-Hill is experimenting with "customization" in books, but also sees applications to magazines. In customization, a college bookstore would have a laser printing unit. A professor who wants certain chapters from different books, maps and other display items orders from a menu of items, and the bookstore puts it together and binds it. "I suspect there will come a day when a publication offers customers similar services," says Ralph R. Schulz, senior editorial vice president for McGraw-Hill. "An editor or publisher will say, 'in the next issue we're offering this menu of stories. What do you want?'"

General Media Publishing Group, which publishes *Penthouse*, is set to publish electronic editions of all its magazines. The New York *Times* reports that several thousand *Penthouse* readers, responding to ads, have asked for free software that allows them to talk electronically to the Pet of the Month or to write electronic letters to the editors.[15]

The "selective binding" process allows publications to meet individualized needs of subscribers. Based on predetermined interest, an extra section or so is dropped into the subscriber's magazine while it goes through the assembly line. Many magazines tailor advertising inserts to geographical locations and demographics. However, *Newsweek* became the first to customize editorial inserts and target them to specialized interests through selective binding.

The specialized sections of newspapers are competing with magazines. For example, 416 newspapers, representing 48 million readers, can now use six standard ad sizes in their weekly TV magazines, according to a June 1990 report in *Editor & Publisher*, thus spelling more competition with *TV Guide* for the TV ad dollar.

The loss of advertising pages, so evident in magazines at the beginning of the 1990s, looms as a big factor in shaping the style and destinies of magazines. Publishers Information Bureau reported a drop of 8.7 percent in ad pages in magazines for 1991. The Bureau said this was the third-largest decline in total advertising pages for magazines for a year since the organization

14. See "The Era of the Big Blur," *Newsweek*, May 22, 1989, p. 73.

15. Deirdre Carmody, "New President at Penthouse Looks Beyond Printed Page," New York *Times*, Dec. 2, 1991, p. D1.

began keeping tab of figures in 1950.[16] Watch a publication's ads; they will tell you something about the publication's readers and policies.

Publications are being merged into giant chains and conglomerates, and most will be centralized into eight or 10 great companies in the future, observers believe. Current groupings include Australian Murdoch's News Corp. and Media Partnership International, which still publishes *TV Guide*, although many of its holdings have been split off. There's also Hachette Publications of France, which bought the Diamandis Communications group, which included *Woman's Day* and 105 other magazines in 19 countries. On the rise is K-III, whose jurisdiction embraces some former Murdoch magazines. The European Community unification is expected to make more cohesive the concept of global publishing.

"It's a wacky world of international publishing," says Russell J. Melvin, vice president/education for the Magazine Publishers Association. *Woman's World*, *First for Women* and a woman's magazine in England are owned by a German firm, the West German Bauer Group. *Essentials* in England is going to Spain and Canada. *Marie Claire* in France is now also in England, Canada and Brazil. "*Elle* [France] is all over. And Americans are doing it, too. *Fortune* is now in Italy and France." And, of course, big American magazines have long had editions on all continents — *Reader's Digest*, *Time* and *Newsweek*. *Reader's Digest*, *Journal of Commerce* and *Business Week* launched Russian editions in 1990 and 1991. Lee Eisenberg, former editor-in-chief of *Esquire*, went to England to be editor-in-chief of a British version of *Esquire* launched in February 1992. *Vanity Fair* also launched a British edition in 1992. In addition, some publications are starting wholly new magazines, but not with certain success. *Reader's Digest*, for instance, inaugurated *Budgets Famille* in France in 1990 and shut it down six months later.

The movement is not just cross national, but also cross media. Murdoch at his peak had 150 media properties on four continents; in the United States these included TV stations, the 20th Century Fox film studio and the Harper & Row publishing company. The Chicago *Tribune*, buying into a new national paper in England, was engaged in a joint TV venture with the German Kirch Group. Capital Cities/ABC gained close to a majority interest in Telemunchen, a German TV production and distribution company. Knight-Ridder acquired Dialog Information Services, which serves 89 nations.

Citing Time Inc. talks with Warner Communications before the merger that formed Time Warner Inc., the managing editor of *Fortune* (a Time Inc. company), Marshall Loeb, noted that the companies "have to merge to keep up with Murdoch. A simple publisher has no leverage. There is a move toward global companies. You have to have size to compete in the global [market]. We've got to be ready for the 21st century."

Survey the markets, understand trends, know for whom you are writing. A publication is a target, and you want to hit the bulls-eye — write something

16. "Magazine Ad Pages Off 8.7% Last Year," New York *Times*, Jan. 15, 1992, p. D15.

so much on target it will be hard to refuse. Knowing all nuances of your market and aiming specifically at a publication you understand are the first steps to scoring success.

The following chapters will take up the steps in making actual contact with publications, research tips, introductions to various kinds of articles, the actual writing — organization and style and other matters. Now it's time to come up with those ideas.

ASSIGNMENTS

1. Find examples of as many kinds of newspaper/magazine articles as you can and look for variations in each category; clip so that each conforms to standard 8½ × 11 typing paper; paste up and fasten the pages in a term paper binder.

   Make section dividers for (1) samples of hard news, feature news, hard news with feature leads, (2) anecdotes, (3) profiles, (4) how-to articles, (5) genres, (6) columns, (7) longer articles dealing with a topic or issue.

   Begin this project now — and add examples as each category is discussed throughout the course.

2. Take a news story or feature in the daily newspaper and rewrite the lead various ways; if it's an anecdotal lead, consider writing it to reflect different "points of view" — "I," "you," "he," "she" or "it."

3. Redesign and lay out a newspaper feature story as it might appear as a magazine article.

4. Study three newspaper feature articles. Suggest how each might be divided into three parts: the main story, plus two sidebars.

5. Interview a writer in town. Ask about how he or she gets ideas, picks a market, interests an editor, makes the article interesting, meets deadlines.

6. Consult a newspaper or magazine directory (*Editor & Publisher Yearbook*, *Writer's Market*, etc.), and choose three publications for which you would like to write. Using the directories and your observation of the publications themselves, write a summary paragraph on what appears to be each publication's needs.

7. Pick one magazine for which you wish to write, examine and analyze its contents and patterns for the past year, and give a report.

8. Write what you think might be the guidelines for a publication; then contact the editor for a set of guidelines to compare.

9. Study magazine racks — pay attention to the kinds of magazines and what they have on the covers. What trends can you see?

10. Study the "Media Business" page in the weekday New York *Times*, *MagazineWeek* or *Folio*. What are the new publications? Which ones have folded? Which have merged? What overall trends can you describe?

11. Propose and describe a new magazine that you think can be started based on the trends.

12. Review the magazine section in your Sunday newspaper. Sample the copies over the past several years. Any trends?

13. Of all the magazines you read or have access to at a library or elsewhere, which do you consider the worst magazine and which the best? Why?

14. Determine the advertising policy of a magazine. If time permits, write for information and rate cards. Discuss advantages and disadvantages of a magazine's being supported by only one advertiser throughout.

15. Study a regional or city publication. Discuss how the format might change or articles be adapted to a publication serving a global market.

CHAPTER 2

Getting Started: Ideas and Queries

You are probably most comfortable writing in an area in which you have some expertise, because of your experience, education or a hobby. Or you might decide to write about a topic that interests you so that you can learn more about it.

When you don't have an idea, you can jump start your mind. Look around you. If you're in a room, you see walls. Use the word to start brainstorming.

Walls, walls, walls. Write about some of the most famous walls. How have walls been used throughout history to make news announcements? How about the walled cities of the world? Consider offbeat ways of decorating walls. And walled communities: Prisons? A prison lawyer profiled? Some innovative solutions to prison overcrowding? How about the changing lives of nuns and monks within walled convents and monasteries? The walls of the mind — ethical limits in society and what's changing? New ways to fence a yard?

Turn to your own life. The problems and needs of those around you open up inestimable possibilities. Maybe there is a rare disease in the family.

Write about it. An occupation—what is learned on the job that might be worth sharing with another? Group relations—how can one better relate to the boss? How does one become the boss? Your hobby—magazines exist for a good many hobbyists, for the quilter and stitcher to the tennis and racing enthusiast.

Turn to your favorite music, TV program, book or movie for an idea. One student was inspired by Robin Cook's murder thriller, *Coma*, which was about to become a movie. In the story a young woman doctor is chased through an auditorium and halls and ends up hiding among the cadavers in the hospital's "freezer." The student wrote a feature article for the Philadelphia *Daily News* on the storage and use of cadavers in Philadelphia hospitals. A sidebar on how to donate your body to science accompanied the article.

Turn to the library. Scan the card and computer catalogs and the publications. Turn to your favorite newspaper. Take one page and subject it to close analysis.

For example, take a news page. The New York *Times* front page on a somewhat non-eventful summer day had stories on rebellion in Myanmar (Burma), a free-needle plan for addicts, military budget vote, the drought's effect on the grain crop, suffering through a heat wave compared to living in a rain forest, church people in Russia helping in hospitals, charges of police brutality in a neighborhood demonstration and vast human-made fires in the Amazon jungle contributing to the greenhouse overheating of Earth. Each of these could stand as a subject for expanded magazine treatment. Each also triggers other ideas. For example, a spinoff for each could be: Rebellion in Myanmar—"How Today's Rebellions Are Different"; needle-free plan for addicts—somehow the word *addicts* stirs thoughts of habits, and so why not "Ten Ways to Break a Habit"; grain—"How Much Fiber Do You Need?" or drought—"Ways to Garden in a Dry Season"; church people helping in Russian hospitals—"volunteerism," such as "The New Young Volunteers" or "20 Places Where You Can Volunteer"; police brutality—"How to File a Complaint"; Amazon fires—"Is Your Fire Protection Good Enough?" Just take any front page.

Look out your window. Suppose you see a sunflower. Why not write about the history and use of sunflowers, as one writer for *Kidbits* did, or about all the places in your yard you can accent with a sunflower or other flowers and shrubs?

It doesn't take much imagination to glean nuggets of ideas from the ads and the classified pages. From fashions to fish stores, from help wanted to hardware, from refrigerators to restaurants, you can set your imagination free. Go through the alphabet—A is for "animals" (pet subjects, etc.), B is for "bed" (sleep topics), C is for "car" (driving tips) and so on.

Magazines are always looking for the right ideas. A few magazines have long processes to produce just the right idea. The old *Realités* magazine had stages through which an idea had to percolate. Ideas would go through market-research testing, with a certain level of favorable response necessary before a story would be assigned. *Cosmopolitan* keeps an "idea book." Established writers are invited to look through a book of ideas created by brainstorming staff. According to one *Cosmopolitan* writer, "The ideas are any dumb thing, one after another: 'Are You a Jealous Lover?' and so on. They tell you to go through the idea book and pick any five ideas, and then the editor runs to Helen Gurley Brown [the editor] for final approval." Even there, beginning writers have a chance. A university graduate student received a go-ahead letter from *Cosmopolitan* on the strength of an over-the-transom query letter for an article on natural beauty aids. The right idea from a writer who has researched the magazine and queried intelligently and grammatically does, more often than not, get attention.

SOME BASIC QUESTIONS

Once you know what you want to write and for whom, you still have more questions to ask.

Is the article feasible and manageable? Are you the one to write it? Can you write it? Do you have the time and money to do the research? Analyze what the time demands are. Check your schedule. If you're working, can the research and interviewing be done during off hours?

The secret to free-lance writing is to "over research," while at the same time using shortcuts. You can look as if you've covered more ground than you have. Questionnaires and phone interviews are legitimate shortcuts. Your planning of time and resources can be crucial.

What's been done on your subject? Start your research by checking the various reference books and indexes in the library. Most important is to know what has been done recently by the publication you are targeting and by its competitors.

In addition to card catalogs, microfiche and computer listings and the offerings on current magazine racks, check *Reader's Guide to Periodical Literature*, *Popular Periodical Index*, *New York Times Index* and *Facts on File*. See Chapter 3 on the use of a library.

THE QUERY LETTER

Essential to success in a writing career is mastery of the query letter, which is simply a letter asking if a publication would be interested in a specific article. If the answer is yes, you proceed to prepare the piece, following any advice offered by the editor. If editors say no to your idea, then abandon it or file it for another day. Writing a query letter prevents you from wasting time. You're writing only those pieces that editors say they want to see.

If you prepare articles at your whim and fire them off to editors, you take a considerable risk. The editor may not like the idea. Your story may be returned with a note saying the idea has already been used or should be approached differently. Don't waste time writing an article that nobody wants.

Can You Call Instead of Writing?

Of course, you can call editors and talk to them personally. But, in many cases, you risk alienating an editor, for you may be calling at a bad time. On the other hand, a one-on-one conversation allows you to say, when you submit the completed article, "This is the article we talked about on the phone, and I have followed your suggestions."

More often than not, the successful phone query is made by an already-established writer, who might even know the editor. Because an ordinary person doesn't call an editor from across the country, some editors — particularly of middle-size or small publications — might be likely to regard the author who calls as an established one. But be advised that editors can get irked even at the experienced writer who is bothering them on the phone.

Big-circulation magazines screen their editors from phone calls. "Phone queries annoy the heck out of me," says Rebecca E. Greer, articles editor of *Woman's Day*. "I get about 150 pieces of mail a day. Perhaps 50 or more calls come in every day." She just doesn't have time for calls. She also takes a dim view of people who try to seek an editor out personally, such as by an invitation to lunch. "Why should I go?" she asks. "I don't always have time to go out for lunch. When I do go out, I can use my own expense account and choose whom I have lunch with."

Greer points out that phone calls cannot be equated with written queries. "I like receiving written queries from writers and read them all myself," she says. "A proposal in writing gives me both an idea on how the person can write and something to pass on to my colleagues for comments. A phone query does neither. Phone calls take a lot more of my time than letters and they often come at inopportune moments — when I'm eating lunch at my desk, finishing up a rush project or discussing an important matter with a colleague. And when I say 'no,' many writers argue. Even if I like the idea, all I can say is 'Put it in writing,' so the call is a waste of time for both of us."

Bob Barnett, who handles nutrition articles for *American Health*, says, "I don't mind phone calls, if you know why you're calling." But Ellen Sweet, of *Ms.*, says, "I hate calls. Only if the story is so hot . . . but I'd still want a query letter. Calls get mixed in with PR calls. All we want to do is just clear our desk. A call may get an editor at a really bad time." But she does add that it's acceptable, as far as she is concerned, to call an editor about a query if you haven't received a reply after a month.

Format and Wording

Most editors agree that a good query letter should be:

- *Neat.* A sloppy letter writer or typist may be sloppy in all things, including use of facts. Wouldn't you get a message if you saw coffee rings or spills on the query letter; ink smudges; the "o's" hollow, punched out by the typewriter; the imprint on paper too light; no margins; bad spacing; inconsistent paragraphing, etc.? Make your letter look professional.

- *Compact.* Short letters won't bore an editor. Professionals often write the shortest letters. Amateurs go on and on. Keep it to a page. Judith Kahn, managing editor of *San Francisco Focus*, says she likes a query letter of three paragraphs.

  Yet some editors prefer long, even very long, queries. Peter Bloch, executive editor of *Penthouse*, says he doesn't mind long queries. "The more you send in, the better chance you have of getting accepted. Send long queries or completed articles to *Penthouse*."

- *Grammatically correct.* Mistakes in grammar and spelling are warning flags. Typos, such as a "th" for "the," do occur; but typos also cause a letter or manuscript to be suspect. They signal that you weren't careful enough to check what you wrote. If you spell *receive* as *recieve* or *you're* as *your* or *its* when you mean *it's*, or if your nouns and verbs don't agree, then you can be sure an editor is saying, "My God, another letter from an illiterate!" Make one mistake in spelling a name, place or a word basic to your topic — like *forrest* instead of *forest* — in the title of a proposed article, and you might as well immediately surrender. The editor will expunge from memory any awareness of the letter or else will exhibit an unpleasant disposition if your name emerges again.

- *Knowledgeable.* The letter should demonstrate briefly that you know a great deal about your topic owing to your expertise or access to top authorities.

- *Simple and modest.* Children are endearing because they are straightforward and to the point. So should your letter be. Don't try to impress by using jargon. Say it simply. Go easy in listing your own credits. Give enough to convince the editor that you're the one to write the article.

Five magazine editors formed a panel on "The Art of the Query" at an American Society of Journalists and Authors (ASJA) meeting in 1991 and told what it takes to grab their attention. Panelists were *Penthouse*'s Peter Bloch; Susan Kane, executive editor, *New Woman*; Michael LaFavore, executive editor, *Men's Health*; Thomas Lashnits, senior staff editor, *Reader's Digest*; and Susan Ungaro, executive editor, *Family Circle*. Ungaro reported that *Family Circle* receives 200 queries a day.

Panelists said query letters should have:

- "An excitement potential . . . some element of controversy . . . a story that makes a difference. Some kind of gripping detail. Putting a lump [emotion] in the throat always works." — Susan Ungaro.

- "An emotional grabber . . . a conversation [sample dialogue] is a great way to begin [a query letter]. Needs some zip. Your excitement has to come through." — Susan Kane.

- "Unique insight and unique information. So many queries just reflect what the author saw on TV or elsewhere." — Peter Bloch.
- An idea that the editor can "sell" to the top editors. "When you write proposals, see 'through' to the editor-in-chief, not just hit with [or try to convince] one editor. Visualize how it will stand up when all the editors see the query." — Thomas Lashnits.
- "One idea [instead of multiple ideas] thought out." — Susan Kane.
- Something extra. "When you are a first-time writer, you have to prove yourself. When breaking into a magazine, you have to go the extra mile." — Thomas Lashnits.
- A clear idea how the article will fit into the magazine. "Don't just send it [article or query] in and expect them [editors] to find a place for it." — Thomas Lashnits.
- An angle. "You'd want it clearly defined." — Susan Kane.
- "A lead, like an article, is needed in queries." — Michael LaFavore.

You can start a query many ways, even by listing your credentials, or with a few lines of sample quotes, according to Susan Ungaro. "There is no formula. Do it a little more unique, that's a challenge."

Marlane Liddell, member, board of editors of the *Smithsonian*, told members of the American Society of Journalists and Authors, in February 1992, what she likes in a query letter. "It should show that you've looked at the magazine," she said. "We want a variety of writing style, a lot of original sources and a reason to do it. It just catches our fancy." When you query, she said, "think of what your friends take to the beach — timeless articles." She said for her magazine you can look for original ideas in the obvious. "What happens when you dial a telephone? Look at crane operators, mannequins. What happens when you mail letters?"

A Basic Query Letter

In a query letter, you use a standard business format (Figure 2-1). Your *address* and the *date* (if you're not using printed stationery) go in the upper right of the page; skip four lines; type the *name* and *address* of the person you're writing to, flush left, single space; skip a line and type the salutation (Dear _____:); skip a line, then enter the *body of the letter* in single space, perhaps skipping a line of space between paragraphs; skip a line; type "Sincerely"; then skip four lines before typing *your name* — the space allows for your signature.

Of course, you can use personal stationery, or business or newspaper stationery, if permitted. Newspaper and journalism school letterheads show an editor that the writer is active in the writing field; business letterheads might suggest that you're an expert, or at least that you have a job in the area of an expertise indicated on the letterhead.

1811 Albatross Blvd.
Heron City, FL 33156
January 1, 1991

George Lyon
Editor, Pet Magazine
1111 Zoo Center Rd.
Philadelphia, PA 19001

Dear Mr. Lyon:

Would you be interested in an article on "How to House-Train Your Parakeet" on speculation?

I am owner of Animal Haven, a pet store here in Heron City, and have observed and worked with parakeets for 20 years. I would suggest about 20 techniques to target your parakeet's droppings at selected locations. Among the techniques is a chemical put on the desired spot in the cage or room. This harmless chemical triggers a silly reaction in the bird, making it aim for the spot and defecate there.

I am also a graduate of the College of Aviary Science at Wingham University, New York City, and have written articles for Bird and Bees Magazine, Your Child's Pet, Birds, Fowl and Timber, Sports Today, Popular Technology and Your Baby Magazine.

With appreciation for your consideration,

Sincerely,

F. J. Flight

F. J. Flight

FIGURE 2-1 Sample format of basic query letter.

To whom do you send your query? Says Carolyn Kitch, senior associate editor for articles at *Good Housekeeping*: "One way to get mail read is to pick a name in the middle of a department. Generally, if it is sent to a middle person, they will think they know you and can't figure out why you wrote and will report. Also, one in the middle doesn't get as much mail."

A good way for an unknown to start: "Would you be interested in an article on (proposed title), on speculation?" Call attention to your article with a snappy working title, but one that doesn't fail to tell what the article is about. Provide a title that would also be a real "grabber" on the cover.

"Have something to say, a point of view, something fresh," says Ila Stanger, former editor-in-chief, *Food & Wine*, and now editor-in-chief, *Travel & Leisure*. "Have an idea. There is a difference between a subject and an idea." Says Lee Eisenberg, former editor-in-chief, *Esquire*: "You have to ask, is there an original idea? You have to feel it. Not just a notion, like 'Dan Quayle.' You have to pursue it, at least provide a counter-idea, an insight." Julie Campbell, senior editor of *Sports Illustrated* and coordinator of the annual swimsuit edition, talks of selling "the power of an idea." At her magazine, she says, "If we understand the potential, we are willing to go out on a limb."

When you say "on speculation," it means that the editor will consider the article, with no obligation to use it. Some editors assume all articles they receive are on speculation anyway and will say so in their letters. "Why volunteer that you're willing to write with no guarantee?" said one editor. So, there are two points of view on saying "on speculation," but to say so does clarify the relationship.

Editors also worry about leading an unknown writer on. Says *Good Housekeeping*'s Carolyn Kitch: "We are careful what we say about 'speculation.' We don't want to say to the writer to go ahead unless we really want it. We don't want to lead him or her on." But if the unknown writer gets the attention of an editor, the "speculation" clause is a protection for the editor. *Ladies' Home Journal* uses a form letter—with address and salutation keyed in—to respond to "on speculation" proposals in which the editors are interested. A letter from the *Journal*'s executive editor, Lynn Langway, told a graduate student who queried: "Thank you for letting us consider your proposal. I would be interested in seeing your article on speculation. I look forward to reading your piece. Sincerely, Lynn Langway, Executive Editor."

"Speculation" is different from an assignment, where the editor is requesting work for pay. If an assigned article is completed successfully and published, the writer gets the promised amount; if it's not published, editors often pay a "kill fee," a percentage (sometimes a third of the agreed amount) that helps to cover the writer's time and trouble.

After a statement of idea and title in the first paragraph, a brief second paragraph in the query letter can tell something about the proposed article, perhaps how the writer will proceed.

A third or final paragraph can give a few lines of your credentials — previous experience, training, publications — anything to help convince the editor that you can deliver. Remember you are selling an idea and the fact that you are the one to write about it.

When you finish saying what you need to say, stop; don't ramble on. However, a brief cordial line or part of a line, such as "With best wishes," could precede the "Sincerely."

"Most queries are doomed because of the sloppiness of writers," says Mike Schwanz, associate editor of *Sports Afield*. "For example, a lot come to us wanting to do something like world cup soccer, but we are not a spectator sport magazine. We do a lot of hunting and fishing. We get a lot of computer outlines and some do not even say 'Dear Editor.' Address a specific person and spell the name correctly.

"We prefer queries of two or three paragraphs, and that's it. A laundry list of 30 ideas we don't take seriously.

"We're a little broader, including wildlife and safari articles. We're for age 40 and the well-to-do and are not interested in what a 13-year-old boy would do." For *Sports Afield*, you have to think a year ahead — partly because pictures are seasonal, and you can't prepare an article and get accompanying photographs in time for this season's issue.

Schwanz cited three good query ideas: (1) One writer said, "You have not done anything on boundary water fishing since 1984." At least you know the reader is taking you seriously, commented Schwanz. (2) Another wrote: "You guys never have done an article on falling in the Rockies." Schwanz observed that hundreds do die falling off cliffs, and the writer had statistics and backup. (3) Another had an interesting fact: "There are 30 percent more timber wolves than at the start of 1985."

Like other editors, Schwanz suggests the writer look for ideas at home. "Everybody wants to go to Alaska and ignore his own hometown. Send us a proposal of something you know about intimately. Grasslands in Kansas." And he adds that a "little bit of homework can go a long way."

Whether it's a query, or a cover letter with the article, Schwanz wants a phone number and Social Security number included. "I've lost 10 years of my life tracking down writers now in Africa or South Africa. Do anything that will make life easier for an editor."

He wants to know in the letter if you can provide photos. "We're one of the few left that does want the writer to send in photos. When a writer goes to Africa or the Northwest Territories, it's too expensive to send a photographer. Also a *Vogue* photographer might not have the stamina!"

In a query don't wax eloquent on why the editor should want your article. Editors know what their publications need. Says Judith Kahn, of *San Francisco Focus*: "The worst thing you can say is why we should read it. I almost see red. I know my readers so much better than they. It's a big 'no-no' — telling us what to be. They should know what we are."

Among other taboos, Rebecca Greer, of *Woman's Day*, reaffirms her suggestions made some years ago in an article in *Writer's Digest*. Her taboos include:[1]

- *Your opinions.* Every writer thinks his or her article is just what readers are looking for, or a great service to humanity, or a sure-fire circulation booster, or even all three. So what else is new?

- *Other people's opinions.* What your mother, husband, teacher or pet mynah bird said about your idea doesn't mean a thing to an editor. Neither do the comments of other editors who've seen the query or manuscript already.

- *"Important" names.* Mentioning the names of other editors or writers you've met socially is a complete waste of space. It not only fails to impress anyone, but most of the names dropped on me are ones I've never heard of anyway.

- *Your reasons for writing.* The fact that your psychiatrist thinks it will be good therapy or that you need to get published in order to pass a course may be important to you, but it's guaranteed to bore an editor.

- *Market surveys.* Writers who claim that "nothing has ever been published" on a certain subject are invariably wrong — even when they cite *Reader's Guide* as proof. . . . *Woman's Day* and *Family Circle* are not indexed in *Reader's Guide*. Chances are editors read more magazines and know far more about their competitors than you do. How many times do we get queries on a piece we just did? You should look over at least one year of copies.

- *Appraisal of the magazine.* Flattery will get you nowhere. Neither will such comments as, "I know you never publish articles of this type, but you're making a terrible mistake. . . ."

- *Irrelevant experience.* If you're proposing an article on hospitals, your experience as a surgical nurse is useful. But a degree in history, a former career as a teacher or marriage to an accountant are not.

- *Outdated research.* While you may be able to use certain material gathered from encyclopedias and old issues of *Life*, you should never admit it. Editors are looking for fresh ideas and new research.

Greer also warns against "insults" ("I never read your magazine, but . . .") and "ultimatums" and "threats" ("If I don't receive a reply in two weeks, I'll send it elsewhere.").

If an editor "bites" on a proposed article idea, Greer adds, then the prospective writer should keep in touch. If there is a "definite assignment or just an invitation to submit on speculation," she says, "be sure to send an acknowledgment that includes the date when you expect to deliver the manuscript. Then, if you can't deliver on schedule, keep the editor posted on your progress. Otherwise, you may find that the magazine has encouraged another

---

1. Rebecca Greer, "How to Query an Editor," *Writer's Digest*, October 1973, p. 10.

writer to pursue a similar topic — or has lost all interest in the idea — during the time you spent struggling and procrastinating."

Enclosures

Many things — some of them junk — show up in query letters arriving on an editor's desk. Greer says she frequently gets enclosures such as snapshots of pets, fabric scraps for new drapes, clippings about an honor to the author. These definitely label the would-be writer as "amateur," she says. Also, she adds, don't include a check-off card of responses that can be returned without the editor writing a letter. "It rarely saves time, and in many cases none of the choices apply anyway."

Whether enclosures should be used may depend on the type of article suggested, what's available to send and the taste of the editors. Some editors encourage the inclusion of an outline, clippings of previous published work, a projected source sheet, synopsis, lead paragraph, and so on.

Betsy Carter, editor-in-chief of the now-defunct *New York Woman*, suggests: "Write a page [of the article] and let us see your 'voice,' and write in the style of the article."

Whatever you decide to send should be of high quality. If the clippings your have are inferior, don't send them. It does the beginning writer little good to send a run-of-the-mill, smudged clipping from a neighborhood weekly. It's better to impress the editor with your professionalism in the quality of the query letter.

Sending Outlines

Most writers don't like to send an outline, since it doesn't accurately convey what the article will look like when finished and because it's difficult to convey life and enthusiasm in an outline.

If you elect to send an outline with a query letter, consider sending a formal one. Such an outline at least gives the impression you are well organized. (Yet some editors prefer a more spontaneous, less rigid approach.) You've seen the formal outline with Roman numerals. Remember, you must follow through — that is, if you have an "I" you must have an "II," an "A," then also a "B," "1," also a "2," "a" and "b," etc. (See Figure 2-2.) Or the outline can be more of a synopsis — two or three paragraphs in summary under each point — or a list of anecdotes or highlights. (See Figure 2-3.)

Variations in Query Letters

A query letter could offer to expand an article you've already published in a local newspaper. Instead of sending random clipping samples, you send a clipping showing the work you've already done on a proposed idea.

One kind of story that beginners could do, according to Greer, is like that of a senior citizen program where high school kids helped. Another topic,

St. Albans, WV 25177
June 11, 1981

Hiley Ward
Editor
Ross House
Suite 305
Head House Square
401 South 2nd Street
Philadelphia, PA 19147

Dear Mr. Ward:

Recently, I talked with Virginia Kirkpatrick, who at one time ran a business called Detect-O-Pet. She was a detective for missing pets. Besides offering her services 100% of the time until the pet was found, Ms. Kirkpatrick provided a consultation service, where she would train the owner to do what she would do.

Before she started her business, Ms. Kirkpatrick had contacted John Keane, author of Sherlock Bones, who is supposedly the only pet detective in the country. Keane supplied her with the detail on strategies and procedures for running a pet detective business. Although Ms. Kirkpatrick is no longer operating Detect-O-Pet, she discussed the following points with me, which I believe would be helpful to any youngster who is trying to locate a missing pet.

I.   How to keep your animal from getting lost
     Things to do, things not to do
II. Steps to take if your pet becomes lost
     A. Within twenty-four hours
        1. Call local animal shelters
        2. Call local police department
        3. Call emergency veterinary hospitals
        4. Decide on a reward
        5. Print up 1000 posters with b/w photograph of missing
           pet and put up within a twenty-block area.
     B. Daily
        1. Visit animal shelters
        2. Visit police department

FIGURE 2.2   Query letter with formal outline.

      3. Run newspaper ads
      4. Read lost and found columns
      5. Keep someone by the phone with a map of the area
  III. Pet napping rings
  IV. How to pay reward
  V.   How to recover your pet

    According to Ms. Kirkpatrick and Mr. Keane, the chances of recovering your lost pet are 90%, if you follow all their suggested procedures, unless the animal has been carried out of state or fallen down a hole and died. Please let me know if you would be interested in a story on how to find your missing pet.

                                    Sincerely,

                                Melanie Vickers

Enclosed: SASE   Melanie Vickers

she says, would be a unique latchkey program. Would-be writers forget local subjects. "Keep your eyes open and read newspapers."

When you send in one of your newspaper clippings to be developed for a national publication, write the editor, "Would you be interested in my fleshing out the enclosed clipping for your magazine? The approach could be. . . ." A professional newsperson, who wrote the original newspaper article, would work this way.

Another way to query is to offer the editor three ideas at once — ideally, "three ideas he or she cannot refuse" — three ideas carefully tailored to meet the magazine's current editorial interests. (See Figures 2-4 and 2-5.) "Surely, the editor will like one of these," you reason.

Logic would suggest that the multi-idea query letter increases one's odds. Most editors do not object to this kind of query. But some, such as Ian Ledgerwood, editor of *Modern Maturity*, questions them. "Maybe they're OK," he says, "but my thinking is that they might indicate that one has too many irons in the fire. If there is one idea, the editor might be more likely to think it is a field the person knows something about."

In another kind of query letter — not an approach normally to be recommended — the writer offers a list of ideas. In this case, the writer risks being

Tampa, FL 33612
December 9, 1987

Hiley H. Ward, Editor
<u>Media History Digest</u>
11 W. 19th St.
New York, NY 10011

Dear Hiley H. Ward:

In 1925, my grandfather was tried and convicted of teaching evolution in the highly publicized Scopes Monkey Trial. For most of the summer, the trial was front-page news, and a surprising amount of the publicity was humorous in nature.

"CRANKS AND FREAKS FLOCK TO DAYTON" was the headline of the July 11, 1925, New York <u>Times</u>. Other stories that summer included: 1) H.L. Mencken would be "roughed-up" for calling the citizens of Dayton "yokels." 2) "God--Or Gorilla" and "Hell in the High Schools" were best-sellers in Rhea County, Tennessee. 3) Clarence Darrow and William Jennings Bryan exchanged monkeys carved from peach pits. 4) A three-foot-tall man arrived in Dayton, claiming to be the "missing link."

I would like to propose writing a 1600-1800 word feature on my grandfather's trial for <u>Media History Digest</u>, emphasizing the humorous reports that appeared in newspapers around the country. Also, I can provide several photographs and cartoons from the trial that my grandfather saved, if illustrations are desired.

Enclosed is a self-addressed, stamped envelope for your reply. And thank you for considering my query.

Best regards,

FIGURE 2-3   Straightforward, simple letter, including list of highlights.

Houston, TX 77036
August 17, 1981

Mr. Hiley H. Ward, Executive Editor
KIDBITS
Suite 305
Ross House, Headhouse Square
401 S. 2nd Street
Philadelphia, PA 19147

Dear Mr. Ward,

Thank you for your guidelines. I am very impressed with the issue of KIDBITS which you sent.

I would like to propose three different articles for your consideration:

1) "Shaka-Shaka Song"-- a craft of approximately 200 words on how to make an African musical instrument out of a stick, bottle caps and some nails. There are three 8 × 10 line drawings for illustration.

2) "Metal Chess Men"-- a 450-word craft on how to construct a chess set out of nuts and bolts. Actually, I make chess sets out of many items--bottle caps, spools, drawer knobs, etc. BOYS' LIFE October 1980 issue carried my article "Make Your Own Chess Sets." The rights to that article have been returned to me. I have b&w photos but could obtain color slides. I would be glad to feature the metal set (a favorite of the kids who come to my house) or any of the others you wish.

3) "Growing Oil Beans and Gasoline Trees"-- a non-fiction piece about some desert plants which may help solve the energy crisis. Length 300-500 words, as you choose.

continued

FIGURE 2-4   Multiple-topic query letter.

continued

The first few articles and activities of the June issue were on the subject of dragons. If you have a theme list for upcoming issues, I would like to obtain that. Currently I am a regular contributor to R-A-D-A-R Magazine (Standard Publishing, Cincinnati, OH) for puzzles on assigned themes. I would like to construct puzzles for KID-BITS also.

I look forward to working with you.

Sincerely,

Mary Wade

(Mrs. Harold Wade)

---

pegged as a factory outlet instead of a quality source. Yet this overkill technique works for some. One is Raymond Schuessler, of Venice, Fla. (See Figure 2-6.) His lists work like brainstorming. If you're an editor of a children's magazine, for instance, always looking for new offbeat ideas to entertain and educate 8- to 14-year-olds, you don't care if the idea grabs you from a single-query letter or from an inventory of ideas such as Ray's.

Some writers personalize their stationery with pictures. One would-be writer's letterhead included a caricature of himself. However, trying to be humorous, this query writer from Canada made himself appear overweight and slovenly. This, of course, didn't inspire the editor with confidence. And when this writer did send an article on speculation, he followed with a letter correcting an error of fact in his science article. The editor decided to ignore him in the future.

One writer in Washington state sends a "Writer's Quick Query." This one-page questionnaire includes boxes the author checks to tell what kind of article he is proposing; included at the bottom is a coupon on which the editor can reply. The editor is expected to check, "Yes, let's have a look," or "Would be interested with changes indicated at right," or "Send complete outline," and so on. Editors, as we have seen, generally do not like these. Such an approach assumes that the editor is a bit of an idiot and can't write a letter.

Figures 2-7 through 2-10 are additional real query letters that, like Figures 2-2 through 2-5, brought at least an initial reply of interest from an editor.

Altona, IL 61414
Aug. 28, 1981

Hiley H. Ward
KIDBITS
Suite 305, Ross House, Headhouse Square
401 S. 2nd St.
Philadelphia, Pennsylvania 19147

Dear Hiley,

Parties are fun, especially when they're different. My article, "Let's
Have a Party," will give ideas which youngsters can use for their
clubs or when giving a party for their friends. My ideas include:

1. Backwards Party--wear clothes backward, do everything
   backward, serve refreshments first.

2. Traveling supper--go to one house for an appetizer, to
   another house for salad, to another house for a vegetable,
   etc.

3. Come As You Are Party--An impromptu party where
   everyone comes looking exactly as he or she did when
   invited.

4. Baby Party--Secure baby pictures of each invited guest. Have
   guests try to identify pictures. Play games with baby's toys.
   Serve baby food for refreshments.

My writing credits include articles in MODERN MATURITY, GRIT,
PEOPLE ON PARADE, CAREER WORLD, YOUNG WORLD, JACK AND
JILL, and many juvenile religious publications.

Would you like to see my article?

Sincerely,

Dianne

Dianne L. Beetler

FIGURE 2-5 Multiple-topic query letter.

Venice, FL 33595

Dear Editors:

Would you care to consider illustrated articles on any of the following subjects? I have been collecting material for such stories for 30 years. I have written for hundreds of national magazines including Boys Life, Cricket, Ranger Rick, Popular Mechanics, HOW TO, Science Digest, New York Times, American Heritage, etc. See WORKING PRESS OF THE NATION.

1. Tracking animals by footprints
2. Archery, how to
3. Astronomy as hobby
4. Backpacking
5. Quick shooting skill with BB gun
6. Badminton
7. Training with barbells
8. Barbershop quartet, form
9. Beachcombing, things to find
10. Beekeeping
11. Biking for health
12. Biking games
13. Bird watching
14. Attracting birds to garden
15. Bowling, fundamentals
16. Imitating animal calls
17. Hunt with a camera
18. Techniques of deer hunting
19. Camping safety
20. Can you canoe?
21. Cave hunting
22. Ham radio operators
23. How to play harmonica
24. Hockey, fundamentals
25. Safety on horseback
26. Train a hunting dog
27. Horseshoe pitching
28. How to collect insects
29. Kite flying
30. Lost in woods, what to do
31. Games with matchsticks
32. Meteorology as a hobby
33. Meteors, all about
34. How to win at checkers
35. Coin collecting
36. How to dive
37. How to train your dog
38. Bringing up a puppy
39. How's your fishing psychology?
40. Ice fishing
41. Fossil hunting
42. Hunting for gems (and rocks)
43. Genealogy, hunt for ancestors
44. How to prospect for gold
45. Fun with a microscope
46. Mountain climbing for beginners
47. Raise a parakeet
48. How to sketch a face
49. How to read faster
50. How to sight-in a rifle
51. How to handle a rowboat
52. Sculpting in clay
53. How to ice skate
54. Skeet shooting
55. How to ski
56. Prevent skiing accidents
57. How to water ski

FIGURE 2-6 Query letter with list of ideas.

58. Fun with a slingshot,
    tourneys held
59. Snow sculpturing
60. Fundamentals of soccer
61. How to pitch a softball
62. How to hit a softball
63. Stamp collecting for
    beginners

64. Swim the crawl
65. Volleyball
66. Walk for health
67. How to whittle
68. Beachcombing as a hobby
69. Make friends with a creek

Sincerely,

R. Schuessler

Raymond Schuessler

Simultaneous Query Letters

Some authors send query letters for the same article idea to more than one publication at once. These writers argue that they are merely asking a question and that they have no obligation to any particular publication at this stage. If a writer sends a proposal to one publication, however, and then withdraws it to prepare the article for another publication, the slighted editor probably won't want to work with the author in the future. In fact, the regular free-lancers probably have enough things in the fire that they don't have to double up on queries, unless the article has a real sense of urgency.

While authors differ on whether queries should be sent simultaneously, editors generally are of one mind. Put yourself in the place of the editor, who doesn't want to waste time reviewing something that might not be available. The editor assumes your query is submitted in good faith. Yet some editors are not bothered about a simultaneously submitted query, if they know it has also been submitted elsewhere. "If you do it, say so," says *Penthouse*'s Peter Bloch. "That's fine. It's a real world. I have no problem, if you're up front. If the editor is interested, the editor can call the writer" (to see the status of the article idea). Says *Family Circle*'s Susan Ungaro: "If you say this is a multiple submission, I then have no problem with it."

Wellington, CO 80549
July 11, 1981

Hiley H. Ward, Exec. Ed.
Hug-Verlag AG
Ross House, Suite 305
Head House Square
401 S. 2nd St.
Philadelphia 19147

Dear Mr. Ward,

Lichens are unusual plants often used as classic examples of symbiosis in biology classes. Lichens also, however, produce totally unique compounds that have antibiotic properties. I propose a short feature for Kidbits about these plants tentatively titled: "Lichens: strange plants with a healthy chemistry."

I have written articles for The American Biology Teacher and The Friend and wrote, illustrated and did much of the photography for a three-filmstrip series on lichens produced by Photocom Productions, Inc. in California.

I can provide color transparencies of various lichens and the crystallized forms of their organic acids (which form beautiful patterns in polarized light).

Thanks for your consideration.

Sincerely,

Gary Raham

FIGURE 2-7   Simple query letter.

Arlington, MA 02174
November 9, 1981

Dear Hiley,

Hope that the semester is progressing well for you and that teaching is not taking up most of your time.

I've given some thought to your suggestion of possibly putting together an entire issue on the world of fishes and I must say that I would be interested in participating in such a project.

Depending on your final lay-out as to contents, I could produce for you articles in the following areas:

1. Evolution of fishes (their sheer magnitude in numbers, remarkable adaptations, etc.)
2. Ecology of coral reef fishes
3. Anatomy of a fish (how do freshwater fishes differ in construction from saltwater fishes?)
4. Where to easily find fossil sharks' teeth from sharks 19 million years old and what it means
5. How to maintain a freshwater and/or saltwater aquarium (supplies needed, how to purchase tropical and marine fishes wisely)
6. Shapes and colors of fishes (how do they differ?)
7. Deep-sea fishes (why do they look so strange?)
8. Fishes with animal names (parrotfish, catfish, dogfish, seahorse, etc.)
9. How to catch sunfish
10. Different methods for catching fishes
11. Fishes that can walk on land (there are several . . .)

Well, the list could go on _ad infinitum_, so I'll conclude here. I have access to many slides of fishes and fishing and know three illustrators who could illustrate any article with fish sketches, water colors, etc. All three have done fish paintings in the past.

continued

FIGURE 2-8   Query letter including list of ideas on one theme.

continued

> Another nice idea for an article might be the art of gyotaku--oriental fish prints made by pressing rice paper over an ink-covered fish.
>
> In any event, please let me know if any of these ideas might be of value in a fish issue of <u>KidBits</u>.
>
>   Sincerely,

GETTING THE WRITING DONE

Writers may be tempted to delay the writing. Real or perceived barriers loom everywhere. The slightest interruption — a phone call or an oven timer — lures the writer away from the job at hand.

A functional working outline can help shore you up against interruptions. Get down on paper the subjects and subtopics you want to take up and connect them. You can begin a functional outline by listing the topics and facts gathered from research. Then draw connecting lines between the ideas, with arrows, and follow the arrows from one idea to the next. Turn this into a more formal outline, if you wish.

For larger projects, lay out your note cards or pieces of paper for each aspect of the story in separate piles. Number the piles in the order you want to take them up, and follow the numbers.

The secret to getting the writing done is to start on it early. In fact, let the article write itself. If you have thoroughly researched the subject and have an effective outline, the words will fall into place. Some writers like to bang out the first draft of an article or a book chapter in one sitting. It's important to get words down on paper. Circle the words that need further checking for spelling or accuracy or put a mark after them, such as "ch." Read over what you've written right away to smooth out the typos and obvious errors; do a light edit. Let the article sit a week or so, and then give it a heavy edit and revision.

Make a schedule. Decide how much time you need for each task, what you realistically can do. Schedule in some extra time for unforeseen difficulties — everybody catches the flu or a cold; everybody has unexpected guests

Tampa, FL 33612
July 5, 1988

Hiley H. Ward, Editor
Media History Digest
11 W. 19th St.
New York, NY 10011

Dear Mr. Ward:

Many thanks for mailing payment to me for the article I wrote on my grandfather. It's always encouraging to get a check in the mail.

Enclosed is an article proposal that I'm hoping might find its way into Media History Digest. Next year will be the fiftieth anniversary of the disappearance of Richard Halliburton, probably the most famous American explorer of the 1920's and 1930's. While I can't claim I have "insider information" on Halliburton, I have long been fascinated by his colorful life and exploits.

I've also enclosed a self-addressed, stamped envelope for your reply. (I'm probably moving within the next month or two, but my mail will be forwarded.)

Thanks again for the check, and thank you for considering my latest query.

Best regards,

FIGURE 2-9   Query letter with proposal.

ARTICLE PROPOSAL

RICHARD HALLIBURTON AND THE PRESS

Summer 1989 marks the fiftieth anniversary of the disappearance of Richard Halliburton. Today, Halliburton might be considered little more than a historical footnote; in his lifetime, however, he was one of the most famous people in America, and his books sold millions.

Consider these adventures:

*Richard Halliburton is the only person to have swum the Panama Canal, and his toll — 36 cents — is the lowest toll ever paid to the Panama Canal Commission.

*The first aerial photos of Mt. Everest were taken by Halliburton, and they almost cost him his life.

*Halliburton once posed as a prisoner on Devil's Island, and when he "escaped," his exposé of the conditions there caused a scandal in the French government.

*In 1939, Halliburton disappeared somewhere in the Pacific while sailing a replica of an ancient Chinese junk from Hong Kong to the San Francisco World's Fair.

What I propose is a 2,000-word article on the life and adventures of Richard Halliburton, with emphasis on the press coverage of his exploits. (His Panama Canal swim, for example, was front page news.)

Sources for this proposed article include Halliburton's books and newspaper accounts of his adventures.

Berwyn, PA 19312
January 22, 1987

Ms. Ruth Hillhouse, Editor
"Think Smart"
McCALL'S Magazine
230 Park Avenue
New York, NY 10169

Dear Ms. Hillhouse:

    Can you use a "tips" article on protecting credit cards?
    Last week, after making a hurried call at a cluster of open tele-
phone booths in Philadelphia's Market Street East Station, a
woman on a nearby bench indicated that she had something to tell
me. "When you made your call," she said, "the man in the next booth
took down your credit card number as you gave it to the operator." I
thanked the woman and immediately called the appropriate telephone company office and canceled my card.
    This caused me to do a little thinking about other ways that
careless uses of credit cards might place us at unsuspecting risks.
    Do we insist on retaining the carbons after each transaction?
Generally, we have nothing to fear from the merchants involved.
But those carbons go into outside trash where they can be re-
trieved, the numbers recorded, and merchandise ordered from mail-
order houses to be delivered to vacant addresses for retrieval.
    And when gasoline is purchased, it isn't enough to check the
service station attendant's written figures. One should always look
at the machine printed numbers in the upper right-hand corner--
the ones used for billing.
    What about the many credit card insurance offers? Are they
worth the costs? They could be. How can you create a handy alert
file yourself by using any standard copying machine?
    Do most people carry far too many cards--more than they re-
ally need--which multiplies their risks? These are just a few
thoughts for a brief feature on a subject of continuing interest.
Please let me know. SASE enclosed.

Very truly yours,

George L. Beiswinger

George L. Beiswinger

FIGURE 2-10   Query letter with list of questions.

drop in. Don't see the writing project as a complete whole with one deadline. Know where you should be in the schedule at certain times. Use the programmed slack time to catch up. Equate x amount of time (a week, a day, an hour) to x amount of productivity. For example, you might allot 2 hours to producing 500 words of a draft, even though you know you can write that much in an hour or less. You've built in slack time. Some prefer rigid schedules set day by day, with slack time added at the end before the deadline.

Ideally, you want to avoid interruptions. If they work at home, magazine free-lance writers can create some semblance of isolation. The newspaper feature writer will likely be interrupted by phone calls and will have daily articles and routines that may make it difficult to work on the feature at a sustained pace.

Here's some advice for those who are faced with interruptions. When the phone or doorbell rings, wait a moment before you answer. Quickly scribble on a piece of paper the beginning of what will be your next sentence plus the next few ideas in the order you want to take them up; or, if you're using a functional outline, mark your place. Then, when you finish your conversation, you can jump right back to where you were. It's surprising how quickly you can forget where you were before you were interrupted unless you give yourself some guideposts.

MANUSCRIPT FORMAT

For both newspaper features and for magazine articles, start in the middle of the page. (See Figure 2-11.) This format lets editors use the top of the page (if the article is accepted) for instructions to printers and for writing in blurbs, titles, headlines, etc.

The first page should have:

- A suggested title centered in the middle of the page.

- A byline centered under it.

- In the upper left corner: Your name, address, phone number. It's probably best to include your Social Security number, usually required by the business office before a check can be made out.

- In upper right corner: (1) Word count. Allow 250 words to a page (if pica type; about 320 if elite). Estimate — don't count every word. (2) Many writers use a "rights" line. (See Chapter 15 for a discussion on rights.) Usually "First North American Rights" is listed, which means the publication can use the article first, and one time only, in North America; and then the writer can resell and use any way he or she wishes thereafter.

- Paragraph indention — five spaces is usual.

- Margins of an inch or inch and a quarter.

John P. North

12 Army Drive

Hill Top, PA 18976

215-111-0001 (H)

215-222-2000 (O)

First North

American Rights

Word count 2500

Gettysburg Revisited

By J. P. North

You recall those words:

"Fourscore and seven years ago our fathers brought forth on

this continent a new nation conceived in liberty, and dedicated to

the proposition that all men are created equal.

"Now we are engaged in a great civil war testing whether that

nation, or any nation so conceived and so dedicated, can long

endure.

"We are met on a great battlefield of that war. We have come

FIGURE 2-11   Sample manuscript first page.

On the second and continuing pages, put in the upper left corner your name and a slug. A slug is a key word that identifies your article. If your name is Smith and you're writing about birds, then use "Smith/birds." In the middle of the page at the top, put a page number. At the end of the article, use some end symbol, such as ###, 30, End or zeros (-00-).

Use a good white stock of paper. Avoid erasable bond, because it smears and it is difficult to mark with a ballpoint pen.

Neatness is important, even more so in the computer age. A clear, clean, dark-type copy is needed by many publications, as the computer reads (scans) type off the page and loads it onto a disk from which it can be edited.

Do not use paper clips or staple your final draft. If the pages have been folded back around a staple, or if a paper clip has been moved around, the article will look as if it's been through the mill and handled by other editors. Send your manuscript flat in a 9 × 12 envelope, with some backing — a piece of cardboard or simply a file folder.

Enclose an SASE, a "self-addressed stamped envelope." Query letters, of course, can be sent in standard letter envelopes, folded like any letter. Some editors prefer an SASE with a query letter as well.

ASSIGNMENTS

1. Take any page from a newspaper; in fact, each student in the class could take a different page from the same paper. Let your imagination range — from idea to idea — and see how many inviting ideas you might find for articles.

2. Using one idea, consider how it might evolve to fit specific needs of different magazines.

3. Prepare a one-page query letter for an article your class elects to do first (for instance, a how-to article, profile or longer article), and mail it. Give a copy to your professor for evaluation.

4. Write sample query letters (you could try several formats) aimed at three publications. Evaluate one another's query letters in class.

5. Prepare a list of questions you have about query letters; collate all those from the class and invite a magazine or feature editor in to answer them.

6. Compile a class list of ten "do's" for query letters and another of ten "don'ts."

7. Look at the sample query letters in the book; decide which you like best, and explain why in a few paragraphs.

8. What is the least effective query letter in the sample? Rewrite it to improve it. Be sure also to give attention to "how it looks."

9. Outline a published article two ways, using both the formal Roman numeral procedure that you might send with a query and also a "listing with arrows" or "mapping" approach that you might use when starting to write.

10. Make a one-month time-use schedule that allows time for writing. Compare outlines in class. Can they be revised to maximize writing time and also to allow work in marginal periods?

CHAPTER 3

Using the Library

A trip to the library can help you with most articles. But remember that library research is just part of the picture. For the modern article you'll also need to convey the sense of an experience and the voices of knowledgeable people — usually through interviews. You're not writing term papers but articles for consumers.

To get information about libraries in your area, consult the *American Library Directory*. Arranged geographically, this guide lists libraries and special collections across the United States, including collection sizes, staff, locations and services. You can use this directory to locate the libraries in your area and to determine how to arrange in advance to use them.

Some libraries provide services to only users who are affiliated in some way with their institutions. When visiting any library, particularly one that is not public and with which you have no affiliation, you should always call ahead to find out what restrictions the library applies to visitors.

Note: Much of this chapter was written by Gwen Arthur, desk services coordinator in the reference and information services department, Paley Library, Temple University, Philadelphia.

Don't discount the non-public libraries. Even if they do not allow circulation of materials to visitors, most allow visitors to use materials on the premises and most provide reference service to all.

INTERLIBRARY LOAN

You're probably used to discovering that books and articles you need aren't available at the library you're using. The Interlibrary Loan (ILL) Department can use library networks, some computerized, to locate and borrow the requested items from another library. The library may absorb some of the costs for postage, teletype and insurance and other costs or pass them on to you.

Interlibrary loan materials may not arrive for several weeks, so you should (1) always check as many local libraries as possible first and (2) allow enough lead time for any materials you request through ILL to arrive. When you make a request to ILL, you must have a reference for a specific item, that is, you must have the author, title, date and publication information for a book, or the author, title, journal title, volume, page numbers and date for a periodical article.

STARTING WITH REFERENCE SOURCES

Start your research with "backgrounding" — getting an overview of the subject and some feeling of what has already been done by checking periodical indexes (for articles on particular subjects), books, encyclopedias, biographical directories and other specialized directories.

Periodical Indexes and Abstracts

Periodicals, also known as serials, issued on a regular basis (weekly, monthly, quarterly — that is, periodically) are good sources for updating information found in other places such as books or encyclopedias. (But, remember, even a current issue of a magazine or journal may be three months to a year out of date, because it takes time to prepare, edit and publish periodicals.)

Indexes and abstracts list references to periodical articles published in a given time period, usually by subject and sometimes by author. They provide the bibliographical information for each article, including title and author, and the journal title, volume, date and page numbers where the article appeared. Indexes range from general, covering articles in popular magazines, newsmagazines and newspapers, to specialized, covering only one field.

Abstracts provide summaries of articles in addition to providing bibliographical information. Here are some samples of indexes and abstracts:

General — *Humanities Index* (1974 to present); *International Index to Periodicals*; *Magazine Index* (microfilm or computerized); *Reader's Guide to Periodical Literature*; *Social Sciences Index* (1974 to present); *Infotrac* (computerized).

News indexes—*National Newspaper Index* (microfilm), which lists recent articles in the New York *Times*, *Christian Science Monitor*, *Wall Street Journal*, Washington *Post* and Los Angeles *Times*; *Christian Science Monitor* (1960 to present); *New York Times Index* (1851 to present); *Wall Street Journal* (1972 to present); Washington *Post* (1971 to present).

Specialized indexes—*America: History and Life* (1964 to present); *Applied Science and Technology* (1958 to present); *Bibliographic Index* (1937 to present); *Biography Index* (1946 to present); *Business Index* (micro); *Business Periodical Index* (1958 to present); *Education Index* (1929 to present); *Film Literature Index* (1973 to present); *General Science Index* (1978 to present); *Historical Abstracts* (1955 to present); *Index to Legal Periodicals* (1908 to present); *Modern Language Association International Bibliography of Books and Articles in the Modern Languages and Literature* (1921 to present); *Philosopher's Index* (1967 to present); *Psychological Abstracts* (1927 to present); *Public Affairs Information Service* (1915 to present); *Sociological Abstracts* (1953 to present).

Subject headings in different indexes and abstracts are not always the same, so think of as many terms as possible that might apply to your topic. A well-organized index will refer you to the appropriate heading if you look under an alternate or unused term.

Entries in periodical indexes include the same basic bibliographic information—that is, author and article title and, of course, the journal or magazine title, volume, date and page number where the article appears. However, entry formats are not always the same. When you're learning to use a new source, consult the introduction at the beginning of each volume; it will tell you about the kinds of materials indexed there and how the entries are arranged and interpreted.

Encyclopedias, Directories and Bibliographies

Besides general encyclopedias, including *Encyclopedia Britannica*, *Encyclopedia Americana*, *Collier's Encyclopedia* and *World Book Encyclopedia*, specialized volumes cover almost every discipline. Among them: *Encyclopedia of Business and Finance*; *Encyclopedia of Education*; *Encyclopedia of Philosophy*; *Encyclopedia of Religion*; *International Encyclopedia of Communications*; *McGraw-Hill Encyclopedia of Art*; *McGraw-Hill Encyclopedia of Science and Technology*; *New Grove Dictionary of Music and Musicians*; *Oxford Companion to American History*.

Encyclopedia entries often end with short bibliographies, giving additional references to books or articles about your topic.

Students sometimes overlook the value of directories and dictionaries about people. Considerable detail about a person can be found in these. Among them: *Biography and Genealogy Master Index*; *Contemporary Authors*; *Dictionary of American Biography*; *Who's Who in America*; *Who's Who in Finance and Industry*; *Who's Who in the World*; Who's Who . . . the list goes on and on; these cover living persons only.

Bibliographies contain lists of publications about different topics. To determine if there are major bibliographies on your topic, first check the *Bibliographic Index*, which is a master list of bibliographies, arranged by subject and published twice a year. Second, search in the catalog for entries under your subject with the subhead "Bibliography."

DATABASE SYSTEMS

Databases are the newest option for researchers, and the lightning speed by which they produce information can save many hours, even days. Databases can be full text or bibliographic. Full-text databases produce every word of a document. Bibliographic databases, producing indexes and abstracts, give a thorough picture of what is available.

The systems are not inexpensive. Online access — via long-distance telecommunications connections — can cost from 25 cents to $5 per minute, depending on the database used. It's not hard to run up a bill of $50 per use. Because of the expense and the specialized computer commands each system requires, most libraries still have librarians perform searches on these database systems for patrons. Check with your library's reference department and ask which computerized services they have and which are appropriate for your research project.

Before you begin a search, you need the key words of your topic and any synonyms. Look in a book, such as *The Synonym Finder* (published by Rodale Press). For example, if you want to identify some weird sports, you might check "games."

Online Databases

Two popular databases used by libraries are DIALOG and Vu/Text.

DIALOG, operated by a subsidiary of Lockheed Missiles & Space Co., Inc., offers access to 200 different databases and to articles and stories in more than 40,000 publications. World affairs databases are included. Among its specialized databases is an American history file with 43,000 records.

Vu/Text is a newspaper database prepared by Knight-Ridder Newspapers. At this writing, it includes 55 newspapers in 27 states. Among them, in a "major papers" category, are the Boston *Globe*, Chicago *Tribune*, Detroit *Free Press*, Los Angeles *Times*, Miami *Herald*, Newark *Star-Ledger*, *Newsday*, Philadelphia *Inquirer*, San Francisco *Chronicle*, and Washington *Post*. Another category groups papers by regions.

Another Vu/Text grouping, "Business, Wire and Magazine Databases," offers access to the Associated Press, *Fortune* magazine, *Kansas City Business Journal*, Knight-Ridder Financial News, *Life* magazine, *Money* magazine, *People* magazine, *Time* magazine, *Wall Street Transcript*, Business Wire, Business Dateline and several sports magazines.

Among other useful commercial databases:

- BRS — DIALOG's main competitor; this contains a slightly smaller number of databases but many important ones; mostly bibliographic.
- NEXIS — A system that covers the New York *Times* and several other major newspapers full-text; also indexes 100 popular magazines.
- LEXIS — Full text of federal court cases and case law for the United States, France and Britain.
- NEWSNET — Full text of 175 newsletters of all kinds of organizations; a way to get inside information from agencies and lobbyists.
- PR NEWSWIRE — Full text of releases for 7,500 companies back to 1983.
- ERIC — An abstracting of 700 publications and project reports in education.
- DATAMAP — 13,000 tables of statistical data.

CD-ROM (Compact Disk/Read-Only Memory)

Libraries that can afford the necessary microcomputer equipment and the database subscriptions are now providing patrons access to computerized databases on CD-ROM (Compact Disk/Read-Only Memory). Subscriptions to these compact disks, which contain thousands of pages of information, are quite expensive, but libraries tend to absorb the costs into their materials budgets without passing them on to library users. The advantages for you, the researcher, are that the disks are usually free to use and you can do the search yourself.

The major disadvantage of the CD-ROM is that each CD-ROM contains only one database, not the wealth of databases available on an online system from a vendor. However, librarians try to purchase or subscribe to compact disk indexes or abstracts that they know from past experience will be most heavily used.

Perhaps the most popular CD-ROM, subscribed to by public and academic libraries alike, has been *Infotrac*, which indexes many of the popular magazines indexed in print by the *Reader's Guide to Periodical Literature* and on microfilm by *Magazine Index*. Academic libraries subscribe to a variety of specialized databases that index scholarly journals in the social sciences, humanities and sciences. These CD-ROMs include *Social Sciences Index, Humanities Index, Public Affairs Information Service, Psychological Abstracts, MLA International Bibliography, Index Medicus* and others.

Just as a number of vendors provide online systems, a number of companies also produce these compact disks. Again the plethora of products and the accompanying lack of uniformity of computerized products from different vendors may cause some confusion. Ask your librarian whether these sources, if available, will be useful for your search. Also keep in mind that, in spite of advances in technology, many computerized sources provide only bibliographic references.

GOVERNMENT DOCUMENTS

Each year federal, state and local governments publish thousands of documents covering a wide range of topics. Under the federal depository library system, some libraries, as full or partial depositories, receive many U.S. government documents free for the purpose of making them available to the public. Don't overlook these sources. They also are valuable for statistical information on a variety of topics.

Because many government documents are not recorded in library catalogs, you need to be aware of the specialized indexes and catalogs that include them. The *Monthly Catalog of the United States Government Publications* (1895 to present) lists publications issued by all branches of the federal government and includes subject, author and title indexes, among others.

Another valuable source of government information is the *Congressional Information Service's Index to Publications of the United States Congress* (1970 to present), which indexes and abstracts congressional publications dealing with committee hearings, House and Senate documents and reports and other areas.

These sources are available not only in print but also in computerized versions, and there is at least one popular microfilm version of the *Monthly Catalog* (cumulative from the late 1970s). Another useful source is the *Index to U.S. Government Periodicals* (1970 to present), listing articles from 150 periodicals published by the federal government.

State governments issue a checklist of documents that they publish. In addition, the Library of Congress publishes the *Monthly Checklist of State Publications* (1910 to present), which lists the state publications the library receives.

However, because published lists of local government documents in particular can be irregular or even nonexistent, the *Index to Current Urban Documents* (1972 to present) provides libraries with easier access to these. It lists local materials published by city (and some county) governments across the United States and even includes some in a microform set.

The Public Affairs Information Service Bulletin or PAIS (1915 to present) indexes journals and books on public affairs, including federal, state and local publications. Although PAIS doesn't provide as much in-depth coverage as do the specialized indexes, its breadth and general availability in libraries make it a useful source. Libraries that do not have extensive documents collections may have this index, which can serve as a reference source for researchers who can then turn to their interlibrary loan services to obtain the items they need.

Libraries also collect international documents: reports from various countries, United Nations documents and others. PAIS also can serve as a starting point for researching these international documents, since its index-ing includes materials from other countries.

STATISTICAL SOURCES

For statistics, consider three sets of indexes published by the Congressional Information Service.

The *American Statistics Index* (1973 to present) indexes exclusively U.S. government publications, including the U.S. Census, which contains a variety of statistical data.

The *Statistical Reference Index* (1980 to present) has statistical informa-tion gleaned from publications of state governments and private organiza-tions, including associations, commercial publishers and business organizations.

The *Index to International Statistics* (1983 to present) indexes statistical materials published by international intergovernmental organizations, such as the United Nations and the Organization for Economic Cooperation and Development.

THE LIBRARY OF CONGRESS

The Library of Congress located in Washington, D.C. is one of the largest libraries in the world, containing 85 million items. Although its first respon-sibility is to provide service to the Congress of the United States, in its role as national library it also serves libraries and patrons around the country.

Although materials in the Library of Congress cannot be borrowed, its extensive collections are available for use by visitors. The library also provides extensive reference services to the public; in a year its reference staff answers nearly 2 million inquiries. The library also publishes bibliographies and other guides to its collections.

The library is a part of a federal library system, the Federal Library and Information Center Committee (FLICC), which operates FEDLINK, the largest library network in the country in terms of staff and budget (over $40 million).

The Information Service of the Library of Congress (Washington, D.C. 20540) provides brochures and pamphlets explaining its services upon request.

SAMPLE ARTICLE TOPICS

Let's take several possible article topics and see how you might develop back-ground at the library.

Suppose you want to write on "Teen-age Marriages: Can They Work?"

Check the *Library of Congress Subject Headings* (or other subject heading list used by your library) to determine if this is the correct heading for you to use in your research. In this case, checking LC headings reveals that "Teen-age marriage" is an official heading that you can use when checking in the card catalog or online catalog for book titles.

Because writers may frequently address the topic of teen-age marriage, you need to check periodical indexes for magazine and journal articles. Indexes that might be useful here include *Social Science Index* for scholarly journal articles and the *Magazine Index* or *Reader's Guide to Periodical Literature* for recent articles on the topic in popular and general interest magazines.

These indexes may be available in your library either in print, on microfilm or CD-ROM, or online. All of these use the standard heading "Teen-age marriages." However, remember that not all sources use the same standard headings; if they don't, watch for cross-references in the indexes to the appropriate headings.

Government documents often are kept in special collections and may not be cataloged in the regular online or card catalog; nevertheless, they cover a surprising variety of topics and can be of particular use in locating statistics about a topic such as this one. Sample searches in the microfilm version of the *Monthly Catalog of U.S. Government Publications* under the subject "Teen-age marriage" and the *American Statistics Index* under "Marriage and divorce" reveal government publications that might be worth consulting.

Consider another topic, presidential lore: "Presidents Who Have Killed: Military Presidents and Others."

This topic (presidents) is primarily historical. You could focus largely on books rather than periodicals (although you certainly could check historical periodical indexes). Also, because of the wealth of published biographical reference sources, you may want to start with these and dispense with the more general encyclopedias. Ideally you would want to check one biography on each president, using the index at the back of each book.

Consulting the *Library of Congress Subject Headings* reveals that books about American presidents are entered under the subject "Presidents — United States." Checking the card catalog or online catalog under this topic will reveal another useful subdivision: "Presidents — United States — Biography." Under this complete heading in your catalog you may turn up any number of books on presidents; some will be biographies of individuals, others will be collected biographies in one volume. By skimming information in the collected biographies first, you can pinpoint individual presidents whose biographies are worth investigating for further details.

A sample search on this topic turned up a variety of useful sources, including two biographical collections that specifically contained sections on the military service of all the presidents. Bush's war record was well documented in newspapers and newsmagazines during the 1988 election. A quick perusal of some of the biographies turned up references to one president who killed another man in a duel (Jackson) and one (Cleveland) who as sheriff of

Erie County, in New York, personally released the gallows trap on condemned criminals.

Consider writing on "Latin America: Has U.S. Policy Ever Worked?"

Since our hypothetical article focuses on foreign relations and has a historical and contemporary slant, you again need to consult *Library of Congress Subject Headings* to ascertain proper headings to use in locating both new and old books. Checking under "Latin America" in the subject headings list reveals that this is a heading, complete with subheading, "Foreign relations — United States" (the entry also notes a narrower, related heading "Monroe Doctrine" and an unused heading "Good neighbor policy"). You can also locate a related heading "United States — Foreign relations — Latin America," but only if you check under headings for the United States.

You can also use a specialized periodical index such as *Public Affairs Infomation Service Bulletin* for articles, books and some government publications on the topic. In addition, PAIS has a cumulative index from 1915 to 1974, which makes it useful and convenient for 20th-century historical research as well. *Facts on File*, updated each month, has summaries of the latest news developments. Flipping through a newsmagazine and checking the relevant sections for the past six months will help you keep abreast of what has happened in recent months on the subject and may suggest some names you can contact on your own.

A combination of any or all of the following can be used to research the latest developments in Latin America: *Magazine Index*, *Reader's Guide to Periodical Literature*, *National Newspaper Index*, all of which are news or magazine indexes updated on a regular basis. Indexes for individual newspapers such as the New York *Times*, Washington *Post* and *Wall Street Journal* can be used for the same purpose. Again, most of these sources are available online; however, computer costs may mean that online searches on this broad topic are not practical.

This kind of topic might also be covered extensively in government documents. Although you can find some government documents on this topic in PAIS, you also may want to check the *Monthly Catalog of U.S. Government Publications* (again under the heading "Latin America") or the microfilm or computerized versions of this source.

Remember, however, in this topic and the others, interviews with experts and authorities may be needed. Library resources, of course, can lead you to the right persons to contact for information and interviews.

ASSIGNMENTS

1. Using this chapter as a guide, determine what is available at your college or university library. What special collections or services does your library offer?

2. As a class, do a library research plan for a topic such as "New Ways to Care for the Elderly at Home" or "How to Live to Be 100" or something you're interested in. Each student could report on one facility or library research service that is applicable.

3. Examine government publications in the library. Suggest five article ideas that are inspired by perusal of the government material.

CHAPTER 4

The All-Important Anecdote

An anecdote is a little story, and like any story, an anecdote has dimensions and development.

Anecdotes are so important that some editors think they are nearly all you need in an article. When he was editor of *Family Weekly*, Mort Persky once told a writer: "Just come up with a lot of anecdotes. We'll string them together for you."

At *Avenue* magazine, they talk about anecdotes as "chocolate chips." If you don't have the "chocolate chips" in the cookies, the batch will be plain and unexciting. "We want to know, where are the chips?" said Susan Roy, when she was senior editor at *Avenue*. She is now executive editor of *Allure*.

CHARACTERISTICS OF ANECDOTES

An anecdote is more than a mere description of place, more than a character sketch, more than a compilation of facts. Whatever else it does, an anecdote adds life to your article. Like a story, all anecdotes should have certain elements of a story.

Subject, Hero or Protagonist

The focus of an anecdote is usually a human being or another living creature. However, the subject or protagonist can be something inanimate that is perceived as living. One student at Mankato State University was assigned to study the floor at the Minneapolis bus terminal all night and describe its evolving, changing nature. Another student walked some distance along a river in Minnesota and presented it as a living entity, watching what it was doing, what was happening in the water and along the banks. Both features were for daily newspapers.

The Philadelphia *Inquirer* dramatized the life of a hapless bald eagle. "He was the guy that flew the coop," began an article on the rescue of the bird. "All the way from a nesting tower near Albany, N.Y., to a construction site in Chester County. He hadn't eaten for 14 days and was near death. . . ."[1]

Most anecdotes re-create a dramatic moment in a person's life. This story recapitulates a suspenseful moment and the tragic outcome:

> BERGENFIELD, N.J., March 20—Dinner was ready at the Rizzo home when the telephone rang that Tuesday night. Cheryl Burress and her sister Lisa were calling to see if Thomas Rizzo and his friend Thomas Olton wanted to go out.
>
> "Save dinner," Mr. Rizzo told his mother, as the two got into Mr. Olton's gold Camaro. "We'll stick it in the microwave when we get back."
>
> Noreen Rizzo was up past midnight waiting for her son. When she woke up the next morning and saw that he had not returned, she assumed he had spent the night at a friend's house. She got her youngest child, Michael, ready for school and chatted with her husband, Tom.
>
> Around 7, the Rizzos heard the front door rattle and thought Thomas had forgotten his key. Instead, standing in the doorway were a police officer and a chaplain. They said that the Rizzos' son was dead, that his friend Thomas was dead, that the two Burress sisters were dead, that it was not an accident. . . .[2]

Place

In anecdotes, as in all narratives, a sense of place helps us to "see." "John Henry is an accountant" is a statement of fact. But "John Henry is tall, balding, with ringlet-like sideburns; he sits in the park on the first bench late in the afternoon as the sun sets" approaches being a story. With a sense of place, you feel you are there.

1. Shelly Philips, "Rescued Eagle Will Fly Back to New York—on a Plane," Philadelphia *Inquirer*, Sept. 16, 1987, p. 7B.

2. Esther B. Fein, "After Suicides, Bergenfield Seeks Answers and Solace," New York *Times*, March 23, 1987, p. B1. Copyright © 1987 by The New York Times Company. Reprinted by permission.

Note the sense of place in these two leads to articles in the *Wall Street Journal*:

> WASHINGTON — The whine of power tools signals the renaissance of the once run-down public housing project. Workers in hard hats toil where drug dealers once preyed. The bullet-proof barrier that separated managers from tenants is gone; today, the tenants are the managers.
>
> The people in Kenilworth-Parkside's 464 homes are taking an historic step. This soon will become the nation's first public housing project to be owned by a tenant organization. . . .[3]

> The owner of a Dairy Queen franchise in Wilmette, Ill., refuses to march in lock step with other outlets. He insists on serving hamburgers instead of the standard Dairy Queen food menu of hot dogs and barbecued beef. He doesn't provide chairs or benches; customers can sit on a guard-rail near a busy road.
>
> Such behavior may not sound like the gravest matter, but it violates a basic rule of modern franchising: Every franchisee must conform to the pattern. Above all else, customers expect consistency. . . .[4]

Significant Detail

Lively anecdotes make use of significant details. But remember that not all details are significant. For example, knowing that a person has several hundred dollars and some coins in a pocket is not useful. But if a rich man carries no money and has to ask for 25 cents to make a phone call, that reveals something about his personality. Among the famous pictures in American history is a photo of presidential candidate Adlai Stevenson sitting on a stage, legs crossed, and a hole in the sole of one of his shoes. When Pope John XXIII met the press in the Sistine Chapel, you noticed how the gentle old man tapped his red-slippered feet incessantly. Billy Graham usually appears calm and collected but one reporter interviewing him in a New York hotel noted how he piled pillows over the phone to deaden the rings in his desperate attempt to get some peace and quiet. A significant detail helps construct an image and direct the course of the story or a particular anecdote.

Significant details can give your anecdote an imaginative or suspenseful feel. Notice how the details in the Bergenfield youth suicide story add to the poignancy, suspense and drama: the ringing phone, the dinner, the microwave, the gold Camaro, normal chatting with husband, the rattling of the door.

3. Joe Davidson, "Pride of Ownership: Takeover by Tenants of Housing Project Makes Place Livable," *Wall Street Journal*, July 6, 1989, p. 1.

4. Barbara Marsh, "When Franchisees Go Their Own Way: Dairy Queen Seeks to Rein in Unruly Empire," *Wall Street Journal*, July 6, 1989, p. 1.

Stephen King knows the power of the significant detail and how it fuels imagination. Describing a creepy house in his novel, *Salem's Lot*, he doesn't use words like "spooky" or "sinister" or an abundance of details. Instead he includes a few salient details, such as the paint being weathered away and many of the shingles being ripped off. Never does he say how many stories the house has, how many steps, whether it has a weathervane. "Imagery is not achieved by overdescription," he says. "Imagery does not occur on the writer's page; it occurs in the reader's mind. . . . Leave in the details that impress you the most strongly; leave in the details you see the most clearly; leave everything else out."[5]

Character Traits

Characters should be real. In an anecdote, as in a short story, a believable character can have both positive and negative traits. While some anecdotes are too abbreviated to flesh out a character with different traits, a longer dramatic scene or an accumulation of anecdotes — in a profile, for instance — can present many dimensions of a person. In the Bergenfield dramatic anecdote, note the devotion of the mother (a positive trait), but also how being a trusting person could have some pitfalls. In reality, of course, one would be at a loss to be able to prevent such tragedies.

Immediacy

Using the simple past or present tense allows your readers to feel they are in the midst of the action. When you use the present tense — some would call it the historical present tense — the past seems to be happening again. Note the use of the present tense and the sense of immediacy that was achieved in the two examples from the *Wall Street Journal*.

Movement

When you have living creatures, you have movement. Living creatures have heartbeats; they breathe, lean, walk, gesture; their eyes, head, feet and hands move. In a larger sense they take action. Movement implies plot, although an anecdote may not complete the plot. Notice movement — a person who reacts and takes action — in this lead anecdote from a *Cosmopolitan* article:

> Gina, a twenty-three-year-old graduate student at the University of Minnesota, knew her parents weren't the happiest of couples, but she fully expected to join them in a celebration of their twenty-fourth wedding anniversary. Just two weeks before the event, however, her father announced he was leaving her mother because he could no longer stand his wife's nagging, petty ways.

5. Stephen King, "Imagery and the Third Eye," *The Writer*, October 1980, p. 11.

Gina was devastated. "When Dad packed up and moved out, the world became a much less safe place for me," she said. Her grades started to suffer as a result, and she sought help from her school's counseling service.

An extreme reaction? Yes. A rare one? Not at all. "Adult children are frequently very disturbed by their parents' marital crises," says Judith Sills, a Philadelphia psychologist. . . .[6]

Plot

A good anecdote, like a full story, often has a plot of its own. In its most rudimentary form, a plot has three ingredients: a protagonist, a barrier (a problem to overcome, such as a hurdler having to get over the hurdle as he or she runs) and a climax that leads to a resolution of the problem. For instance, consider anecdotes from *Reader's Digest* with abbreviated "plots":

> When in London, author P. G. Wodehouse solved the problem of the long walk to the post office by tossing letters out his window. He believed that the average person, finding a stamped, addressed letter on the pavement, would naturally pop it into the nearest mailbox. Never once was he proved wrong.[7]

Another from the *Reader's Digest*:

> A teacher was having trouble with his bank. Neither the bank's accuracy nor its mode of expression lived up to his standards. The last straw arrived in the form of a letter from the bank which read: "Your account appears to be overdrawn."
>
> To this, the teacher wrote back: "Please write again when you are absolutely certain."[8]

Constriction of Time

The best anecdotes — and usually the best short stories — constrict time. The shorter the time span (and the fewer the number of scenes), the stronger will be the sense of drama. For instance, even though a serious auto accident happens in a flash, those involved often see their lives passing before them. For dramatic effect in movies, action takes place in slow motion — someone crashes through a window, a car plunges into the deep, a touchdown is scored.

6. Myron Brenton, "When Your Parents Aren't Getting Along," *Cosmopolitan*, July 1989, p. 70.

7. "It's Human Nature," *Reader's Digest*, September 1988, p. 153, item from Stephen Fry in *The Listener*, England.

8. "Report Card," *Reader's Digest*, September 1988, p. 158, item from John J. Creedon, quoted in the *Wall Street Journal*. Reprinted by permission of the *Wall Street Journal* © 1988 Dow Jones & Company, Inc. All rights reserved worldwide.

Condense the time span, dissect, stretch out the tissue of action. Consider the excitement of this golf shot in slow motion:

> LIGONIER — You're not supposed to make noise when a golfer is reading a green.
>
> Someone 220 yards across the fairway broke that rule when Arnold Palmer was crouched on the 18th hole at Laurel Valley Golf Club.
>
> "Make it Arnie!"
>
> Palmer just laughed, put his hands up and turned around, much to the delight of a huge throng of Western Pennsylvania friends and neighbors.
>
> It would be nice to say he did make it. But he lipped out from six feet for a two-putt. He finished par for a 77, 5 strokes over for the round. . . .[9]

Consistent Viewpoint

An anecdote, like a story, gets its unity largely from a consistency of viewpoint (or point of view). Used most often is the single point of view — telling the story through one mind — the first person "I" or the third, "he" or "she." Other viewpoints include the omniscient (appearing in everybody's mind at will) and the reportorial, the observer/narrator point of view. Note that the reader identifies with the narrator's first person viewpoint in this anecdote from the Philadelphia *Inquirer's Inquirer Magazine*:

> As the Amtrak train rolled into Philadelphia from the north, a voice over the speaker system announced its arrival.
>
> "Ladies and gentlemen, in approximately three minutes, at 5:54, this train will arrive 30th Street Station, Philadelphia, the only stop in the Philadelphia area on this train."
>
> While departing passengers gathered their belongings, the voice crackled once again.
>
> "Ladies and gentlemen, this is Philadelphia, we are now arriving Philadelphia."
>
> After a pause, there it was again. "Philadelphia, this is Philadelphia."
>
> A conductor standing next to me checked his watch and smiled. "That's the engineer," he said. "He must be proud he's on time."
>
> "What's wrong with that?" I asked.
>
> As the train lurched into the station, right on schedule, he explained, "People will start to expect it," he said.[10]

A self-contained humorous episode, this compact story could serve as a lead into an article discussing the punctuality of train schedules and efficiency of train systems in general.

---

9. Rick Xander, "Palmer Evokes Nostalgia," Doylestown (Pa.) *Intelligencer*, July 3, 1989, p. B-1.

10. Nena Baker, "Oh, I Think I See What You Mean," *Inquirer Magazine*, Philadelphia *Inquirer*, "Our Town" section, Nov. 9, 1986, p. 8.

CAN YOU MAKE UP ANECDOTES?

Like any good story, an anecdote should sound real. Of course, because you're writing nonfiction articles, your anecdotes should be factual. But even an absolutely true anecdote will undermine your piece if it doesn't sound as if it really happened, if it isn't believable, says Rebecca Greer, *Woman's Day* articles editor. Furthermore, she says "We usually insist on real names in anecdotes, but do make occasional exceptions — especially for sensitive topics (like incest) where people might not want to reveal their names."

Says Liz Logan, articles editor, *Mademoiselle*: "I think the truth is alway more interesting than fiction."

Terry McDonell, editor-in-chief of *Esquire*, says simply that made-up anecdotes are "unacceptable." Ronald P. Kriss, executive editor of *Time*, says he feels the same way about made-up anecdotes as about made-up quotes: "Verboten. One may occasionally use a device like: 'An apocryphal story making the rounds . . . ,' but inventing an anecdote and presenting it to readers as something that actually happened is dishonest and therefore unacceptable."

There are some ways of using the "made-up" anecdote or the ones that are almost true. But pay careful attention to these exceptions to the truthfulness rule. Their use does not entirely suspend the sense of truth and reality.

Anecdote as a Model

You're sitting down to write your article, and you need just the right anecdote to start. You create a "model." You write the kind of anecdote you want and then go looking for the real version. You call around and ask people if they know about a person or story like the one you have in mind. For instance, you're doing an article on upwardly mobile young people, and you want to tell someone's story in the lead or in a sidebar — someone who is upwardly mobile and disabled. Or you're assigned to do a feature on barbershop quartets. You know exactly the kind of person you want to highlight. Or you're trying to personalize an article on newly released statistics, such as the increased enrollment of college freshmen. You want an athlete, a non-athlete, a minority student and so on. You call the appropriate offices until you find just the right persons. You have already created the scenario; now you're fitting people to it. You then discard the model, the fake anecdote, and insert the real.

Getting into the Mind of a Person

Giving someone else's thoughts in an anecdote seems to provide an element of fiction. You can do this with historical persons more easily than with contemporaries who might challenge you.

If you stick closely to the facts concerning a deceased person, as do writers of historical novels like Gore Vidal, then you can give depth to your main characters by showing their thought patterns. You don't violate the known facts, and you fill in the gaps in a manner consistent with research about the person and historical period.

For instance, in a feature recapturing the death of Gen. George Armstrong Custer and his troops at Little Big Horn in Montana territory, you could safely say that "Custer looked up as the swarm of horses and warriors came in as if from the sky. He gave a command. The little circle of horses and men tightened." You should not venture to guess at Custer's words, but you can dramatize the facts and still be true to them. If you put words in a historical figure's mouth that are not substantiated verbatim in the records, make clear that you're doing so. Vidal adds a postscript to his works, indicating what is known and what is interpolation.

If you're trying to get into the mind of a living person, limit your endeavor to people you interview or can contact. Then, you simply ask what the person was thinking at a certain time in a given situation. What was the gubernatorial candidate thinking on the night the primary returns were coming in? What was the football star thinking when he broke free and zoomed toward the goal line? Work their thoughts into your re-creations of the episodes.

Protecting an Identity

As Greer suggested, you might mask the identities of people in anecdotes to protect them from unnecessary embarrassment or possible danger if their names are used. Using just a first name indicates that you have disguised the identity, while the details make it clear that the person is real. In an article on the many facets of addiction, Gloria Hochman, writing in the Philadelphia *Inquirer*'s Sunday magazine, starts off with a triple punch to show the variety and persuasiveness of addiction. She used fictitious names, although the anecdotes are very real:

> When Lauren awakened in the morning, the first thing she thought about was food. When she went to bed at night, she thought about what she'd eat the next day. A typical breakfast might be a dozen doughnuts, half a gallon of milk, three bowls of cereal overflowing with crumbled cookies, bananas and a scoop or two of chocolate chip ice cream.
>
> "I would eat so much I would have to unbutton my blouse and my bra," she says. "I would get to a point where I was so stuffed, I couldn't breathe. So stuffed my chest hurt. . . .
>
> "I knew something was wrong with me, but I wasn't sure what it was."
> *Today, I know that I am an addict and that I am powerless over my addiction.*
>
> When David was a shy, sensitive 13-year-old, a friend showed him how to masturbate. Like most boys his age, David loved the feeling it gave him, and he began doing it every day. Soon, he discovered pornography magazines; they gave him an "incredible ecstasy" that temporarily reduced the sadness in his life. "I would look at the pictures and masturbate . . . every chance I got. It

was all I could think about. I didn't care about school any more. Nothing else mattered."

Then came X-rated movies. He would slink into a theater, glancing over his shoulder to make sure no one saw him enter, and watch the film and masturbate under a raincoat. "My need was impossible to ignore," he says.

Even after marriage, and after becoming a father, he needed continuous sex away from home. It might be in massage parlors. It might be with hookers who did exactly what he told them, and did it fast enough to get him back to work before people noticed his absence. When he wasn't engaging in sex, he was fantasizing about it. He was obsessed. It was costing him several thousand dollars a year, and he still couldn't satisfy his craving.

Today, I know that I am an addict and that I am powerless over my addiction.

Angela Marshall called herself the V & V girl. Vodka and Valium. She had her first drink — a whiskey sour — when she was 16. She still remembers the kick it gave her. "I felt smarter, more attractive, more self-confident. I knew I never wanted to lose that feeling."

For 20 years she pursued that euphoria. First it was drinking on weekends, then it was a couple of V.O.'s on the rocks in the evening — every evening. Then it was a martini at lunch, or two or three. For a while, she drank vodka from tumblers made of Waterford crystal. Later she slugged it down right from the bottle.

The slightest upset was an excuse to drink. An argument with her husband. A friend forgetting her birthday. Alcohol "fixed" it all.

Today, I know that I am an addict and that I am powerless over my addiction.

Addiction is one of modern medicine's most provocative riddles. Everyone knows that substances like alcohol, Valium and nicotine can be addicting. But what about food, as in Lauren's case? Or sex, as in David's case? Or any of a multitude of other activities such as jogging, working or dancing? Done in excess, are these things equally addictive? . . .[11]

Hochman tells how she gets her "real anecdotes": "I'll ask experts to select someone or I go through PR people. In the addiction article, I got the alcohol person from a center, the food addict from another center via the PR people; the sex addict from a psychiatrist. I interviewed 12 persons [by tape] and narrowed my choices to three. I left out one of the 12 because the case would be recognizable. Some poured their hearts out to me. They wanted to be helpful." Incidentally, she called back the nine she did not use to explain why. "I know they will be disappointed if they are not in the article. I call them and say, 'your story turned out too long, or 'it doesn't fit the focus, but your words are useful and helped me.'" It's not only considerate and thought-

11. Gloria Hochman, "The Dangers of Desire," *Inquirer Magazine*, Philadelphia *Inquirer*, Feb. 21, 1988, p. 17.

ful but also good public relations. You may want to go back sometime and pull out an interview for another article, she says.

Constructing Composites

A counselor or doctor wants to talk about certain people but can't because of the need to protect the confidentiality of the individuals. But to make a point, such as to describe an "average" subject or patient, the professional draws information from a number of cases and compacts it as if there were one person; and a fictional name is given. For instance, you want to describe a typical person in a home for unwed mothers. You draw facts from various backgrounds so that no one is recognizable, and you call the composite "Sarah" or some other name. You indicate clearly in your article that this "typical" young lady is a composite of several people. The facts are real; you are honest; the point is made. Yet "Sarah" is not one person, in name or character. However, as useful as they are for certain types of articles, composites usually sound more rhetorical than real and just aren't convincing. "I never use composites," says Hochman. "Sometimes I might change a name; sometimes I might change a location, for example, from southeast Philadelphia to northeast Philadelphia. Every time you change something, you lose something."

Myth, Parable or Allegory

A myth is a story, often based in history, that explains something; a parable is a story based on common knowledge that conveys a lesson or moral; allegory takes familiar things and creates a symbolism-laden story with several levels of meaning. Used in articles, these all work as anecdotes. They should be clearly marked as fictitious. Often, as in the following parable, they are printed in italics so that they stand out — another way of indicating that the story is fictitious and is being included to make a point.

> *Perhaps a movie will be made in which a much harassed business traveler finds, as Jack Lemmon did in* The Out-of-Towners, *just how much can go wrong on a trip.*
>
> *The updated version would be more outrageous, though, since the list of security breaches has grown much longer in the 15 years since Lemmon appeared in the classic comedy.*
>
> *The woes would begin at home, as he finds his closest aides, despite protective measures, are stealing from him and the company. People are able to wander in and out of his company's secret sessions and secret files as if they were invisible. Raiders lurk everywhere. The ultimate secrecy of computer codes has also been transgressed, even by teen-age hacks.*
>
> *As he goes to the overseas office, his plane is hijacked, he is terrified, but emerges alive. On the return flight, the great jet crashes; but he's in the tail section, and he survives with some injuries. Within a month, one arm still in a sling, he is gunned down by some extremist wing of a liberation group.*

A hapless man, he compacts into a nutshell the imagined — and real — fears of the business traveler.

More than 8,000 incidents of terrorism have occurred since 1968, according to the State Department. Terrorists struck 5,175 times in the decade from 1973 to 1983, leaving 3,689 dead and 7,791 wounded. Forty percent of some 500 attacks in 1983 were aimed at the U.S., with 271 Americans killed and 116 wounded, the biggest number reported since record keeping started in 1968. More than 50% of incidents over that period were directed against U.S. interests. In 1984, the incidents were up 30%, even though total casualties were down.

Business executives accounted for 14% of terrorist victims in 1983 (another 48% were diplomatic and government personnel of the U.S. and other countries).

The most publicized strikes against U.S. citizens have been the taking of the hostages in the U.S. Embassy in Iran for 444 days; the burning of the U.S. Embassy in Pakistan; the blowing up of the embassy in Beirut; and six months later the blowing up of the Marine compound in Beirut, killing 241; the bombing of the U.S. Embassy annex in September 1984, and this past summer, the hijacking of TWA Flight 847 en route from Athens to Rome. Forty were taken hostage, many of them businessmen, and a Navy diver in the group was murdered.

Figures to be released by the State Department this fall for 1984 show 600 international incidents of terrorism (40% of them in Europe) with 1,526 casualties (483 dead). Figures for the first four months of 1985 show 265 terrorist incidents, compared with 214 for the same period last year. . . ."[12]

Note how Robert Benincasa clearly and immediately labels the following anecdote from an article on a southeastern Pennsylvania quarry debate as fictitious:

Two residents of Plumstead Township bump shopping carts in the produce section one Thursday afternoon: "Oh, hi, Bill. You going down to the firehouse tonight? I hear they're talking about acoustical physics."

"Acoustical physics? I was sort of hoping to hear a little more about grout injections, and perhaps kick around some of the more significant debates in contemporary hydrogeology. I guess I'll go, though. See you there, Jane. Oh, and uh, don't forget your No-Doz."

The conversation is fictitious, but may as well be real.

On 29 evenings thus far, township residents have shown up at the Plumsteadville Fire Co. to listen to lawyers and scientists labor over the technical details of operating a crushed stone quarry on Point Pleasant Pike.

The subject matter, it might be said, is obscure enough to make a VCR instruction manual read like a comic book.

Were it not for residents' fears of noise, traffic, dust and pollution from the would-be Miller & Son Paving Inc. quarry on Point Pleasant Pike and Valley

12. Hiley H. Ward, "Risks of Business," *Travel Weekly*, September 1985, p. 17.

View Road, this protracted and expensive "curative amendment" hearing might well play to an empty room. . . .[13]

A few magazines allow fictitious anecdotes to be used as if they were real, and some successful writers admit to using them without labeling them fictitious. Questioned about an article she wrote in *Cosmopolitan*, one writer said, "I started with three case histories. One case history was about a friend. I had worked with her at *Glamour*. The second was also about a friend who lived in the Village, also a writer." The article used just first names without identifying occupations. Regarding the third case history, the writer said, "Well, I don't know who this is. I suspect I made it up. I needed a case history to round out the other case histories. I knew from interviews with a sex therapist [the article dealt with sex problems] that this was possible. Writing for *Cosmopolitan* is very close to writing romance novels. Do you want to be a writer or journalist or a little bit of each? It's fun [writing for *Cosmopolitan*]. You can exercise your fiction writing. It's a 'good read,' a 'juicy read.'" This author argues that the made-up anecdote has the effect of myth, capturing the essence of a bona fide situation that could exist. Yet most editors would insist the fictitious anecdote should be labeled or should be obviously fictitious, as in a composite.

Be advised that—despite what some writers do for certain kinds of publications—if you make up an anecdote without labeling it as fictitious, you likely will be in very deep trouble very quickly.

THE PARTIAL OR FRAGMENTED ANECDOTE

Anecdotes are not always complete, rounded out, with action resolved. An anecdote can depend on imagination and memory. An anecdote can exist by implication.

The One-Word, One-Phrase Anecdote

One poignant word, one descriptive word, one metaphor or simile sometimes acquires the status of story or anecdote. Virgil's classic metaphor, the "rosy-fingered dawn," suggests a sky, animated, moving, becoming. Alice Walker's "Spanish moss" mustache (in her story, "To Hell With Dying") suggests an unruliness and a feisty personality. Stephen Crane's stream becoming "a sorrowful blackness" (*The Red Badge of Courage*) and Thomas Hardy's "perfect silence" (*The Mayor of Casterbridge*) are observations, but they convey more in the imagination. A feature on racing could start with just the imitation in a

13. Robert Benincasa, "Both Sides Stand Ground in Tedious Quarry Battle," Doylestown (Pa.) *Intelligencer*, Jan. 6, 1991, p. A-1.

word of the whining sound of a car taking the winning curve or the sound of a sickening crash and crunch. Sometimes a word tells a story.

The Sentence Anecdote

A story can be summarized in a sentence. Consider this lead in a story on Joel Hyatt and his legal services firm in *USA Today*. Notice much is said in the first sentence:

> Lawyer Joel Hyatt has heard all the jokes about his Hyatt Legal Services —
> McLaw, Laws-R-Us and Microwave lawyer.
>
>   He's prepared for more derision after he appears live tonight on Cable
> Value Network — the USA's second largest home shopping network — to be-
> gin pitching his prepaid legal insurance plan. . . .[14]

You could stretch that first sentence into a full anecdote of several para-graphs. You could tell the jokes in all their detail. But things are very tight in the *USA Today* format and one sentence does the trick as well, with the force of a full story.

The Implied Anecdote

Like a nuance, a feeling, ambience, an implied anecdote does not derive from any special wording, but from what is not said. Perhaps it's the context, a situation, or what we already know about some things, our suspicions, our expectations. We sometimes expect the worse, readily creating scenarios and stories in our mind. John Kennedy, Gary Hart, Bill Clinton linked to or just in the presence of beautiful women suggest romantic scenarios, although sus-pected trysts may not have any ground in fact. A bedridden president: The mind wanders — what if he dies? The implied anecdote that most journalists would avoid using is used with skill by the tabloids and inadvertently even by major media. When an alleged mobster has his day in court, how much is implied in just the tone of the article?

WHERE TO USE ANECDOTES

If you can write an article almost entirely with anecdotes, as Persky suggested, then the anecdote can probably be used almost anywhere in the article.

    Certainly anecdotes can be used in the lead, grabbing wary readers by telling a story and leading them into the article. Note how the following two anecdotes, which led an article in *Psychology Today*, tell you that the article will be about "traveling offices":

> Sandra Gill, an independent health-care consultant in Illinois, travels by
> plane four out of five days a week. While on the road she keeps in constant

14. Ken Myers, "Hyatt Makes a New Pitch," *USA Today*, Sept. 9, 1988, p. 2A.

touch with her clients and her office by phone and fax machine. She uses spare time on airplanes and in hotel rooms to write speeches and papers on her portable typewriter. Her productivity "has zoomed," she says, since she began this system.

Andre Delbecq, dean of the School of Business Administration at Santa Clara University in California, uses his time on airplanes for reflection, not for writing. But when he drives 56 miles two or three times a week to San Francisco, he spends the time answering his correspondence. "When you're going eight miles an hour on a congested freeway, you can make very good use of a Dictaphone," he explains.

In the old days, traveling business executives knew that they would be incommunicado for much of their trip. . . . Those days are gone. . . .[15]

Make sure your opening anecdote doesn't just catch the reader's eye but that it also hints at the subject of the article. A rule of thumb with anecdotes: they should not be so entertaining that they let the reader forget the rest of the article. Remember that the human model standing next to a new car in a commercial might make viewers fail to notice the car.

Anecdotes can be used throughout the article to make a point or to expand on one. But don't get lost in a labyrinth of anecdotes. Make sure they make the point and propel the reader into the rest of the article.

Anecdotes can be used at the end of an article as a summary, conclusion or punchline. Bob Greene, writing about the generally unknown composer-musician, Richard Berry, summarized his *Esquire* article with an anecdote that encapsulated the essence of Berry:

I thanked Berry for his time and for the information, and I said that I had to bother him with one more detail. I told him that *Esquire* has a research department that fact-checks everything that goes into the magazine. So I asked if he could help me out with a seemingly minor question: Was there a comma in "Louie Louie"?

"A comma?" Berry said.

"Yeah," I said. "Is it 'Louie, Louie,' or is it 'Louie Louie'?"

"I don't know," Berry said. "I never thought about it."

"They're going to want to know, and they're going to drive you crazy until they find out," I said. "Could you look on the original song?"

Berry laughed.

"You must be kidding," he said. "That piece of toilet paper that I wrote 'Louie Louie' on fell apart many years ago."

That made sense. "Could you make a decision, then?" I said.

"Okay," Berry said. "'Louie Louie.' No comma."[16]

Anecdotes can also be used in a sidebar (a boxed item) to make a point or add information. They can be read for their own value without distracting

15. Ellen Hoffman, "Have Office, Will Travel," *Psychology Today*, September 1988, p. 42.

16. Bob Greene, "The Man Who Wrote 'Louie Louie,'" *Esquire*, September 1988, p. 67.

from or interrupting the flow of the article. Ian Ledgerwood of *Modern Maturity* cautions against overworking the anecdote in the body of the article. "You can have too much of one thing," he says. "I like anecdotes as sidebars."

HOW TO GET ANECDOTES

Because the anecdote generally centers on people, it follows that you get anecdotes from people. You can use your friends, as the *Cosmopolitan* writer quoted earlier admits, without saying they are your friends. But go further, or else your article will sound and be unambitious.

If you want someone to give you an anecdote, ask the kinds of questions that will elicit one. (See Chapter 5 for techniques of interviewing.) Go looking for stories, keep asking the person interviewed for one story, then another. You don't want ordinary stories, but rather the best stories a person has to tell.

"Superlative" questions work, and they're good for pulling out anecdotes: "What's the funniest, worst, best thing that ever happened to you? When were you in the most danger?" Help them along. Ask a pilot, for instance, not just were you ever scared, but also did you ever jump out of a plane? Did an engine ever conk out? Did you ever have a problem with landing gear? Ask a sports hero not only what was the most embarrassing moment, but also "Did you ever run the wrong way? Did you ever read the signals wrong? Did you ever misspell a fan's name when autographing a ball? Did you ever forget your wife and leave with her still at the stadium?" Ask a scientist not only to describe current research and especially difficult experiments, but also about hypothetical situations — using DNA to create organisms that produce ozone and close up the holes, for instance.

You can get good anecdotes by going on site. Sit, listen, watch. A writer doing an article on "creative loneliness" for *CGA World* (the CGA stands for Catholic Golden Age) dropped in on a monastery that fed the poor every day, many of them elderly. The writer joined the men at the tables, listened to their stories and sought from them the ways they used their lonely years creatively. For a book on communes some time ago, the same writer visited communes coast to coast — both by arrangement and incognito — and listened to real stories.

If you have the time, participation can work for certain stories. If you're writing about waiters and waitresses, train conductors or garbage collectors, sign on as one; if you're writing on the elderly, become an orderly in a senior citizens' home.

You can pick other people's minds. Let them tell you not only their own stories, but also stories about others they know. For the *CGA World* article, the writer also dropped in on a welfare officer at city hall, heard her stories and came away with stories she had heard elsewhere in the country. The welfare officer also gave the writer phone numbers of people across the nation to call for stories. That article began with a rapid-fire series of one-sentence anecdotes about persons fighting loneliness.

The local newspaper will have articles related to the subject you're writing about. If you're writing about how to live to be 100, look for the centenarians featured. One writer enlisted the help of newspaper editors and columnists across the country to get clippings about oldsters featured in the local papers. In researching a newspaper piece on high-achieving children, one writer contacted parents of kids who had been in the paper for their achievements (such as 4-H winners).

Library books are good sources for anecdotes. Rummage through the biographies. In researching an article on how to see a famous person, one writer found delightful stories in a biography of W.C. Fields. The book described how people succeeded in getting through to the eccentric comedian. Also using *Who's Who* and other listings, the writer wrote to some celebrities who sent their stories, among them Eli Wallach and Alec Guinness.

You need to collect anecdotes as well as information. Save items from the paper — sometimes just because that item will be good for use as an anecdote.

A recent article in the paper concerned a man who was trying to create some mystery around his suicide. In fact, he was trying to make it look like murder. He had tied a balloon to the gun he was using to shoot himself, intending that after he pulled the trigger, the gun would soar away with the balloon. There would be no death weapon. But the balloon got caught in a nearby tree and was discovered. The death was easily ruled a suicide. Filed away, that item could emerge not only as an idea for a fictional mystery but also for an article on "How to Get Mystery Ideas from Real Life" or as a part of an overall imaginative article on "Life's Almost Mysteries."

Consider the bright little story in the paper about a new police recruit being received into the force by the officer who had delivered the recruit as a baby. It could find its way into an article on police duties, the ironies of time, coincidence and so on. The same issue of the New York *Times* that carried the police story had a report on the head of a photo agency who, facing a number of lawsuits over finances, disappeared without a trace. The story could lead off a discussion of miscreants who disappear or the beginning of a look into tighter controls on accounting.

Begin a topical file. Most writers clip voraciously. Under A in such files you check for stories about "abuse," "aged," "altruism," and so on; under B, "babies," "birds," "bravery"; under C, "cats," "Christmas," "crack" and so on.

SELLING THE SHORT, HUMOROUS ANECDOTE

You can also write a short, simple anecdote and sell it by itself. Newspaper Sunday sections, such as the Philadelphia *Inquirer Magazine*, will pay $25 for a short anecdote. *Reader's Digest* pays $300 for anecdotes used in its variety of humor sections. A class at Temple University sold this group of anecdotes to *Campus USA*:[17]

17. "Campus Humor," © *Campus USA*, Spring 1988, p. 69.

Campus Humor

First Impression

On his first day of class, Bob arrived to find a young man reading a sign posted on the door of the classroom. Bob read the sign out loud: "Speech 66 cancelled today. Will resume next week in Room 603."

The young man standing next to Bob groaned and said, "That's terrible."

"That's great!" said Bob, who was trying to postpone academia as long as possible. "Why do you care?"

The young man looked at Bob and said, "Because nobody told me and I'm the professor."

— Pam Scheer

Sign Language

University Park, Pennsylvania, home of Penn State University, boasts a trio of stores aimed at the college crowd: a decorating center (Walls 'N' Things), a plant store (Plants 'N' Things) and a salad bar (Sprouts 'N' Things). The local college chaplain, dissatisfied with attendance at morning services, amused his students with the following sign, which he hung on the chapel door: "Forgiveness 'N' Things."

Bookish Hint

A student who neglected to pre-register for a required course faced the prospect of standing in long lines at the registrar's office.

"I'm going to register," he told his roommate, who had already braved the ordeal. "How are the lines today?"

"Well," his roommate said, "there are copies of *War and Peace* on the waiting room table."

— Marjorie Preston

Cool Streak

After a particularly difficult final in the spring of my freshman year, a group of us gathered in the dorm room next to mine. The heat, the humidity and the test just passed begun to play on our minds and, as one idea led to another, one thought in particular sprang into our heads.

Our plan was to "streak" through the university's student center. But little did we know that the center's air conditioning had broken down. Instead of the large mid-afternoon crowd we expected, there were few people to see us.

We did, however, get mentioned in the center's end of day log. One of our friends who worked there made a copy of the report and read it to us later: "A group of students protested the lack of air conditioning by successfully negotiating the corridors without the hindrance of clothes."

— Anthony R. Edwards

Bank Note

Late last semester, my friend decided to forego her weekly jaunt home to give tours of the campus for a little pocket money. This was only the second time all semester that she had stayed. When she started running low on cash, her weekend visits were replaced by calls home asking for money.

Several days later, "Jane" received her requested $25, along with a gentle reminder from the CEO of "Bank of Mom and Dad":

"Dear 'Jane':
As a valued customer of this organization, we are happy to comply with your request. Since this transaction was a telephone request, we are concerned with the security of your account against unauthorized withdrawals. In the future, all telephone requests for the withdrawal of funds will require your use of the code word 'PLEASE.' I am sure you recognize the importance we place on the security of your account, and trust the timely use of the above named code word will in no way inconvenience you."

Sincerely
J. Doe, Jr.
Special Executive
in Charge of Funds
— Stephanie Koretski

Touching Gesture

The week before Christmas Break was always hectic at the University of Pittsburgh. Students were frantic trying to get some necessary holiday shopping completed, while also cramming for finals. That's why my roommate Sherri and I were especially touched by the lovely poinsettia plant we received from our downstairs neighbors. The note attached to the plant said, "Happy Holidays and thanks for being such good friends."

Feeling a rush of guilt that we hadn't thought of buying our friends a gift, we ran downstairs immediately and thanked our friends profusely.

The next morning, all dorm residents received a memorandum underneath their doors. From the staff of the dorm dining hall, it read: "It has come to our attention that many residents are 'borrowing' poinsettia plants from the dining hall. These decorations were to be donated to Children's Hospital. Could you please return the plants, so that others will be able to enjoy them? Best wishes for a happy holiday season."

— *Pam Scheer*

A series of humorous anecdotes can make an article. The idea for "'I Couldn't Get to Class Because . . .': Some of the Greatest Stories Ever Told" began with the observation that students come up with the most outrageous excuses. From there, writing the story was merely a matter of collecting excuses. The author remembered excuses he had heard in the classroom, asked university colleagues for their best excuse stories and picked up stories when he was in other cities and on or near other campuses.

In the "excuses" article, note the detail that adds realism to some of the anecdotes.[18]

"I couldn't get to class because . . ." Some of the Greatest Stories Ever Told

By Hiley H. Ward

It was 5:40 p.m. and grad students who had made their way through the teeming jungle of traffic to J621 (media history) at Temple University's near north campus in Philadelphia were straggling in. They politely volunteered excuses.

A tall fellow with glasses intoned: "Sorry I'm late. I saw this cat stranded in a tree. I climbed up, and spent the last hour trying to get it down. But the cat jumped at me and scratched me." He held out his arms with thin blood streaks — a student excuse signed, sealed and delivered in blood!

In the same class, another student said he was delayed because somebody threw a bottle in front of one of his tires and he had a flat. Still another latecomer apologized for her tardiness by claiming she had to put out a fire under her car hood.

continued

---

18. Hiley H. Ward, "'I Couldn't Get to Class Because . . .': Some of the Greatest Stories Ever Told," © *Campus USA*, Spring 1987, pp. 28, 30.

continued

Student excuses form a great body of American lore, and some day somebody is going to pull them all together and sell a handy how-to booklet, "All the Excuses You Should Know and Haven't Tried" or "How to Back Up the Tides of Classwork with Stories That Even Mark Twain Would Never Have Thought Of."

Consider an excuse that worked at the University of Indiana in Bloomington. At Spring Break, a young lady wrote to her professor: "The boat we rented (to take us sailing in the Bahamas) was stranded and we can't make it back in time to I.U. to take our test on Monday." The prof let her take the test a week later and the same excuse worked for four others on the same boat. Perhaps the prof wished he was stranded on a Bahamian island, too.

Another Spring Break excuse, given with a straight face by a journalism student at the University of Kansas: "I have to leave school early for Spring Break because my father is flying me and some of my sorority sisters to the Virgin Islands in his corporate jet. He doesn't want to have to pay the pilot overtime, so we have to leave early in the morning."

Still another Spring Break excuse. "My sister is getting married and I have to leave early to attend."

The professor (at Temple) wasn't satisfied.

"Where is the wedding?" she asked.

"Fort Lauderdale," said the student.

Another Temple excuse, penned recently by a magazine article writing student: "I tried to phone your office. . . . A kid I've been covering came out of his coma late last night and is being transplanted to a rehabilitation hospital. . . ."

Grandmother excuses work very well: "My grandmother died and the funeral is Wednesday. Can I take the test tomorrow?" Such lines are always suspect; yet grandparents and other relatives do die. A professor at Wichita State always tells his students at the outset of a course that they are allowed only FOUR grandparents, and two parents, with some allowance for extended families.

The deaths of "family" as commonly perceived are not the only death excuses students use. Dog excuses are common. At the City University of New York, a student begged off coming to class because, she said, her dog had suffered a heart attack. A more familiar excuse: "My dog chewed up my term paper!" At California's University of Santa Clara, a student told Shelby H. McIntyre, a marketing prof, that her dog ate the diskette containing her paper.

Some excuses are "hairy." Joan Bastel, a newspaper editor who teaches part time on Temple's suburban campus, reports that a girl who missed a class wrote: "I had to miss the session due to my own vanity — my hair has turned a putrid orange as a result of my own in-house experimentation. I made an emergency appointment to try and fix the problem."

Some students plead allergies. A junior and pre-physical therapy major at Central Michigan University told a skeptical professor: "I was dragging this deer out of the woods. I had been hunting. I got this terrible reaction. My nose was running. I went to the doctor and he said I was allergic to fur."

At Washington State's Central Washington University, one of the deans reports, "There was this student who lost his term paper because his car went off a bridge into a river." The student saved his dog but, naturally, the term paper was lost. Then there was the young woman who said she left her term paper at her aunt's house, went back to retrieve it, but accidentally set off a burglar alarm and was arrested.

Car excuses continue to be good. "My keys got locked in the car" has worked on more than one campus. At the University of Georgia, a grad student in Soviet studies reported that "a plane landed on the highway and traffic was held up." It worked.

Students have their version of what makes a good excuse. "Pure honesty has great shock value and can be the best excuse," said the University of Georgia grad student. "Like, 'I was hung over,' 'I was very bored with the work,' or 'I went to the races.'"

There are students who write an honest confession, "Mea culpa, mea culpa," on a late paper. One student wrote in turning in a late second draft of an article: "This draft is late because the first draft was late."

In telling and presenting an excuse, it's important to be convincing. There is no worse downer than to be telling the truth and not be believed.

When presenting excuses, students have some ideas on how to encourage their acceptance. Students at Central Michigan suggest:

- If you're saying you are sick or have been sick, look sick—wear sweats, etc. "Cough a lot, sneeze."

- Get on the good side of the prof. Prepare him or her for a forthcoming excuse—stay and help after class; volunteer to run off copies; say nice things when you leave class, like "Have a nice weekend."

- "Keep things close to reality. Take an ordinary incident and blow it up a little."

- Use significant detail. Like, "I had an accident, swerved and bent the rim of my front right wheel."

And last but not least:

- Look prof in the eye.

ASSIGNMENTS

1. Study one newspaper feature article and one magazine article. Underline the anecdotes. Indicate their purpose. Identify other information in the articles that also could have been conveyed by anecdotes.

2. Write and prepare for mailing two anecdotes aimed at one of the anecdote sections of *Reader's Digest* or other publication.

3. In class, compare anecdotes prepared for class or gathered elsewhere. Vote on the best one. What elements make it the best (conciseness, recognizable character and problem, suspense, surprise, cleverness)? Are there elements of humor (timing, pacing, word play, a put-down, hyperbole, Freudian slip)?

4. Interview fellow classmates—or a guest—and write the entire article with anecdotes. (A guest could be offbeat. One university journalism class invited a local go-go dancer to class for an interview.)

5. Bring to class the longest and shortest anecdotes you can find. What do they have in common?

6. Study a public figure. Compare the "same" anecdotes about that person as they are used in newspapers, newsmagazines and magazines in general.

CHAPTER 5

Interviewing

A journalistic interview differs from the matter-of-fact interview employers, government officials or social workers might conduct, as they seek to collect a wide range of facts about a person. The journalist who interviews someone is selectively looking for specific information and traits.

The interview achieved full bloom, scholars believe, with the Penny Press mass circulation papers of the mid-1800s; they cite an early James Gordon Bennett interview with a madam of a house of ill-repute and Horace Greeley's interview with Mormon leader Brigham Young. Yet the question-and-answer format is as old as history; historians have always asked questions of older generations and passed along the stories they have heard.

In the 20th century, the interview has attained the status of art form. The modern interview is designed to pry loose interesting and sometimes previously unknown information; it proceeds along selective lines, depending on the intent or theme of an article. A good interview takes intelligence and an understanding of the reasons for the interview and what is expected from it.

WHOM DO YOU CHOOSE?

The person you interview is determined by the purpose of the article. Unless they are in charge of a beat or special section, newspaper reporters have little say on the choice of the subject. The editor determines the subject and sends the reporter out on assignment. On the other hand, the free-lance writer usually chooses the subject and interviewees.

If you're using the interview to bolster a position or supplement information in a topical article, you want to pick persons in authority or experts whom the reader will believe. It's also necessary that the person be cooperative, give you the time you need and be expressive. If potential interviewees are hesitant, you can ask them to suggest colleagues or friends more willing to talk to you.

Having backup interview subjects is a necessary strategy when the deadline is tight and you absolutely need a certain viewpoint or dimension. Subjects do cancel at the last minute — they get sick or are called out of town; more often than not, when you're dealing with corporate executives, a meeting is called and the subject can't see you as scheduled and will have to work you in the next week. If you have a backup — a second person — to interview, you can get along without the one who cancels.

Students in university news and magazine writing classes at times come up with the excuse that the subject canceled. "I can't see that person until he gets back from vacation. I'll need another two weeks for the assignment." Deadlines are deadlines. You can be spared the wrath of a professor or editor if you have backup interview possibilities to fall back on instead of coming up empty-handed.

TECHNIQUES OF INTERVIEWING

The skills needed for interviewing are akin to those needed by the professional psychologist or actor. In fact, some writers think that a good course in acting and mastery of stage presence can help an interviewer become confident and skilled — that is, a good manipulator. For that's what interviewing is. You graciously manipulate someone into giving you what you want to know about her or him, often more information than the interviewee may want to give — and usually in a very short time.

You will develop techniques of your own and fine-tune them with practice. As a starter, here are 30 tips for interviewing:

1. *Be prepared.* The more you know about a person ahead of time, the more wisely you can use your time and zero in on new or keen interest areas. Check newspaper file clippings, résumés (if available), magazine articles and *Who's Who.*

2. *Have the basic vital information.* Know about the person's residence, family status, age, and so on. Don't overlook basic background information.

   Make *sure* you have the name of the person spelled correctly. If it's a difficult name, put it in your notes in block letters. Repeat the spelling slowly to the subject. Use some words to get the right letter. Some letters, b and v, f and s, t and p, m and n, are easily confused orally. For "Trautman," for instance, say T for Tom, R, A, U, T for Tom, M for mother, A, N for Nelly. Watch the double consonants: F and N are tricky. Is it Hoffmann, or Hofmann, or Hofman; Tanenbaum or Tannenbaum? Watch F and HP. Adolph or Adolf, Rudolph or Rudolf? Watch simple names. One student didn't check the spelling of what sounded like "Lee" in a telephone interview. It appeared in print as "Lee," but it should have been "Leigh."

3. *Get right to the point.* The subject's time is valuable, and so is yours. Get on with the questions. People basically appreciate a professional attitude.

4. *Avoid interviewing someone in a press room.* Meet in a quiet place where you can interview the subject alone. You don't want other reporters to interrupt or steal the good answers you get to your questions.

5. *Have some questions ready.* Some writers plan on having all the questions ready, including questions that might help the subject open up.

6. *Identify yourself and your purpose fully,* if possible indicating where your story will be published. Subjects tend to be more comfortable if they know what is going on.

7. *Avoid off-the-record conversations.* If a person says certain matters are off the record (and can't be used), remind that person to keep it on the record or not to say it. (There are variations to this, depending on how badly you need the information, but usually the subject will provide the information anyway.)

8. *Keep yourself out of the interview.* Some subjects are such charmers that they get you talking about yourself instead of the other way around.

9. *Pretend to be on the interviewee's side.* In fact, you are on nobody's side, but a subject who thinks you are with her or him will talk more readily. If you're seen as the enemy, you might as well go home. In other words, don't be negative or rude when it isn't necessary. Sometimes you'll need to vary your attitude; but, in general, appear sympathetic, a good interested listener.

10. *Camouflage note taking for some interviews.* If the subject is uptight for some reason, pretend you are writing in full the answers to the innocuous questions and aren't paying attention to the answers to penetrating questions. Of course, it just looks that way. Ask a tough question, then don't write anything; follow with a simple question, about the family or a hobby, and write down instead the answer to the tough question.

11. *Don't be intimidated.* So what if you haven't read the subject's latest book? Maybe the subject hasn't read what you've written either. Ideally, you prepare as much as possible before the interview. Some magazine pieces allow you time for a crash course on the interviewee's books or films, but how do you completely prepare for somebody like the late Isaac Asimov, who wrote over 400 books? Newspaper reporters with daily assignments find it virtually impossible to read an author's books before the interview. But they do take a quick look at file clips.

12. *Do some fishing.* Get what you came for in the interview, but float some questions that might open up unexpected areas.

13. *Include "superlative" questions.* Such questions are useful in getting anecdotes, as we've noted. Ask what was the *most* dangerous moment, the *happiest* moment, the *best* time, the best "whatever" and the worst. These questions can reveal fascinating aspects of a subject's personality.

14. *Repeat questions, persist.* If you're dealing with an adventurer or an explorer, for instance, ask what was the most dangerous moment. But also ask about what was the second and the third most dangerous moment. Sometimes the persistent third question yields an anecdote or facts that can give your story a real spark.

15. *Always ask "why?"* Somebody was scared, somebody made a decision or has a certain attitude — why?

16. *Collect documents.* If the subject has a copy of a speech or a book, ask to take it with you.

17. *Think pictorially.* If you're setting up a photo to go with your story, be imaginative. Don't just put a book in the person's hand or stand your interviewee against a wall map.

18. *Avoid fragmented quotes.* Take down enough so that your quote is a sentence. Fragmented quotes are suspect; it's better to paraphrase than to use fragments.

19. *Get good quotes.* Help the subject to use metaphors or similes. Say "That is like what?" and so on. Quotes are good only if they are interesting. When you write, don't put quote marks around information. Quotes should be alive; they should stand up on their own.

20. *Get the full quote.* Sometimes you need to get down an important statement or declaration by the subject exactly as it is said. A governor chooses not to run again, for instance. Readers — and history — will want the words down just right.

    First of all, you have to recognize the statement's importance to your story as soon as you hear it. You acquire that skill, of course, from experience and from being prepared. One way to get a verbatim quote (without using shorthand) is to take down the first letter of *every* word and write about the fifth word out in full. Then go back after a few sentences or so and fill in the other words before you take more notes. You should be able to get the important quote in full.

21. *Understand the context.* Maybe what a person is saying isn't quite what he or she means. What did the person say just before the quote in question? What is there in the person's background that would shed light on the words? If you report words, without understanding intent and meaning, you can mislead the readers.

22. *Keep a sense of place.* Readers relate to an interview subject if they feel they are there, if they can see the person. Describe the subject in a few words (avoid bromides such as "blonde, blue eyes" for women). Give readers some idea of where the interview takes place. If it's over the phone, say so. If it's in a conference room, mention an elbow on the table, or the turtleneck sweater, but don't try to be Charles Dickens or Victor Hugo.

23. *Be sensible in restaurants.* Some people don't like to interview their subjects over a meal. But a restaurant provides a relaxing atmosphere. Your subject is captive for a definite period of time. The interview lunch also offers a chance to kill two birds with one stone — have lunch and get the interview at the same time (in reality, you're probably taking a longer lunch and may not be saving any time). Don't order too much food. You don't want to take up too much space and crowd your note taking or recording. If you're feeding your face, you'll be talking with your mouth full; you might even get drowsy. Remember why you're there. Get to the interview right away; otherwise you might chat away much of the time. Save the niceties and idle banter for whatever time is left after the interview.

24. *Have a neat appearance.* Nobody respects a slob. One campus reporter at Michigan State University put on a dress and hose before she went to talk to people in the university business office for a sensitive article. She said they were used to talking to business types, and so she planned to look the part.

25. *Pursue the subject.* If you can't get a person all to yourself for an interview, then stake out the path to and from the auditorium or press room and get in your questions. The placing of police and security types will usually give the route away. The assembled press herd will be waiting at the end of the line. Catch the subject as he or she materializes at some distant escalator in the hotel. You'll get in some exclusive questions. You could always get a long walk with Martin Luther King, Jr., this way or with a chief justice of the Supreme Court (Earl Warren) or even a vice president (Nelson Rockefeller); some quick shuffling of the feet and you get a word from Ted Kennedy or the pope.

26. *Get phone numbers.* In one interview, Martin Luther King alluded to the possibility of a new demonstration that could shut down one of the automakers in Detroit. The reporter couldn't pin him down but knew where

he could be reached by phone. The desk at the newspaper had the reporter call King to pursue the question. Sometimes your profile subject can give you other numbers. One interviewee gave a reporter the unlisted phone number of Betty Shabazz, Malcolm X's widow. The reporter got an exclusive phone interview on the anniversary of the black leader's death.

27. *Keep cool.* If a subject becomes insulting or patronizing, just keep a level head. There is nothing to lose by keeping calm, everything to lose if you blow your top. You lose the interview and sources, and word of *your* temper might get back to your editor.

28. *Verify facts.* If your subject quotes another person or a book, don't include it in your article without checking. Invariably, the quote is inaccurate. Nobody quotes accurately from memory, and facts conjured up in an interview can be wrong. Ask for sources for facts, quotes and statistics. If the interviewee is an absolute authority who is normally the last word, then you can go with her or his facts, attributed, of course. But repeated quotes, or excerpts, bear checking. Quotations from Scripture or literature need checking if for no other reason than to have the punctuation right. "To be or not to be. . . ." Maybe there's a comma in there?

29. *Ask an open-end exit question.* At the end of the interview, you might ask, "Is there anything I should ask you that I haven't asked?" Some reporters would bristle at this, but in some instances this final question has elicited a startling response. Sometimes if the subject doesn't warm up to this one, an aide in the room might say, "Ask him about . . . ," and you're off and running on something exciting.

30. *Send a clipping.* Most subjects are flattered and happy with the prospect of another story about them. They will ask you to send a clipping. Tell them you "plan" to send a clipping. But you have a lot to do, and maybe when it is published, your reminder note to send it will be lost. Try to remember.

TAPING AND NOTE TAKING

Most interviewers have to decide whether to tape. Many reporters and writers are working with tape recorders, although older writers tend to stick with taking notes, which is what they're used to. Most reporters and writers agree that the tape recorder is especially valuable in getting down the sensitive quotation or the controversial remark that a subject might try to deny later. Many use both. The tape recorder makes the subject believe that he or she will be quoted accurately. The reporter takes notes to be used while writing and the tape recorder is available for backup. Some free-lance writers, such as Gloria Hochman, will check back with their tape recorder on all quotes, making sure the ones they are using are verbatim. The newspaper reporter does not always have that luxury of time. Theoretically, when out in the field, a reporter could have the tape's content sent back electronically to the newspaper and transcribed by a rewrite person. Of course, breaking stories require that the reporter dictate a story or notes personally over the phone, usually from written notes.

Travel Weekly would have its free-lance reporters tape over the phone key travel executives and corporation heads across the country. A pool of secretaries would transcribe the tapes, and then an editor would take the story from there, keeping a question-and-answer format. This approach at *Travel Weekly* was usually used in special issues, with the regular weekly issues using standard, one-on-one interviews shaped by the interviewer.

Should the other party in a phone interview be told that you are taping? Federal law (*Lopez* v. *United States*, 1963) allows one party in a phone conversation to record and make known what transpired without telling the other party. The Crime Control Act of 1968 allows an interception (taping) in a conversation if it is not for a criminal purpose. However, state law is also applicable. Some states, such as Florida, require the consent of both parties in taping; many have no regulations concerning consent.

The novice reporter and writer would be wise to get used to taking written notes before starting to rely on tape recorders. There are times when you have to jot down notes — when you're in a hurry, when you don't have the tape recorder or when it won't function.

Popular for taking notes is the "Professional Reporter's Notebook," the narrow flip-over spiral pad, which can be ordered in quantity from Portage, P.O. Box 5500, Akron, Ohio 44313 (800-321-2183) and other suppliers.

Most reporters develop some form of partial shorthand — using symbols from various disciplines, such as the pyramid of three dots from mathematics for "therefore": or the angle signs for "lesser" or "greater." Some create abbreviations by using several letters of a word, such as "bg" for "background." Some words lend themselves to a one-letter symbol, such as "with" becoming a "w."

Sometimes you need to flag yourself in your notes. You might not be sure of a point, a spelling; you might need more information, or something must be verified. You can write "ch" for "check" or "CQ" or put a question mark in the margin. Sometimes you'll use these marks when you write your copy, then edit them out after the checking. (In finished copy, if you have a strange spelling, put "CQ" or "folo copy" and the name in the margin so that a copy editor knows you've already checked it.)

Read your notes as soon as possible if you're not going to write from them that day. Handwritten notes have a way of becoming obscure and hard to figure out later. As you read them over, fill in the gaps, but use a different pencil or pen or color for the fill-ins. If you have doubts about the notes later, you will know what you took down at the moment and what was filled in later to smooth them out. Sometimes your shorthand or notehand can confuse you. For instance, does "diff" mean "different" or "difficult?" If you read your notes right away, you'll probably remember what you meant. A week or so later, you might not.

PREPARED QUESTIONS

Writers don't agree about whether you should take prepared questions to an interview. Some feel they stifle the interview, getting in the way of its spontaneous development. Others feel a list of questions is handy, at least for glancing over at the end of the interview to see if everything has been covered. Nearly all reporters have wished "if I had only remembered to ask. . . ."

You can settle for a compromise that allows spontaneity and thoroughness. Take in the questions, but use them with a sleight of hand. The interview subject doesn't know you have a list.

Here's how to do it inconspicuously: Fold a piece of typing paper vertically. Run one side through your typewriter. Type one-line questions that cover the gamut of topics to be covered. You might even number the ones you want to take up first, so that if the interview is shorter than you expect, you have what you want most. You can also underline key words. Place this list of questions under your narrow, vertical reporter's notebook. With knees crossed, you can place the list on your thigh so it can't be seen. The notebook, which is shorter, can be moved up and down over the questions as you take notes.

The following list would work with a celebrity in the news — let's say an entertainer, a film star:

- Bg (background: name, age, family, home)
- Latest film?
- How got role?
- Compare to your other films?
- Next film?
- Why? Whom working with? Why?
- Costars, comments?
- Best actress, actor worked with?
- Best role?
- Worst role? Why?
- Upbringing, parents?
- Reviews, opinions of?
- Local angle: Been to town before?
- How do you stay looking young?
- What will you be doing 5, 10, 20 years from now?
- Who are your friends?

- Enemies?
- Most embarrassing moment?
- Happiest moment?
- Any person turn you around in life?
- If you had it to do over . . . ?
- Hobbies, recreation?
- People you met — president, queen, etc.?
- Going to write a book?
- What else have you written?
- More on family, kids, girl or boy friends?
- Religion, guiding values?
- Opinion on today's events (whatever is current)?
- Travels?
- Your house, vacation house?
- Theater projects coming up?
- Charities?
- Your greatest honor?
- Any close call in your life?
- Your favorite books?
- If there were one role you could play, what would it be?

SPECIAL TECHNIQUES

Most reporters and writers have their own special techniques. Joan Bastel, managing editor of the Doylestown (Pa.) *Intelligencer* and a writer of many feature articles, says, "I always ask if there was a turning point or catalyst. The Olympic swimmer, for instance, might say, 'Oh yes, there was a time when I had polio.'" She also asks what she calls the "or" questions. "If you ask a person if he likes apples, he might just say 'yes.' But if you ask if he likes apples *or* oranges he will have to choose and will tell you why."

Bruce Selcraig, investigative reporter for *Sports Illustrated* based in Austin, Tex., says he tries to find "some obscure detail" on the subject before he does the interview. Doing so not only shows the subject that Selcraig has done his homework but also can compel a reluctant interviewee to answer questions. "I also contact people away from their home city where they may be more inclined to talk."

"Don't get discouraged if some people won't talk to you," adds Selcraig, who worked for Dallas papers and also served as a staff member for the U.S. Senate Permanent Subcommittee on Investigations. "I have a little respect for them; I wouldn't talk to reporters either. But do not give up." He uses "mailgrams," Federal Express and special couriers to take requests to some of the subjects he wishes to interview. "Talk to the person's comrades. Be nice [about the person], and word will get back [to the subject]. You just want a foot in the door. Smith will tell Jones that you, the reporter, are not so bad."

At the Investigative Reporters and Editors national conference in the summer of 1989, where Selcraig gave his remarks during a panel discussion on interviewing, Barbara Walsh, of the Fort Lauderdale *News* and *Sun Sentinel*, also gave her views. Walsh shared in a Pulitzer Prize for stories on prison furloughs when she was a reporter at the Lawrence (Mass.) *Eagle-Tribune*.

Walsh distributed this set of guidelines for interviewing:

I often mention things about myself that are relevant to that person. When I go into a grieving home I usually say, "I'm terribly sorry this happened to you. I have five sisters and can't imagine something like this happening to one of them."

But whatever you say, be sincere. They'll see through you otherwise and most likely toss you out on your ear.

Don't be afraid to empathize. It's okay to start off saying, "I'm terribly sorry this happened to your family or your boyfriend or whatever. . . ." When approaching grieving families, be gentle. Put yourself in their shoes. And often if you show some concern they will eventually open up to you.

Give to get. If the source is reluctant to talk, I often give him a bunch of information that I have collected, ease the notebook out and ask, "So, what have you heard about this?"

But use caution in what you give out. Don't give them anything you won't be printing the next day. Keep vital information for future stories to yourself.

Be especially wary of politicians, cops, officials in general. Don't tip them off to investigative pieces you're doing.

Don't get too chummy. Watch out for crossing the line. Does the source think you're his friend or personal public relations hack? Cops, politicians are especially good at using reporters. Use caution.

The Gospel truth. Don't believe everything your source tells you. Check it out. Don't be a pawn in a feud among politicians.

Lies. If the source is new to you throw them a curveball. Ask a few questions you know the answer to and see how they respond. If they lie, tell them you've heard differently from another source. Don't gloat, but be firm about wanting the truth.

Tape recorders. Don't use them. Somehow things will screw up and either your machine's batteries will die, the tape will get chewed up or you'll hear the traffic instead of your source. Avoid them whenever possible.

Take the time. Make sure you have enough time to do a thorough interview. This isn't possible all the time, but when it is, don't sell yourself short.

Get their phone number. Never leave an interview without the source's work and home number. Tell them if you have any further questions or want to clarify something they've already said, you'll call. They'll appreciate your thoroughness.

Be ethical. Don't use quotes you've promised to keep off the record. You could land in a messy court suit and your source will probably never speak to you again.

Don't take quotes out of context to fit your story. It's not fair and will also earn you a bad reputation.

ASSIGNMENTS

1. Pick out a celebrity or famous personality in the news. In preparation for an interview (you might want to decide which publication you are writing for), make a list of questions you want to ask. Decide what you want to know most and include follow-up questions.

2. Make a list of the 10 biggest problems students have had in interviewing, and brainstorm for solutions together.

3. Bring in examples of the best—and worst—published interviews and discuss why they were so good or so bad.

4. Role-play some great personalities in history and "interview" them.

5. Compare interviews with a famous person as handled by the daily press, wire services and newsmagazines. Discuss any noticeable differences or slants.

6. Play a game on accuracy of names. Type 25 or so of the most difficult names from a phone directory. Divide the names, and then each student writes down the complete list by asking other students to say the names. How accurate are the resulting lists?

7. Interview a person, such as a city official, in class. Without discussing the interview, each student should write an article on the interviewee. Compare student articles—leads, theme, development, quotes.

CHAPTER 6

The Profile

All publications—from weekly and daily newspapers to magazines and books—use the profile or personality article. Even when an article is not primarily about a person, profile material and personal vignettes may contribute to its success.

But don't approach the profile thinking it's a rote form based on an easy interview. "Profiles are becoming a major problem in the magazine business," James Lloyd Greenfield, recent past editor of the *New York Times Magazine*, told a meeting of the American Society of Journalists and Authors in September 1990. "All are sounding alike. We must begin to do them more interestingly and in depth. Most seem to be done by rote, and they are becoming a blur."

He warned those who would write *New York Times Magazine* profiles: "People sell a person so hard that we reject it. It sounds like a PR job. Many ideas are turned down because they are so hard sell and one-sided and predetermined."

The genres for which profiles are written may determine the style and effect. The sports personality feature will likely be breezier, with some jargon;

the lifestyle personality feature might have a self-help focus; the men's and women's magazine profiles will reflect the concerns of each; children's publications and some religious publications probably are looking for a message in the story of a person's life.

COMMON CHARACTERISTICS

A successful profile—whether for newspapers, magazines or a book biography—has certain qualities.

A Significance

Something should distinguish the subject of the profile from any other person and should be so significant that people will want to read the article. Does an artist or writer ever sell anything? For instance, a writer can pay a "vanity" press to print a book. Unless the self-published book wins a prize or gets good reviews from recognized critics, you have little or no significance.

New leaders may be significant for the change they represent and what they plan to do, but too often the subject is described in terms of skin color, national background or gender. Unless the person is really the "first"—the first black governor, the first woman governor or first woman Supreme Court member—the visible tags are not the most significant. Describe the substance of the person: How does she react, what does he believe, what will she do to change the status quo? It's amazing how eloquent a student can sometimes be about a "tag" while neglecting the substance of the person being profiled.

However, some subjects may be too important for you to consider. It would be difficult for a newcomer and most non-staffers to publish a profile on an extremely visible person, such as a state official, a member of Congress or a rock star. Such persons will already have been covered, most likely by writers on regular full-time beats. A publication will assign the leading politicians to its own political editor and staff, the top musician to its arts and music writers.

Major publications have local bureaus and can get to the obvious celebrity themselves. Eighty percent of the article ideas that Robert Smith received when he was managing editor of *TV Guide* were a waste of time, he says. "These people are not even thinking." Somebody is in Cincinnati and wants to write about a Hollywood personality. "If they look at the masthead, they will see we have a bureau in LA."

Smith suggests that "what you know about locally that has national acclaim or interest is good. Humor is good." Although humor is being done less, he observed, "still, it is something you can do from Missoula, Montana." What makes a subject significant might be founded in humor, style or basic human concerns. One student published a stylistic short piece in the Philadelphia *Inquirer* magazine on an obscure clown who passed out flowers on the street.

A Purpose

The "significance" can also deepen into a purpose. The clown article tapped into universal concerns for peace. Some magazines that don't publish many profiles want to make it clear why they are running a certain profile. That is the case with *Mother Jones*. "We do only about 10 profiles a year," says *Mother Jones* editor Douglas Foster. "So we try to do something really new or something not given exposure before, something important. We do not want to look at a celebrity to give a lift but to generate new ideas."

Foster cites as an example a feature on lawyer Danny Sheehan who, with his Christic Institution, has put together "a massive civil conspiracy suit" against 29 members of an alleged ominous secret group, serving, as they see it, the interests of the government. The article on Sheehan and the Institute, "The Law and the Prophet," by James Traub (February/March, 1988), purports to present a relatively unknown lawyer and his organization and their challenge to a secret, nefarious operation, consistent with the ongoing concerns of the liberal magazine. The purpose is spelled out in a contents page blurb: "Lawyer Danny Sheehan of the Christic Institute has become a hot item on the Left: in a tone blending '60s politics and '70s theology, he says that a 'Secret Team' of spies, smugglers, and killers has run U.S. foreign policy for 25 years. He's about to put the team — and his own view of the world — on trial."

A sense of purpose may be one of the things that distinguishes a magazine profile from a newspaper profile, says Robert C. Smith, who has written profiles for the *New Yorker* and *TV Guide*, where he is the recent past managing editor. "A news feature does not need much excuse; somebody is in town and the newspaper does it right away. Therefore, as a rule, newspapers are shallower. Yet the very best newspaper profile might be better, if you do it for some reason and give it time."

The *New Yorker* looks for profiles that offer something more than entertainment and information. Says Smith, who wrote "Ratcatcher" about Scotsman Brian Plummer for the *New Yorker* (Feb. 15, 1988): "I established [in a query letter] that Plummer [the ratcatcher] was not only interesting [in his rat-catching techniques and in his books on dogs and hunting] but had an attitude that led him to live more effectively and intensely. I like to do people who are driven. I said I did not want to just write on an English eccentric."

Information

As with all other features, you write a profile to convey information. Readers want facts. However, in selecting facts to fit a theme or emphasis, you can err by leaving out background. It takes skill to handle essential background information.

Carol Horner in *Inquirer Magazine* of the Philadelphia *Inquirer* shows how to deal with a central question or theme and sweep up background facts in one paragraph. Note the quick short history of George Bush in the 10th paragraph, starting with "Surely . . ."

The question posed to George Bush, flying home one cold twilight aboard Air Force Two, is where has he left his mark in life?

"Friendships with people," he says.

Friendships with people.

"Yeah. They're strong."

But what about in his public career?

"Friendships with people," he says.

Leaning toward him across a small table in his private cabin in the plane, you find yourself expecting, perhaps hoping for, something else. This is Bush's chance for a neat riposte to the critics who say he hasn't proven himself a leader — who say that despite his unrivaled political résumé, he has no string of major accomplishments to point to.

While some ridicule him, question his manhood, and call him weak, George Bush, running for president, is talking about friendships.

It's curious.

Surely there must have been proud moments — votes cast, ideas advanced, policies developed and implemented — in a career that has placed him in some of the most visible, influential, potentially powerful positions the country has to offer. Congressman. Ambassador to the United Nations. Chairman of the Republican National Committee. Envoy to China. Director of the Central Intelligence Agency. Vice President.

One such moment is well-known. It was an April night 20 years ago, when he went back to his Houston congressional district to face constituents who were furious with him for voting in favor of open housing. They packed a high school auditorium, muttering angrily, some hooting and catcalling. Bush, steady and unapologetic, spoke to them of justice. At the end they rose to their feet in thunderous, sustained applause.

In his 1987 autobiography, *Looking Forward*, Bush wrote: "More than twenty years later I can truthfully say that nothing I've experienced in public life, before or since, has measured up to the feeling I had when I went home that night." Bush's admirers see that moment as quintessentially Bush — a time when his innate sense of decency and fairness and his quiet, unadvertised courage intersected to produce an action that bucked the tide.

But detractors say his looking back 20 years for such a moment only underscores his failure, in the intervening years, to define what he stands for . . . [1]

Sometimes you need to work in a good bit of information — especially when the subject is unknown. Note the weaving of extensive background into the lead of this article on a surgeon, Vivien Thomas, in Katie McCabe's article, "Like Something the Lord Made," in the *Washingtonian*. The article won the award for feature writing in the 1990 National Magazine Awards competition sponsored by the American Society of Magazine Editors.

Say his name, and the busiest heart surgeons in the world will stop and talk for an hour. Of course they have time, they say, these men who count time in

---

1. Carol Horner, "George Bush," in *Inquirer Magazine*, Philadelphia *Inquirer*, Feb. 28, 1988, p. 14.

seconds, who race against the clock. This is about Vivien Thomas. For Vivien they'll make time.

Dr. Denton Cooley has just come out of surgery . . .

No, Vivien Thomas wasn't a doctor, says Cooley. He wasn't even a college graduate. He was just so smart, and so skilled, and so much his own man, that it didn't matter.

And could he operate. Even if you'd never seen surgery before, Cooley says, you could do it because Vivien made it look so simple.

Vivien Thomas and Denton Cooley both arrived at Baltimore's Johns Hopkins Hospital in 1941 — Cooley to begin work on his medical degree, Thomas to run the hospital's surgical lab under Dr. Alfred Blalock. In 1941 the only other black employees at the Johns Hopkins Hospital were janitors. People stopped and stared at Thomas, flying down corridors in his white lab coat. Visitors' eyes widened at the sight of a black man running the lab. But ultimately the fact that Thomas was black didn't matter, either. What mattered was that Alfred Blalock and Vivien Thomas could do historic things together that neither could do alone.

Together they devised an operation to save "Blue Babies" — infants born with a heart defect that sends blood past their lungs — and Cooley was there, as an intern, for the first one. He remembers the tension in the operating room that November morning in 1944 as Dr. Blalock rebuilt a little girl's tiny, twisted heart.

He remembers how that baby went from blue to pink the minute Dr. Blalock removed the clamps and her arteries began to function. And he remembers where Thomas stood — on a little step stool, looking over Dr. Blalock's right shoulder, answering questions and coaching every move.

"You see," explains Cooley, "it was Vivien who had worked it all out in the lab, in the canine heart, long before Dr. Blalock did Eileen, the first Blue Baby. There were no 'cardiac experts' then. That was the beginning."

A loudspeaker summons Cooley to surgery. He says he's on his way to do a "tet case" right now. That's tetralogy of Fallot, the congenital heart defect that causes Blue Baby Syndrome. They say that Cooley does them faster than anyone, that he can make a tetralogy operation look so simple it doesn't even look like surgery. "That's what I took from Vivien," he says, "simplicity. There wasn't a false move, not a wasted motion, when he operated."

But in the medical world of the 1940s that chose and trained men like Denton Cooley, there wasn't supposed to be a place for a black man, with or without a degree. Still, Vivien Thomas made a place for himself. He was a teacher to surgeons at a time when he could not become one. He was a cardiac pioneer 30 years before Hopkins opened its doors to the first black surgical resident.

Those are the facts that Cooley has laid out, as swiftly and efficiently as he operates. And yet history argues that the Vivien Thomas story could never have happened. . . .[2]

2. Katie McCabe, "Like Something the Lord Made," *The Washingtonian*, August 1989, p. 109.

Human Interest

A profile is more than a case history or dossier. While the concept of "human interest" must factor in nearly all your writing, it should certainly be prominent in a profile. Readers want facts fleshed out with narrative. When you write profiles, you're telling stories, albeit true ones. Stories or anecdotes hold attention, involve the reader and entertain.

Joe Dendy, when you get right down to it, probably isn't very important, and his name carries no special significance. But the stories he tells about his long-term relationship to a highly visible racetrack make him interesting. Consider the beginning of the report on Joe in the weekly Winston-Salem (N.C.) *Chronicle*:

> When the National Association of Stock Car Racing (NASCAR) was born in 1949 at Bowman Gray Stadium, Joe Dendy was just a kid picking up bottles out of the stands to make a few cents in change.
>
> Dendy was unaware that he would go on to spend nearly 40 years of his life there, rubbing elbows with young drivers who would go on to be legends in the sport, and saving some lives as well.
>
> The 54-year old Dendy can't remember that far back very well, but there have been some times during his 39-year love for racing that he will never forget.
>
> He remembers the time Herman Rush flipped behind the guardrail one fateful Saturday night. Dendy ran across the track, jumped the rail, and crawled into the car.
>
> "I unbuckled him and was trying to drag him out of the car while gas was running up my nose," recalls Dendy.
>
> "I sort of carried him across the track, and no sooner than we'd got out, the car caught on fire."
>
> "I guess I was pretty lucky," he grinned.
>
> He recalls another accident that did not end on such a happy note.
>
> "Bill Justus Jr. was hit in the rearend and gas from the tank right behind the seat spilled all over him. We tried to get him out, but he was tied up in there with some bailing wire.
>
> "The car caught on fire," Dendy said with a solemn voice.
>
> "He never got out."
>
> "That next year, that boy's daddy was the chief inspector for all the cars out there."
>
> The days of bailing wire and loose gas tanks have long since passed. They've been replaced with safety harnesses and fuel cells. . . .[3]

Timeliness

There should be some reason the profile is running *now*. The article might reflect what is happening in the world. A new leader on the world scene or yet another hostage taking might occasion a profile. Sports figures who reach a

3. Randy Pettitt, "'Ol Joe': His Love for Racing Makes Bowman Gray Stadium a Safer Place to Race," Winston-Salem (N.C.) *Chronicle*, May 7, 1987, p. B1.

new pinnacle, who help win a championship game, who set a new mark are "timely."

Anniversaries in the lives of personalities can be timely. Old politicians are easily forgotten, but when they reach milestones in age — or the anniversary of an event with which they are associated is celebrated — then the past, by linking with the current date, is timely. Alf Landon, Republican candidate for president, swamped by Franklin Roosevelt in 1936, marked one birthday after another generally unnoticed. When he turned an even 100 just before his death in 1987, the world paid attention to him once again. The president was at his doorstep.

Elliott Almond, of the Los Angeles *Times*, profiled a mountain climber but used an upcoming climb of Mt. Everest for the news peg. Look for the news peg or "update" angle in paragraph six:

> Jean Ellis was imprisoned in a dome-shape tent on the edge of the world, helpless to do anything but listen as screaming gales sent snow down in opaque sheets and shook the shelter so hard he expected to be wafted aloft like a hang-glider.
>
> He and nine compatriots were stalled on their six-week climb up the glacial walls of Annapurna IV in the eastern Himalayas of Nepal, trapped in a makeshift campsite, only two days away from the summit.
>
> Now, after the long haul that started six months earlier with the organizing of the expedition in the United States, they had a life-or-death decision to make. Should they wait for the storm to subside as food supplies run perilously low or should they turn back after being tent-bound on this 21,000-foot-high ledge for four days?
>
> They headed down.
>
> "It hurt to do that, but you knew it was the right decision," said Ellis, an emergency room physician at the Mission Hospital Regional Medical Center in Mission Viejo. Heavy snows arrived the next day and "had we stayed . . . the return route would have been obliterated."
>
> The climb up Annapurna IV in 1986 was Ellis' second trip to Nepal and his first full-scale attempt at climbing a Himalayan peak. But it was only a tuneup for late this summer and fall when he takes on the fabled peak that has totally absorbed him since he first stood before its wonder seven years ago — Mt. Everest. . . .[4]

Student Lindsay Taylor wrote about an ordinary grocer, but "everybody" in town knew him. His store was about to mark its 45th year. The article, nearly as long as a *New Yorker* piece, ran in a Pennsylvania weekly in two installments, beginning:

> At 6 a.m. on Independence Day, village grocer Dale Bowers will be the only witness to a milestone event in the life of a rural Chester County community. When he unlocks the door of Bowers' Food Market in Sadsburyville that

4. Elliott Almond, "Magnificent Obsession: Adventure, the Specter of Death Will Dog Physician's Attempt to Conquer Everest," Los Angeles *Times*, June 2, 1989, Part IX, Orange County Life, p. 1.

morning, the 65-year-old proprietor will mark the 45th anniversary of the grocery shop his father and mother opened on July 4, 1943.

"We're more than just a store," says Bowers, who, with his wife, Dot, has owned the shop since the death of his father, Milton, in 1969.

The market, located in a two-storied stucco building on Business Route 30 near Old Wilmington Road, has always been a gathering spot for a town in which the main intersection isn't busy enough to warrant installation of a traffic light. The pedestrian traffic in and out of Bowers' Market, 600 people on a good day, makes up for any lack of auto activity. Bowers' customers, however, aren't always there just to shop.

Says Carol Witman, a 26-year resident of Sadsburyville, "I just drop in to visit. It was the same way for my father when I was little. He would bring me along while he visited with Dale's dad."

Behind the checkout counter, Bowers and his wife preside over a clearing-house of information from the innocuous to the inexplicable.

Sunday morning, 9 a.m. Coffee klatch prime time. A half-dozen parents are discussing the senior prom attended by their sons and daughters the previous evening. A local paper is selling like griddle cakes — five at a time — the prom account and photographs made front page news.

A local fellow pokes his head in the door to inquire how far he can drive his car with a broken water pump. "As far as you can get to home," Bowers quips.

An elderly woman wearing a sunbonnet steps in. Bowers quizzes her. "Did the boss let you walk all the way down here by yourself?"

"He doesn't know I'm here," she answers quietly and stands by the door awhile.

Bowers questions a youngster. "Where's your mother this morning?"

"At our yard sale," the boy replies.

"Well, if she sells the yard, you won't have to mow it, will you?" The boy grins.

The prom parents interrupt their conversation when a black Lincoln Continental with tinted windows and New York plates pulls in. . . .[5]

A Focus

The best profile — especially one concerned with showing what makes a person tick — will settle on one aspect of a person's life.

The reader doesn't need to know everything. When David Friedland, a fugitive former New Jersey state senator, was returned to the United States to face fraud charges, there was much public interest in this flamboyant politician who absconded with union funds, faked his scuba diving death and moved about the jet set on most of the continents before he was apprehended in the Maldives Islands near India. The reader didn't care about Friedland's legislative voting record — just about how he pulled off his scam and what kind of character could be so clever and successful for so long in his hedonistic pursuits.

5. Lindsay Taylor, "Browers' Market — Sadsburyville Celebrates 45th Anniversary," Parkesburg (Pa.) *Post*, June 30, 1988, p. 1.

In *Premiere*, "The Movie Magazine," Fannie Weinstein focused on the political life and attitudes of actor Alec Baldwin. She starts off asking him about his chief fantasy. He explains that he wants to be a top movie star so he can lead a voter registration drive in this country. She talks about his political interests and pre-law training, then moves into other aspects of his personal life, career and ambition.[6]

An Effect

By selecting, grouping and corralling the facts, anecdotes and quotations, the writer leads the reader to a conclusion about the personality, a kind of judgment. You can call it a point of view, although this term, as we have seen, is used in different ways in writing. You also can talk about "meaning." A person's life is about something, even if it's only about boredom. A breathing human being has an effect on others. Since you're steering the article, you have a say in shaping that effect.

In their profile on Chris Zorich, All-America football lineman, James Kunen and Grant Pick focus on his devotion to his mother and suggest that altruism and self-sacrifice form a basis for happiness.[7]

All-America Chris Zorich Starred in the Orange Bowl and Returned Home to Find His Courageous Mother Dead

James S. Kunen and Grant Pick

It is unlikely that anyone would call Notre Dame nose tackle Chris Zorich a mama's boy — at least not to his face. But in a sense that's exactly what the ferocious 270-lb. All-America lineman has always been. So right after his team's heartbreaking 10–9 New Year's night loss to the University of Colorado at the Orange Bowl in Miami, he telephoned his mother, Zorka, back home in Chicago. As usual, she made him feel better, proudly telling her only child how well he had played. "Mom, I love you," he said before hanging up.

His 10 tackles had earned the quick, tenacious Zorich the honor of being chosen by NBC Sports as the game's outstanding player for the Fighting Irish. "I played the best I ever played,"

continued

---

6. Fannie Weinstein, "Actor Alec Baldwin," *Premiere*, September 1988, p. 23.

7. James S. Kunen and Grant Pick, "All-America Chris Zorich Starred in the Orange Bowl and Returned Home to Find His Courageous Mother Dead," *People*, Jan. 21, 1991, pp. 105, 106. *People Weekly* © 1991 — the Time Inc. Magazine Co.

continued

he recalls. "But I didn't know why until I got home."

When he arrived there the next day, Zorich discovered that his Orange Bowl performance had been the last gift of glory he could offer the woman who had raised him on her own. After his mother failed to answer his knocks, he broke down the door to find her in the hallway of their South Side flat. At 59, Zorka, a diabetic, had died unexpectedly of natural causes. "She was just lying there," says her son. "I knew she was dead. I gave her a kiss on the lips and said, 'Bye, Mom.' I didn't freak out." In fact, the 21-year-old Zorich turned calmly to his distraught Uncle Blaise, who had driven him to the apartment, and said, "I made her happy. She made me happy. I know she's in a better place." Only later did tears overcome him. Now, says Zorich, "she can watch over me as my guardian angel."

That, after all, was what Zorka had done while she was alive, with the same single-mindedness that her son would bring to the football field. "Chris was her life, her everything," says Zorka's sister Anna Radick. A coatroom attendant at George Diamond's Steak House in Chicago, Zorka became pregnant at age 38. When she told the father, he left her. "I never knew his name," says Radick. "She would not discuss it. 'I can take care of my son,' she said." Zorich knows his father's name. He also knows that he was a black man with a gold tooth. But that is all he knows. He has never spoken to the man and has no idea if he is dead or alive.

Forced to quit working to raise her child, Zorka subsisted on welfare. Though one of her six siblings is the successful character actor Louis Zorich, the husband of actress Olympia Dukakis, Zorka stubbornly refused to ask for help—though her family would sometimes send her money. "Just about all she would accept was food and hugs," recalls Chris's cousin Barbara Radick. For the past 12 years Zorka and Chris have lived in a one-bedroom apartment with peeling walls and a patched ceiling; a towel is stuffed into a crack in the front window to keep out the cold.

It is a tough, mostly black and Hispanic neighborhood, and it was especially tough for Chris. "I got picked on a lot because I was mixed," he says. "I got the crap beat out of me." By the time he entered Chicago Vocational High School, Zorich desperately wanted to succeed at football. But Zorka resisted. "She wouldn't sign the consent form," says Zorich. "I begged and begged, but she didn't want her baby to get hurt." Finally, as a sophomore, he forged her name and joined the team. When she found out in midseason, "I told her I didn't want to let the team down, so she let me play," Zorich recalls. His high school coach, John Potocki, soon recognized that Zorich had a shot at a college football scholarship. "What he lacks in height [Zorich is 6'1"], he makes up for in heart and desire," says Potocki. "He has a hate, an anger that comes from the streets, but he channels it in a positive direction." Potocki believes that crucial self-control came from Zorka. "She gave him enough love for two parents," he says. "She gave him a base."

Throughout Zorich's career at Notre Dame, where he majors in American studies, he maintained that closeness with his mother. "I called her whenever I felt like it," he says. "School can be scary, but I didn't have anything to worry about because she was always there. She was my best friend. I would talk to her about girls, football, anything." Says Zorich's roommate, guard Tim Ryan: "They would talk like boyfriend and girlfriend."

Zorich has told his real girlfriend, Notre Dame sophomore Jessica Fiebelkorn, 19, not to be surprised if she finds him carrying on imaginary conversations with his mother. "Obviously I miss her," he says, "but I feel I can still talk to her all the time—and not have an enormous phone bill."

Zorich, winner of the Lombardi Award as the nation's best college lineman of 1990, will be a possible first-round pick in this spring's NFL draft. "There are many things with which I want to make my mother proud," he says. "I want to have a big family. And in my house, above my fireplace, I'm going to have a big picture of my mom."

A Context

Articles that don't have a sense of place can be as boring as an instruction manual. Describing the setting and appearance, however briefly, brings the reader into the subject's presence. Providing a sense of place allows for some dynamics, some movement; it makes the subject appear to have life off the page. You've slowed down enough to see and capture with some of the senses the world of the subject.

Note the sense of being someplace, achieved by giving the location and detailing items in the room and personal appearance in this article on comedian George Burns from the San Francisco *Chronicle*:

> Las Vegas
>
> God was right on time.
>
> The doughty little show-biz deity — aka/Natty Birnbaum, aka/George Burns — shuffled into the bedroom of a lavish suite in the Centurian Tower of Caesars Palace, slowly eased himself into a chair and greeted the assembled faithful of six reporters, who felt like standing, bowing, kneeling, something.
>
> As one writer said, "It's like meeting the pope." Only more fun.
>
> At 92, the Yoda of showbiz puffed his cigar, peered around through his owlish black frames, searched for an ashtray and a glass of water, sat back and fielded questions about his new movie, "18 Again," opening April 8, and inspired by the song he sings onstage, the theme of his act and his life, one in the same.
>
> If there is another, secret George Burns, nobody can find it and, to be honest, nobody really wants to find it. The on-stage, on-camera, on-reruns Burns is such a consummate artist that he has managed to blur the line between life and art so that, one suspects, not even he can tell if there is one.
>
> During a 40-minute interview — Burns talked to the press all day Saturday, gleefully respinning anecdotes he has told 5,000 times on stage and off, wherever one or more people gather, then did a 50-minute show that night at 10 — the only sign of aging in the five years since I last met him is that he's more stooped.
>
> He now does most of his act in a chair. He could do it from a bed and it would still be wonderful. It's the same act, plus one new song and two new jokes; it's enough.
>
> At the interview, in a gray coat, dark blue ascot and snappy hanky in his jacket pocket, he looks dapper but frail and, to be sure, they were treating him at Caesars like priceless, breakable crystal. As he says, "Most people 92 are dead."
>
> His legs are spindly and you have to speak up, but he misses nothing and, just when you think he has, Burns waits a beat, looks up, hits you with a gag, and puffs his cigar. The smoke, he explained later, is a laugh cue, but you'd laugh even if the cigar wasn't lit; the puff just frames the laugh. . . .[8]

You feel you are on the street corner with singer Barry White in this article from *Essence*.

8. Gerald Nachman, "George Burns: 92 Going on 18," San Francisco *Chronicle*, March 8, 1988, p. 81. © San Francisco *Chronicle*. Used by permission.

Standing on 33rd and Central Avenue in southeast Los Angeles, the downtown skyscrapers a distant backdrop to the bleak city streets, Barry White towers over his old block. He's dressed in black—long flowing black coat, black silk shirt, black draped trousers. Sunlight glistens on his curly-permed hair, long in the back, a lion's mane, as his eyes fill with tears that now streak down his cheeks. For several seconds he says nothing. You wait for his honeyed bass voice, an instrument of tremendous power and feeling, to elucidate the pain.

"This is where my brother was murdered," he finally says. "It happened on this very spot. He was my best friend. We were a two-man gang, respected and feared. We fell into devilment. For years we ran and ruled these streets. No one ever has, no one ever will, love me any deeper than Darryl did. I saw it coming, I predicted it, I said, 'Darryl, some motherfucker crazier than you will blow you away.' Happened on December 5, 1983. Shot through the heart. Right next to the rooming house where Daddy lived. All my life I worried about how I was gonna tell Mama her son was dead. And here Mama was telling me. I went into seclusion, canceling an appearance before the United Nations to protest apartheid. For nine days and nine nights I didn't move, didn't speak. No one could understand the bond between me and Darryl. I struggled to understand the forces that drove his soul in one direction and mine in another. That struggle continues."

White's recent struggle to end a decade-long slump has just proven successful. The 47-year-old artist, an eccentric sex symbol in the seventies, has been rediscovered in the nineties. . . .[9]

PROFILE "FORMULAS"

The following formula is one approach to writing profiles. Start with an (1) *opening anecdote* that gets across the *essence* of the person or a *theme*. (2) Next bring in a *"nut" paragraph* that sums up where the article is heading (see Chapter 8). Then, in another paragraph (3) sum up the *credentials* of the person or at least indicate the subject's *significance*, the reasons why someone is reading this article.

From there, (4) continue to make the *points* and (5) *subpoints* of the theme with anecdotes, preferably *building* with the anecdotes so that they progress like the actions of a character in a play to a (6) ringing *conclusion*. As with a play, the profile may reveal that the subject has shortcomings.

The profile approach used by the late Robert Ruark, who produced hundreds of articles about famous people, is remembered in an article in *Folio* magazine:

> The [Ruark] "formula" starts with a lead anecdote (the head). Next is justification, in which the reader is told about additional achievements of the subject (the neck). Amplification (the upper body) is made up of present-day doings and achievements. This is followed by "a nosepicker" or "wart" to

9. David Ritz, "White: The Long Day's Night of Barry," *Essence*, April 1992, p. 76. Reprinted by permission of the author's agent, the Aaron M. Priest Literary Agency.

make the subject believable; flashback with another anecdote (lower body); another "nosepicker"; and a "get out of town" anecdote (the feet)."[10]

The final "get out of town" conclusion needs some explaining. Writes J.T.W. Hubbard, who did the piece in *Folio* on Ruark's techniques:

> Like the lead, this ["get out of town"] should be an anecdote or incident that brings out the essential quality of the subject. In many ways it may resemble the lead, and set up a distinctive resonance with it that brings the intervening material into focus.
>
> Selecting such an anecdote is not always easy, and I have heard writers say, "I've got a great lead, but nothing for the kicker." If there is clearly no available material, then it can only be for one of two reasons. Either the writer has not done sufficient research or the opening anecdote does not hook into one of the subject's central traits.
>
> Conversely, if the lead derives four-square from the center of the subject's personality, then there is bound to be a wealth of affiliated anecdotes for "getting outa town." . . .[11]

Joan Bastel, who has edited feature sections in newspapers and written many profiles, says, "If the person is interesting, I like to start with the name and a present tense. . . . If the person's alive, why not?" She remembers that one started, "Dr. Marvin Hunter works in a lilliputian world. It is a world. . . ." And she went on to tell of his work as a microsurgeon.

"A person is a living breathing person as you speak," says Bastel, managing editor of the Doylestown (Pa.) *Intelligencer*. "To bring along the reader it is important that it seems as if he can walk through the door any moment."

Gary Provost, in *Writer's Digest*, leaves the profile process open. "I can tell you how to write a profile in 23 words," he says. "Find a subject. Do research. Imagine a reader. Create a slant. Query an editor. Do more research. Conduct an interview. Write a profile."[12]

VARIATIONS IN FORMAT

By now it should be apparent that there is no one approach to take in writing a personality profile. The following sections describe some formats commonly used.

One on One

You sit down with the subject and ask questions. The newspaper writer who has multiple assignments and deadline pressures may have little time to go

10. J.T.W. Hubbard, "Writing the Personality Profile," *Folio*, September 1983, p. 134.

11. Hubbard, pp. 138, 214.

12. Gary Provost, "Writing and Selling the Personality Profile," *Writer's Digest*, November 1981, p. 21.

beyond the one-shot interview. Yet one-on-one profiles can be enhanced by doing some advance preparation and checking with other people about the subject.

Sans Subject

Someone you want to profile might not be available for an interview — because of hostility to the press, illness, busy schedule, fear of being misquoted. But lack of availability won't stop an enterprising editor and reporter. Some interesting profiles and biographies, including a book on Frank Sinatra, have been written in depth without cooperation of the subject. When freelancer Kitty Kelley proposed to do a book on Sinatra, he not only refused to be interviewed but also filed a $2 million lawsuit in 1983 against Kelley before she had done the book. She proceeded (and won) with her uncomplimentary blockbuster *His Way: The Unauthorized Biography of Frank Sinatra*. She also did not have access to Nancy Reagan for her book, *Nancy Reagan: The Unauthorized Biography*, and will not likely have access to the Royal Family, her next unauthorized biography. Gay Talese wrote famous pieces on Sinatra and Joe DiMaggio without formal interviews. Someone like Sinatra or Nancy Reagan has many friends and enemies — and a considerable public record of comings and goings. Using such contacts and sources — and observing them over a period of time — probably produces a more multidimensional view of a subject than would relying on interviews with the subject.

The Q and A

Playboy is noted for its extensive profile articles, which appear up front in each issue. Usually featuring a celebrity, the profile is simply a transcription of a question-and-answer session. Questions are sometimes asked by one person, although they may have been prepared by staff and researchers. Sometimes a panel of interviewers asks the questions.

Politicians are often profiled using the Q and A technique. A panel of editors sits down with the candidate or officeholder and fires off questions. Sometimes the questions are limited to an agreed-on subject. A blurb or précis accompanying the article explains who asked the questions. In all, it's a see-saw effect, a question, an answer; a question, an answer.

Conversations

Ms. magazine inaugurated a conversations feature in February 1988. Explained Editor Anne Summers in her up-front "Editor's Essay": "We start a new feature — conversations between well-known and interesting women, with Martina Navratilova and Billie Jean King sharing memories, and talking frankly about themselves and each other."[13] A blurb accompanying the article, called simply "*Ms.* Conversation," read: "In this, the first of a series of

13. Anne Summers, "Editor's Essay: Continuity and Change," *Ms.*, February 1988, p. 7.

woman-to-woman dialogues, Martina Navratilova and Billie Jean King discuss life, sports, politics, and the passage of time." The article began:

> Buried in the midst of the news stories about Wimbledon last summer was a small item: Billie Jean King, it said, had been trying to talk Martina Navratilova out of her season-long court slump. Since Navratilova went on to win, we can assume that King's words were helpful. But King's role as the elder stateswoman of tennis made us wonder not just what King and Navratilova said to each other, but what both would like to tell the *next* generation of women players.
>
> *Ms.* invited them to talk together about their sport and themselves; about facing the impending twilight of an athletic career; the generation gap between those who fought for women's tennis rights and the naive youngsters who today reap the benefits; the second-rate media coverage of first-rate women's competitions; and the prejudice each has encountered because of their lifestyle choices.

> BILLIE JEAN KING: I don't remember when we first met.
>
> MARTINA NAVRATILOVA: I remember when I first *saw* you. It was at Queens, in front of the clubhouse. And I was like . . . oh, yeah, there's Billie Jean!
>
> KING: I remember Martina, when Owen Davidson and I played Jan Kodes and Martina in the quarterfinals in mixed. . . .
>
> NAVRATILOVA: On Court Two. . . .[14]

In the rest of the article, King and Navratilova move on into a discussion of substantive questions.

"Walk Ins"

If you can't get enough human interest about a person through an interview or interviews — or if the person has no time to sit down with you for an interview — consider doing "a day in the life of. . . ." If you follow someone around for a day, you can catch him or her off guard and pick up little tidbits, anecdotes and humor.

Student Dana Bartlett produced a story on a night with an emergency room doctor; another student made the rounds with a visiting nurse in a hospice program as she called at the homes of the terminally ill. Another chronicled a local politician in a typical day on the stump. You might consider following the spouse of a politician for a day.

"A day in the life of . . ." gives structure to a story. Seeing subjects across the span of a day yields a cross section of their lives, as if the tissue of their existence were examined on a slide under a microscope.

Sometimes you can follow a person — or family or group — and observe actions and record conversations over a period of time. Dave Curtin, of the Colorado Springs *Gazette Telegraph*, won the 1990 Pulitzer Price for feature

14. Michele Kort, interviewer, "*Ms.* Conversation," *Ms.*, February 1988, p. 58.

writing by "profiling" over a period of time a family badly scarred by a pro-
pane gas explosion in their Ellicott (Colo.) home. He monitored the father
and two of his children when they were in the hospital and watched the 4- and
6-year-old children deal with the reactions of other children when they returned to school. He ate with the family and spent one night in the home as he
watched the rehabilitation over a five-month period.

"As told to . . ."

A writer takes information and details about someone and makes the story
seem as if it came directly from the subject. *Reader's Digest* and *Guideposts* —
magazines dealing in personal adventure and inspirational stories, among
others — make good use of this format. If the story is about an adventure of
John Smith, and the writer is Jean Johnson, then the byline reads: "By John
Smith as told to Jean Johnson" or "John Smith with Jean Johnson."

A feeling for detail is important in all writing, but perhaps even more so
in the "as told to" approach. In a discussion on this format, Lois Duncan
notes you have to be a kind of detective. She says it takes explicit details to give
a first-person story its intimacy.[15]

Wrap-Ups

Joan Kron, editor-in-chief of the upwardly mobile *Avenue*, says she likes to
use profile articles that are "wrap-ups." She gets a group of people to talk on
one subject, for instance, telling what they bought in antiques.

Variations on this include, especially in newspapers, the candid-camera
technique. The reporter and cameraperson on the street secure pictures and
comments on a topic from passers-by. *USA Today* uses this format on its
editorial discussion page, including a panel of pictures and comments from
people selected at random. Each gives a view on an issue discussed on that
page.

Another variation of the wrap-up is the group interview. On the one
hand, it's hard to stand before a group, small or large, and elicit creative
material you can use while keeping proper track of identifications. On the
other hand, there are times when you would like the views of everyone in a
group — kids in a classroom, adults in a workshop, people on a panel. Using
the right psychology and a little charm to get the cooperation of the person in
charge of the group, you make sure that each person gets a simple one-page
questionnaire. Each person quickly fills out the form. You compile the best
and most interesting responses for your article, a "composite profile" on an
issue, if you will.

If you have no prior discussion about the questions with the group, you
maximize the variety of answers, for one person's views will not influence
another's. Limit this kind of one-page questionnaire to five or six questions,

15. Lois Duncan, "Writing the 'As-Told-To' Article," *Writer's Digest*, April 1985, p. 31.

with two or three questions covering the most basic information you need. At the beginning of the page identify yourself and your purpose. At the end, get the name, title and location of the respondent, with a line for a signature authorizing the use of the information and comments.

CASE HISTORY

Peter Sikowitz is an editor at *Diversion* (a travel magazine for physicians) and writes free-lance pieces. He tells how he produced his profile article on tennis player Yannick Noah for *Penthouse*:

> During early April 1986, I pitched an idea to Kim Jones (not real name), as editor at *Penthouse*, for a story on a California video company that was re-releasing the best of the worst films of the 1950s on video (an old college friend and fellow writer gave me her name; he had written some things for her front-of-the-book section in the past). I phoned her (not recommended since editors are often too busy to handle this type of call and, if they like the idea, they usually need something on paper to show their editor) and made the pitch. She thought it would work, but wanted to see the idea in writing.
>
> The idea on the video company was accepted and I signed a contract. Kim knew I wanted to write more for *Penthouse* and suggested the best story ideas "might be in my own backyard." Since I was an editor at *World Tennis* magazine at the time, she wanted me to consider writing a tennis story, perhaps a Q & A with a top pro, since I had good contacts. I told her there was a tournament coming to nearby Forest Hills next month, and, since the tournament is much smaller than the U.S. Open, it might be easier to talk to players, or at least set something up. I suggested two players that would make good stories: Mats Wilander of Sweden (the alleged heir to the throne of Bjorn Borg), and Yannick Noah of France. She preferred the Noah story.
>
> Since the idea was to do a major piece, she suggested sending my clips and whatever else would help my case, when presenting the idea (and the idea of me to write it) to her editor. Her editor liked the idea, and thought I was qualified to do the interview.
>
> The Shearson Lehman Brothers Tournament of Champions was held at Forest Hills May 5–11. At the beginning of the tournament, I put in a call to Noah's agent to see if he could set up the interview. The agent said Noah was very busy and it would depend on his schedule — he said he'd check with him.
>
> Within the week, I spoke with Noah's agent who said he had checked with Noah and that he was just too busy to do it. Agents, like any extra cog in the works, should be avoided whenever possible — it's not sensible to have someone else do your work for you. So, during the tournament, I charted Noah's progress anyway — I attended his matches and press conferences whenever I could in case I would need the material. Fortunately, he won the event. After the final, I asked him if he would agree to be interviewed by me for *Penthouse*; he said we could do the interview in two months . . ., prior to the U.S. Open, after he played the Italian and French Open championships. (Judging from Noah's response, I suspect his agent never asked him about the interview.)
>
> I signed a contract to do the story in early June (the interview would take place around late August, early September). In the meantime, I researched

my subject and got around 100 questions together on aspects of Noah: his life, his family, issues in the game, on being an international celebrity, etc. (My editor was helpful in suggesting areas *Penthouse* readers would be interested in—she also gave me similar Q & As the magazine had done in the past.) She approved my questions and I was all set to do the interview when he returned to the States. (Noah and I both live in New York City, home of the U.S. Open, so this made it all easier.)

When Noah returned to the States, I contacted him via a mutual friend and we set up a time to do the interview during the U.S. Open. Unfortunately, Noah retired in an early round, but it didn't matter—he gave me four hours of very good material (we talked in cafes around his home in downtown Manhattan).

In early September, I handed in my tapes—*Penthouse* had them transcribed. My editor looked at the material (around 120 pages of Q & A which would have to be trimmed down to around 20 pages) and liked it very much. Her editor liked it too, but he now wanted the story turned into a 5,000 word *profile*. He had his reasons, and that was that.

I went to work on the piece, and in early November, I turned the profile in to my editor. The piece was accepted.

Because of a backlog of stories, my profile was scheduled for the August 1987 issue, just before U.S. Open time. A few minor revisions were necessary to update the story.

The story ran in the August 1987 issue of *Penthouse*.

End of story. I would not advise journalists just starting out to try this; since I was an editor at a tennis magazine, I had a tremendous advantage. If someone has something similar in their favor, fine. If not, try a smaller market—*Penthouse*, like most big magazines, [is an] extremely competitive market for freelance writers.

Here is the beginning of Sikowitz's article in *Penthouse*:

ROLAND GARROS STADIUM, PARIS, JUNE 5, 1983. The final of the French Open. On the hot, dusty red clay of *le court central*, game, set, and match rest on the racket of 23-year-old Yannick Noah. With his acrobatic and emotional style of serve-and-volley tennis, the six-foot-four-inch, 180-pound tower of power has been playing the match of his life, and if he can serve out the game, he will become the first Frenchman since Marcel Bernard in 1946 to win the honor. His opponent and antithesis is the defending champion, 18-year-old Mats Wilander of Sweden. The crowd of 17,000, which has cheered its native son throughout the dramatic two-hour and 24-minute contest, is silent as he prepares. He serves, Wilander responds with a forehand that sails long, and the stadium erupts. Noah thrusts his arms to the sky and screams. He pushes the frenzied fans, who have overtaken the court, out of the way and runs to his father, who is among them. Tears stream down his face as they embrace, creating an unforgettable image of triumph.

In sports-mad France, Noah becomes a larger-than-life hero, a major deity and then some. The French press hails him as the "Black Panther," the "Indomitable Lion," and "*Le Sex Bombe Extraordinaire*." He is hailed as the heir apparent to French tennis legends Rene "le Crocodile" Lacoste, Jean

Borotra, Jacques Brugnon, and Henri Cochet. He is hailed as a celebrity, constantly monitored by a French press that dutifully reports his every move. He is hailed by fans wherever he goes. He is hailed by strangers, who leave dozens of messages on his telephone answering machine.

After his spectacular performance, he is rich (the French Open victory alone was an $87,656 payday), famous, and — repeat — 23 years old. Clearly, he holds *tout le monde* in the palm of his callused hand.

A few months later, Noah calls a press conference in Paris. He breaks down, weeps, and tells stunned reporters that life has become almost unbearable. He doesn't sleep at night and wanders the streets crying. The adulation has become suffocating, and he has even had thoughts of ending it all by jumping into the Seine. He announces he will move to New York, where he can take the subway if he feels like it, where he can be anonymous, just another face in the crowd. He must go to find himself, to focus on his tennis so he can be not among the best players in the universe, but *the* best.

The So-Ho section of New York, once a mecca for impoverished artists, is now home to upscale art galleries, chic eateries, high-priced real estate, and the world's No. 4 tennis player, who I'm supposed to meet at his loft at 11 a.m. I give him a few extra minutes before pressing a buzzer that's off to the side of an undistinguished metal door. Through an intercom, he says he'll be down in a minute. He comes down looking disheveled in an old, faded denim jacket, a peach-colored T-shirt printed with a large American Indian's head, white sweatpants and unlaced tennis shoes. No sunglasses. He doesn't seem to notice, or care, that his wristwatch is upside down. *Elle* magazine named him one of the world's ten most electric men, but I'm pretty sure he was asleep 15 minutes ago.

We stand in the street for a few minutes and talk about some of his recent matches. There was a pretty good one, he says, that he lost, but there were many great shots and the crowd was entertained.

The crowd was *entertained*? Hell, what's more important, entertaining or winning?

"I like to win — winning is the ultimate pleasure," he says in soft, French-accented English, a sharp contrast to his overpowering style of play. "But it's great to lose and feel good, too. You have to be strong enough to lose and still enjoy the game."

I guess, but I've seen him play. Although he has a deserved reputation as a first-rate sportsman — he's exceptionally quick to concede a point to an opponent that he feels was incorrectly called in his favor — and is one of the nicest players off court, when at work, he's all business: ferocious, cursing at himself in whatever language suits him at the time, slapping his thighs hard when he makes mistakes. He can also rival any of the more demonstrative players on the tour when confronting a spectator who has gotten under his skin. Like other top athletes, when he's doing the thing he must have been put on earth to do, the man is intense. . . .[16]

16. Peter Sikowitz, "PROFILE: Out of Africa, Soaring to the Top. NOAH'S ARC," *Penthouse*, August 1987, pp. 67–68, 70, 74, 147. Reprinted by permission. © 1987, Penthouse International, Ltd.

ASSIGNMENTS

1. Compare profiles of comparable length in both a newspaper and magazine.

2. Take a popular personality and, with the aid of library indexes, find five different feature and magazine articles on the same person. What different slants did each take? Why? Which did you like the best? What additional slant can be taken? Suppose you were assigned to write a personality profile on that person. Decide what publication it could be for and explain your approach.

3. Analyze a profile with color pencils. Underline the anecdotes in blue; quotes in red; facts and background information in yellow.

4. Cut out a profile article paragraph by paragraph and mix up the paragraphs. Have another person in class arrange the paragraphs in an intelligible, effective order. With the puzzle complete, compare with the original published article.

5. Take 10 anecdotes about a famous person and string them into a personality profile.

6. Pick a person who comes from a small town (such as a college athlete); write an updated profile on the person and send it (with a picture from an information office) to a newspaper in the person's home area. Here's a chance to publish (most small-town newspapers are interested in profiles of hometown men or women making good).

CHAPTER 7

The How-to Article

One of the easiest articles to produce — and one also in considerable demand — is the "how-to" article. These describe how to make something, or how to do something. Sometimes referred to as "service" articles, these provide a service to the reader. "Service" articles can be as undramatic as a "round-up" of information, and some service articles may look more like a directory than an article.

"How-to" articles are usually short. They draw from a body of expertise, preferably on a subject that the writer knows a good bit about. The article can be as simple and matter-of-fact as the directions on how to assemble a new swing set, golf cart or cabinet.

Don't be misled by the paucity of form. You must know the subject thoroughly or at least know someone who does. You must know the requirements of specific magazines and target the piece. You need a sense of logic and order; also, you must know how to give clear and complete directions, not leaving any gaps. Above all, you have to be intelligent and creative, because coming up with the right ideas and suggestions is paramount.

ON BEING AN EXPERT

If you're an expert on a subject or have a special interest in it, that's the best place to start. You're an expert if you're at home with the subject. Some amateur historians are as good as the academics, for instance, because they have read as much and have tremendous collections of primary materials. Movie buffs may know more about films — the older films in particular — than do many young critics. You're an expert if you're close to the subject.

Sometimes people become an expert, without knowing it, as they grow into their expertise. This is true of general assignment reporters who write on all subjects. Experts aren't born; they're created. The many routes are obvious — hobbies, academic training, volunteer work in an area of interest, internships, plus extra attention to the subject of interest in libraries and journals.

If you're a college student, concentrate in school on one or two subjects that interest you the most. If you're a journalism major, make sure you know a great deal about one or two other subjects. Many schools don't have double majors or minors, but you can create you own areas of concentration.

Developing a specialty is good advice for all would-be writers. If you're going into newspaper work, you might latch onto a special beat in labor, politics, education, religion, the arts, business, real estate and so on. The same advice applies to those who go to graduate school. Specialize and concentrate on an area other than your undergraduate major. A student with several areas of expertise will have more options in landing jobs and in free-lance writing — in producing "how-to" and other articles.

WHERE TO GET HOW-TO IDEAS

One professor tells of a student in a magazine writing class who reported no special interest, training or hobby. She was, curiously, the editor of the college newspaper and had been for several years. Somewhat reluctantly, she found herself enrolled in the magazine writing course, which was proving to be a challenge much different from rehashing administration and student organization releases for the rather dull campus newspaper. She was encouraged to come up with an idea that would make a person pick up a magazine and read her article. No success. She just didn't have anything to write about. In life, she spent much of her extra time slaving at the student paper; she didn't have a car . . . ah, there was an idea. How does a student who doesn't have a car transverse hilly landscape and attend a rural school? How does a student without a car and other amenities get by in this rapid world? You could expand on the idea — "How Do You Go to College and Grad School When Mom and Dad Won't/Can't Give Any Help?" Or, "How Do You Find Good Part-time Jobs?" or "101 Things to Do Instead of Studying." The student finally wrote a fairly commendable piece on how to survive in a rural campus town without a car.

If you're a political science major, flip through a textbook and look at subheads for inspiration. You might come up with ideas on "How to Run for Office," "How to Meet a Governor or President," "How to Launch a Lobby," "How to File a Complaint," "If You Have to Serve on a Jury," or "If You Have to Testify in Court—20 Things to Know." There are manuals, such as those for police, with just these kinds of "how-to" lists that could get you started.

If you're an English major, try "How to Increase Your Vocabulary," "How to Write a Novel," "How Best to Understand Shakespeare," "How to Write a Poem." If you're a psychology major, the sky's the limit. One author wrote a book on the concerns of early adolescents. He created his own list of ideas but also picked the brains of teachers and principals. He looked for ideas in the youth magazines, such as *Seventeen*, which about every three years seems to cover every concern teens have. Each chapter, quoting kids, teachers (from surveys of classrooms), psychiatrists and clinical experts, offered help on these topics and how to deal with them: anger and temper, boredom, brother/sister relationships, clothes, cults, death, drugs, embarrassment, friends, health, homesickness, jealousy, loneliness, low self-esteem, money, neighbors, shyness, single parents, swearing, values, video games, winning/losing and happiness. Several dozen topics were left over for another book.

For science majors, again, the sky's the limit on ideas. In biology, something humorous on "How to Raise an Insect Pet," or more seriously, "How Do You Prevent Osteoporosis?" or another disease, or "How to Select a Doctor," "How to Take Better Care of Yourself." Informed articles on dieting and fitness are perennial winners. In botany and horticulture, "How to Prepare Your Garden for Winter," as one student wrote for a magazine, or "How to Take Care of a Tree." One student wrote about "How to Protect Your Child From Household Plants That Can Kill." In chemistry, consider environmental issues: for example, the effect of toxic chemicals—"How to Purify Your Water System." In physics, "How to Protect Yourself from Radon Gas"; "How to Work with Electricity"—how to change the wiring in your home, how to avoid electrical overloads.

If you're a journalism major, you can write for the media journals, although you should leave journalism as a topic to the professors and grad students with assignments for research in certain areas. For instance, you can write about how a newspaper in your locale developed one of its big stories or you could profile an interesting editor. *Editor & Publisher* will use such timely fare from new writers. But journalism, at least for the beginner, is best conceived of as a technique and a profession, not a topic; seek out the content areas with down-to-earth topics that will grab the mass reader.

Here are some additional "how-to" articles that students have written drawing from their training and interests: What you should know when your child travels alone (the student had been a TWA flight attendant); how to take the bite out of moving; you, too, can be president; how to dress retro;

how to teach your dog tricks; how to prepare for an online computer search; how to predict stock market trends; how to make chili delight; how to market management ideas when marketing plans fail; how to write your child's birth plan; how to make interfaith marriage work; how to survive a career crisis; how to give a stand-up presentation and feel good about it; how to buy a condominium; how to leave your job; how to cope with homemaker limbo; how to get the market information you need for free—almost; how to use self-service storage; 10 ways to reignite your job search; what every young woman should know about combining career and family; how to brighten your home with suncatchers.

In searching for ideas, keep an eye on the new books. A constant stream of how-to books is published in the United States. Look at *Publishers Weekly* in the library. Check out its weekly summaries of forthcoming books. Their titles can set your creative juices churning. Sunday book sections sometimes include a round-up on new how-to books. For example, Carlin Romano in the Philadelphia *Inquirer* recommended the following how-to books to readers and included paragraph synopses: *How to Teach Your Dog to Play Frisbee, How to Make Love to the Same Person for the Rest of Your Life and Still Love It, How to Play Popular Piano in 10 Easy Lessons, How to Start and Run Your Own Word-Processing Business, How to Find and Buy Your Business in the Country, How to Survive on Land and Sea, How to Shoot a Gun, How to Cut Kids' Hair, How to Save Your Hair, How to Afford Your Own Log House, How to Make and Sell Your Own Record.*

Take a new book list like this one and let it inspire you directly or indirectly. Looking at Romano's list, you can come up with your own "how-to" about business, such as, "How to Start an Antique Furniture Business" or a commercial art gallery. Instead of how to cut your kids' hair, "How to Trim Your Dog."

Of course, you can just look at your life and decide what *you* don't understand. Begin to read about the topics, and search out those "in the know" to interview. If you don't know anything about the stock market, you might be interested in writing "20 Tips for the Beginning Investor." If you need to make a will, or a special kind of will, you can get the information you need and write about it at the same time.

QUESTIONS TO ASK YOURSELF

A "how-to" article should have substance. Just providing a list of obvious directions doesn't contribute much, and editors won't buy how-to articles without any real meat in them.

To make sure you're on the right track, use the following checklist. If you can answer yes to all the questions, you're on the way to a salable piece.

- Do I know which magazine I'm shooting for? Have I studied the magazine and written a query?
- Do I know what has already been written on this?

- Did I do any research whatsoever (or did I just sit down and write it off the top of my head)?

- Am I aware of the complexities (or did I just simplify and generalize everything)?

- Are there any specifics, such as naming relevant organizations and how to find them?

- Did I follow a logical pattern in structuring the article?

- Have I said anything new about the subject?

- Do I have any authority base? Am I an expert, or did I rely on experts?

- Is there any relevant primary material (such as interviews with the right people) or updated secondary material (studies, statistics, case histories) I might cite from the literature on the subject?

- Finally, is there any reason for someone to read this article?

BASICS OF THE HOW-TO FORMULA

The following factors are common to most how-to articles:

- *The how-to article is concise.* The reader wants clear information, not entertainment.

- *The how-to article has a progression,* an orderly movement from one step to another.

- *The how-to invites very short leads* or no leads at all. Simply get right to the directions, promised in the title.

- *The how-to article has a visible quality.* The reader has to be able to see how to do something. Clear diagrams or pictures depicting the main steps in the directions should accompany the manuscript. Ideally the art and pictures should be of high quality; but if not, they should at least be intelligible enough so that an artist or photographer assigned by the editor to illustrate the article will know exactly what to do. You should also "see" the structure of the article, know at a glance how it is organized.

- *The how-to article has some kind of parallel structure,* a repetition of style. This aspect of how-to is one of the most important. In the most simple approach, start the beginning of each point or step you are making the same way. If you start off your first point with an imperative verb form, such as, "*Buy* such and such a product," then the next points follow the same approach — for example, "*Choose* your store carefully," then, "*Total* your expenditures daily." Note that "buy, choose, total" are imperatives or commandments, "do" and "do not." The pronoun *you* is omitted in the imperative case.

- *The how-to article seeks to give approximately the same amount of space to each point.* If your first point is two paragraphs, the second point or step should be two paragraphs of comparable length.

- *The how-to article has few quotations.* You can mention other authorities, and often by so doing you strengthen the article, but you may not need quotes. Just attribute information. Quotes interrupt and dilute the progression of the hands-on information.

- *The how-to article may be broken into components.* You might have several lists and each could have a title. A directory of whom to contact can be in a separate box. *USA Today*'s how-to features in the Life section are generally split into three parts.

Phyllis Marcuccio, editor of the National Science Teachers Association's *Science and Children*, published in Washington, uses many how-to articles. She has her own suggestions for writers:

- "If you think you know how to make something and are writing about it, *try it first.* Do it, before you turn the article in." [The Rodale Press, in Emmaus, Pa., which prints magazines and books, makes its how-to book editor create anything in a book he or she edits: a greenhouse, a solar heating unit, etc.!]

- *"Don't forget the parts.* Enthusiastic persons leave out paragraphs. Read the article aloud. What your eye will pass over, your ear will not forget. We editors need to know more than we need. We will edit it down to size."

- *"Be aware of safety* and include any precautions or safety steps that should be taken." [An example from fiction makes the point. When I was creating a comic strip, "Inez, the Invisible," I needed to show how Inez became invisible at times. Marcuccio, an adviser for our magazine, *Kidbits,* said not to let Inez ingest anything because kids imitate and might swallow something dangerous in imitating Inez. We decided to let Inez become invisible and visible again by blowing a dog whistle—the result of an experiment that went wrong at a school science fair. Also in *Kidbits* I once wanted to have a feature on "How to Hang Glide" to go with a beautiful set of hang-gliding pictures taken against the sunset. But, again, safety was a consideration. Some kids who saw the article might sail over a cliff in a less-than-adequate improvised vehicle.] Always consider your audience and tailor your article to its age level and its taboos; make safety issues central.

- *"Keep the directions simple.* You don't need an erector set to push a toy across the room."

- "If *diagrams are involved, they have to match what is going on.* So often something is happening in the diagram totally off the wall and foreign to the article."

- "Normally *the shorter the better*—like a list . . . [telling] how to put a bicycle together at Christmas time, with a few paragraphs of introduction. But if the article first of all is dealing with a concept—such as a science principle—discuss the concept before telling how to do it."

There is, of course, "no absolute format for the how-to article," as Judith Nolte, editor of *American Baby* and former president of the American Society of Magazine Editors, points out. And as Joel Gurin, former editor of *American Health*, says, in summary: "Generally just give useful information."

VARIATIONS OF HOW-TO ARTICLES

You'll probably recognize most of the formats for how-to articles, even though you may not have paid much attention to them. In a good how-to article, the way you say it is very much part of what you say.

The Simple Parallel Structure

In this basic format, you make each point in the same way, using parallel sentence structure. As we've seen, this approach is one of the most common. Sometimes each point is numbered. Usually the points total up to a round number: Ten ways to do something (like a Ten Commandments) or 20. . . . However, some editors like an odd number. "It's the mystique," notes writer Linda Murray. And perhaps "Seven Early Signs of Cancer" has a sharper edge to it than does the smooth "Ten Early Signs of Cancer."

Each new idea can start with an imperative or commandment, can be marked by a number, can start with a full sentence or can start with a subtitle.

The *imperative* or commandment approach was used by journalism graduate student Linda Knoll in her article, "Get the Market Info You Need for Free — or Almost," for *Entrepreneur*. The parallel wording pattern — imperatives — and type design (boldface, caps), make the points stand out.[1]

Get the Market Info You Need for Free . . . Or Almost

Linda Knoll

The old saw that "success is one percent inspiration and 99 percent perspiration" applies to most businesses. There is another ingredient, however, that can make all the difference — information.

A great deal of market information is available to you, and most of it is free, or close to it. All you have to do is use your eyes and ears, and take a few tips from the pros.

Conduct a market survey and gather information about all aspects of your market. In doing so you will learn about your customers, their needs and wants, their habits, and how to find and satisfy them. You will learn about your competitors,

continued

---

1. Linda Knoll, "Get the Market Info You Need for Free — Almost," *Entrepreneur*, July 1982, pp. 49, 73, 74.

continued

their strengths and weaknesses, their plans for the future. Most importantly, you will learn about your business, where it is, where it's going, and why.

The basic steps described here will expand your understanding of your market and your business without punishing your pocketbook.

CHECK YOUR OWN RECORDS. Your business records hold valuable information. Sort your sales receipts and take a good look at your mailing list. Just looking at your records (or a sampling of them) can give you answers: Who are your customers? What geographic area do they cover? How many are there? Are they similar in sex, occupation or age? Potential customers will have much in common with existing ones — so get to know your customers as a group. Knowledge will help you tailor your product, prepare your advertising and determine your pricing.

Take a close look at sales or order records too, noting the size and contents of the transactions. You may find easy ways to build sales and profits.

Suppose you find a pattern. For example, if your business is a retail-garden supply store and nursery, your sales slips may show that customers who buy plants occasionally buy fertilizer at the same time. Why not consider a cross-selling program, asking plant purchasers at the checkout whether they need fertilizer? You may boost sales and do your customers a favor at the same time.

Sales receipts can also indicate seasonality in your business. Do half your sales fall in the summer months? At the end of the year? Although you may be generally aware of seasonal patterns, a closer look will clarify them and show when you should build inventory, add sales help or reduce business hours.

SUBSCRIBE TO TRADE MAGAZINES. From *Entree* (gourmet cookware dealers) to *Hardware Age* and *Restaurant News*, there are magazines aimed at dealers, manufacturers and suppliers in every industry. Many are free to sub-

scribers. Find out more about these publications and the information they offer you.

Subscribe to as many as you can, and read them — not just those aimed at you but those directed toward your suppliers and customers as well. You will learn more about general trends affecting your business and benefit from in-depth specifics. Trade magazines commonly feature statistics about industry size, results of expensive, professionally designed research surveys, and interviews with industry experts. Consider hiring a part-timer or a student to help clip articles and arrange them by topic.

JOIN TRADE ASSOCIATIONS — and go to meetings. Whatever your business, there is probably a local chapter of a trade association serving your field. As a member, you'll pay modest annual dues, plus hotel charges for meals served at monthly meetings. In exchange, you'll hear speakers on topics related to your community or your business. Opportunities to make informal but valuable contacts with suppliers, competitors and customers are other benefits.

If you're unsure whether an organization is the right one for you, go to a meeting or two to check it out; you need not join right away.

Marketing organizations are also worth checking out. The American Marketing Association, Marketing/Communications Executives International and Business/Professional Advertising Association are a few that have many local chapters. Their monthly speakers feature marketing techniques, successful programs and new approaches to marketing problems. You'll get good ideas for your business from marketing professionals, for little cost.

STUDY THE COMPETITION — diligently. Tack their ads up on your bulletin board and make a list of common themes and ideas. Look at your competitors' price lists, order forms, catalogs and brochures. You'll learn how others have chosen to solve many of the problems you face: pricing (what to do about freight or what volume discounts to offer); advertising (what points to emphasize, what not to say); product development (what additional products to sell, which to drop).

You may not agree with your competitors' decisions on these questions, but you can still benefit from their thinking because you know the problems they face. It may even be possible to become a customer of one of your competitors — and experience exactly how they treat you.

Talk to your customers and your suppliers about your competitors. Those who sell to or buy from you are probably well-acquainted with your competitors, and would be flattered if you asked their opinions. You may be surprised at how much you can learn about the competition's strengths, weaknesses and plans for the future.

One word of caution: Be sure you know who your competitors are. Do not be guilty of "marketing myopia." The railroad industry, the automobile industry and the record industry have all suffered major business setbacks by failing to anticipate competition from outside the immediate industry.

If you sell takeout sandwiches, you compete with McDonald's, Burger King and also the local Chinese restaurant. If you sell data-processing services, the day may not be far off when your most serious competition comes from desk-top microcomputers rather than other data-processing services. Be aware of trends both inside and outside the industry that affect your business.

USE YOUR STOCKBROKER. The research department of your brokerage firm can provide you with all sorts of valuable data. Annual reports of companies that own your competitors, industry summaries for your industry or those of your suppliers or customers, and informal discussions with industry experts may all be there for the asking. You'll learn how objective, professional analysts see your business, and become more familiar with an overview of the marketplace and growth expectations for the future.

USE THE PUBLIC LIBRARY. If you live near a metropolitan area or a college, you are probably close to a large, modern library well-stocked with information and people who know how to use it. Take advantage — it's free.

Look in the card catalog under subjects related to your business. Use the *Reader's Guide to Periodical Literature, Business Periodical Guide,* and other indexes to find published articles on your type of business. Thumb through stock-market reports, directories and newspapers with strange but interesting names. If you market a consumer product, read back issues of *Consumer Reports* (completely indexed) to find analyses of product categories related to yours.

Many larger libraries also offer, for a small fee, computerized data-base searches. At the press of a few buttons, your friendly librarian can probably provide a listing of dozens of recent magazine or newspaper articles relating to your business.

USE THE GOVERNMENT. You do pay taxes, and some tax funds are used to gather information you have access to.

If you sell mail-order umbrellas, you may want to know which U.S. cities get the most rainfall. The *Statistical Abstract of the United States,* published annually by the Department of Commerce, will tell you. It costs less than $20. If you sell residential real estate in Utica, New York, you may want to know more about expected migration patterns for that area. Government Printing Office reports can tell you — ask for the "geographic mobility" series.

If you live in a major metropolitan area, a Census Bureau office or Government Printing Office bookstore may be at your disposal. If you live near or occasionally travel to Washington, D.C., you're even luckier — you have access to the Library of Congress. Take the time to call your local government bookstore, or the Library of Congress if you're in Washington. The amount of available information is matched only by the assistance provided by the experts in charge.

By following these steps you can survey your market thoroughly — and spend next to nothing doing it. Now finish off the job with another free but professional step: write it down.

A 50-page, typed and bound document may not be necessary. A simple outline organizing
continued

continued

what you have learned will help you and others involved in your business to gain real benefits from your efforts. Once the information is written in black and white you can always refer to it.

One way to organize your survey is to divide it into five parts, covering the "5 Ps" of marketing:

- Product — Exactly what is it? How is it used? And by whom? Weigh each word carefully. This is the key section.

- Pricing — What is it and what affects it?

- Promotion — How do advertising, publicity and merchandising affect sales?

- Packaging — In what packages, quantities and related sales is the product sold? How important is this?

- Place — How is the product sold to end-users? How does this compare with competitors? Can distribution be expanded?

In each section consider your own business practices and those of your competitors.

After you have written down your key findings, you may discover other questions that you are not able to answer. This may be the time to call in a marketing consultant. The consultant's charges will most assuredly not fall within our definition of "free or almost."

If you decide to take this step, however, you'll be able to spend your money wisely and your consultant's time effectively because you have an organized, written summary of your market survey.

Journalism student Bonnie McMeans added numbers to emphasize the parallel points in her article, "Leaving Your Job? Do It Right!" for *Career World.*[2]

Leaving Your Job? Do It Right!

Bonnie McMeans

When Harry was 16, he got his first job working part-time in a shoe store. "See?" he told his friends. "Getting a job is easy. I just talked with the guy."

A few weeks later, Harry had a disagreement with the store's assistant manager. After the argument, Harry left for lunch and never went back. "I'll get another job," he said.

This time it was at a restaurant. But, after five months of bussing heavy trays, Harry decided the money wasn't worth it. He told his supervisor he found another job and had to start immediately. "The guy wanted to kill me," he bragged. "But, so what? He wasn't even paying me anything."

Then a friend told Harry about a great job working in an arcade. The position paid above minimum wage and his friend was already hired so they could work together. Harry applied for the job.

"Have you worked before, son?" the owner asked Harry during a brief interview. Harry told

---

2. Bonnie McMeans, "Leaving Your Job? Do It Right!," *Career World*, February 1983, pp. 14, 15. Special permission granted by *Career World*, published by Weekly Reader Corporation. Copyright © 1983 by Weekly Reader Corporation.

him about his last two jobs. "Sounds good," the owner said. "I'll call them and if everything checks out, you can start Monday."

But everything didn't check out. Harry had earned a reputation for quitting a job without giving notice. Now, finding a third job was going to be difficult.

Burning Bridges

Like Harry, many people new to the job market make the mistake of underestimating the importance of leaving a job the right way.

According to Burton Adler, career counselor and author of the book, *Arming Yourself for Part-time and Summer Jobs*, "Leaving a job appropriately is just as important as looking for a job appropriately. It's important for every work experience to contribute to the 'slingshot effect' that occurs when you use each job as a tool for getting a better job. Even the job that pays poorly or seems beneath your potential can come in handy later when you are building your 'reference biography.'"

People burn bridges when they leave jobs for many reasons, says Larry Brown, president of 70001 Ltd., a national youth employment training program. "If someone is new to the job market, he or she may not realize what's expected when the person wants to resign. Sometimes, someone will just follow the advice of a friend and leave without telling anyone or not show up for work the next day. In other cases, the employee could be embarrassed or afraid of a confrontation with the supervisor over the resignation, and avoid the situation altogether."

Nadler says resigning from a job at any age can be difficult. "It takes a secure and assertive person to confront someone who's been paying you to do a job, day after day, and tell the person you're leaving. Some employees even feel they're 'stabbing the employer in the back.'"

Smart Steps

Regardless of the anxiety that might surround quitting a job, personnel directors and career counselors advise the following steps to make someone's resignation a positive experience:

1. *Always give the employer notice that you are leaving.* How much notice depends on the personnel policy and your position in the company. Usually two weeks is enough. Giving proper notice is important for several reasons.

   First, it means you are treating the employer with the same respect that you, as an employee, would feel entitled to. "No one likes to be laid off or fired from a job without warning," says Brown. "The employer deserves the same preparation time to hire and train your replacement."

   Second, giving proper notice can help you get a good recommendation when you want to use the job as a reference at a later time. Personnel directors agree that in most cases, when someone leaves without notice, it is recorded in their personnel files. Even if you feel you'll never need an employer's good words, leave on good terms anyway. This way, if you want to refer a friend or relative to the company sometime, your reputation as a solid employee will come in handy.

   Third, failure to give proper notice could result in the loss of any earned benefits or vacation pay, as well as the opportunity to return to the company at a later date for another position. Valerie Titus, a human resource developer (personnel specialist) for Shared Medical Systems in Philadelphia, says that high school students who mislead an employer by promising to work past the summer just to get a summer job are inclined to quit without notice as September approaches because they feel guilty or embarrassed. "However," Titus says, "if you give them notice as the summer comes to an end, maybe that job will be waiting for you next summer."

2. *Give notice in writing.* According to the personnel director of a national retail company, most employers want to know the reasons behind someone's resignation as well as the date the person intends to leave. This can be accomplished by writing a personal letter or *continued*

continued

by filling out a form supplied by the company that asks the employee to explain the reasons for leaving.

3. *Tell your immediate supervisor first.* "A supervisor never likes to hear from the personnel department that one of the staff is quitting," says Robert Cardillo, assistant administrator of the Sacred Heart Hospital in Norristown, Pennsylvania. "Therefore, we always encourage our employees to first notify their supervisor who in turn will notify the personnel office."

4. *Be honest with your supervisor about your reasons for quitting.* If you're leaving the job to return to school or take another job, make sure to say thanks for the opportunity to work. If you're leaving because of a problem with a co-worker or even the supervisor, politely and tactfully explain the situation. Your honest feedback or input may help to remedy a bad situation.

5. *If the employer reacts angrily, keep your cool.* As long as you are giving proper notice and are following the procedure outlined in the personnel policy, you are on solid ground. Stay calm and be polite. After the employer has thought about it, he or she may realize you did the right thing by leaving and you won't lose out on a good reference.

6. *Offer to help the employer find a replacement for you.* You might suggest a friend you think would like the job. Offer to show your supervisor any system or procedure you used to get the job done so training your replacement will be easy.

7. *Continue to do your job well, even up to the last day.* Remember, you are being paid to produce during those last two weeks and how you finish off your employment will remain fresh in your supervisor's mind when he or she is asked to be a reference for you. Complete any previously scheduled assignments or reports prior to your leaving.

8. *Participate in or request an "exit interview."* This is the time when you discuss with your supervisor or the personnel director how you felt about working for the company. "It's a time for mutual feedback," says Cardillo. "An opportunity for us to evaluate the employee and for the employee to evaluate us. It's also a good time for discussing how any earned vacation or benefits will be handled, as well as collecting necessary equipment such as keys or uniforms." And it gives you a chance to ask how and when you'll receive your final paycheck.

9. *Ask for a letter of recommendation.* Should the company close down or move, or the supervisor you reported to leave, a letter of recommendation may be hard to obtain when you need it.

10. *Don't "bad-mouth" former employers.* Dolores Brien, director of career planning and guidance for Bryn Mawr College in Pennsylvania, says, "Don't fall into the trap of criticizing your former employers just because you left a job under unpleasant circumstances." Titus adds, "Employers support employers," so if you speak against another employer or supervisor, chances are you're the one who looks bad.

If these guidelines for leaving a job the right way seem too complicated or too official for just a part-time or summer job, remember that being successful in the job market means learning the necessary skills early. These skills include using every job to your advantage by moving on in a professional way.

A *question* led off each point in Nick Bollettieri's article in *World Tennis*. The questions served as subheads in bold type, each introducing a section of discussion. The question subheads included: "Should you set goals at the start of each lesson?" "Should you set up drills?" "Should you talk more and hit less?" "Should you ever lose your temper?"[3]

   Subtitles indicate the individual points in undergraduate student Sharon Taft's "Ski Touring Under the Stars," written for *Nordic World Magazine* when she was a student at Mankato (Minn.) State University.[4]

Ski Touring Under the Stars

Sharon Taft

Imagine a calm, moon-lit winter night. Fresh snow blankets the landscape and stars twinkle in the sky. You're not tired enough to go to bed. What's the logical next step if you're a cross-country skier? A ski tour under the stars, of course.

   Few people realize what an enjoyable and safe adventure skiing in the dark can be. It is easier to see in the dark than most people think. It's simply a matter of letting your eyes adjust to the night light. Even on a moon-less winter night, there is generally enough light reflected from the stars for you to be able to move around slowly but safely.

   The snow is particularly fascinating at night because of the many tracks left in it. It is possible to follow these tracks and read the stories they tell. You might even come upon the little animals that made them. If you do, treat these animals with interest and respect.

   Cross-country skiing at night can be a richly rewarding experience if the necessary steps are taken to prepare for the tour.

Kind of Night
The choice of night for your tour should be made with great care. It should be a night with a relatively bright moon. And, of course, there should be little or no wind. Skiing in blowing snow is difficult and unpleasant enough in daytime. At night, it can be positively foolhardy.

Trail
Preferably, you will choose a trail that you've skied before. A familiar trail is best because you'll know of any obstacles to be encountered such as a swift downgrade or possibly barbed wire fencing. Both of these could be very dangerous, especially if you aren't aware of them. The trail could be located in any one of several areas. Fields, golf courses, or woodland are all possible areas for night-time skiing.

   You might want to pick out and scout a trail during the day, checking to see, among other things, where a shelter is located. You could stop at the shelter and collect wood to build a fire. This way you won't have to take time in the subdued light to gather wood later. When your group gets to the shelter that night all you will have to do is light the fire.

   In choosing the trail, be sure to take the length into consideration. The distance should be kept relatively short. Possibly one to two miles would be best. If the trail is short, you'll have time to stop and listen to the sounds around you, and generally get in much closer contact

continued

---

3. Nick Bollettieri, "Teaching Your Child Is No Kid's Stuff," *World Tennis*, December 1984, p. 29.

4. Sharon Taft, "Ski Touring Under the Stars," *Nordic World Magazine*, December 1975, pp. 14, 15.

continued

with nature and your surroundings. With a longer trail you may find yourself having to race over it from start to finish.

Group Size

The group should be limited to a smaller number to make it possible to enjoy the animals and the sounds of the night. A smaller group would also be desirable in a forest environment because of the threat to the ecosystem a larger group would pose. On the other hand, the group should not be so small as to leave no avenue of assistance if there is an accident. There should be one person to stay with the injured and one or possibly two to seek help. Therefore, for safety's sake, you should have at least three or four people in your group.

Clothing

There's an extremely wide range of clothing one could wear. But whatever you wear, make sure that it fits loosely so you'll be able to move with ease.

Clothing should be breathable. This allows the body to maintain an even temperature. Nylon is a material to stay away from because it does not "breathe." Wool is the best material to use because it is breathable and if it should get wet, it will still maintain your body heat.

The amount of clothing you take will depend on temperature. However, heavy clothing shouldn't be necessary, as you'll be generating body heat as you ski. But be sure to take a jacket to put on when you stop.

A hat or earband should be worn. You can always stuff them in your pocket if you get too warm. It's also advisable to have mittens or gloves with you.

Gaiters are a very useful article to wear over your boot tops to keep the snow out. When you first go out into the snow, stand a minute or two and let your boots cool off. This will help prevent cold feet. Avoiding cold feet can also be accomplished by keeping your boots waterproofed.

Equipment

In making a last minute check of your equipment, be sure that the bindings are in place, all screws tight, and your boots have the proper laces.

An extra ski tip is a useful piece of equipment to take along. This is a curved piece of plastic or metal that can be slipped on a ski when you break a tip. The danger potential of a broken ski tip in the heart of wilderness is obvious. You're not likely to be very far away from civilization on a ski tour at night. Nonetheless, an extra ski tip is a handy item to have with you — particularly if the snow is deep.

Safety

Beware of hypothermia. Hypothermia is a lowering of the body core temperature due to the body losing heat faster than it can produce it. Unchecked, this condition can result in death in less than two hours.

To guard against hypothermia, carry enough clothes to keep you protected against the effects of moisture, wind and temperature changes. Eighty percent of the body's heat can be lost if the head and neck gets cold. If you should get cold, cover these areas. If you get wet, eat high energy foods such as gorp or granola, and drink plenty of hot liquids such as tea, coffee, soup or cocoa. Change out of your wet clothes as soon as possible.

It's a good idea to take along a few extra items in the interests of safety. This might include a flashlight, a knife, compass, matches, a first-aid kit, a trail map and a portion of gorp or granola.

Should you get lost, don't panic. Retrace your tracks. This is the best way to find out where you went wrong.

Stars

The sky is clearest on a cold, sparkling winter night. On a night like that, even the faintest stars can be seen. The winter constellations contain some of the brightest and most easily recognizable stars. These constellations center around Orion, the Great Hunter. The belt of Orion acts as a pointer. To the northwest, it points toward the Pleiades and in the opposite direction, toward Sirius, the dog. You can locate Orion by noting the time and checking with a star chart. . . .

Wilderness Music

At first, most of us lack the sensitivity to hear wilderness music. But if one listens carefully, it is possible to raise our consciousness. There are many types of music, each different from the rest. A pack of coyotes and the wild beautiful sound as they tune their voices; the sound of wild geese flying in the night; the hooting of an owl; the sounds of hemlocks whispering with the breeze; the cracking of ice on streams and lakes as it forms or is disturbed; the swish of your skis gliding over the snow. Wilderness music is there for those who have ears to listen.

One of the most unusual experiences I have enjoyed is combining night skiing with catching the sunrise. This can be accomplished by skiing around 5:30 in the morning; you're able to enjoy the late night and yet see the sunrise as well. The beauty of this is something you should experience for yourself.

Checklist and Quiz Structure

Wendy Stehling used checklists in her book, *How to Find a Husband in Thirty Days* (Pinnacle, 1985), and the checklists appeared in magazine articles based on the book. For instance, Stehling discusses what to do on the first three dates, and the discussion of each date is followed by a checklist.

In a newspaper feature, Barbara Burtoff conveyed information for the traveler going abroad in the form of a quiz: The 25 multiple-choice questions, plus a sidebar of "Answers and Advice," took a full page in the Doylestown (Pa.) *Intelligencer*.[5]

A series of rate-yourself aptitude tests was designed by I. Orrin Spellman, of Philadelphia, for *Family Circle*. Spellman, a semiretired head of a public relations business, prepared the article in a university graduate course in nonfiction writing. He more than recovered his tuition with the sale to *Family Circle* for $4,000. The magazine gave his article, "Discover What You're Best At: Free Career Aptitude Test," a great deal of space and featured it on the cover. He tells how it all came about:

> It started as a classroom exercise. As the professor asked us to do a consumer magazine piece, I decided to try one about aptitude testing based on my past experience in this field. Since *Family Circle* is one of the largest women's magazines in the world with about 8 million circulation (23.5 million readers), I decided to try there.
>
> Here are the steps I took:
>
> 1. My first submission to class. Some of the prof's comments included: A question about the working title. Originally it was: "How to Find Out Who You Are." But the lead dealt with examples of people who were dissatisfied with their careers. The prof asked: "Is the subject 'awareness' or dealing with 'dissatisfaction?'" He suggested a title something more along the line of "How to Find Out What You Really Want to Do in Life," or "What You Should Be Doing in Life." Other comments: "Let's

5. Barbara Burtoff, "A Quiz for Travelers," Doylestown (Pa.) *Intelligencer*, July 2, 1987, p. 41.

target one group, such as mid-life. To get into high-school testing and later career change testing blurs the article. . . . Try to hold together more by transitions, such as repeating of subject. . . . A lot of stuff — and useful — is here. . . . For a sharper focus and to help each to get a handle on it: (1) target it to one group — age level — of people; (2) in each category, work in some anecdotes; (3) you might create some case or model histories and give the conditions, etc. and then the 'prescriptions' in each case; (4) could include some sample questions for each test."

2. I gave the rewrite to the prof along with a letter to Lawrence Kane, executive editor of *Family Circle*, packaged and ready for prof to mail.

3. In a letter dated exactly a week after my letter to Kane, Susan Ungaro, articles editor, replied to me showing interest in the idea of aptitude testing but wanting a miniature version *Family Circle* readers could take and score themselves.

4. As she suggested, I got in touch with Barry Gale, author of a "do-it-yourself" book on aptitude testing called "Discover What You're Best At." About a month later on April 9 I took him to lunch at New York's Meridien Hotel ($70). At the luncheon table he signed permission for me to condense his book.

5. A month later on May 7 I sent Ungaro a brief outline of my suggested excerpting of Gale's book of 176 pages into 8 pages of *Family Circle*.

6. About six weeks later, on June 24, not hearing from Ungaro I wrote a follow-up.

7. Shortly thereafter, Ungaro called me, asking me to go ahead with a piece effectively condensing the do-it-yourself aptitude testing book into no more than eight *Family Circle* pages. I did not receive a letter approving my written outline.

8. I worked on the condensation, off-and-on all summer. Based on what I knew about testing, it was tough to put together what I regarded as an adequate test. I finally eliminated all tests for those under 21, since most FC readers were adult. My editing experience with the mechanics of type size, character counts and line counts per page was very helpful.

9. Finally, on Sept. 30, I sent the MS to Ungaro, with a copy to Gale. Gale okayed my material with only two small changes.

10. Nine days later, Oct. 9, I received a contract for the story; about a month later I got a check for $4,000.00. It was the first check I'd ever received for a magazine free-lance story. (I was a stringer for the *Chicago Tribune* when I was 16; high school sports) and while I was at Northwestern University I covered the North Shore as a stringer. (This journalism course was the first I'd ever taken.)

11. The March 24 issue of FC carrying the story came out on March 3, 1987, almost exactly a year after my first submission to the magazine. The piece ran ten pages and was on the cover as the top feature in the issue.

The public relations firm promoting single-copy sales asked me to do some talk shows promoting the issue. They paid me per diem for my time . . . I did four or five interviews.

Incidentally, during the month of publication, March, the sales of Gale's book soared from about 3,000 monthly to more than 7,000.

The Case History Structure

Charles Salzberg talked to a number of top college athletic trainers across the country and gave their background and their advice one by one in "How to Shape Your Student Body" in *Semester Magazine*. *Parade* magazine carried an article on how to be successful after 60, told through the eyes of senior citizens explaining their new projects and jobs. Another article in *Parade*, "Why You Should Run Too," by Colin Greer, March 29, 1992, gave case histories of ordinary persons—a plumber, nurse and others—who have run successfully for office. A sidebar gave the reader 10 pointers on "How to Run for Office."

Mervyn Kaufman told how senior citizen couples can make a successful and happy move as they realized their retirement plans. These couples' case histories or stories offered a primer for others. Kaufman's article, "Making the Right Move," with the blurb, "If you explore your options and plan well, relocating can be a great adventure rather than a bad mistake," appeared in *New Choices for the Best Years*. A sidebar of questions, "What to Ask Yourself Before You Move," appeared with the article.[6]

Making the Right Move

Mervyn Kaufman

A dream house at last! The chance to be closer to the children and grandchildren . . . a more favorable climate . . . a less hurried pace . . . scaled-down living space. These are among the goals of nearly 4 million mature Americans who have relocated during the past decade. Some have moved across town, others have wound up halfway across the continent, but all have had to begin by weighing options.

The trouble is, too many of us don't fully consider what our needs are likely to be once we stop working 9 to 5. "Eighty percent of people approaching the retirement years have never even discussed where they want to live as retirees," reports Leon Harper of the Consumer Affairs Housing Section of the American Association of Retired Persons. By not considering important lifestyle questions and planning properly, Harper adds, we risk a move that could well turn into a mistake. "Being stuck alone in a strange new community, with no family and no friends, is nowhere to be," he warns.

To help you avoid the pitfalls, here are the stories of a number of recent retirees who made
continued

---

6. Mervyn Kaufman, "Making the Right Move," *New Choices for the Best Years*, December 1991/January 1992, pp. 32–34.

continued

winning moves, along with some expert commentary on why they succeeded.

Ruth and Herb Ignatov hadn't thought seriously about retiring until they took a vacation on Sanibel, an island off Florida's Gulf Coast, in February 1987. Enchanted by the surroundings, they found themselves touring model homes. "We saw that building costs were lower than in West Orange, New Jersey, where we lived," recalls Ruth. "And the price of lots, even those facing water, actually seemed reasonable."

Back home, Ruth worked as a clinical social worker and Herb as a psychoanalyst. Though they were devoted to their careers, their workdays seemed to be getting longer and longer, and both were tired of the grind. Here in Florida, however, their future plans suddenly began to jell. Herb said he felt better where the climate was milder, particularly in the winter. Ruth wasn't sure she wanted to leave family and friends behind, though she agreed that a lifestyle change was needed. So after building their house — not on Sanibel but in nearby Cape Coral — they tested it first, taking a series of vacations until they were both convinced they would enjoy living there full-time. "We made sure to spend a few weeks there in the summer, too," Ruth notes, "so we'd know if it was too hot or humid."

The Ignatovs enjoyed the fact that they could live among people of all ages; only a third of Cape Coral's residents are retired. They also were close enough to the Northeast to visit children and grandchildren easily. Pleased with their decision, the couple made their permanent move in the summer of 1990.

Like the Ignatovs, Naomi and Bob Eber lived for years in New Jersey, in their case the town of Maplewood, a suburb of Newark. But when they decided to seek a new community to retire to, the couple opted to stay in the Northeast. "I was retiring first," notes Bob, a former stockbroker, "while Naomi wanted to continue her career as a lawyer. We wanted to be near a major metropolitan area so she could continue to do her thing. And we liked New England because of the recreational facilities." Loosely translated, this means Bob wanted a place to sail his boat.

After visiting towns along the coasts of Maine, New Hampshire and Massachusetts, the Ebers happily stumbled on Guilford, Connecticut, nestled on Long Island Sound. They liked the natural beauty of the area — the house they eventually bought faces a pond — as well as the convenience of the location: "Our boat is a thirty-minute drive away, along a lovely rural road," notes Naomi. "And we're just twenty minutes from New Haven, which is not only home to Yale University but also a very active cultural center."

Naomi didn't waste any time getting reestablished in Guilford; she immediately joined the Connecticut Bar. "Since then, I've been doing special projects for the American Civil Liberties Union," she says. "It's not the same as getting involved on a full-time basis, but there are other compensations. And we're free to travel whenever we wish."

The Ebers' story is a reminder that spouses may have widely different needs. "One of the big mistakes couples make when relocating is not giving equal consideration to both partners," says Rose Dobrof, executive director of the Brookdale Center on Aging of Hunter College in New York. "I knew one couple who had moved to Florida, and the wife was considerably younger than her husband. The retirement community was wonderful for him, but as she told me, 'You know, it just isn't fun being the youngest kid on the block.'"

That wasn't a problem for Nicki and Jim Sindt. The couple had lived for 27 years in Minneapolis, when Jim worked as a manager of technical manuals. But there was one catch: "The older we got, the tougher the winters were for us," Jim recalls. "We hated dealing with all the snow and ice, the constant digging out, and the cold. We had a lot of friends who either moved to or vacationed in Arizona, so we were encouraged to come down and check it out."

The Sindts fell in love with Tucson because of its pure air, uncrowded streets and proximity to mountains. They bought property in Saddlebrook, a retirement community 22 miles northeast of the city, and moved in two years ago.

"Everybody here is in the same boat," says Nicki. "We've never had trouble meeting like-minded people. Of course, it helps to first get to know your neighbors and then find out what social organizations are in the area. We joined the Lions. Then, along with golf and tennis, there is our bridge group and block parties, socials and dances. We don't have enough time to do all the things we like."

Marion Heffner, a friend of the Sindts', moved to Saddlebrook from Woodinville, Washington, in April 1990 as a single. When her husband had died of heart disease two years earlier, she'd found herself alone in a neighborhood that was populated increasingly by young families. "I wanted to be in a community with other retirees," she says, "preferably a place with lots of sunshine. I had lived in Arizona years before, so I knew it would be ideal."

While there are other singles in Saddlebrook, Marion had to seek them out. "Our society is basically couple oriented," she notes, "and many of the activities here were geared for twosomes. But now we're starting a support group for singles so we can all meet and plan activities together."

"A support group is a terrific idea," says Dobrof. "If someone relocates and finds the adjustment tough, he or she should seek help to understand and ease the pain. Many communities have newcomers clubs to assist people with the transition, or you can talk with a close friend, religious mentor or therapist. The key is to get help."

Ultimately, Dobrof and other experts note, not all retirement scenarios are equally effective for everyone. Jim Sindt admits that his retirement community might not be someone else's cup of tea. "There isn't a real cross-section of younger residents here," he observes, "and a lot of people we know have afflictions—we've already lost one friend to cancer."

And Nicki Sindt recalls that it "did take us a while to establish ourselves with physicians here. For the first year we waited till we visited Minneapolis to see our doctors and dentist."

"Medical considerations aside," says Dobrof, "some people are geared to be more successful movers. These are people who don't have an enormous emotional attachment to the place they've lived in, and they either establish close relationships easily or don't need them at all.

"Of course, it helps to have a sense of adventure," she adds. "After all, moving is one of the great adventures of our lives."

The Personal Experience Structure

Nena Baker speaks firsthand about getting a job in journalism in her entertaining "How I Began My Brilliant Career" for *Mademoiselle*. Note how putting the article in the first-person point of view—"I"—and giving attention to step-by-step details in her job search she creates empathy with a laugh and suspense and a sense of drama. Baker's article has most of the ingredients of a short story, including a protagonist or hero, a conflict or a problem to solve, a climax and solution.[7]

7. Nena Baker, "How I Began My Brilliant Career," *Mademoiselle*, April 1984, pp. 204–205, 270, 298, 300.

How I Began My Brilliant Career

(This article was originally published in Mademoiselle.*)*

Nena Baker

July 20

Now that I'm out of school, it's time to begin the rest of my life. I've been looking forward to this for years. With my newly minted diploma in hand, I'm going to look for my very first *real* job.

Of course, I know it won't be easy. I want to be a journalist—a writer—and I've been doing a little reporting for a local newspaper here in Portland, Oregon, for the last two years. But the editor's already said he doesn't have a full-time job for me, and there aren't too many publishers around these parts. That's why I've decided to leave here—and travel across the country—to try and make my mark in the capital of the publishing world—New York City.

My mother's not too happy about my plan and most of my friends think I'm just plain crazy. They all tell me people just don't move to New York without a job or a place to live. Successful job searches aren't conducted while living like a gypsy. In fact, this whole notion would be impossible to carry out if I couldn't stay at my uncle's Manhattan apartment—rent-free—while he's away. Right now, I keep thinking about Frank Sinatra singing, "If I can make it there, I'll make it anywhere." But what if I don't? I'll waitress. It wouldn't be the end of the world. I guess what scares me about as much as not getting a job is being alone in that big, tough city. Except for Amy, a college friend who lives in New York, I won't know anybody. But if I want the career I've always dreamed of, I've got to take this chance, and take it now. Don't I?

August 28

(Twin Falls, Idaho) With all of my belongings that my compact car could hold, my dad and I pulled out of the driveway this morning and pointed the nose of the car east. Dad's helping me drive the 3,000 miles from Portland to New York City. Then he'll take a plane back home.

I'm glad he's with me, although we didn't talk much today. I just sat and watched everything that's been familiar—and safe—zipping by. I hate to admit it, but I can't help fantasizing about the car breaking down, delaying or maybe even preventing my move. That way, it wouldn't be my fault if I didn't get there.

September 7

I arrived in New York today feeling somewhat as the immigrants who came through Ellis Island must have felt—like a stranger in a strange land, hoping for prosperity.

It's hot and crowded, but there's a frantic pace—a beat—to this city that makes it invigorating and exciting. The potential for getting a great job exists here. It's time now to make a full-time job out of finding one.

Having contacts is important, so first I'll call my uncle at his country house. He's a playwright and he's lived here a long time, so he probably knows a few people in the news or publishing business who might be able to help with job leads. I'll also answer classified ads in the paper every day and register with employment agencies. It probably wouldn't be a bad idea, either, to stop by the personnel offices of the major publishing houses. There's a lot to be done, that's for sure.

September 8

Dad flew home this morning. "Call anytime—collect," he said just before he left. Boy, how I needed to hear that. I was doubting everything about myself and my decision to move.

Driving back to the apartment, I thought he'd have some astronomical phone bills in the future.

September 9

I called Uncle Jerry this morning. Off the top of his head, he knew of three people who might have an inside track on job openings. One is a researcher for a literary magazine, another is a TV news producer and the third is an editor at a national weekly.

"Call them," Jerry said. "They're very nice people."

I'm sure they're very nice, I thought. But they're also busy people who might not have the time to talk to me. So what's the worst that could happen? They'd just tell me that.

I decided first I'd call the researcher, a woman who — my uncle told me — grew up in Seattle — my neck of the woods, and perhaps a topic for some small talk. I dialed her number. Patty answered (a stroke of luck, because I didn't have to fight my way through a secretary). I told her who I was, that I had just arrived from Portland in search of a job.

Well, the conversation took off. We were talking about colleges, New York, our home-towns and different publishers. Then Patty mentioned that there was an opening at her magazine. They need someone to compile the weekly listings of movies, plays, exhibits, concerts and other events in the city.

As Patty suggested, I wrote a covering letter and took it to her office that very afternoon, along with my résumé, which I'd had typeset back in Oregon. Just as I walked into the apartment, my credentials delivered, the phone rang: It was the magazine calling to set up an interview!

September 11

Today, with my first interview scheduled for next week, I turned my attention to my presentation and appearance. My letters of recommendation and my newspaper clips are arranged neatly in an easy-to-handle portfolio. The skirt, blouse and linen blazer I plan to wear have been cleaned. I replaced the slightly run-down heels on my pumps. But my hair was a problem. It was shaggy and didn't fit the neat image I plan to project.

I was lamenting the problem to Amy, a New York native with lots of city savvy. She had an idea that was definitely worth a try. A well-known hair salon offers free haircuts one night a week if you model for a hairdressing class. I figured it was safe since it was a reputable and somewhat conservative salon that probably wouldn't be teaching wild and crazy styles.

So I went and waited with some three dozen other hopefuls as the teachers and students milled around the group, tousling heads of hair. One student kept coming back to me. Finally he brought over his instructor, who ran his fingers through my mop and decided to take my case.

Four hours after I walked into the place, I emerged with the best haircut of my life. Every strand, every layer, every angle was made as perfect as possible. I feel ready for action.

September 19

New York is unfit for humans. The Indian-summer heat and humidity drives them away. Those who remain are subhuman types — such as whoever picked my wallet from my handbag on the subway home from my interview. I was so absorbed in replaying my job interview over and over that I didn't see the guy sulking around me — until it was too late.

Things weren't going too well even before the interview began. I arrived 30 minutes early, so I had coffee at a luncheonette. The caffeine assaulted my already-queasy stomach, and I wound up in the restaurant's grimy little bathroom — getting sick.

I got to the interview but I felt shaky and feverish. My interviewer, a long-time employee of the literary magazine, explained the job to me: compiling the entertainment listings every week. It sounded dull but maybe it would lead to bigger and better things. So I asked her about the company's policy of promoting from within.

"Frankly, my dear," she said, "the kind of promotion you have in mind doesn't occur often at all." With that the interview ended.

I went straight to a phone booth and called Patty. "How did the interview go?" she asked.

"Okay," I told her, "but I've got my heart set on a job with a little hands-on writing and edit-

continued

continued

ing attached—something that offers a chance for advancement."

"Look, nobody finds her dream job on her first interview," Patty said. "I've got a good idea of what you're after and I'll keep my ears open."

September 21

I couldn't even make it to the employment agency today. The trouble began with a subway track fire that interrupted downtown service, which created an overload on downtown buses with angry commuters acting like nervous livestock. With big-city aplomb—I thought—I wriggled my way through the rear door of a crowded bus and was congratulating myself on the move when at the next stop, exiting passengers pushed me out and the bus pulled away. I was in trouble!

If I walked to the agency I would have been inexcusably late. And cabs are an unthinkable luxury. So I came home, called the agency and rescheduled the appointment. I spent the rest of the afternoon getting up the nerve to call the other two contacts my uncle gave me. They *were* very nice, but they didn't have any ideas about where I might look. Then I called Amy because I needed a little support.

"The longer I'm here, the crazier it all seems," I told her. "I'm thinking about going back home."

"Don't!" Amy said. "You've got to get in as many interviews as possible before you need another haircut."

September 22

All day I visited agencies specializing in editorial placements. After completing an application, taking a typing test and explaining my job interests, agency personnel would pitch me secretarial jobs camouflaged by titles such as "administrative assistant" or "editorial aide." '

My money is going too quickly. I've got enough to last maybe three more weeks. After that, I'll have to find work slinging hash at some restaurant where the tips are good. Better that than settling for a secretarial job. . . .

September 27

My first agency-arranged interview today was infuriating. It was for an "editorial assistant" at an advertising agency although they wanted a secretary. At my second agency-arranged interview, the director of a public relations office told me he was looking for an assistant. But the way he smiled at me convinced me he was looking for something more. Lasciviously, he fingered my portfolio, then said: "You'd do a great job, wouldn't you, honey?"

"You creep," I thought. "What did you tell the agency you wanted? Or are they running an escort service, too?"

October 1

I've written answers to at least 50 classified ads and I haven't received one single response.

What's going to happen to me? I'm down to waiting for responses to ads—and a few hundred dollars.

October 3

I had an interview with a nonprofit cultural arts agency that's looking for an assistant publicist. My friend Amy had a connection there. The job consists of writing releases, researching grants and basic "gofering" stuff—it might be fun. But the pay is paltry and it's a job in public relations—not journalism. If they offer it to me, though, I think I'll take it.

October 5

Today, my answering machine played back a message that was music to my ears. The copy editor of a national men's fashion magazine, a friend of Patty's, wants me to get in touch with him. He needs an assistant copy editor.

I called Patty. "How can I thank you?" I asked.

"Take me to lunch when you get the job," she said.

October 6

As Patty suggested, I went to the library to prepare for the interview. I pored through two years of back issues, so I can refer to specific columns or issues, offering comments or asking questions. I want my interviewer to know I have a genuine interest in his magazine. This is the most intriguing job lead I've had and I've got to make the most of it.

October 10

Today, I interviewed for the job I want. I walked into the men's magazine office, expecting to see everyone wearing Italian designer suits and haughty attitudes. But the dress was casual and the atmosphere relaxed. My job would be entry-level, with its share of typing, filing and photocopying, but I'd also be expected to do some copy editing and writing.

George, the copy chief, gave me a copy-editing test. I passed, but not by much. I think the interview went well enough, though, to make up for that. I feel like I fit in and I'm hoping they feel that way, too.

October 14

Today I had to sell the gold pendant my great-uncle gave me. I got $450 for it, so I should feel happy, but I feel awful. It was stupid of me to come to New York with so little money.

I've *got* to get that magazine job! I know I can handle it. Why doesn't George call to tell me what's going on?

October 17

I couldn't stand waiting any longer, so I called George. He told me I didn't get the job. Says he needs somebody with "more experience." Damn. I really thought I was going to get it. Everything about the job felt so right.

It's funny. I knew I'd be disappointed if they didn't offer it to me, but I didn't realize I'd feel panicky. What's left now? I'm afraid if I call my parents now, I'll hear myself saying, "I'm coming home."

After receiving the bad news, I called to cancel my dinner plans with Amy, telling her I'd be miserable company.

"Come anyway," she said. "Misery loves company."

I poured my heart out to her. It was such a relief to talk about it. "Call this guy back," she said.

I thought she was crazy.

"I'm serious. You've got absolutely nothing to lose," she said. "Convince him he's making a mistake by not hiring you. He is, you know." Sounded a little unrealistic. "I've got to think about this," I said.

October 18

I slept terribly, but I made my decision. I got up early and paced around the apartment until 8:45. Then held my breath and dialed.

"Hello, George, this is Nena Baker calling. I wanted to tell you that I'm still very interested in this job — I believe I'm the best candidate for it, because I'll work so hard — and I think if we can meet one more time, you'll see that, too."

"This is a little unusual," he said, after a pause.

"Have you offered the job to anyone else yet?"

"No," he said.

"Well —" I said, holding my breath.

"Come by the office at four-thirty," he replied.

I was there at 4:25, took another copy-editing test and improved my score. "Nobody wants this job more than I do," I told him.

October 20

I was offered the job at the cultural arts agency today. I said I would tell them tomorrow if I would accept it. The men's magazine job is really the one I want. Maybe with this other offer I can force their hand. If I call George and explain the situation, he might finally be convinced of my value because somebody else wants me. . . .

Of course, this could also be his chance to get me out of his hair for good, but I've got to take the gamble.

I dialed George's number, wondering where all this courage was coming from. Have my six weeks in New York made me a crazy person?

continued

continued

"Ah, George, this is Nena Baker calling . . . again. I've received another job offer and I'm going to have to accept unless we can work something out soon."

"I see," he said. "Why don't you stop by here around five. I want you to meet with our managing editor."

When I got there, I explained to George about the offer and that the job at the magazine was still what I wanted.

George went in to talk with the managing editor and finally, after 15 agonizing minutes, they called me in.

"George has told me about you," the managing editor said as we shook hands. "I've got to say that your tests were only a little above average."

My heart sank to my stomach.

"But you've got guts. And the way you've hounded George," he said, smiling and shaking his head.

My heart began to rise again. "I really want to work at this magazine," I told him quickly. "I just didn't want to let the opportunity slip by."

"Well, looks like you've won yourself the job."

I thought: "Looks like I owe somebody lunch."

Humor, as Baker demonstrates, can be an effective approach to giving how-to information. Much depends on the subject and whether a magazine thinks its readers will accept a humorous treatment. People like to laugh at others — older adults laugh at young people or children, or vice versa. Some groups don't mind a good laugh on themselves; humor certainly makes a pill go down more smoothly. But humor in a how-to article sometimes serves more as entertainment than as real how-to help. It lends itself to satire, such as when syndicated Chicago columnist Mike Royko and others told how to become a vice president (in light of the initial Dan Quayle flak of 1988) with tongue in cheek. But humor also helps get some serious thoughts across. One writer took a light approach in a piece called "How to Take a Teen to a Movie." It was hilarious, but a few pointers of more serious intent could be gleaned from it.

The "Within-a-Larger-Article" Structure

The following article looks like a profile of Judge Joseph Wapner of TV's "The People's Court," but it's really about his advice concerning how to proceed with and win a court case. Joanne Morici wrote it for *Family Circle*.[8]

8. Joanne Morici, "'The People's Court' Judge: How to Wage — and Win — a Lawsuit on Your Own," *Family Circle*, April 30, 1985, pp. 26, 28, 61. Reprinted from the April 30, 1985 issue of *Family Circle* magazine. Copyright © 1985 The Family Circle, Inc.

"The People's Court" Judge: How to Wage — and Win — a Lawsuit on Your Own

Joanne Morici

When Judge Joseph A. Wapner takes the bench on "The People's Court," over 15 million viewers watch and listen intently. Now in his fifth successful season on television, Judge Wapner presides over real-life cases that have been filed in small claims courts in California; the decisions he renders on the air are legal and binding. Although rules governing small claims courts vary from state to state, the principles are the same: The claim must be *small* (the maximum amount can vary between $500 and $5000), and people usually represent themselves.

With more than 20 years' experience on the State of California Municipal and Superior Court bench, Judge Wapner knows what it takes to make a "winning" case. His following tips are the best free legal advice you'll ever get.

- Try settling your differences out of court first. Talk to the person you're thinking of suing. Outline your grievance and what you want done to solve the problem. Inform him that if an agreement can't be reached, you'll then go to court.

- Follow up your talk with a letter (keep a copy) stating the exact nature of your grievance. For example: "On April 9, 1985, I took my blue silk dress to XYZ Cleaners, Inc., to have it dry-cleaned. When I picked up my dress on April 11, I discovered a 2″ hole on the front of the dress that was not there before. Since the dress cannot be repaired, I would like to be reimbursed for the cost — $185. If I do not hear from you within 10 days, I will be compelled to sue." Writing such a letter serves two purposes: It states all your facts clearly and can be used as documentation if your case must go to court.

- If you're not sure you have a legitimate legal claim, talk to a lawyer who specializes in cases such as yours. (If you don't know a lawyer with the kind of expertise you need, local and state bar associations can give you a referral.) For a small consultation fee (usually $35 to $50), a lawyer can tell you whether you've got a case, what your chances are of winning and how you should proceed.

- To find out where to file a small claims suit, check your phone book or call the state court. The court clerk will give you the appropriate forms and tell you how to fill them out. Filing charges are usually between $5 and $25.

- To file a claim, you must know the name of the person you are suing, where that person lives, and how much you are suing for. This information is not always as easy to find as it sounds. Using the dry cleaner example, you could be suing XYZ Cleaners, Inc., or John Doe dba (doing business as) XYZ Cleaners, Inc. Judge Wapner's advice: Sue everyone who might be even slightly connected with your case. This will help you collect any damages awarded. The correct address is equally important, because before your suit can begin, the person you are suing must first be served with a claim (notification he's being sued).

- When your claim has been filed and the defendant served, the next step is collecting all the necessary documents, facts, witnesses or affidavits you'll need to prove your case. This

continued

continued

is called "marshaling the evidence." For example, in suing XYZ Cleaners, you would need a store receipt for the dress, noting the price you paid for it, the ticket from the dry cleaner, proving you did indeed take it there for cleaning, and the damaged dress itself as evidence. In certain cases, such as a damaged automobile, photographs are acceptable evidence.

• Witnesses who appear in person are better than signed affidavits. Affidavits are hearsay, and while some courts allow this as evidence, others don't. Having the owner of *another* dry-cleaning establishment testify that your dress was cleaned improperly is much stronger than having that same person sign a statement to that effect. A witness can also be cross-examined by the judge, if necessary.

• Expert witnesses — people who are knowledgeable about the matter at hand and are willing to corroborate or back up your claim (such as that owner of the other dry-cleaning establishment) — should be chosen carefully. Select an expert witness who is reputable, credible and articulate, and who is willing to take the time to appear in court. Some states may require you to pay a witness fee, so it may not be worth the extra money if your claim is for a small amount. You can also have the court subpoena a witness and legally *make* him appear in court. However, having a reluctant witness may not be in your best interest.

• Dress for your day in court as though you were going on a job interview. Men should wear a suit and tie; women should wear a suit or a conservative dress. Although the judge's decision is based on fact, it does help to make a good first impression.

• Speak clearly and courteously. Always address the judge as "Your Honor" or "Judge." Look directly at the judge when you are speaking.

• State your case simply and in your own words. Don't resort to legal double-talk. It will not impress the judge and may end up confusing you both.

• Always answer a direct question with a yes or no. If you need to explain something further, ask the judge if you may do so. A rambling, disjointed or imprecise answer takes up time. It can also signal to the judge that you are unsure of your facts or are hiding something.

• Don't argue every point. Sometimes what the other person says may actually help your case. Allow the judge to ask you to clarify any contradictory statements between you and the person you're suing.

• Never read a written statement. It's best simply to jot down a few notes or points you want to introduce in court. If the judge asks, "Is there anything else you'd like to say?" you can then refer to your notes and say, "Yes, Your Honor, I failed to mention this."

• Judge Wapner's final word of advice — and a rule of thumb everyone should follow when doing business or making an agreement: *Get it in writing.* Most cases would never even reach court if people would remember to do this. Whether you're sharing an apartment with a roommate or sharing your lawnmower with a neighbor, write out the terms of your agreement. Some people balk at having a written agreement with a friend, but many people in small claims court start out as "good friends" and end up as enemies.

Georgia Witkin Lanoil discussed obscene phone calls in her "Heavy Breathing" article for *Health* before she concluded with tips on how to handle the phone call and then how to deal with the emotional stress afterward.

Carl Navarre discussed backgrounds and breeds of hunting dogs for *Esquire* before concluding with "how to buy" a hunting dog.

Francine Klagsbrun defined words such as *intimacy* and gave a framework for the discussion before giving how-to advice obtained from interviewees in her "Secrets and Pleasures of Long-Lasting Marriage," excerpted from her book *Married People* for *Ms*.

The "Mostly Pictures" Structure

A university student published an article with only pictures and cutlines/type blocks on "How to Prepare Your Boat for Winter" for a boating magazine. *Allure*'s March 1992 article, "Rain Check," tells the young woman, mostly with pictures, how to dress and put on makeup for a rainy day.

Kenneth Pulomena in *Cook's* describes "How to Fillet Fish," using mostly pictures. He starts by discussing which fish is the most easily filleted; then he describes the dozen steps to follow to fillet a fish; finally, he rounds out the article with recipes for filleted fish. One full page of the three pages of the article—right in the middle—is a panel of 12 pictures, each showing a step in fish filleting. The pictures, with numbered cutlines beneath them, could have stood on their own as a how-to article.

ASSIGNMENTS

1. Select five possible "how-to" topics. Match up a magazine to each idea and explain why the ideas should work in the magazines you selected.

2. Examine covers of magazines for the current month. Report on the most common "how-to" article subject—an idea used in more than one magazine. What are the variations? What is the most unusual "how-to" article announced on the covers?

3. Analyze a "how-to" article and report on: Why the particular author wrote it; what research might have been used; what form and logical structure it has; what variations—in topics and approach—are also possible; how could the article be improved?

4. Convert a "how-to" article in a magazine to an alternate format, using one of the formats suggested in this book or one that is not mentioned.

5. Draw up a research plan for your proposed "how-to" article. Granted you may be an "expert" or hobbyist in the area, but how can you get three or four more sharp ideas for your article?

CHAPTER 8

Structuring the Longer Article

Although the specific formats used to structure profiles and how-to articles can also be extended to other types of features and magazine articles, longer topical articles have traditionally been characterized as exposition, narration or argumentation.

The *expository* article explains something. An expository article might start: "The book publishing business operates this way. . . ." Or an article could explain a new development: "The voting dynamics came together in such a way Tuesday to defeat Mayor Nogood. . . ." Or the background of an international incident might be examined.

The *narrative* article tells a story. Sometimes these are about people: "John Babbler started writing books at three. He hadn't yet started nursery school when he first took up a pen. . . ." Or the narrative could be the story of a battle or even the story of an industry. While exposition proceeds point by point or logically, a narrative is a tale unfolding, not unlike a short story or letter written home.

The narrative approach is often more entertaining, even more whimsical, than is a straightforward analysis. The reader gets caught up in the unfolding story. Sometimes exposition and narration merge — the causes of World War I explained in chronological terms with an emphasis on personalities and important events, all building to a climactic conclusion. If you write features about history, you'll often combine narrative and exposition — and sometimes argumentation as well.

When you use *argumentation*, you set out to argue, to debate, to persuade. The format works well when you're dealing with a political topic. A question is raised — often asked outright in the lead: "Should Supreme Court nominee Waite Aminute take himself out of consideration?" All sides are given, views of the bipartisan devotees, the ethicists, the radical and conservative coalitions, friends on both sides. Yes, eight people say, he should be confirmed, for these reasons. . . . No, say another eight. The pros and cons can be alternated. In a *TV Guide* article on whether there were UFOs, Isaac Asimov labeled alternating paragraphs "pro" or "con."

In newspapers, the lean point-by-point exposition article often provides background to the news. The narrative article is likely to be found in national magazine articles where the point is made by a story and where even the point may be the story: a narrative mostly for entertainment. The argumentation article is alive and well on newspaper editorial and op-ed pages, which seek to give dimensions and alternatives to the events of the day. Argumentation also gives a kind of electrical pulse to issue-oriented magazines. *Ms.* uses many argumentation pieces: for example, "Blowing the Whistle on the 'Mommy Track,'" with the blurb — "A tortured muddle of feminist perceptions and sexist assumptions that should never have been taken seriously" in July/August 1989.

THE CONSENSUS ARTICLE

Especially in magazines, most articles don't conform to any single category. Modern articles combine expository, narrative and argumentative characteristics. The staple of many modern magazines is what might be called the "consensus" topical article. While it might flow along in narrative style, it probably also explains and argues for a direction or point of view.

A consensus topical article usually announces a theme, often indicated by the title, then informs the readers, and entertains them with stories — leaving the matter up to the readers to resolve.

We might refer to the fullest, the main article, in a publication as simply a "longer article." These often are topical. A longer consensus topical article might merge various genres, formats and techniques.

Note the mix of narrative, exposition and argumentation in this *McCall's* article on "dehaunters."[1]

1. Joyce and Richard Wolkomir, "Ghost Busters at Work," *McCall's*, July 1989, pp. 104, 106, 109.

Ghost Busters at Work

Joyce and Richard Wolkomir

When Fred and Trudy Duncan saw the house for sale in a prosperous Toronto suburb, it was love at first sight. A substantial ranch, built in 1956, the fine construction indicated the builder had taken great pride in the house. And it was only a few minutes from their hardware business and a quick subway ride from their son and daughter's arts high school. In April, 1984, the Duncans moved in. They never dreamed their new home would haunt them — literally. But their experiences in the house have so shaken their image of their family's normalcy that they have asked *McCall's* not to use their real names.

Norman Rockwell might have painted the Duncans. Fred, sandy-haired and ruddy, is an avid baseball fan and a golfer. He also plays the bagpipes, as did his Scottish forebears. Trudy handles the family store's accounting. Petite and vivacious, she likes to invite neighbors over for summer barbecues and Christmas cookie exchanges. Their son, George, now 21, works in an art shop. Daughter Donna, now 19, is a college student. Says Fred, "We'd be the last people to believe in ghosts."

Soon after moving into their new home, the Duncans began renovating the basement, turning an old sewing room into a bedroom for their son. One morning, George was astonished to catch a hazy glimpse of a stranger in his new room.

"It looked like an old man, dressed in white pajamas," remembers George. In a moment, the "visitor" vanished. But one day not long afterward, Donna complained to her mother that she and some high-school friends had felt a frightening "presence" in the basement.

Meanwhile, Fred had set up a workshop in the basement. "Almost every time I went down there to work, I felt someone was watching me," he says. But Fred kept the feeling to himself.

Then it was Trudy's turn. One morning, from the corner of her eye, she saw a man in a tuxedo walking down the stairs to the basement. She assumed it was her son. Puzzled, she went downstairs to ask George why he was dressed up. But George was in his room, wearing a sweatsuit. "It was odd," says Trudy, "but I wasn't frightened."

Still, she decided to tell her husband about the eerie feelings the house was eliciting. "You're not going to believe this," she began. When she finished her report, Fred said, "You're not going to believe this either." Then he told her about his own feeling of being watched. When the basement renovations were completed, however, the haunting waned to only occasional feelings of a "presence." "It really died down for a couple of years," says Trudy. Then, in September, 1988, the Duncans began redecorating the house's first floor, painting, wallpapering and installing new wainscoting. Almost immediately, the ghost was back.

George began having encounters in his basement bedroom. "I'd be in my washroom shaving at six a.m., getting ready to go to work," he says. "I'd look in the mirror and see someone walking by. I saw it every day for a week and a half."

Too worried to keep silent any longer, Trudy told a couple of her neighbors about the experiences. To her relief, "nobody seemed to think we were crazy," she says. Then she recalled hearing a radio interview program featuring Ian Currie, a professional "dehaunter."

Trudy called the station. "They told me he was legitimate and that their phone lines had lit up the day he was on," she says. When she called the "ghost buster," her first words were, "We don't believe in ghosts, but. . . ."

"That's what everyone says," Currie told her. "But if you think you've got a ghost, you probably do."

For 20 years Ian Currie was a sociology professor at the University of Toronto and the

University of Guelph in Ontario. Today he is a parapsychologist with a special interest in de-hauntings. "People call me as a last resort," he says.

Currie is one of a small band of independent dehaunters, men and women with some psychic insights and abilities and, perhaps most important, a firm belief in the existence of ghosts, a willingness to fly in the face of skepticism and a desire to help the often disbelieving but badly frightened house owners who seek them out. Ghosts, they say, are lingering spirits who, for one reason or another, refuse to accept the fact that they are dead and are sometimes reluctant to leave the premises to which they were once deeply attached. Often, all they need is a firm but sympathetic push into the other realm. And sometimes, despite the ghost busters' best efforts, they will not be pushed.

Currie himself has dehaunted more than 90 houses, and he guarantees success. He distinguishes six kinds of hauntings, including fraudulent hauntings, delusional hauntings (squirrels in the attic, branches against the window) and poltergeists, which involve objects that fly around. "With poltergeists, there is usually an adolescent in the house and there is lots of kinetic energy," says Currie. "It has nothing to do with the dead." He also cites "thought-form" hauntings, caused by psychic energy from a living person, and "retro-cognitive" hauntings, when dramatic events that occurred at a site endlessly replay, like a psychic videotape. The sixth type is genuine hauntings.

"Forty percent of ghosts have unfinished business — they won't rest until it's communicated," says Currie. He says ghosts can appear to four of our senses: "You can see, hear, feel or smell a ghost," he says. The most common signs are sounds, like knocks or footsteps. Ghosts also can move objects.

"If you see a ghost, it usually looks exactly like a real person," says Currie, adding that it also can be incomplete, have holes or be monochromatic. "You know it's a ghost," he says, "because it disappears into thin air and goes through walls."

After listening to Trudy, Currie told her their ghost sounded agitated. Currie promised to come that evening with a psychic, through whom the ghost could speak. Then, via the psychic, Currie would talk to the ghost.

Trudy was apprehensive, envisioning the psychic showing up in fortune-teller's robes. But that evening, when Currie arrived, he proved to be a deep-voiced man with a flamboyant mustache, impeccably dressed in a business suit. With him was psychic Elizabeth Paddon of Toronto. Trudy was struck by her normal appearance. With her golden-red curls and quick smile, she could pass for Fergie, the Duchess of York.

Paddon said she felt the ghost all through the house. Fred was surprised. He had thought the basement was the ghost's territory. Then Paddon said, "He's showing me the house being built — a lot of trees in the area being cleared. I see the blueprints."

She felt the ghost was the house's first owner. But then she "lost" him. She led the family downstairs to George's basement bedroom. They chatted. "He's back." Paddon announced. Did the family observe the old Scottish custom of leaving sherry and shortbread for Father Christmas? she asked. She said the ghost would like that. She said the ghost liked the family, and he feared that if he left the house they would sell it.

The Duncans were thunderstruck. Trudy had been looking at a house for sale just down the street. Currie and Paddon then tried to convince the ghost to go away.

"Most ghosts don't know they're dead," says Currie. "I tell them they're dead — they usually give me an argument." He directs ghosts to go toward the welcoming light that psychics claim marks the portal into the dimension where we go after death. "It breaks their concentration," says Currie. Then the ghost "crosses over," leaving our world.

Paddon was rubbing the right side of her head. She said she sensed that the ghost had died

continued

continued

of a head pain. And she said the ghost felt undeserving of going "into the light." Meanwhile, Fred was thinking, "They're taking me — they're a couple of Hollywood actors." Afterward, however, when he walked into his workroom, he knew the ghost had gone. "He just wasn't there," he says. "I felt lonely." The "presence" has never returned.

Later the Duncans met a man who had known the house's original owner, a developer, and learned that he had died of a brain tumor in the house 15 years before. He was especially proud of this house, which he built for himself. When he lived there, adultery had been rife in the area, and he had been divorced, perhaps the reason for his guilt.

Currie says ghosts often are stirred up by house renovations. "Ghosts are pathetic and confused," he says. "They are frozen in time — a ghost is a perfectly ordinary person with no physical body." His studies show 83 percent of all ghosts died suddenly. "Sudden death often confuses people," says Currie.

Ed and Lorraine Warren of Monroe, Connecticut, have spent nearly two decades crisscrossing the U.S., speaking at universities about their encounters with ghosts and helping hundreds of distraught homeowners dehaunt their houses. Their work has been chronicled in a series of books. But their unusual career actually began when Ed was only six years old and heard — unmistakably, he says — the presence of his grandfather, who had recently died.

That episode left Ed with a permanent interest in ghosts. When he was 18, he met and married Lorraine, who had an odd talent. As a child, she had seen around people the colored lights that psychics call auras. At the time, she assumed everyone saw them. Ed served in the Navy and completed art school. Lorraine, too, became an artist, and they earned their living traveling to tourist sights, selling their paintings. But Ed kept an ear open for tales of haunted houses in every town they were in. He also did a series of paintings of haunted houses. An exhibit of these paintings in the little Connecticut town where he and

Lorraine lived led to a request to speak at a local college. That led to more speaking engagements and to requests for help from people living in houses they believed were haunted.

At first, Lorraine was skeptic. "Ed, all those people have read the same books," she would say. But then, seeing several ghosts herself in houses they visited, she became a believer. And her latent clairvoyance returned. She says she learned to make contact with lost spirits so that she and Ed could help them shake free of their ties to the physical earth.

In one of their first cases, a Newtown, Connecticut, policewoman called the Warrens for help. She was about to leave the house her grandfather had built. Apparently, he objected, although he was dead. A one-time sailor, he loved the house so much that he repeatedly vowed that if anyone but his descendants ever moved in, he'd haunt them. He lived to be 98.

In 1970, long after his death, his granddaughter, Marie, and her husband decided to move to New Hampshire. They sold the house. On one of their last nights there, Marie heard something smash in the pantry and went in to find that a cup and saucer had jumped from a shelf to the floor. Sweeping up the shards, she couldn't figure out how it happened. She returned to bed. An instant later she heard a deafening roar from the pantry. The family ran to the room, then froze in horror. Cups, saucers, pots and pans were flying from the shelves and smashing on the floor. A heavy stein sailed through the air and struck Marie on the forehead. Clearly, the house harbored an invisible — but angry — "presence."

The next day Marie called the Warrens, already known locally because of their lectures. Ed taped an interview with the family. When he played the tape that evening, it sounded as if someone had been banging on a pipe while the recorder ran. "When I heard that, I knew we had something here," he says.

He returned to the house with Lorraine. While they were there, Marie's son saw a luminescent form descending the stairs, an old man with a white beard. Then Marie saw the apparition, which she recognized as the likeness of her grandfather. Meanwhile, clairvoyantly, Lorraine heard the ghost's voice say that he did not want the family to move from his house. But Marie was not about to let her dead grandfather dictate where she would live.

The next few days were a battle of wills. Once the family heard a loud thump in the kitchen. Investigating, they found that a knife left in the sink had flown across the room, nearly penetrating the door. "He'd had a favorite bronze ashtray, shaped like two hands linked together, very heavy — I saw that thing take off from the mantel and smash a picture of him and his wife," says Ed.

When Marie finally moved, she told the Warrens, all the way to New Hampshire in the car she periodically heard her grandfather's voice command: "Marie, turn around and go back home! Turn around and go back home!"

Boyce Batey works at an insurance company by day. In his off-hours he's an avid psychical researcher and executive secretary of the Academy of Religion and Psychical Research in Bloomfield, Connecticut. His interest in parapsychology, particularly in whether the consciousness survives death, began when he was a student at Princeton University. After graduating, he studied for a time at the pioneering parapsychology laboratory started by Duke University. When Batey investigates hauntings today, he usually works with a team that may include Brian Riley, a nuclear physical chemist whose hobby is parapsychological investigation; a psychologist; a medium; and a clairvoyant (Batey works with various people).

A typical case Batey's group investigated involved a house belonging to a young Manchester, Connecticut, couple with children. At first, only the wife experienced the peculiar phenomena: odd noises, footsteps, the feeling of a "presence." Her husband heard and felt nothing out of the ordinary. Yet the couple's three dogs persistently converged on one spot in the master bedroom, where they would scratch on the floor. One day the wife's sister was visiting, totally unaware that her sibling was experiencing eerie happenings in the house. At the spot where the dogs scratched on the floor, the sister spontaneously announced that she felt "something wrong."

One evening, as the family was watching television, an invisible tornado seemed suddenly to grip the wife. As her startled husband watched, the tornado whirled his wife around and around, into the master bedroom, and slammed the door. The wife had heard about Boyce Batey's ghostbusting hobby and called him immediately.

Batey arrived with a medium and a clairvoyant, who said they sensed a "presence" in the house — that of a confused elderly man. "They said the center of activity was focused on that spot in the master bedroom," says Batey.

Entering a trance, the medium spoke with the ghost's voice: "What are you doing here?" Batey replied, "You're frightening the people in the house." "Why?" the ghost asked. "Because you're dead," Batey said. "I'm not!" the ghost insisted.

"We discussed the situation for a while," says Batey, adding that eventually he began to convince the ghost that he was indeed dead, clinging to the earth in his confusion long after he should have left physical reality. "I told him to call for a loved one who had died," Batey says. Then they heard the ghost cry, "Mom? Mom? Mom!" Clearly, says Batey, the ghost's mother had appeared to him. "I don't need to be here anymore — I'm leaving," the ghost announced. Simultaneously, the woman of the house, the medium and the clairvoyant said, "He's gone." And he was.

Skeptics are . . . well, skeptical about all this. James Alcock, a professor in the Department of Psychology at Glendon College, York University, in Toronto, who has studied paranormal events extensively, says, "I think a belief system that we develop as children and that is deep in our emotional heritage can lead us to think we've seen or heard things. Our perceptions are very subject to suggestibility." Alcock, who has often debated Ian Currie on television shows, says, "I don't believe in ghosts for a second," adding that

continued

continued

people do believe they have seen what they describe.

Another scientist who distrusts ghostly experiences is psychologist Robert Baker, recently retired from the Department of Psychology at the University of Kentucky in Lexington. He has investigated some 60 claims of hauntings. "There are no haunted houses, only haunted people," he says. "We all have perceptual expectations, so we do see and hear things that are not there — we see what we expect to see."

Ghosts often appear at night. "Most of them," says Baker, "appear during hypnopompic sleep," which occurs as we awaken, partly asleep, partly awake. In that state, we may think we are wide awake, seeing a ghost. "It is like a waking dream," says Baker. Also ripe for ghost viewing is hypnagogic sleep, which occurs when we are dozing off, again neither fully awake nor asleep, he says.

But even skeptics find hauntings fascinating. As James Alcock puts it, "They should make us look at the excitement and mystery our own minds can produce." Ian Currie says ghosts can be as skeptical as scientists. "Most [ghosts] deny it when I tell them they're dead," he says. "I've been called crazy by more dead people than living people."

The first 11 paragraphs of this "consensus" article set up the problem with a story. The 13th and 14th paragraphs introduce the main subject, the work of "dehaunters." The rest is largely development, a mix of exposition and narration. Other dehaunters are introduced. Argumentation enters in at the end when the views of critics also are considered.

Notice how the article includes brief profiles of the people living in the haunted houses as well as of the "ghost busters." In addition to profiles, consensus articles frequently include "how-to" advice; a sidebar may detail some technique or a list of ways to respond to a problem.

THE VISIBLE STRUCTURE

In the profile, the eyes go from anecdote to anecdote; in a "how-to," from enumerated point to point. Like shorter articles, such as profiles and how-to, the fuller article is seen as much as read. People don't read with their minds as such, although the mind interprets the symbols and objects that register on its "screen." The eyes do the reading. The eyes see the words, and the eyes see not only the segmented words (rushing them together in a scanning motion and transferring the symbols to the brain) but also the whole page or spread at once.

How do you read a magazine? Do you flip through the new issue and notice articles (sometimes back to front), glancing at the art, photos, title, blurbs? Of course, you might look up an article that is mentioned on the cover, but your first encounter with it might be as a unit — how it looks to you. Subheads and white space divide up the article. Your eyes skip along to these markings or "flags." You are seeing the visible unity of the article, its created image. You relate to the effect — the design, illustrations, the words, sentences, groupings of paragraphs.

Rapid readers zip through it all; slower readers pause, look back, look ahead, depending on the signposts of words and art and design. They also "see" the article. How many people really read words anymore? It's difficult to do so in a visual TV and video-oriented culture. Reading a magazine is a seeing experience.

MODELS FOR THE LONGER ARTICLE

How you develop your longer article will probably depend on the subject, genre and market as well as on your own preference and writing style. Among the most common structures are the three-part model, the three-parts-plus-an ending model, the cyclical model, the question/answer model, the "waves" model, the "chunks" model and the straightforward (news-oriented) model.

Three Parts

You've heard the statement—Julius Caesar said it when he wrote about the Gallic Wars— *Gallia est omnis divisa in partes tres*, or "All Gaul is divided into three parts."

"Every article contains three sections: lead, establishing section, and development," says a *Guide to Writing a Popular Science Article*, distributed to *Popular Science* magazine's regular and promising writers. This three-fold structure, the *Guide* explains, "makes the information contained in the article easily accessible to the reader. It must be in logical order. The reader must get a clear grasp of exactly what the article will be about with the first few paragraphs. And he must understand not only the subject, but the angle—the precise point the article will be trying to make. The first two parts give him this information. The third gives the evidence to support the first two."

According to the *Popular Science Guide*:

> Part One is the lead. Its purpose is to give the reader some grasp of the subject matter in as concise and interesting a way as possible. It can take many forms: a statement of fact, an anecdote, a striking description (highly effective, and much underused), a "multiple hook" lead in which several short, provocative sentences indicate the breadth of the subject.
>
> The second, *and by far the most crucial*, part of the article is the establishing section. It is sometimes confused as part of the lead. It can be thought of in that way, but we have found it helpful to consider it as a totally distinct and separate element that performs quite a different job. . . .[2]

The establishing section—usually a paragraph, sometimes only a sentence—is also commonly called the "nutgraf" (for "nutgraph"); it summarizes

2. *Guide to Writing a Popular Science Article*, cover letter by editor-in-chief C. P. Gilmore, distributed by *Popular Science* magazine, p. 8.

the article in a nutshell. Or it's called the "summary paragraph" or the "billboard" paragraph. You could also think of it in terms of a pivot or a drive wheel around which the whole turns or as a bull's eye or target or focus paragraph. Some call it a theme paragraph. Others see the key summary statement between lead and body of an article as a "bridge." In the "Ghost Busters" article earlier in this chapter, the 12th and 13th paragraphs bridge to the third part of the article, though perhaps the 13th paragraph alone would be called the nutgraf.

The *Popular Science Guide* continues:

> The establishing section tells clearly and succinctly what the article will be about. It also gives the news peg — why we're bringing up this subject now. . . . It outlines all territory to be covered, sets boundaries, tells what the article will be about. It prepares the reader to understand the material to follow without having to wonder what point the writer is trying to make. Once the reader has read the establishing section, nothing in the article will surprise or confuse him. . . .
>
> Nothing that has not been forecast or that does not relate specifically to the point or angle as stated in the establishing section can be included in the article.
>
> The third element in a *Popular Science* story . . . is the development. This is 90 percent of the article, and it is the part where the writer presents his material, supporting the theme he set forth in the establishing section. This material should be presented in a clearly organized and logical way that will justify the theme stated in the establishing section. . . .[3]

Three Parts Plus an Ending

Most writers would modify the *Popular Science* guidebook formula somewhat. According to Nancy Rubin, who writes for *Parents*, *McCall's*, *Newsday* and *Ladies' Home Journal*, "there also needs to be a finalizing section, or conclusion. An article without a conclusion leaves the reader puzzled."

Lorene Hanley Duquin, who writes for *Redbook*, *Seventeen* and *McCall's*, notes that the three-part formula "excludes conclusions. Endings are very important." Says Ellen Alperstein, who writes for the Los Angeles *Times*, *Islands* and Whittle Communications publications: "Most articles have a lead, a middle or thesis development and a conclusion."

Duquin would divide an article into these four parts: "Lead, statement of theme, elaboration on central theme (quotes, examples, anecdotes, etc.), conclusion . . . and sidebars when applicable." Rubin suggests these four parts: "Lead, thesis, explanation (or development), conclusion."

Note in the "Ghost Busters" article how an ending pulls together points of view with a lighter sign-off tone. See also the discussion and samples of endings in a discussion of a "straightforward" model later in this chapter.

---

3. *Guide to Writing a Popular Science Article*, pp. 9–10, 14.

Cyclical

You lead a young son or daughter around the block and point out various sites. You end up at the same place you started — home. The child is richer for the trip around the block.

You state a thesis at the beginning of an article. You walk through the literature, the statistics, the stories and examples. You continue to support the thesis and amplify it with added points. Then you summarize and you are back at the start, having clarified your thesis.

Consider an article that starts off: "The three-toed frog is nearing extinction. . . ." You corral your facts, describe how the frog's habitat is being destroyed, and allow authorities to further explain the problem and alternatives. At the end of the article you can say the frog faces extinction unless certain actions are taken. You're back making the same statement, but it's more forceful now than when you started. In effect, Kenneth Brower uses this structure in his extensive article, "The Destruction of Dolphins" (*Atlantic Monthly*, July 1989) as he describes the destruction of dolphins netted with tuna. The article ends up with the prediction that because things aren't changing, thousands more dolphins will be killed in the next several years.

Question and Answer

We've already considered the long Q and A format sometimes used in profiles. In addition, some general consensus articles embody a similar structure, although the article may not be written in the dialogue form used for *Playboy* profiles. One such consensus article is Linda Murray's "Sexual Destinies" in *Omni*. According to the blurb that accompanies the title: "Homosexuals are born, not made, claims one physician, who says he has proof positive that sexual orientation is sealed in the womb." Murray, in fact, prints some of her questions, even though that's not standard. But on occasion, as a structural device, questions work as signposts to carry readers through the longer article.

Murray was intrigued with a report by a doctor who told a London meeting that homosexuality was determined biologically before birth. She queried four publications: *Omni*, *Penthouse*, *American Health* and *Smithsonian*. "I submitted multiple queries because of the short lead time before I was to go abroad. I had the letters hand-delivered. In three days *Omni* called and they had been considering an article on Dörner (the subject). Two days later *Penthouse* called!" She, of course, went with the first to respond. She explains the 15-point structuring of the article, which hinged on answers to her questions:

1. "I wanted the sensational part up front — a scene setter." Her article opened with a ballet scene in which homosexual dancers displayed female behavior.

2. The second paragraph is her "establishing paragraph," which she calls "paragraph 2." She quotes the doctor: "They were behaving more like

females than like heterosexual men." And that leads to the questions through which the article is plotted.

3. "Then I backed into the science — his [Dörner's] theory and his argument and how he came to that."

4. "Then you have to early on bring up the universal that affects all our lives, no matter what the hell he is doing." So (in paragraph 8) she pointed out that "Single-handedly Dörner has touched off the most provocative debate in the field of sex research."

5. She talks with Dörner the day before he is to give a paper to the International Academy of Sex Research in Amsterdam. (She and other press are barred from his actual presentation.)

6. She delves into his background, how he grew up, his marriage, children.

7. Then she covered his wide research interests. "He would rather talk science and medicine than eat."

8. The *Omni* editors advise that she may have a profile article, not a topical article, because she hasn't turned up critics, and she casts about for opposing views.

9. Editors wonder what society would find objectionable, and she tries to find out.

10. Dörner's research has not been replicated by others, which raises some questions about it.

11. Her further research finds that one group did replicate it, another could not.

12. Then in the article, she says, "I opened it up. I talked to any expert, and considered the politics and raised implications."

13. She contacted members of the gay community for comment.

14. "I raised every intriguing possibility I could, and discussed it this way and that."

15. "Finally, I came around to a final quote," which noted, "As complex as we are, we are still mammals." This summarizes the subject's point of view, Murray suggests, that "there is solid basis to his argument on a strong biological orientation."

Note the use of an anecdote and the sense of immediacy at the beginning of the article by Murray, who is a public relations consultant in New York and a former managing editor of *Sexual Medicine Today*.[4]

4. Linda Murray, "Sexual Destinies," *Omni*, April 1987, pp. 100, 102. Reprinted by permission © 1987, Omni Publications International, Ltd.

Sexual Destinies

Linda Murray

Günter Dörner and his wife were watching the Ballet of Vienna on television, when he had a sudden revelation that would throw the field of biology and gender into turmoil. "There were some homosexual dancers with typical female behavior," says Dörner, who is director of the Institute of Experimental Endocrinology at Humboldt University in East Berlin. What does he mean? "Gestures that couldn't possibly be performed by heterosexual males," he replies quickly. "And there I had the idea that there must be a biological basis to homosexuality."

What kind of gestures? A pointing foot, a hand sweeping forward and upward? "They were graceful. All their movements together — the whole body. But I don't think that's important. While they danced, they were behaving more like females than like heterosexual men. I know most male ballet dancers are homosexual. And because they are homosexual, they are especially capable of dancing."

Dörner is reluctant to talk about this incident, to explain how — and why — he divined this. When questioned, he seems impatient with the obvious; his intuition is enough. Although he is convinced, other members of the scientific community are not swayed so easily. Indeed, to many, his assumption borders on the preposterous.

For 20 years now, Dörner has been antagonizing colleagues with his dogmatic stance that sexual orientation is sealed in the womb and not influenced by early environmental factors. Although sex researchers had entertained the idea that homosexuality is biologically determined, no one had tried to prove it. Enter Dörner. Homosexual males, he insists, are born, not made — the products of maternal androgen deficiency, a lack of masculinizing hormones during a critical period of fetal brain development. In some cases, Dörner states, the hormonal imbalance results from stress in the pregnant mother. He claims he can tell, based on amniotic fluid samples, if the fetus is at risk for being born homosexual, and he can "correct the abnormal" condition in the uterus by injecting supplementary androgens, or masculinizing hormones. Furthermore, Dörner has announced that in the near future he may be able to turn adult gays into straights with an experimental drug.

As evidence for his theory that homosexuality is biologically governed, Dörner points to the LH (luteinizing hormone) positive feedback effect. At puberty a girl will begin ovulating. This is because estrogen has triggered a surge of a brain hormone called LHRH (luteinizing hormone-releasing hormone), which in turn causes the release of luteinizing hormone. Without the LHRH, the brain cannot instruct the ovaries to begin ovulation. Both hormones, however, can be touched off artificially with an injection of estrogen. But give a heterosexual male a shot of estrogen and his LH levels fall or stay flat; there is simply no positive feedback response.

Dörner argues that the brains of male homosexuals become feminized before birth due to a deficiency of androgens, especially testosterone. According to Dörner's reasoning, gay men should respond to estrogen injections the same way females do. In fact, when he performed the LH test on a group of homosexual men, the men's LH levels rose as if the shot of estrogen were signaling a phantom ovary. Dörner contends this is proof that sexual orientation is decided in the womb.

An American team has backed him up. Their findings, published in the prestigious journal *Science* in 1984, confirmed a rise in LH levels in male homosexuals injected with estrogen. "Our evidence shows there is some biological element to sexual orientation," comments chief investigator Brian A. Gladue, assistant professor of

continued

continued

psychology and director of the Program in Human Sexuality at North Dakota State University. But Gladue is not sure he agrees with Dörner on what that element is. "It could be prenatal hormones, or it could be something else entirely," he says.

Single-handedly, Dörner has touched off the most provocative debate in the field of sex research. Simply put: Is there a biological underpinning to human sexual orientation? In the process by which a baby girl or a baby boy is created, the genes at first reign supreme. Sex is decided at the moment of conception by either an X-chromosome-bearing sperm, for a female, or a Y-chromosome-bearing sperm, for a male. Sometime around the sixth week of pregnancy, if the embryo is female, the chromosomes instruct the gonads — collections of germ cells — to develop ovaries, the womb, Fallopian tubes, and the upper two thirds of the vagina. If the embryo is male, however, the Y chromosome oversees the development of testicles, which secrete two crucial masculinizing hormones — including the major one, testosterone.

The brain, too, is prenatally influenced by hormones. Dörner contends that when a male embryo is deprived of high levels of testosterone and is influenced by ovarian estrogen, the brain becomes feminized and the boy becomes homosexual. But when the right amounts of testosterone are available, Dörner states, the brain is masculinized and the boy becomes a heterosexual. When a female embryo is exposed to a high level of testosterone, the brain becomes masculinized and the girl becomes lesbian.

The day before he is to make a presentation to the International Academy of Sex Research in Amsterdam, Dörner is relaxed and affable. We talk at La Rive restaurant in the gracious old Amstel Hotel because the press has been barred from the meetings. If this article were in a question-and-answer format, which qualifies as an "official" interview, Dörner would need to get permission, he tells me as we cross the drawbridge over the river Amstel. Dörner's employer, the German Democratic Republic (GDR), funds his work and issues visas for him to travel to the West. . . .

Waves

Consider a man in the crow's nest on top of a ship tossed at sea. He sees land through binoculars. He watches as gradually the waves hurl the ship toward shore. At last he stands safely on shore. An article focuses in on its ending from the very beginning — in the lead and beginning paragraphs. If the development is convincing, then the point is well grounded by the end.

The waves model underlies articles that rely on anecdotes. Remember the editor who said anecdotes can simply be strung together to form an article? Each carefully chosen anecdote is a wave, bringing the reader closer to shore. The model is seen as ripples: the circle widens until the stories have brought the reader to a conclusion.

Chunks

In his *Writing for Story*, Pulitzer Prize winner Jon Franklin tells about a writing professor, J. R. Salamanca, who told him to write in "discrete chunks." Another way of saying this is "write in scenes" — complete stories, complete images — before moving on in an article.

Salamanca advised Franklin to consider the work of a cinematographer. The filmmaker doesn't settle for a once-over of the crowd on a street. Says Franklin:

> A professional filmmaker would do it differently. He would focus on a single representative face and zoom in on it until it filled the frame. He would linger there, for a moment — long enough for the viewer to perceive the emotional state of the person, to see if he's screaming in anger, or cheering, or crying. In that way the film captures the humanness of the face, a single face, a unique face, with which the audience can identify.
>
> Then the filmmaker would zoom back, and the person who had filled the frame an instant ago would recede to become, once again, a face lost in the crowd.
>
> Then, having panned back, the cameraman would move the camera — just far enough to find another face, and then he would zoom in on that and record whether that face was laughing, or crying, or shouting in anger. . . .
>
> Salamanca gave me a moment to absorb the lesson, then handed my manuscript back to me. I had panned across my story as the amateur pans a crowd, and the result was a meaningless blur, without emphasis; having no emphasis, it had no drama. Having no drama, it had little interest.
>
> Go back, he said, and rewrite it. Only this time tell the story in discrete chunks. I did so, and the difference in my copy was nothing less than astonishing.[5]

Other writers and editors also refer to chunks. According to James Lloyd Greenfield, recent past editor of the *New York Times Magazine*, the writer should create scenes and then weave these "chunks" of narrative together. He was asked, "Is there one approach that works best for the *New York Times Magazine*?"

Greenfield compared his magazine's approach to scriptwriting: "I think of scenes." It's not on target, he said, "unless I see it physically, unless I smell and feel it, unless there are breaks, unless there are scenes. I want to look at it and see scenes, not just a mirror or a newspaper piece."

The reader should be made to feel personally, he said. "A lot (of writers) are good correspondents, but they don't make you feel you are there. . . . I love it when there is a chunk here, and a chunk there, and it is vaguely tied together, but it's a mosaic when you finish the piece."

Straightforward

Newspaper feature writing, in particular, relies on newswriting models. But, in fact, the "descending" development used in writing news stories is not totally different from that used to write some magazine articles. The lead, the establishing paragraph, development (explanation), "quickies" (additional

---

5. Jon Franklin, *Writing for Story* (New York: Atheneum, 1986), pp. 68, 69. Reprinted with the permission of Atheneum Publishers, an imprint of Macmillan Publishing Company from *Writing for Story* by Jon Franklin. Copyright © 1986 by Jon Franklin.

secondary information), the summary or wrap-up and an ending are all elements of a straightforward feature that might occur as well in a cyclic model, a question/answer model, a chunk model and so on.

Lead   It is commonly said that a lead's main task is to hook the readers — to get them to read the article. The function is the same — whether the lead is for a news story, fiction or a magazine piece. Get the reader into your story. If that doesn't happen, all is lost. Once you've hooked your readers, then you can set them up to follow the path where you develop the theme of the article.

Leads come in many forms. They can be as brief as a one-word paragraph, followed by a two- or three-word paragraph; for example, "Zip," then the second paragraph, "He got away." Or the lead can be a long descriptive paragraph, enlisting the senses to make the readers feel as if they're part of the scene.

Anecdotes, as we have seen, serve well as leads — sometimes several of them at once underscoring a point. But the dramatic for its own sake does not work. Says Van Varner, editor of *Guideposts*: "So many start like this: 'The siren sounded. . . .' followed by police radio talk. Then you know there will be a flashback. They think they are creating dramatic effect." He says he likes to know in the first paragraph what the article is about. The writer, he says, "must make a contract with the reader, so the reader knows pretty much the direction it is going." Rather than starting with police taking a call to go to a neighborhood, "I'd have him [the community leader who is the subject of the article] walking in the neighborhood he is going to change, such as 'I walked among people who 10 months ago. . . . These people are something else. . . . ,' and unravel from there."

When you're writing a piece for his magazine, which has strict space limitations, "You can't be all over the landscape. I get confused. There is already a flashback (to the police call), and generally I find I forget about the action." He warns against using anecdotes that appear to only be a writer's "device" and "contrived."

Leads aren't easy to write, and many writers don't recognize their good ones. "I find with new writers that the lead may be in the second paragraph and I get rid of the first paragraph," says Janet Spencer King, editor-in-chief of *Working Parents* and *Mothers Today*. Pam Fiori, former editor-in-chief of American Express's *Travel & Leisure* and now editorial director of American Express Publishing Corp., says "Some give us two or three leads. I choose one. Sometimes page three might be the lead."

Establishing Paragraph   As we have seen, a key paragraph close to the top determines the direction of the article. It's the "who the hell cares" paragraph that must answer the question of why the reader should undertake the article," says Janet Spencer King.

Development   Developing an article is like reporting to work for a day. You know where you have to be, what you have to do and where you want to come out at the end of the day. Most of the direction is set out in the mission you have accepted and stated in the establishing paragraph. It may depend on the model you selected. The "Ghost Busters" article, for instance, is developed by finishing the anecdote begun in the lead and then telling other anecdotes about haunted houses and how they're "dehaunted." Methods, theories and personalities are explained while the stories are being told.

Says writer Nancy Rubin: "Immerse yourself in your material before writing an outline. The material will then lead you to a natural evolution for the story. Although I do outline — at least in my head and sometimes on paper — I do not hold to a strict format because the material varies from story to story, and the story 'evolves' differently each time."

Quickies　Few articles exist as pure narrative. You need supporting information: examples, statistics, authoritative quotes, etc. A simple direct approach can include a catch-all category or section.

You might find yourself with some miscellaneous material that belongs in the article, but it is not highly readable. This material can be boiled down toward the end. Such material ranges from more personal facts about a person in the article to "quickie" summary anecdotes to a summary of additional agenda. You might have a list of addresses or sources that must be included.

This "quickie" bare-fact category, of course, is more applicable to newspaper features, which may be informational rather than theme centered. But even in a thematic article that excises much of the chaff, a place can exist for a catch-all paragraph or two.

Tying It Together　A good mystery writer often ties the story together once the plot reaches a certain point; perhaps the narrator or even one of the characters summarizes the action, the clues and suspects.

Sometimes nonfiction writers also need to stand back and tie all the threads together in the course of the article. If you're going to start describing contradictory viewpoints or if you're going on to another stage in a very long article, a quick summary paragraph can help. Be brief; distill what you've already said; recapitulate with words you haven't already used. While beneficial, sometimes even necessary, in magazine articles, this approach may seem redundant to a newspaper editor.

Ending　A newspaper feature may have a tagline, a clever remark or observation. Note how this article on prostitution in China from the New York *Times* begins and ends with an amusing sketch:

> FUZHOU, China — In dark hotel bars along China's coast, young women in tight dresses and carefully coiffed hair wiggle their ankles as they linger for hours over a single Coke. Nearby, young men in ostentatious jewelry look for clients to whom they can offer the women's services.
>
> Prostitution in China is back and flourishing. . . .
>
> In Canton, the police arrested more than 7,000 prostitutes last year. But it is widely believed that most are back at work after paying small fines or submitting to brief periods of "re-education." In the small town of Deqing,

about 100 miles west of Canton, a man accused of being a pimp was executed after being convicted of using his house as a brothel and luring six women to work for him.

But despite these highly publicized cases, the two women in Fuzhou were unfazed. "We're not afraid," the shorter women said. "My only worry is whether I'm getting too fat."[6]

Because magazine articles are allowed more space, their endings can be more extensive, more elaborate, more purposeful.

"There's no one way to end," says Duquin. "It depends on the article — sometimes summary, sometimes tied into the lead, sometimes a quote or final anecdote."

Writer Rubin agrees:

There is no best way, except to remember that the reader must understand your conclusion. I try to bring him full circle with new understandings or insights. In other words, if I've begun with an anecdote or have posed a question, my ending often provides answers to that beginning, or tells how an individual 'solved' his problem.

A second approach is to write a summarizing statement which evolves from the natural development of the material.

A third method is to end with a quote from an expert or observer which reinforces, or underscores the material in the story. This approach is used much more frequently in newspapers than in magazines, perhaps because of space constraints.

Editor-writer Janet Spencer King says, "I never use quotes in the last paragraph, except stylistically. You can end with the voice of the author again." She believes that endings should never be merely a summary, "never a repeat. I try to use a bit of new information." But, she confesses, she can spend days on getting the right ending. Here's her ending for an article on "Video Game Fever" in *Working Mother*. (She does not like the fact that the editor added the "of" in the "one family I know of.")

In the end, it looks as though, as with everything else in child rearing, nothing replaces parental supervision in handling this video-game craze. You might want to be cautious about supervising too closely while the kids are playing, though. In one family I know of, the kids are complaining that they've lost Nintendo privileges because they can't get the controls away from Mom.[7]

Says American Express's editorial director Pam Fiori: "You have to be conscious that the writer has one [an ending], and that you are not just trailing off into space somewhere." She likes a *Travel & Leisure* article by William Kittredge that has a sense of mystery and lets you know "what it feels like to

6. Edward A. Gargan, "Fuzhou Journal: Newest Economics Revives the Oldest Profession," New York *Times*, Sept. 17, 1988, p. 4. Copyright © 1987/88 by The New York Times Company. Reprinted by permission.

7. Janet Spencer King, "Video Game Fever," *Working Mother*, January 1989, p. 54.

be there in winter and spring. I liked the ending because he really talks and builds to where he lives (Idaho). The idea of home I love. . . . We're all searching and he found it. If he found it, I might find it. The idea of home means peace."

Following is Kittredge's lead and ending for his article, "The Northern Rockies."

> Think of it as a secret kingdom, as I do: wild roses blooming along the fence lines in late spring, shining snowy peaks along the Rockies front, and perfect Indian summer days to remind us of the wintertime to come. Think of the long sweep of the Great Plains reaching to immaculate infinities in the enormous sky to the east; imagine yellowing aspens in the ravines along the great open slopes.
>
> When we talk about the Northern Rockies we mean a specific territory with natural geologic boundaries. It includes that half of Montana west of the Crazy Mountains, Idaho north of the Snake River Plain, Wyoming above the Red Desert and the old Oregon Trail. And, we believe, a certain spirit of involvement with life's own whimsies.
>
> If it sounds like the beginning of a love story, that's right.
>
> There is an intricate, workable combination of personal freedom and natural life I find in the Northern Rockies — trout in clean rivers, elk bugling through the fall in the Sun River country, small decent towns with good schools for the children, no need to lock your car, strangers you can trust. . . .
>
> It is an idea of home, where you fit into the world like a lost piece clicking into place in a picture puzzle. Maybe that's what we all come seeking when we travel, such a home in the world.[8]

THE INVISIBLE STRUCTURE

In addition to its visible structure, an article's success rests on elements that can't be seen — invisible support structures, invisible language, research, subliminal messages.

Inner Structure

When you look at the human body, you don't see the bones, cartilage, sinews, nerves and synapses that you know are there. In the same way, you don't see, although you are conscious of, what holds an article together — the planning, the organization, the arrangements, the outlines that work like poles holding up a tent. You discern the structure indirectly from the harmony and fabric of the result.

8. William Kittredge, "The Northern Rockies," *Travel & Leisure*, March 1989, pp. 107–109. Reprinted with permission from *Travel & Leisure*, March 1989. © 1989 American Express Publishing Corporation, all rights reserved.

Silent Language

You've heard of "unspoken language": body language, gestures, a look in the eye. You sense the mood of a piece from the cast of the sentences. The association of words next to each other, the rhythm, the sound of the words, length of syllables and vowels evoke meanings not explicitly expressed.

Unseen Research

You see the results of research in an article, but you don't see every fact the author learned. Sometimes, indeed, you see a very small percentage of the research; but the author's confidence, understanding of the subject, ease with the subject and ability to draw in just the right facts suggest an abundance of information to which the author has access but does not (and because of space could not) choose to use.

Free-lance writer Caroline Bird, in writing "If Your Child Cheats" for the *Woman's Home Companion* some years ago, gathered information from everywhere—periodicals, books, interviews, a mass mailing to educators, psychiatrists and sociologists. She had about everything you could hope for on the subject. Her editor told her just to throw away all the research and write what came to mind and what she thought. The editor said to bring in anecdotes and comments that fit, but not to worry about using all the material she collected.

She explained in a précis of her article—when it appeared in anthology of best articles—that a magazine article is much like an iceberg that exists eight-ninths below the surface. You go to great depths in getting research, but then discard most of it when it comes to the actual writing.

Deeper Messages

What an article is saying is not always apparent on the surface or in the establishing section which announces the direction and purpose. The final message or messages may be subliminal. Some people wear their emotions on their sleeves; some keep their feelings inside. Like a poem, an article may be subtle. The messages may not be blurted from a tower, but they are there—carefully crafted into the total product. An article on a homeless person on the street may end open-ended—that is, the destiny of the person may not be indicated, but there is an aura of hope in the depiction of the homeless person's attitude.

CHECKLIST OF QUALITIES

Fulton Oursler, Jr., former executive editor of *Reader's Digest*, described for a panel of magazine educators his approach to condensing articles for the *Digest*. In so doing, he also suggested what he thought an article consists of and what might be in the finished, condensed, tighter version:

What I strive to preserve are those elements that touch the reader most deeply; that involve his emotions and intellect; that cause him to react. I try to keep all of the best anecdotes because these mini-narratives are the building blocks of reader interest and identification.

Finally, I do all that I can to see that the article possesses these qualities:

1. A unified theme, or focus that captures the essence of the author's message.

2. An arresting lead that involves the reader.

3. A structure that is developed as it moves smoothly and clearly from a beginning to an end, with a high level of interest throughout.

4. A satisfying ending.

5. Conciseness in every degree.

ASSIGNMENTS

1. Find and report on examples of strictly expository, narrative and argumentative writing; then report on an article that combines all three approaches.

2. Study a general or consensus article and outline its parts and progression.

3. Take a popular magazine and circle the establishing paragraph or "nutgraf" in each case. Note how its position might vary from article to article. Which article has the establishing paragraph closest to the lead? Which one, the farthest? Why?

4. Study a long article and give a "name" to its structure using one given in this chapter or a name of your own choosing.

5. Take a magazine and prepare a list of variations in the kinds of leads and endings in the articles for that issue.

6. Mix up endings and leads from a number of articles. Draw them from a hat or box. Have the other members of the class identify which are leads and which are endings.

7. Take a newspaper feature article and suggest how it might change if it were rewritten into a longer magazine article or vice versa.

8. Identify an article you want to write that is timely, relevant and targeted to a magazine. Of course, write a query letter, but proceed to do a tentative outline. Will one of the models in this chapter work?

9. Write a one- or two-page essay: "I think the hardest part of writing a longer article is. . . ." Why? And indicate how you would solve the problem.

10. Make a research, strategy and time outlay plan — a complete schedule — for a longer article you will write.

CHAPTER 9

Style: The Flow of Words

Style is something everybody wants—in living and in writing. To dress in style means to be distinctive as well as up to date. Nobody wants to wear exactly what another wears.

In the use and wearing of words in style, as in clothing, originality prevails. Yet at the same time, style is something acceptable to the reader, pleasing to the mind and the ear, agreeable to people at large.

A writer's style belongs to the writer and sets off the writer. A style may resemble another and be inspired by another, but like look-alike human beings, differences exist. Style has its own kind of fingerprints, markings and accents on words.

Style has something charismatic about it, and, like charisma, it defies definition. You know when you are in the company of a person with charisma. The person's eyes dance with the sparkle of life, the words are inviting, cheerfulness exudes; so does determination, an innate sense of authority, wisdom, self-assuredness.

DEVELOPING YOUR STYLE

To write in style is to have charisma in your writing, something more than a succession of words and information. The language takes on a life of its own. Although it may be pared down to the simplest of sentences, the language stands up and dances with joy, communicating other qualities, such as clarity of vision and enthusiasm with the reading.

Style, like charisma, is not surface deep. It arises from the being of the person or inner psyche. It is not added like lipstick or eye shadow. Style, like charisma, must be a part of the person and a part of the product. It is not simply laid on.

According to William Strunk and E. B. White in *The Elements of Style*:

> Young writers often suppose that style is a garnish for the meat of prose, a sauce by which a dull dish is made palatable. Style has no such separate entity, it is nondetachable, unfilterable. The beginner should approach style warily, realizing that it is himself he is approaching, no other; and he should begin by turning resolutely away from all devices that are popularly believed to indicate style — all mannerisms, tricks, adornments. The approach to style is by way of plainness, simplicity, orderliness, sincerity.[1]

Learning from Others

When you read what others have written, you become aware of style. If you immerse yourself in the best writing, especially in great literary works, you can't help learning how to write well. You get lessons in the economy of language and in its extravagance, in word choice, imagery, symbolism; in dramatic structure and characterization. But learning from others doesn't mean imitating them when you write your own pieces.

Keeping company with words makes a person at once comfortable with them and awestruck by them, as Robert MacNeil describes in his autobiographical *Wordstruck*:

> Music heard early in life lays down a rich bed of memories against which you evaluate and absorb music encountered later. Each layer adds to the richness of your musical experience; it ingrains expectations that will govern your taste for future music and perhaps change your feelings about music you already know. Certain harmonic patterns embed themselves in your consciousness and create yearnings for repetition, so that you can relive that pleasurable disturbance of the soul. Gradually, your head becomes an unimaginably large juke box, with instantaneous recall and cross-referencing, far more sophisticated than anything manmade.

1. William Strunk, Jr., and E. B. White, *The Elements of Style*, 3rd ed. (New York: Macmillan, 1979), p. 69. Copyright © 1979 by Macmillan Publishing Company. Reprinted with the permission of Macmillan Publishing Company.

It is so with words and word patterns. They accumulate in layers, and as the layers thicken they govern all use and appreciation of language thenceforth. Like music, the patterns of melody, rhythm, and quality of voice become templates against which we judge the sweetness and justness of new patterns and rhythms; and the patterns laid down in our memories create expectations and hungers for fulfillment again.[2]

What specifically can you gain from reading? You can gain a sense of harmony of elements from Ambrose Bierce and an appreciation of imagery, detail and suspense from Jack London. You can learn about the extravagance of language from John Updike and Joyce Carol Oates and about minimalism and leanness from Raymond Carver; you can gain a sense of adventure from Louis L'Amour and John Jakes, a feeling for philosophical rootings from Graham Greene and Morris West, for mirth and existential predicament from the stories of Woody Allen and Tama Janowitz.

Style and Experience

As we have seen, free-lance writers should write about what they know, particularly when writing "how-to" articles. But there are times when all writers, especially staff reporters and feature writers, must tackle topics about which they know little or nothing. Even then there is a common denominator, because people lie at the heart of most topics.

Writing in style has something to do with living. If you relate to people and care, you will have empathy and a meaningful framework with which to write. Those who go through life with feeling for others can write in style. Working with children in camps, serving the elderly, helping on the streets, mixing with people from campus to the military, all help with style. A New York *Times* editor advises that serving in the Peace Corps is great training for being a writer and provides credentials that help you get hired.

While reporting has its straightforward, objective side, it nevertheless introduces the writer to many aspects of life. Many great writers started as journalists: Stephen Crane, Charles Dickens, Jack London, Ernest Hemingway, Theodore Dreiser, Victor Hugo, Mark Twain, Ambrose Bierce, Rudyard Kipling, Damon Runyon, H. G. Wells.

Organization and Style

If the term *organization* with its implications of a preset structure and outline seem antithetical to the term *style*, then think about what style is. Style comes from a flow of words and the harmony thereby created; the effect is more than the sum of the parts, more than counting up the particular feelings and words. Although it seems spontaneous, style is in fact the result of hard work. Style depends on the relationship between ideas and words — blurts, spurts, and

---

2. Robert MacNeil, *Wordstruck* (New York: Viking, 1989), pp. 23, 24.

exclamations do not a style make. Writing that is emotional isn't good writing unless it has continuity and structure, no matter how highly charged the words and ideas may be.

Poetry is a high form of writing in style. You know it from the impact the poem has as a unit. Yet a poet sweats over each word, each progression of a thought; the poet has not only a theme and an effect in mind, but also a form. The poem may sound like a stream of continuity, of spontaneity, but there is an invisible hand of organization at work.

Take a close look at poetry, from the sonnet to the short haiku to free verse. The sonnet has 14 lines. Depending on what kind of sonnet you write, you have prescribed rhyming patterns and meter. One form calls for the first eight lines to be quatrains (with a rhyming pattern, a, b, b, a; a, b, b, a) and the next six lines in another rhyming pattern (c, d, e; c, d, e). The meter is iambic pentameter: that is, one, two; one, two, etc., five times in a line with the emphasis on the second beat. A haiku, a Japanese form, has only three lines — the first has five syllables, the second, seven; and the third, five. Even "free verse" which does not conform to traditional models may have its own method of line divisions and word groupings and its own sense of rhythm.

Doesn't a good poem sound simple and fluid? But take a sonnet at random — say, William Wordsworth's celebrative tribute "To Sleep." Do you see a very obvious structure and set of rules in play?

> To Sleep
>
> A flock of sheep that leisurely pass by,
>   One after one; the sound of rain, and bees
>   Murmuring; the fall of rivers, winds, and seas,
> Smooth fields, white sheets of water, and pure sky;—
> I have thought of all by turns, and yet do lie
>   Sleepless; and soon the small birds' melodies
>   Must hear, first uttered from my orchard trees;
> And the first cuckoo's melancholy cry.
> Even thus last night, and two nights more, I lay,
>   And could not win thee, Sleep! by any stealth:
> So do not let me wear to-night away:
>   Without Thee what is all the morning's wealth?
> Come, blessèd barrier between day and day,
>   Dear mother of fresh thoughts and joyous health![3]

A well-written piece begins with the organization of an idea. "Perhaps it is more of an intellectual discipline" than anything else, says Lee Eisenberg, former editor-in-chief of *Esquire* about writing in style. He attributed the success of Chip Brown's "The Transformation of Johnny Spain" in *Esquire* to a conscious intellectual control. The article won first place in the feature

---

3. William Wordsworth, "To Sleep," in A. T. Quiller-Couch, editor, *English Sonnets* (Freeport, N.Y.: Books for Libraries Press, 1968), p. 141.

writing category of the prestigious National Magazine Awards in 1989. "It was a human drama so powerful and the strength was in the way it was written," says Eisenberg, who is now launching a British edition of *Esquire*. "It could have been maudlin and breathless and political. It could have been ruined by easy viewpoint. The writer chose to remain on the side when he could have made it a black political issue or racism. It's wise to let the story build on its own power and natural momentum."

The awards committee called Spain's article "a gripping story of a man born white in Mississippi who grew up to spend his adult years in prison as a black revolutionary. Writer Chip Brown reconstructs the life of Johnny Spain, a Black Panther and one of the Soledad Brothers, with detail and perspective that even the subject himself had never been able to do. The writer resists the temptation to sentimentalize the tragic circumstances of Spain's childhood. Instead, Brown delivers a complex and compelling profile of a man whose life reflects the painful costs of our country's struggle with racism."

Chip Brown knew ahead of time what he wanted to do and how. He wanted to let the strength and drama of the material stand on their own and avoid didactic and preachy intrusions that confirm stereotypes. His task was to create narrative segments, with a cast of precisely drawn characters and dialogue in vivid settings. With the force of fiction, he let the action propel the reader to the conclusion. That game plan gave clarity and unity.[4]

Here is the beginning of Brown's prize-winning *Esquire* article:

The Transformation of Johnny Spain

Long before the killings, the trials, the fantasies of revolution, Johnny Spain was a six-year-old boy who lived in a small bungalow on the south side of Jackson, Mississippi. His father, Fred, drove a beer truck; his mother, Ann, manufactured TV cabinets. He had an older brother, Charlie, a younger sister, Lissie, a baby brother, Ray. That summer of 1955 his name was Larry Armstrong and he looked pretty much like anybody else's kid except for his hair—"nigger hair," people called it. The children in Choctaw Village liked to put their hands in it, but no barber in Jackson's white parlors would touch it.

Johnny Spain remembers a little from those days, but not much: the time Charlie, his steadfast defender, called him a nigger; the times he hid under the bed when Fred came home; when he heard his father slap his mother and holler, "Take the nigger baby and get out!" He would have entered first grade that fall were it not for his hair, and the talk and all. Even the superintendent of Jackson's public schools knew about

---

4. Chip Brown, "The Transformation of Johnny Spain," *Esquire*, January 1988, pp. 73, 74, 81.

him. Nearly twenty years would pass before children with hair like his would sit in class with whites.

Of what happened next, he recalls virtually nothing. His mother broke the news that he was going to live with a family in California, where he could attend school out of harm's way. She packed his clothes, and then the three of them, Fred and Ann and the boy, piled in the car and eventually he found himself on a train with an elderly woman. He thought his parents would turn up and take him home at any moment, but the sun went down, and morning broke over new country, and the train was streaking west. It was three days to Los Angeles. He would never forget the trestle bridges that traversed the canyons, nor the woman riding with him, but it would be years before he could understand the impact of that journey. This was the child who grew up to be Johnny Spain, the onetime Black Panther, protégé of George Jackson, and sole member of the San Quentin Six convicted of murder. And this is the central fact of his life: a long time ago he boarded a train in Mississippi as a little white boy; when he got off in California, he was black.

Jackson, Mississippi, was burned so thoroughly during the Civil War it got the name Chimneyville, but in the early 1950s "the crossroads of the South" was doing business in furniture, lumber, and cottonseed oil. The population of almost a hundred thousand was two-thirds white and scrupulously segregated. In the 1950 city directory "colored people" were distinguished by a C with a circle around it, and a disclaimer cautioned, "The publishers are very particular in using this, but are not responsible in case of error."

In that year's edition, an Ann and Fred Armstrong are listed. The two children noted would have been Charlie and Larry, and as far as the very particular publishers were concerned, both were white.

Fred Armstrong still lives in Jackson. On a humid June morning I found him sitting in a white T-shirt on the screened-in porch in front of his trailer, a big keg of a man with enormous ears, and the morning paper spread on his lap.

"Mr. Armstrong, can I talk to you about Larry?"

"Larry?" he said.

"Larry . . . Armstrong?"

The name didn't seem to ring a bell.

"Your son . . ."

Finally it clicked. "The nigger?" he said.

We talked through the screen. Fred Armstrong insisted there wasn't much to tell. What's more, he said, at seventy-six some of the details had escaped him.

"Last time I heard, he'd shot a man or something in California. I think he's out of jail now, maybe he's gotten married."

In Germany during the war, Fred Armstrong had been an Army cook. He opened Armstrong's Café on Monument Street when he got back. He worked nights, his wife Ann worked days. They had met at a dance on an Army base, courted by letter, and married on October 6, 1945. He was thirty-four; she was ten years younger.

"At first she took the marriage seriously," he said. "When Charlie was born we were living on Rose Street, we got along pretty good. I was working all the time, she was working. She wasn't bored. We were sleeping together. Then she started slipping out. She come home at 4:00 A.M. one night, and I seen her get out of the car. I slapped her around.

"She got pregnant when I was running the café," he recalled. "I had it two or three years. I sold out in 1948. Then I spent eighteen years in the beer business."

He couldn't remember the name of the man who fathered Larry. He knew him though.

"He come in my café and ate. That boy worked down on State Street at some garage. When he found out I was after him, he skipped."

"What would you have done to him?"

"Back in those days? I probably would have hung him or killed him. Now I look back, it was as much her fault as his. He was about twenty, twenty-five years old. He'd set up at the counter by the cash register. I seen 'em talking, but I didn't think anything about it. She knew all the niggers, they would come in from the cotton mill.

continued

continued

"It happened up there across from the farmers' market. She'd go up there and the nigger went with her. They'd go up in the evening after she got done washing dishes."

"Were you surprised when the baby was born?"

"I was surprised," he said.

"Ann's grandmother was dark-colored," he continued. "I just passed it off. But the boy's hair was nigger hair. I was in the jukebox business, working for Charlie Warren. When that boy was a year old, Charlie told me, 'Fred, that's a nigger baby and you better do something.'

"I said, 'That ain't no nigger baby,' and he said, 'Yes he is,' I really thought it was my own baby until he was a couple of years old. We raised him six years."

"Was he part of the family?"

"Oh, yeah. He ate at the same table and slept in the same house. But the older he got the more he looked like a nigger. People was talking, friends of mine. They'd make remarks: 'When you gonna get rid of that nigger boy?'

"I told 'em after I found out who the father was. Me and her had a talk about it. He didn't rape her, she did it on her own free will. I went down there, I was gonna tell him to take that baby himself. They said he'd quit and went to Chicago.

"I didn't have much to do with Ann after that. I didn't want the boy around. He was a good, disciplined boy. Him and Ray and Charlie played together. But he couldn't go to the white school. Something had to be done.

"I don't know where he is, if he's dead or what. I asked Trina, Charlie's wife, a while ago, 'What ever happened to Larry?' She said he'd shot a man and did some time in California."

"Are you interested in his life?"

"No, no. You get over something like that."

Ann Armstrong and Arthur Cummings converged over a counter top, talking about poetry and baseball.

Arthur came from D'Lo, Mississippi, twenty-five miles southeast of Jackson. He was working as a mechanic. He was a regular at Armstrong's.

There was a wall down the middle, whites on one side, blacks on the other. Ann worked both sides of the partition.

"Do you dare play a game of cards?" Ann asked.

"Why not," Arthur said.

Ann was restless, unhappy at home.

"Fred was very abusive," she recalled. "One night he got really rough and threw me down the stairs. He was jealous, but at that point it was all in his mind."

How did the affair get started?

"One thing led to another," she said.

"I knew the seriousness of it," said Arthur. "The consequences would have been extreme. But I just didn't worry about those things."

Today Arthur lives in New Orleans. Ann lives in the Northwest under the name of her second husband. She's a diabetic and is legally blind.

When Larry was born, she put him in a crib in her room, rocked him, and talked to him more than she had to Charlie. "I felt more of a responsibility to him. I had the feeling that when he got past me, he'd have nothing."

Fred Armstrong sold the café, and in 1951 the young family moved to a small one-story, two-bedroom house on Stokes Robertson Road, in a poor white neighborhood on the south side of Jackson. Larry was two.

His skin was growing darker, but he played with neighborhood kids. There were chinaberry fights in the fields and baseball games on Wayne and Senie Fortenberry's spacious lawn. Senie was friendly with Ann.

"She told me she was never so shocked in her life the day he was born and they brought the child in," Senie recalled. "She told me her husband accepted Larry as his child. As far as we were concerned he was welcome to play in the yard. I had no problem. You'll find prejudice in all people, but I go by the Scripture.

"Pastor Wayne Todd told Ann—for the child's sake, not the church's—if they could move to a northern city, where the child would be accepted, it would be better. If she couldn't do that, then maybe they should send him to a colored family, a fine Christian family, out of this antagonistic situation."

Into my hand Senie pressed a copy of the New Testament and two gardenias graciously clipped from a fragrant bush. It had upset her to learn that Larry Armstrong had spent the last two decades in jail. She confessed that she had always been afraid something bad would happen to him.

"Why do you think all this happened?"

"It's because of sin — the sins of society, the sins of the parents," she said. . . .

[The following concludes Brown's 11,000 word article.]

Now it is the fall of 1987 and freedom tantalizes Johnny Spain. He has served twenty-one years in jail on a single conviction for a murder committed when he was seventeen — nearly twice the average sentence for that crime. He has been denied parole twice, but another parole hearing was scheduled for this December. The prosecution theory that Spain was part of a conspiracy to escape — never very credible among many lawyers and authors of books about the case — was further eroded when Stephen Bingham, the lawyer who had been a fugitive for thirteen years, returned to face trial and was acquitted of charges that he had joined the escape conspiracy by smuggling a gun to Jackson in San Quentin. Spain today is an accomplished electrician. His work has earned parole recommendations and letters of support from ninety-three guards — the very men he had scorned as pigs a decade ago.

Nevertheless, the Marin County district attorney plans to retry him on the original San Quentin charges if those convictions are not reinstated. Parole may well be denied again: there are many who agree with David Ross, of the L.A. County D.A.'s office, when he says, "There's no question he's not the black-hearted ogre that he was when he came here, but he's not Rebecca of Sunnybrook Farm, either."

On East Twenty-third Street, El Santo Niño is closed. Bus benches on the corner of Hill and Venice are covered with the cyrillic scrawl of L.A. gangs. Under the interstate, some partisan,

now no doubt in business school, stopped long enough to write, LONG LIVE THE GREAT PROLETARIAN REVOLUTION.

After a decade of marriage, Pinkey Spain has consented to a divorce. "Johnny is a humanist, he believes in what man can do for man," she says. "I'm a Christian. I believe in God, life after death, heaven and hell." Ann saw her son last spring. She and Arthur sometimes talk on the telephone. Arthur writes to Johnny now and then, but they have not yet met — airfares are expensive and Arthur is a man who stays on the periphery of his children's lives, not wanting to be a bother. When he was hospitalized with a heart condition some years ago, he left blank the lines of the admittance form that asked for next of kin.

Cathy Kornblith talks to Spain at least once a week by telephone. She has traced the outermost branches of his family tree, and her conclusion is, "Lots of relatives, no family." The word *struggle* still pops up in her speech, with an odd and anachronistic ring. But the struggle boils down mostly to one man's freedom.

That man — the product of an interracial union when such affairs were felonies in Mississippi, punishable by ten years in jail — never sought to be a symbol. If Johnny Spain has put aside the grander aspirations of his militant youth, he now yearns as intensely for the consolations of ordinary life. He wants to meet his father before his father dies and play with his children before they grow up. He wants to put his hands on a dog, feel the bark of a tree, make a sentimental journey home.

"I don't want to complain," Spain told me. "I believe I have already participated in the biggest revolution in my life, and that is my life. But it's necessary to go beyond history."

Late in the day at Vacaville, I asked him to draw a map of the childhood house on Stokes Robertson Road in Jackson, but he remembered nothing of it, not even the name of the road, and instead drew a map of the house he did remember, on East Twenty-third Street. After he finished the sketch, he ripped a fresh sheet from his

continued

continued
legal pad and began again, this time to get the scale right. He drew meticulously, from the mind's eye: front yard, backyard, kitchen, stairs, his room, the small garage where grandmother lived. Up welled the past. Once he had tied his grandmother's apron strings to her rocking chair as she sat dozing. There had been an orchard of trees in the yard — limes, oranges, avocados. He circled the spots where trees had stood, assigned them numbers, and compiled a legend.

"I don't know if they're still there," he said, gazing at the map.

I saw the yard later. Like so much else in his life, they belonged to memory.

Imagery

As we noted in an earlier chapter, readers "see" a magazine or newspaper article physically. But the words that are read also provide images. So you will want to consider highlighting words that convey images, even starting sentences with them. How much power can a sentence have if it starts with the vague "there is" or impersonal "it"?

Create images, something that the brain sees, something that can't be skipped over. Words like *boy, duck, fingernail, tile* or *brick* make us see.

In addition to using image nouns as subjects or highlighted in a sentence, you can create imagery by selecting words that involve the reader's emotion (by appealing to the reader's sense of duty and responsibility or by appealing to the reader's fears, hopes, ambitions).

Involving the senses in your writing — touch, sight, hearing, smell, taste — creates images. And, as we discuss elsewhere, the employment of interesting details that have some significance and inspire imagination is useful in creating imagery.

The Sound of Words

Language is not just read but also heard — even when read silently. Some words are more enjoyable, pleasing and effective than others. Words such as *nevertheless, however, furthermore,* don't resound. They have little tonal value. But words such as *night, face, see, take, low, high, go, cow, feel, mice, nice, reel, team, wave,* settle in. Note that most such words are monosyllabic and some of the more sonorous have a long vowel. We can be made excited or sad or can be plummeted into a fighting or loving mood by such words. They are emotive words and are useful in combination with other factors in the total context.

Avoid "Latin" words — those with a Latin base. Most prominent are the "-tion" words — most can be converted to a simpler word: *aberration — flaw; liberation — freedom; trepidation — fear;* and so on. Also convert "-ness" words: *indebtedness — debt.* Avoid words with prefixes and suffixes — short additions such as "ex" or "ad" at the beginning of words, or "tion" or "ish" or "ed" at the end of words.

Some language analysts have developed yardsticks to measure the gobbledygook or fog factors of sentences — short, direct sentences help you score well, as does avoiding prefixes and suffixes. Rudolf Flesch explains these measures in his books, *The Art of Plain Talk*, *The Art of Readable Writing* and *The Art of Clear Thinking*. If your word processing program has a grammar checker, it will probably give whatever you write using the program a readability score and a fog index.

Avoid Bureaucratese

The words you write should sound natural — as if you were speaking. Corporate bureaucracies and public relation staffs using words like networking, parenting, interfacing and so on don't score many points for writing gracefully.

Get rid of, or rather, go easy with, what might be called the "public relations participle." So many public relations releases or handouts overload their sentences with information. One technique of overloading is to precede the subject with a participial phrase: "Working as a butcher at Safeway as a young man in Pigeon, Mich., James Animalfat is the new head of the School of Veterinary Medicine at. . . ." Avoid such hitch-on phrases. Be direct: "In his youth James Animalfat worked as a butcher at Safeway in Pigeon, Mich. . . ."

Quotations

Some teachers and writers encourage variety in words of attribution. Instead of *said*, these people like generous sprinklings of *maintain*, *proclaim*, *declared*, *insisted*, *commented*, *stated* and so on. These Latin-based words, many of them multisyllable, are plain distracting. Most writers will simply stay with the simple, quick *said*. Sometimes, especially when you're writing dialogue or continued exchanges of quotations, you might introduce a little variety. Louise Boggess suggests a "cycle" in the use of *said* to create what she calls "emotional dialogue." At first the attribution is *said*. Then, next time the person speaks, it's *he said how*: "he said timidly." Next: a *said substitute*; "he whispered." Then, no attribution: "'I can't do it.'" Then back to *said*: "he said."[5]

You want to move on with your story as rapidly as possible, not call attention to words of attribution. Identify the speaker and get on with it — the quotation, the anecdote, the facts. Often, simply using *said* is enough.

How about *says*? Usually you elect to use one or the other, depending on preferred style of the publication. *Said* is common in reporting, since the story is usually published the next day; in any case, after the event. *Says* is often used when referring to advice and direction. Thus a textbook writer might use *says*.

Use short quotations; make sure they have zip. But don't fragment quotes — give full sentences. Try not to quote more than a sentence or so at a

5. See Louise Boggess, *Fiction Techniques That Sell* (Englewood Cliffs, N.J.: Prentice-Hall, 1964), pp. 114, 115.

time. Don't merely give facts. You can put facts in your own words. Example of a bad quote: "I was in a plane crash," or "Springfield is 200 miles from Chicago." A good quote: "I could feel the plane coming apart. I lost consciousness. I woke up in the middle of a corn field." Don't string along paragraphs of quotes by breaking in with "he adds," etc. If a long quote is necessary, don't add superfluous words.

Action Verbs

Imagery and sound rely on action verbs rather than on verbs devoid of movement. How exciting is "An explosion occurred . . ."? How much more excitement and imagery in "A blast rocked . . ."? "He drove by at 80 miles per hour." Why not "He roared past at 80"?

Verbs generate the movement in a scene. A good characterization has movement: A person on stage or in a story breathes, leans, gestures, moves about, talks. Morris West describes a village at dawn in *The Devil's Advocate*. It is not static but the scene has people coming out of doors, moving about.

In a later novel, *Lazarus*, West shows again the importance of bringing a scene to life with movement:

> Nicol Peters sat under a pergola of vines on his terrace, sipped coffee, ate fresh pastry and watched the roof-dwellers of old Rome wake to the warm spring morning.
>
> There was the fat fellow with striped pyjamas gaping open at the crotch, whose first care was to take the cover off his canary cage and coax the birds into a morning chorus, with trills and cadenzas of his own. There was the housewife in curlers and carpet slippers, watering her azaleas. On the next terrace, a heavy-hipped girl in a black leotard laboured through fifteen minutes of aerobic exercises to the tinny tunes of a tape machine. Over by the Torre Argentina a pair of lovers thrust open their shutters and then, as if seeing each other for the first time, embraced passionately and tumbled back into bed for a public mating.
>
> Their nearest audience was a skinny bachelor with a towel for a loincloth, who did his own laundry and hung out every morning the shirt, the jockey shorts, the cotton vest and socks which he had just washed under the shower. This done, he lit a cigarette, watched the love-making of his neighbours and went inside to reappear a few minutes later with coffee and a morning paper. . . . Above them, the first swifts dipped and wheeled around the campaniles and through the forest of antennae and satellite discs, while shadowy figures passed and repassed by open doors and casements to a growing cacophony of music, radio announcements and a rumour of traffic from the alleys below.
>
> These folk were the theme upon which Nicol Peters was building the text for his weekly column, "A View From My Terrace." He stacked the scattered pages, picked up a pencil and began his editing.[6]

Movement achieved by action verbs helps quotations spring to life. A person grips a railing as he or she looks over a plain or valley; someone lifts a

6. Morris West, *Lazarus* (New York: St. Martin's, 1991), pp. 68, 69.

coffee cup, gestures, rises and sits on a desk during an interview. Recorded movement helps to give relief to longer quotes and contributes to the setting of a scene.

Normally the simple past tense is used: "He choked the man," instead of "he was choking the man." "He killed the man," instead of "he was killing the man." A simple past action is easily conveyed. A progressive verb form, "he was killing" and even the present tense, "he kills the man," somehow removes the protagonist from the event and makes it seem tentative.

The Touch of Poetry

Develop a keen ear for the language and learn how to prune your words. The result will be a style filled with rhythms and cadences, perhaps approaching the poetic.

Recall some literary devices from your literature studies:

- *Alliteration.* The words in a sentence or phrase repeat the same sound, usually a consonant. "Beside the silent sea she sang a song of sadness." Don't overuse alliteration or you'll sound tongue-tied.

- *Simile.* You use the word *like* when you're making a comparison: "The kid looks like an elephant but eats like a frog — his tongue is like a conveyor belt."

- *Metaphor.* You make a comparison without using the word *like*. "His diamond-shaped face cut through the steely silence of the party." Use metaphors and similes sparingly. Remember, directness and simplicity are the greater virtues.

- *Onomatopoeia.* The sound of a word or series of words suggests their meaning. Tennyson's description of bees sounds like bees: "Murmur of innumerable bees." Virgil in the *Aeneid* in Latin spoke of the roar and ringing sound of trumpets: *Exoritur clamorque virum clangorque tubarum* — "the shouts of men are high and the clang of trumpets."

Poetry — old-fashioned poetry at least — has a rhythm and a beat. Prose writing sometimes achieves a similar rhythm, an almost-scannable meter. Then, word substitution for effect, if done intelligently, adds a little spice of style. Both rhythm and word substitution will be touched on again in Chapter 11 on columns. Here are examples of a familiar kind of wordplay in a newspaper and a magazine.

From the *Wall Street Journal*:

DEBOIS, Maine — The blueberry crop is bountiful here this summer, thanks largely to the labors of migrant workers. Worker bees, that is — hundreds of millions of the industrious little critters, from as far away as Florida. . . .
It can be a honey of a business. . . .[7]

7. Sanford L. Jacobs, "Farmers Are Abuzz About the Benefits of Trucked-In Bees," *Wall Street Journal*, July 6, 1989, p. 1.

From the *Utne Reader*:

Francis Moore Lappé, the nutrition activist who wrote *Diet For a Small Planet* in 1971 and went on to build a national reputation as "the Julia Child of the soybean circuit," admits she doesn't know beans about gourmet dining. . . .[8]

Tightening Process

Condensing and rearranging as a part of the editorial process can change an article significantly. *Reader's Digest* tightens up articles — and, some would say, improves them — by condensing them drastically and rearranging parts.

Compare this short original article, "After a Death," as it appeared in the *Journal of the American Medical Association*,[9] with the even briefer version, "Shining Brightly, Briefly," as it appeared in the *Digest* for a broader audience.[10]

After a Death

I have witnessed many deaths and, loyal to my training, have generally remained objective and appropriately supportive during these events. Death, once a matter between family and physician, is now a public event involving guidelines, consultants, and tests, house officers, social workers, nurses, and students. This change in the nature of dying allows one to be more scientific and less involved when talking with a family, making it easier to review with them the litany of personnel and procedures that have been invoked and that basically mean there is no hope for their child.

I believe that, in general, I am too old to have new insights into myself; however, a death this summer became an epiphany for me. She was a 14-year-old girl, an only child, who three days earlier had been practicing to be a cheerleader, and who on a bright summer day, despite all our best skills and technology, had no life left in her brain. Her mother, a single parent, and her maternal grandmother sat by her bedside and waited for the end.

Her transition from life to death was quiet and private. The nurse and I closed the curtains around the bed; I wrote the order, showed it to the nurse, and turned off the power to the ventilator. The nurse disconnected the alarms, and we took up our stations on opposite sides of the room. While the mother held her child's head and the grandmother her hand, I watched them and the clock. For some reason tears started rolling down my face.

---

8. Peter Carroll, "Frances Moore Lappés Diet for a Better World, *Utne Reader*, May/June, 1989, p. 42.

9. Gregory S. Liptak, "After a Death," *Journal of the American Medical Association*, Dec. 13, 1985, p. 3185.

10. Gregory S. Liptak, "Shining Brightly, Briefly," a part of a collective article, "What Children Teach Doctors," *Reader's Digest*, April 1985, pp. 153, 154. Reprinted with permission. From "After a Death," *Journal of the American Medical Association*, Dec. 13, 1985, v. 253, p. 3185. Copyright 1985, American Medical Association.

It is now considered acceptable for male professionals to cry at such times, as long as it is done noiselessly. Although I usually do not cry, I found myself crying for the life that had vanished, for the indescribable loneliness the mother would come to know, for the loss to the grandmother of a generation of women. I also cried for the child's regular physician who had misdiagnosed the meningitis — was I so vulnerable too? But mostly I cried for my children, two healthy young boys. Like the Chinese who mourn the death of a baby when it is born, I mourned the death of my children while I watched this young girl die. I now carry part of their dying with me.

One of the most disconcerting aspects about disconnecting children from ventilators is that life often leaves with great reluctance. They shudder and gasp and twitch and inevitably lead you to believe that you have made a mistake and should not have disconnected them. She, however, was kind to us, and the rhythm of her beads and braids ebbed quietly.

We stayed in our positions, frozen like characters in an Edward Hopper painting, waiting. When the prescribed amount of time had elapsed for her death to be legal, I talked with the family and encouraged them to spend some time with her. They thanked me for everything we had done, although we had not really "done" anything to save her.

As I walked back to my office I thought about a friend, an obstetrician, who was being sued for the "wrongful life" of a child born with Down's syndrome. He had failed to send the 37-year-old pregnant woman for an amniocentesis. I wondered how life could be wrongful and considered that nothing in my childhood or education or training had prepared me to deal with such perplexities.

When I graduated from medical school I started a crusade to protect life from the dragon of death. Very gradually since then, death has become a fellow traveler — sometimes welcome, although usually not. I have vowed never to help him do his trade, yet I understand him a little more now and sometimes even converse with him.

Driving home, I thought about my children, who had picked raspberries for me the night before. My wife had told them that one of my favorite foods is fresh raspberries for breakfast. No food tastes as good, yet none is as perishable. I decided to stop at a local store to buy a whiffle ball and bat to thank them and to celebrate their living.

Our family lives in the country, surrounded by so many living things that death is a frequent visitor — especially to our canaries, who have been bred for song and beauty rather than for hardiness. We have a ritual: when a bird dies, we make it into a star. We troop outside to the boundary of our yard and throw the small body high into the air and into the adjoining wheat field. The body disappears in the tall grain before hitting the ground and makes no sound. That evening during supper we talked about the girl, and our 3-year-old asked if we had made her into a star. I told him we had and would point it out to him that night if he were still awake. I also told him I had placed a quarter in her hand when she had died in case she had to make a phone call; "or play a video game," added our 5-year-old.

Friends often ask how I can do the work I do, especially the part dealing with death. I never know how to answer because I really do not know. Perhaps, like a gambler, I do it because I enjoy "getting high on the action"; perhaps, like the hangman, I do it because it is a job that someone must do; or perhaps I do it from a sense of duty, borne out by my having been an altar boy and by hearing since childhood stories of family members who had been in the seminary. I thought I usually protected myself, however, by trying not to feel.

That night I dreamed that the girl's mother and I had taken her body to the edge of our yard and swung it back and forth. We heaved it toward the wheat field and like the canaries it disappeared in midflight with no sound. I sat upright, and then walked into our boys' room. I kissed each on the forehead and adjusted their covers. I wondered why I did not feel more grief for this girl than I did, and I realized that I felt immense gratitude toward her. In her dying she was teaching me how to live.

In *Reader's Digest* Liptak's article appeared this way:

Shining Brightly, Briefly

She was a 14-year-old girl, an only child, who three days earlier had been practicing to be a cheerleader. Then meningitis struck. Now, on a bright summer day, despite all our skills and technology, she had no life left in her brain. Her mother, a single parent, and her maternal grandmother sat by her bedside and waited for the end.

The nurse and I closed the curtains around the bed, and I turned off the power to the ventilator. We took up stations on opposite sides of the room. While the mother held her child's head and the grandmother her hand, I watched them and the clock. For some reason tears started rolling down my face.

I have witnessed many deaths, and though I have been appropriately supportive, I usually do not cry. But now I found myself crying for the life that had vanished, for the indescribable loneliness the mother would come to know, for the loss to the grandmother of a generation of women. But also I cried for my own children, two healthy young boys. I mourned their inevitable death someday while I watched this girl die. I now carry part of their dying with me.

When dying children are disconnected from ventilators, life often leaves with great reluctance. But the rhythm of this girl's breathing ebbed gently. Her transition from life to death was quiet and private.

Later, driving home, I thought about my children, who had picked raspberries for me the night before. My wife had told them that one of my pleasures is fresh raspberries for breakfast. No food tastes as good, yet (like all truly precious things) none is as perishable. I decided to stop at a store for a ball and bat to thank them and to celebrate their living.

Our family dwells in the country, surrounded by so many living things that death is a frequent visitor — especially to our canaries, who have been bred for song and beauty rather than for hardiness. We have a ritual: when a bird dies, we make it into a star. We troop outside to the boundary of our yard and toss the small body high into the air toward the adjoining wheat field. The bird disappears in the tall grain and makes no sound. That evening during supper we talked about the girl, and our three-year-old asked if we had made her into a star. I told him we had and would point it out to him at bedtime.

That night I dreamed that the girl's mother and I took her to the edge of our yard and swung her back and forth. We heaved her to the wheat field, and like the canaries she disappeared soundlessly in midflight. I sat upright, and then walked into our boys' room. I kissed each one on the forehead and adjusted their covers. I felt immense gratitude toward the girl. In her dying she was teaching me how to live.

One member of a panel of *Digest* editors meeting with university magazine professors explained that the lead for the *Digest* version was chosen because it was like a "once upon a time" lead. "We like to tell stories, like a Bible parable which can get things across in the simplest of terms," said one of the editors. Some writers write longer articles than the required length, then trim them back, cutting out non-essentials, helping to achieve a firmer style.

Le Mot Juste

A good writing style almost always results from rewriting. Good writing requires not only careful cutting of needless words but also finding the "right" words. It was the 19th-century novelist, Gustave Flaubert, who insisted on *le mot juste*, the right word. In the preface to *Pierre et Jean*, Guy de Maupassant quotes Flaubert: "Whatever one wishes to say, there is one noun only by which to express it, one verb only to give it life, one adjective only which will describe it. One must search until one has discovered them, this noun, this verb, this adjective, and never rest content with approximations, never resort to trickery, however happy, or to vulgarisms, in order to dodge the difficulty."

Rewriting, and rewriting the rewriting, can make all the difference. "If you don't go through three complete drafts, you're not writing carefully," says *New Yorker* writer Robert C. Smith, former managing editor of *TV Guide*. "The organizing and the style come in the process," says Smith. "Usually in the early stages, you want just to get it said. Then you look at it. You admire the sentences; it just lies there, one damn paragraph after another. It is not charged with energy. You do not feel the writer has grabbed you by the arm to 'see.' . . . Logically it is just *this* after *that*, but there is not the feeling that the writer is excited about it. Style is a human voice: 'Listen to this!' The way it works for me is that I let it sit there. Then I say, 'what is really important about this piece?'" The search goes on for the right ideas and words. What's right also varies with the intended audience and market. Although, of course, there are exceptions, some generalities can be observed (see Table 9-1).

FICTION TECHNIQUES

In an article on feature writing in *Style* (published by the American Association of Sunday and Feature Editors), William E. Blundell makes the assumption that feature writing is basically storytelling. But few writers are storytellers, says Blundell, a *Wall Street Journal* editor, because they see themselves instead as lawyers arguing over right and wrong, as scholastics who "try to learn everything" and are "prisoners of their stories" or as objectivists. The objectivist is merely a "fact funnel" whose "work seldom sticks in the memory." Feature writers forget that they are storytellers above all, he says, and "as storytellers [they] are in the drama business."[11]

To enliven your prose with a sense of storytelling and drama, consider the following fiction techniques.

---

11. William E. Blundell, "Feature Writing Fears," *Style*, Summer 1989, p. 11. From William E. Blundell, *The Art and Craft of Feature Writing* (New York: New American Library, 1988).

Table 9-1. Comparisons of Writing Factors for Different Readers

	Public Relations Releases	Columns	News Features	Magazines
Audience	Head of company—editors, consumers	Casual reader, editor	Informational reader, editor	General reader and specialized, editor
Facts	Pack in	Selection	Selection	Selection
Point of View	Third person	First	Third	First, second or third
Anecdotes	Scarce—not a priority	One expanded anecdote	Many	Many
Sentences	Participial phrases	Short	Direct	Direct
Sound of Words	Not important	Very important	Important	Very important
Imagery	Not important	Very important	Important	Very important
Verbs	Past tense	Re-created present	Past tense	Re-created present, also past tense
Attribution	Said and said substitutes	Said	Said	Said

Create Traits

Avoid melodrama, which is peopled by wooden characters and stereotypes. In melodrama, characters are nondimensional—all good or all bad. Let the reader see the various sides of your characters. The good person has at least one flaw; the bad person has some spark of divinity. This doesn't mean you have to resort to character assassination every time you write about someone. By no means. But even Mother Teresa can be made real by discussing some of her controversial causes. An alleged Mafia leader might have irresistible charm and a soft spot for children. A review of James Michener's book, *Alaska*, analyzes his mastery of this technique:

> Mr. Michener is adept at manipulating our sympathies. No one in the book is entirely good or evil, not even the fictional Captain Shransky of the black ship Erebus, who, the author imagines, refined the practice of corrupting Alaska's natives with liquor, and perfected the art of "pelagic sealing," or "chasing down the seals, most of them gravid females, when they were in the open sea totally defenseless, slaughtering them with ease, and ripping from their wombs the partly formed young whose skins had a special appeal in China."

We actually admire the energy and resourcefulness of one Thomas Venn, another fictional character, as he advances in the firm of Ross & Raglan, even though the canning factory he runs is depriving the Tlingit Indians of their native fishing rights and depleting their environment of the magnificent sockeye salmon.[12]

Set the Scene

If readers feel that they're part of a scene or location, they better experience the dramatic impact of a story or article. In one of a series of feature articles for which she won the Pulitzer Prize in 1980, Madeleine Blais very literally set the scene, as she wrote about Tennessee Williams:

> The scene: Tennessee Williams' house on Duncan Street in Key West, a small, simple, white-frame house with red shutters and a picket fence. The time is late February, day's end. The living room is dominated by books and art. Out back is a studio where Williams works every day, seven days a week, waking up about 5 in the morning and sometimes using a Bloody Mary, if need be, "to overcome the initial timidity." He has often said, "I work everywhere, but I work best here." Under a skylight, surrounded by empty wine bottles and paint-caked brushes, seated before a manual typewriter, he awaits sunrise and inspiration. On Key West, there is a great ethic of sunset, but the playwright stalks the dawn.
>
> Williams is sitting on the patio adjoining the house. He has arisen late from an afternoon nap and his face is still puffy with sleep. In a few hours, he will attend the opening of one of his plays at a local theater. From where he sits, there is a view of the backyard, which is dominated by a swimming pool, strangled weeds and trampled plants. Williams glances with dismay at the untended growth snaking toward the pool.
>
> "My gardener was shot, you know. . . ."[13]

Your nonfiction writing should avoid the mistake many beginners make in fiction — stringing out the story too much. Consider a romantic tale of a young man and young woman in the big city. He is coming over to see her. He gets out of the car, he walks into the complex, finds the elevator, boards it, gets off, rings the bell on the door and enters. Better to place him in the apartment or at the door to begin with. Then space can be given to the electrifying dialogue and development of the theme.

From Tolstoy to Hemingway to Ray Bradbury, the single-scene story has power. A Ray Bradbury story in *Playboy*, "Heart Transplant," takes place in one room — in about 20 minutes, marked by conversation and a phone call.

You can learn about dramatic structure from the format of a stage play. Think about the last play you saw. While some productions (*Les Misérables*,

12. Christopher Lehmann-Haupt, "Michener's Cautionary Tale of the 49th State," New York *Times*, June 23, 1988, p. C21. Copyright © 1988 by The New York Times Company. Reprinted by permission.

13. Madeleine Blais, "Three Scenes in the Life of a Tormented Playwright," *Miami Herald*, April 1979.

for instance) become a showplace for rotating and changing sets, most dramatic productions are characterized by space and time limitations. Some plays also are marked by a paucity of props (*Agnes of God* had only a few chairs on stage), as well as tightness in the number of scenes and time span. How many plays have you seen where the program announces three acts — early morning, late afternoon and evening of the same day?

The effects of dramatic limitations can be put to use in nonfiction articles and feature writing. Compression makes anything — almost anything — sharper. Compression does not necessarily have anything to do with length. Franz Kafka's *The Metamorphosis*, a lengthy short story, takes place largely in one room.

Limiting the framework of time, the number of scenes and the "set" itself makes for exciting nonfiction. It works in profiles, even in books on people's lives, as Jim Bishop demonstrated in his books *The Day Lincoln Was Shot*, *The Day Christ Died*, *The Day Kennedy Was Shot* and *FDR's Last Year*. Even a story of an institution or an enterprise can be told as "a day in the life of. . . ." Consider a day in the life of a bouquet of Valentine roses, as chronicled by the New York *Times*.[14]

A Story of 12 Roses on Their Big Day

Before Paula Howard could sniff the dozen red roses she received for Valentine's Day in Manhattan yesterday, they had to be flown from California to Newark with thousands of others, trucked through the Holland Tunnel, sorted on West 28th Street, driven to Second Avenue and delivered to 59th Street and Lexington Avenue.

All in 24 hours.

For Valentine's Day, the biggest day of the year for roses, thousands of roses make their way into New York vases from as far off as South America, France and the Netherlands. This is the story of 12 of them.

Miss Howard's bouquet started its journey at L. Piazza growers in Oakland, Calif. Her flowers were part of a shipment that arrived at Newark International Airport at 9:47 p.m. on a DC-10 from San Francisco. By midnight, Dominic Coppola of D & J Flower Express, a shipping company, was there with his 24-foot truck.

'Little Last-Minute Stuff'

Mr. Coppola, 24 years old, spent the next few hours heaving onto his truck 110 boxes of ice-packed flowers — each about 100 pounds. But Mr. Coppola said it was a light load; the bulk of the Valentine's Day roses had already come.

"Last week, I had about 280 a night," he said. "This is the night before Valentine's — just little last-minute stuff." Last night, he said, the 110

---

boxes were worth about $15,000. Last week, when shopping was at its peak, 30 boxes were worth $30,000.

By 2:50 a.m., Miss Howard's roses were heading through the Holland Tunnel en route to West 28th Street — Roses Row — where wholesale stores like W. M. Kessler were waiting.

At 4 a.m., while many New Yorkers were dreaming heart-shaped dreams, West 28th Street was alive with men in flannel jackets, faded jeans and heavy boots, handling an incongruously delicate cargo of baby's breath, tulips and thousands of roses.

The Day of the Rose

Miss Howard's roses were included in Mr. Coppola's final delivery, to W. M. Kessler's, a smaller outlet on the 28th Street strip between the Avenue of the Americas and Broadway. There, Joe Gulotta, one owner of Kessler's, wasted no time in slapping the boxes on tables and slicing through the twine with a jackknife.

Although the store had stacks of such exotic flowers as birds of paradise from Costa Rica, Liatrus from the Netherlands and gladiolas from Brazil, yesterday was clearly the day of the rose, and the color of choice was no surprise.

"Red is the biggest seller because red means love," Mr. Gulotta said. "Red means passion."

At 7:53 a.m., Andy Turshen, who owns Accent on Flowers on Second Avenue between 58th and 59th Streets, stopped in to buy 125 long-stemmed red Royalty roses. Like most retailers, he had purchased most of his roses days before, and these were last-minute orders.

'They're Beautiful'

At 8:50 a.m., Mr. Turshen pruned 12 of his new roses and arranged them in a box on a bed of white wax flowers with a water well attached to each stem.

At 9:20, a young man named Jimmy delivered the flowers to the arms of Miss Howard, 22, a part-time systems analyst at Bloomingdale's. (They were from her fiancé, Charles.) "They're beautiful," she said, beaming.

But Mr. Coppola, the shipping driver, said that if he had his way, Miss Howard would not be receiving roses at all.

"Now that I'm in the flower business and I know more about flowers," he said, "I like to give girls calla lilies."

An article in the *Times* in August 1989 centered on the day in the life of a drug stakeout team in Times Square.

Select Significant Detail

Already mentioned in several contexts in this book, significant detail is essential to all writing. In magazine writing, the use of significant detail lets the writer meet space limitations as well as construct an image. As free-lance writer Max Gunther once put it:

> As a magazine article writer I battled continually with space limitations. "No more than three thousand words," an editor would say — and in my experience, when he said that, he meant it. I was always looking for ways to say something in as few words as possible. In particular, I trained myself to observe and remember the one or two telling details that would help me describe a person, a room, the mood of a crowd, the emotional aura of a building.

While interviewing somebody I would hunt deliberately for such details. I would tell myself: "I want the readers to see this woman as I see her, but I can't spend a paragraph on her. She gets one sentence. What is it about this face that clutches me?" . . .[15]

Consider the significant detail—the right detail—in this article by David Zucchino in the Philadelphia *Inquirer*. The article is part of a nine-article series that won Zucchino the Pulitzer Prize in 1989 for feature writing.

Note how, in the second paragraph, the "damp dirt" and the clothes smelling of tear gas contribute to a somber mood and how, in the fourth paragraph from the end of the article, the description of the dead man's clothes speaks of the injustices.[16]

Even in Death, the "System" Challenges

TUMAHOLE, South Africa — It was not done the proper way, the old man said. The burial of his son had been spoiled, and it pained him that his final memory of the young man was so stained by discontent.

The damp dirt of his son's grave stuck in the shoes of Joseph Nakedi. His clothes smelled of tear gas. His wife was weeping. He could hear the rumble of police armored vehicles along the dirt path outside his shack.

Johannes Lefu Nakedi had just been buried on Oct. 10 in the windswept veld of the Orange Free State, his funeral watched from a safe distance by a crush of security police with shotguns and bullet-proof vests. The mourners had been tear-gassed. The priests had been bundled into a riot vehicle. "Hippos" — troop carriers — roared up and down the roads, scattering and panicking the black children of Tumahole township.

The confrontation seemed to define the short life of Lefu Nakedi, an activist who had challenged the system and was ultimately killed by it. He was just 23, fresh from another stretch of detention, when he was shot dead by the Green Beans — killed one midnight by the black township police in their distinctive green uniforms.

To the South African police, Nakedi was a terrorist. They said he had attacked a Green Bean with a knife and was shot dead to prevent the officer's murder. They said, too, that the young blacks of the Tumahole Youth Congress, which Nakedi had led, had supplied fellow blacks with hand grenades for use against the authorities.

But Joseph Nakedi believes his son was murdered. The police could not break or silence him even after 15 months in detention, the old man thought, so they lured him to a trap and killed him.

Now Nakedi, a common laborer, totaled up the many ways that "the system" — as blacks call white rule — had encroached on his life. Long

---

15. Max Gunther, "Fiction and Nonfiction Writing — Interchangeable Skills," *The Writer*, October 1980, p. 16.

16. David Zucchino, "Even in Death, the 'System' Challenges," Philadelphia *Inquirer*, Dec. 11, 1989.

before Lefu was killed, there were regular visits by the security police in the dead of night. His shack was watched, photos were taken. Lefu was detained for 13 months, then for two months. Another son, Benedict, was detained for 13 months. It seemed to Joseph Nakedi that the police lived at his place.

And the infringements did not end even with the claiming of his son's life by the system. It claimed his funeral, too.

Since June 1986, South Africa's black townships have been smothered by a state of emergency that now intrudes on the most prosaic aspects of daily life. The emergency dictates whether a book may be read, a pamphlet distributed, a meeting held, a speech delivered, a detainee visited, a funeral held. People may be detained without charge or trial or access to a lawyer. Police need no warrant to break in and search a house. Sometimes an activist is taken away and simply disappears.

Tens of thousands of black families in South Africa have suffered somehow because of emergency rule. About 32,000 people have been detained, and civil rights groups say at least 1,200 of them are still in custody. Countless others live in fear that they or someone they know will be detained, questioned, restricted, banned, informed upon, wounded or killed.

The government says emergency rule is necessary to protect the majority of the country's 26 million blacks from intimidation and death at the hands of black revolutionaries bent on a "total onslaught" against law and order. No government, it says, would fail to take the same action against terrorists who openly seek to overthrow the state. Ordinary laws are not sufficient to deal with these radicals, Pretoria says, but law-abiding blacks need not fear detention or harassment.

Joseph Nakedi has broken no laws. Nor had his son, he insists, but what happened to them happens often to black activists who challenge the state.

Lefu worked at an advice office run by the Tumahole Civic Association, an affiliate of the restricted United Democratic Front. The office supplies legal advice and small sums of money for families of detainees and others affected by apartheid laws or emergency rule. The government portrays such offices as instigators of unrest.

The authorities are particularly suspicious of Tumahole. In 1984, the township, about 75 miles south of Johannesburg, was the first in South Africa to resist rent increases, thus helping to trigger the great township revolt of 1984 to 1986. It is still known as a "hot" township. At least 60 local activists have been detained, and 10 more have been shot dead by the police in the last four years.

Four weeks after Nakedi was killed, another Tumahole Youth Congress leader was shot dead by the Green Beans. The Civic Association released a statement the next day: "We perceive a concerted effort by agents of the system to break the resistance of the people by systematically eliminating activists."

A police spokesman in Pretoria declined to discuss the specifics of either killing beyond brief police statements already released. He said anyone who felt abused by the police could file a formal complaint.

Through the Civic Association, Joseph Nakedi has been provided a Johannesburg lawyer who intends to challenge the police in court. Nakedi said Lefu had been harassed by the Green Beans, who would stop him on the street, search him and threaten to kill him. He said that the night Lefu was killed, he was asked by a young woman to accompany him to a *shebeen* — a nightclub. The woman, Nakedi alleged, is a police informer.

At the *shebeen*, Lefu was shot in the eye, the back and the right arm. He died instantly.

"From that day on, the police have interfered in every single thing we have done," Nakedi said, speaking in the southern Sotho dialect of the area. "We did not have the right to bury our son in our own private way. We were not allowed even to mourn him in the proper way."

The family tried to have a night vigil — the all-night venting of grief at the home of the deceased. The police imposed a time limit and re-

continued

continued

stricted the number of mourners to 80. The Johannesburg lawyer, Priscilla Jana, managed to have the restrictions eased.

The funeral itself was even more heavily restricted. Because of bloody confrontations between mourners and police at highly politicized funerals during the 1984–1986 uprisings, the authorities severely restrict burials. In Nakedi's case, they even restricted access to the corpse at the funeral home. The family was permitted to see Lefu's body only after the lawyer intervened.

The police sent Nakedi a series of letters that quoted at length from the complex emergency laws. There were to be no more than 300 mourners. The memorial and burial could last no more than three hours, from 10 a.m. to 1 p.m. Only an ordained minister could speak. And "no ceremonial gathering, insofar as it takes the form of a memorial service for Johannes Lefu Nakedi . . . shall be held out of doors."

Nakedi was issued 300 slips of white paper. Each contained a number from 1 to 300 — one "ticket" for each guest — and the words *Funeral* and *The late Lefu NAKEDI.* They were stamped with something that offended Nakedi: the official blue stamp of the Suid-Afrikaanse Polisie, the police. Nakedi could not insult his friends and family with these things. He refused to hand them out.

On the day of the funeral, the police surrounded Nakedi's corrugated metal shack and ordered the mourners to disperse. Some of the *amaqabane* — the young men who call themselves "comrades" — began the *toyi-toyi,* the rhythmic chanting and dancing that so antagonizes the police. Tear gas was fired, and three young men were arrested.

The two priests were dragged into a riot vehicle and taken to St. John the Baptist Catholic Church at the edge of the township. There, a rushed memorial service began.

A white Dominican priest, the Rev. Jan Jansen, compared Lefu's work to the work of Jesus. "He sought the liberation of his own oppressed people," he said of Lefu, speaking in Southern Sotho. Though it was illegal, a few comrades stood up and said the revolution would continue in Lefu's name, that the "racist regime" would be toppled.

Across the street outside, police commanders stood in a drizzle, bored, and swung imaginary cricket bats at imaginary balls. An officer with a gun on his hip filmed the service with a video camera so that informers could later identify people in the crowd.

When the mourners emerged from the church, an officer told Father Jansen that no one would be allowed to walk to the gravesite. They would have to take vehicles. But no one had a car; it was a small township.

A nun tugged at Father Jansen's arm. "Can't you talk to them?" she said of the police.

"No, I have tried," the priest said. "It's like Germany before the war. Orders are orders."

Soon some taxis were arranged and everyone piled in, some mourners standing on the bumpers. A few fell off and had to roll quickly out of the street to avoid the huge wheels of the armored vehicles that followed the procession. One Hippo had the words *Kiss Me* painted on the front.

The burial was a brief and chaotic affair held in an open field next to other graves in a pasture where cows grazed in the chilly spring air. The police watched through binoculars from atop their Hippos as Father Jansen said a few words and Lefu's damp-eyed mother, Lydia, wrapped in a wool blanket and supported by two women, tossed a handful of dirt on her son's coffin.

Sharp whistles and shouting broke out, like a sudden stiff wind. There were screams of *"Amandla!"*—"power!"— and *"Voetsek!"*—an expression used to shoo away a dog. It was directed at the police, who stiffened at the sound but kept their distance.

Then it was over, and the taxis and the Hippos roared back to Nakedi's little shack. A funeral tent had been attached to the shack. Inside, guests ate a mourning meal of pap and mince — corn meal and ground meat — and tried to talk over the roar of the Hippos on the pathway outside.

In a burlap bag inside the shack were kept the dead man's clothes. Someone pulled them out. There was a scarlet shirt with a gunshot hole in the arm and a nylon ski jacket stained brown with dried blood.

Joseph Nakedi sat down in a heap. He was worn out. Everything had gone wrong. This was a miserable way to say goodbye to his son.

He knew this was not the end of it. Just two nights earlier, he said, the Green Beans had roused him from his sleep and told him they would rip down his shack if he caused any trouble. He did not consider himself a man easily cowed — a sign in his yard said "Beware of the owner — never mind the dog" — but he feared for himself and his family.

There was a living activist son to worry about: Benedict, just 18, but already familiar with a detention cell. The old man mentioned something the Green Beans had done the other night. They had pointed to Benedict and said: "Careful — maybe he's next."

Atmosphere

Atmosphere is often thought of as geographical or environmental. The mist from the sea, the sun striking through the clouds, the grinding and sinking of sand beneath the feet. But atmosphere — whether a sense of dampness (as cited in the Zucchino article) that affects the soul or a brightness and airiness throughout — may be more of an illusion than a tangible reality. Whether real or conjured, atmosphere involves the senses in a real way.

Tone

Tone is embodied in the resonance and position of words. Tone in writing is akin to "tone of voice" in speech.

Tone (attitude) can be different from theme (which is a statement such as "injustice abounds") or atmosphere (gloominess). The opera *Carmen* has a lightheartedness, but underneath all the gaiety of music is a somber tone and voice. You know all is not well. The opera *Faust* has its moments of celebration and festiveness and even a triumphal ascension into heaven at the end for the wronged heroine, but the tone is foreboding and tragic. The composer wills it so, and the symbols and the direction of development prepare for the characters' tragic destiny.

Tension

A story or article establishes tension by contrasting the character traits of a subject, producing and sharpening a conflict. A profile on a sports figure or politician, with the various good and bad traits given in contrast prior to resolution and conclusion, has tension. Tension in writing is achieved in part by the choice of subject, characters, setting; events that are anachronistic or sudden might put things off kilter and "tense" the story or article. Mysteries create suspense as a way to charge the piece with tension. If a writer withholds clues, promises information that is not readily delivered, asks puzzling questions with implications for the future, the reader is on edge.

Foreshadowing

Only if a piece has a sense of continuity, of connectedness over time, will your attempts to create tension and atmosphere — and, to some extent, tone — succeed. One way to achieve continuity is through the technique of foreshadowing — "planting" ideas and clues that anticipate the outcome.

Methods of foreshadowing include symbolism (clenched fists, a broken vase, a near drowning), description, dialogue and parable. Frames, like a Greek chorus or flashbacks or flash-forwards, point to an outcome. Authorial intrusion in a narrative hints at or reveals an ending and creates tension: "If he only knew what would happen, he would not have made that choice." Whatever the case, foreshadowing aids suspense and adds to clarity of direction and continuity. The technique works in nonfiction: An article on safety, be it with motorcycles, airplanes or elevators — a hint of a violation can be given at the beginning of the article or extended anecdote and the predictable result seen later.

TRANSITIONS

Good writing flows from point to point; this kind of movement requires transitions. *Transition* comes from Latin words meaning "to go across," thus "get there from here." In effective writing, sentences flow into sentences and paragraphs into paragraphs.

Common criticisms of new writers — in news, feature or magazine writing — include the tendency to abruptly move from subject to subject between sentences and paragraphs. Remember, people don't just read articles. They "see" them. Repeating a subject — a name or an idea — from sentence to sentence — re-anchors the reader.

Repetition is used to the maximum — and effectively — in the newsmagazines. Readers have no doubt where they are or what's being talked about in newsmagazine articles. The subject — the lead noun — is repeated verbatim or as a pronoun. Note the repetition of the subject in this piece in *Time* on Mikhail Gorbachev [**boldface** is ours]:

> What Mikhail Gorbachev wants, whether it is a policy change or an official appointment, **Mikhail Gorbachev** usually gets. Through nearly six years in power, **he** has put together an almost unbroken winning streak at contentious parliamentary sessions and Communist Party meetings. **He** did it again last week in the Congress of People's Deputies — taking some nasty thumps along the way — when he managed to ram through another political reorganization that further strengthens his hand. But **he** acknowledged this hard-won victory with a tone of finality and a warning. "I intend to act as President," he said, gathering up his papers on the final day of the session. "So don't be surprised."
>
> **Gorbachev** has accumulated unprecedented powers — on paper. In practice, **he** is finding it increasingly difficult to rule. Only a week earlier Foreign Minister Eduard Shevardnadze had shocked everyone by announcing his res-

ignation in protest against what he called an approaching dictatorship. **Gorbachev** then proceeded to behave as if determined to lend substance to that prediction. **He** pushed through constitutional amendments last week that subordinate all government departments and policies to the will of the President, then forced the reluctant Deputies to accept his choice of a colorless communist loyalist as the county's first Vice President. . . .[17]

Other methods of transition are used to effect here—the words *again, another, then*—and also, the juxtaposition of "on paper" and "in practice."

Connecting words, such as *and, but, however, nevertheless, according to* can be used sparingly. Ordinarily you would steer clear of the multisyllabic connector (*nevertheless, however*) and opt for the simple word. But in newsmagazines the writing is so lean that the writers and editors get away with using transitional words that would seem dull in most prose.

Highlighting a theme—literally and figuratively—keeps a reader on track. If a person has a "cool" personality or a "hot" temper, repeat the words "cold" or "hot," maybe even allude to the cold or hot environment to keep the special feeling alive in the article. *Time* magazine has used "heating up" vocabulary—literally and figuratively—in profiling a "hot" new entertainer.

An orderly sequence gets the reader to the next point without effort. If you have a first point, then look for the second, and so on. Words like *then* and *next* and numbered lists help.

Typographical devices—such as "bullets" (dots)—preceding a sentence or paragraph help to group ideas and create a logical path to follow. Italicizing the first words in a list (as done here) is another way to indicate the grouping of ideas.

Contrast sets up the next stage. If you give a woman's viewpoint, you might also need that of a man; a Republican, a Democrat; an adult, a youth. Provide expert opinion from each end of the spectrum.

Narrative development has its natural beginning, middle and end to provide structure and movement.

Poetic devices, in addition to repetition (a strong poetic device), can be signposts that point the article forward, such as use of alliteration, similes, metaphors and a sense of rhythm.

Interruptions, if dramatic and clear-cut, ironically make a reader leap into what follows. Sometimes a real gully—some extra white space on the printed page—is left between paragraphs or segments, in effect telling the reader to now start again.

Familiar tags work in some cases, but beware of doing very much labeling or stereotyping. You try to get away from clichés and generalities, but some universal characteristics persist that are not offensive to particular groups: the antics of children, the scenes and humor of family life, the stress and boredom

17. Bruce W. Nelan, "Soviet Union: A Slippery Slope," *Time*, Jan. 7, 1991, p. 60.

of corporate life can be anticipated in particular articles by analogies and familiar words and thus have the effect of transitions. Words like "white collar," "upwardly mobile," "pin-striped" suits — clichés and stereotypes — conjuring up a familiar image might be used in a feature on junior executives, from paragraph to paragraph.

Creating a scene or setting allows description and significant details to hold the reader to a confined place. If you can see a room, or an area, even a town or city, where the article is happening, and see all the action in this context, you will feel you are there and move forward with the article.

As you write an article, check to see which of the methods — or others you might think of — are getting you from paragraph to paragraph, even from sentence to sentence.

VOICE

An article without a "voice" is like an ice cream sundae without a flavor. An article without a voice has no vocal cords, no body language, no way to express feelings or disposition.

"Voice is the sound of a writer," says *American Health* senior editor Robert Barnett. "You can read any great novelist, and in three sentences, you will know whether it is Hemingway or Faulkner or another."

Voice is the sound of you. It catches up your experience, your outlook, the regionalism and charm of your speech, your disposition. While voice may come through various points of view (that is, the eyes through which you tell the story), there is still no getting away from "you," the author.

Voice, like charisma, cannot be adequately defined. Like the essence of a person, it cannot be pinned down and dissected.

Lee Eisenberg, *Esquire*'s former editor-in-chief, says voice is an "attitude. It's not writing by the book. You express your self. It's idiosyncratic. It's playing a little and opening up for some magic."

A writer may use different voices for different pieces. "Voice can change," says Madeleine Blais. "There are different kinds of voices: a comic voice, minimalist voice, no voice (pretending not to have one), ethnic, feminist. The problem with journalists writing, they think they should have one voice: a conscience, a stern voice. Some assume the same tone for all they write."

Carey Winfrey, editor-in-chief of the popular but now defunct *Memories* and new editor of *American Health*, says voice reflects a "star quality — all eyes go to that person." Voice also is "the way you string it together, the point of view, idiosyncrasies, twist, the unexpected. You approach the material from 8 or 12 degrees out, from an unconventional tack, because a person has his own unique way of looking at it."

A magazine will seek to include diverse voices.

Patrice Adcroft, former editor of *Omni*, says "*Omni* is not exactly a Greek chorus. It's very eclectic, with a lot of voices. We try to maintain a writer's personality."

Writers have their views on "voice."

- "'Voice' is the center of gravity of your expression that characterizes the mood of the piece." — Richard Cummings, who writes for New York *Times* and *Newsday* among others.

- "It is both the special choice of material one chooses to write about and the special style and mood that one brings to an article. It has centrally to do with emotional feelings an author brings to his/her article." — Harriet Harvey, *New Yorker*, *Vogue*.

- "'Voice' to me is a stylistic characteristic that comprises grammar usage, one's point of view, the structure of a piece and how it is approached. It's something eccentric, often idiosyncratic and above all individualistic." — Bob Diddlebock, San Francisco *Examiner*, Los Angeles *Times*, Dallas Morning *News*, Boston *Globe*.

- "I consider my 'voice' to be my personality — pace, rhythms and point of view — which comes through no matter how I approach a piece." — Pam Hait, *Ladies' Home Journal*, *Omni*, *Working Mother*.

Writing in "voice" has its obstacles. Diddlebock cites as an obstacle "adhering to the strictures of 'objectivity,' if you're writing a newspaper story, or not having researched your subject matter thoroughly enough to gain command of the topic in order to speak authoritatively on the issue at hand." According to Harvey, what makes voice difficult is being courageous enough to bare your soul — expose your own feelings, without relying on others' evaluation of the project or circumstances." She cites Tolstoy in effect: "'One ought only to write when one leaves a piece of flesh in the inkpot each time one dips one's pen.' This is imperative." An obstacle to "voice," says Cummings, is "not having an emotional response to your material."

Does "voice" have anything to do with the "point of view" (first, second, third person) from which the article is written? "To a certain degree (voice is distinguishable from a literary point of view), but it cannot be isolated or divorced from the fabric of the story or article," says Diddlebock. Says Harvey: "Yes, it's different. A 'literary point of view' is more an analytical approach which has more to do with knowledge and reason than with emotional response. The two, of course, can't be separated completely. They influence one another, but 'voice' is the emotional thumbprint of the author and has more to do with synthesis rather than analysis." Yes, "voice" and "point of view" are distinguishable, says Hait: "It ['voice'] is the written 'voice print' — a strong voice always is recognizable regardless of style of a story (i.e., objective, reportorial, etc.)."

FIRST-PERSON POINT OF VIEW

You will likely use various viewpoints for your articles, but there's always the temptation to put yourself into an article, to tell the article through the first person, "I." This first-person technique is difficult for many writers to master; too much of the writer can find its way into the article. However, when you write for slick national magazines, "I" is a serviceable point of view. "'I' gives you immediate contact with the reader," says *Guideposts'* Van Varner. "There is no intermediary, nobody in the way."

Since writing in the first person is difficult, editors advise the beginning writer to consider the third-person point of view. "You can hide behind the third person," says Pamela Fiori of American Express publications. And that is what the beginner should do, she says. "Start writing third person and know the techniques. Keep a distance from the subject, then as experience grows, you come 'out of the closet,' so to speak. As an inexperienced writer, one really doesn't have much to say. Build up experience. When I started I had nothing to say. Now I have a lot to get off my chest."

Early in her career as a writer *Mothers Today*'s Janet Spencer King found it difficult to put herself into an article. "And usually I edited it [I] out. Then I learned how to pace and then did so sparingly: One problem in a first-person essay, it bogs down with detail. Does a reader really need to know [all the details]? First person has to be a little tighter, and not too serious."

Good writers temper the ego inherent in the first-person point of view with humor and a glimpse of their own vulnerability. Diddlebock says you avoid "'sledge hammering' the reader with all your knowledge and grasp of the subject matter. Low-key, subtle use of the language usually helps."

The following three examples show how point of view works as a literary technique.

In this article that starts with a second-person or "you" lead, consider the sense of drama and immediacy:

> At 7 p.m., the phone rings.
> *Hello, Mr./Ms. Your Name, this is Sweet-Voiced Complete Stranger from the Please Buy Our Product Co. How are you tonight?*
> Oh, no — not again.
> *Mr./Ms. Your Name, the reason I am calling is to see if you know about the complete line of quality goods offered by the Please Buy Our Product Co., such as the Unbelievably Wonderful X and the Terrifically Practical Y. Are you acquainted with our products?*
> About now, dinner has turned tepid, the family is yelling and you're not feeling too charitable toward that insufferably peppy voice on the phone. Every available epithet springs from your lips before you slam down the phone with nary a "thank you" or "goodbye." . . .[18]

In this first-person example, note the sense of involvement and a greater appeal to the emotions.

> The results of my blood-cholesterol test in January jumped out at me from the laboratory report: total cholesterol of 236. That's only 4 points short of

---

18. Karen Heller, "A Job with Hang-ups," Philadelphia *Inquirer*, Jan. 25, 1989, p. F1.

240, the level that marks the beginning of the borderline high-risk zone for heart attacks.

My levels fell in the 201 to 239 range, which is associated with a moderately high risk of a heart attack. Above 240, the risk of heart attacks rises steeply. Cholesterol measurements are given as milligrams of cholesterol per deciliter (a deciliter is nearly 3½ ounces) of blood.

But I recalled what Dr. Gustav Schonfeld, director of Washington University's Division of Atherosclerosis and Lipid Research, had told me once: "You can have your high cholesterol 'cured' just by going to a different laboratory." . . .[19]

In this third-person lead, the author creates a mood, as well as a little distance from the subject.

SURIN, Thailand — "Elephant boy, what's your name?"

Seated 12 feet above the ground, on the neck of his elephant, the young man pondered the question a moment from behind a pair of dark sunglasses. "Me? Or my elephant?" was his reply.

He was Theing. His elephant was Bunmah — "bearer of merit." And this was the Surin elephant roundup.

The roundup is a national event that is a sort of combination trade fair, festival and barebacked elephant rodeo. . . .[20]

STYLE COMMANDMENTS

Writers were asked to give five rules for developing a good style:

For Johanna Garfield, writer for *McCall's*, *Reader's Digest*, *Seventeen*, New York *Times*, these rules would be:

- Brainstorm
- Organize ideas
- Start to write
- Revise
- Revise

Carol Weston, *Cosmopolitan*, *Glamour*, *Woman's Day*, *Young Miss*, *McCall's*:

- Read what you've written aloud to make sure it sounds OK.
- Let what you've written rest for a day or more so that you can edit it with a fresh eye.

19. Roger Signor, "The Cholesterol Roller Coaster," St. Louis *Post-Dispatch*, June 28, 1988, p. D1.

20. Rod Nordland, "A Thai Rodeo, of Sorts," Philadelphia *Inquirer*, Dec. 16, 1979, p. D1.

- Always have a notebook in which you can jot down anecdotes or turns of phrase.
- Let someone you trust look over your work before submitting it for publication (with luck this person will be critical, but gentle, too).
- Strengthen and tighten. Get rid of mamby pamby words like "nice," fancy words like "hence" and long-winded phrases like "at this point in time." Search for *le mot juste* instead of padding your article with adjectives and nonsense.

Linda-Marie Singer, King Features Syndicate:

- Once you establish what your style is, it's almost like asking that sophomoric question, 'Who am I?' You write the way you write, and it's unnecessary to copy the speech patterns of, let's say, Hemingway. There's only one Hemingway, and only one you. Live with it. Stop trying to fit someone else's mold.

ASSIGNMENTS

1. Report on your favorite writer — drawing from your own reading (books, magazines, newspapers) or from readings in a literature course. What characterizes this person's style?
2. See how many examples of *le mot juste* you can find on a feature page in a newspaper or magazine.
3. Analyze what you as a person bring to "style" from your philosophy, personality and experience.
4. Find an article that could be an inspiration for a good short story or novel and discuss why.
5. Take a *Reader's Digest* article and find the original from which it was condensed. Try your own condensation of the original, then compare your version with the lean *Reader's Digest* version.
6. Take an effective newspaper feature or magazine article and underline the significant detail.
7. Take a page of *Time* or *Newsweek* and underline the transitional words, ideas and devices.
8. With a paragraph or two from a famous writer in front of you, write a paragraph definition of "voice" independent of other class members. Compare definitions.
9. Compare a paragraph of your writing to a paragraph from the work of a famous writer.
10. Find what you consider a dull piece of writing in the media. What "stylistically" would make it more interesting?

CHAPTER 10

Investigative Articles

The term *investigative reporting* (or *investigative writing*) sometimes frightens people. On the one hand, the persons who are subjects of these reports worry that the results will be negative. However, investigative reporting can be positive: it can describe how to shop wisely for a particular product or how to file a complaint in court.

On the other hand, writers themselves may be uncomfortable with the term. After the Watergate investigations of the early 1970s when Bob Woodward and Carl Bernstein helped topple a president, investigative reporting acquired a certain cachet. Investigative reporters, it seemed, wrote mostly about powerful people and organizations; their research took months or even years. But, in fact, investigative reporting isn't always so epic in scope. Even beginning writers can find a manageable subject and produce a piece in a reasonable amount of time.

Some journalists dislike the standard definition of investigative reporting. They feel that it's not just exposé reporting. These journalists prefer to equate investigative reporting with in-depth reporting that leaves no stones unturned and uses multiple sources. New York *Times* investigative reporter Selwyn Raab, for instance, says he doesn't like the term *investigative journalism* and prefers to talk of "enterprise and patience." Wes Gallagher, former general manager of the Associated Press, believes that if writers do a competent day-by-day job, there is no need for investigative reporters. Earl Caldwell, former New York *Times* investigative reporter, argues that all reporting worth anything is investigative.

Pulitzer Prize–winning feature writer Madeleine Blais says, "All writing is discovery. Even the smallest brite [short bright item] can be investigative of something — the way the ocean looks in autumn. Lengthy features are by nature investigative; for example, an article on crack overtaking a neighborhood, an article on abuse."

Says Kathleen Neumeyer, who writes for the Los Angeles *Times*, *Los Angeles Magazine* and economics and legal journals: "My definition of an investigative article is a story which cannot be told by talking to only one person or researching in only one area. To do an investigative story, the reporter must talk to many different people and conduct original research. The result is a new creation — something which did not exist before. Most of the investigative stories I write are a result of talking to 10, 20, even 50 different sources and integrating the information I have culled into one cohesive article."

Samuel Greengard, who has written for *Los Angeles Magazine* and *Playboy*, makes a distinction on another level. Investigative articles, he says, "are far more work;" they involve "a greater level of responsibility" and "potential legal problems." Douglas Foster, editor of *Mother Jones*, prefers to think in terms of "exposure" rather than "exposé." He's interested in articles of systemic dimensions that get at the heart of institutionalized and corporate society.

While *Mother Jones*, *Common Cause* and other such "watchdog" publications deal largely with investigative pieces, most general magazines include them as well. For example, consider these articles: *New York* ("What Really Happened in Central Park?" — reconstructing the lives of alleged assailants in a brutal attack on a female jogger), *Modern Maturity* ("Murky Waters" — evidence of new exploitation of the oceans), *Cosmopolitan* ("Morning Television: The Mayhem Behind the Scenes"), *Woman's Day* ("How to Get the Most out of Medical Insurance"), *Vanity Fair* ("Investigation: How General Zia Went Down," an in-depth look at the crash that killed Pakistan's president), *Southern Exposure* ("Ruling the Roost: What's Bigger Than Tobacco, More Dangerous Than Mining, and Foul to Eat?" — a group of articles on the dangerous and degrading conditions and abuse of workers in the chicken industry) and *Consumer Reports* ("Beyond Medicare," an untangling of the muddle of Medicare services and how to fill the gaps). The last two magazines won awards for their articles in the 1990 National Magazine Awards competition.

THE FORMAT

All investigative pieces have elements in common, whether they appear as hard-nosed news or background pieces or as features or magazine articles.

Investigative writing deals with particulars. Significant details support the point of the investigative article. An investigative article especially needs to make the complete context — the larger picture — as clear as possible. A sense of story, of narrative, of chronological development, usually prevails. Because investigative articles are often long, graphic design — layout, display, photos, illustrations, sidebars — can help the reader get a sense of the whole.

The following sections discuss some approaches for structuring the investigative article.

Categorical Summary

When a newspaper decides to publish an investigative article or series, it has considerable space available. A series can stretch over a number of days, a luxury that type-squeezing magazines do not have. Despite the space, in the categorical-summary approach, the newspaper treats the main or lead-off article in an investigative series as a hard-news story; it summarizes the most important facts at the top of the article, draws a conclusion from all the facts gathered at the outset. However, the newspaper gets the best of all worlds by using a number of side stories and boxes to carry additional information and separate narratives.

The formula for the lead or the lead article in a series is likely to be a simple statement of the facts, sometimes following an anecdote, and then a catalog or list of proof statements. Note how the marshalling of summary information makes the case in the first article of a series on child neglect and abuse by Mary Hargrove in the Tulsa *Tribune*. Each summary statement is marked by a bullet:

> Oklahoma's children need a messiah.
> Never in the state's history have so many youngsters been abused, locked in psychiatric wards, committed so many serious crimes, or killed themselves.
>
> - 54 children died from abuse or neglect in the last two years. Oklahoma was ranked eighth nationally in the number of reports of abuse in 1985, the latest data available.
> - 81 children, including 17 in Tulsa County, killed themselves in 1987. Suicide is the second leading cause of death for Oklahomans 21 and younger.
> - 1,111 children in fiscal year 1987, an increase of 151 percent since 1983, were placed in private inpatient psychiatric care for unlimited amounts of time.
>
> Beginning in 1982, youth gradually were shifted to psychiatric care as the state closed its large juvenile-training centers and did not replace them with smaller treatment facilities.
>
> - 1,911 juveniles in fiscal year 1988 were declared by the courts to be delinquent, in need of supervision or in need of treatment, a 22 percent increase from the previous year.

The state has only one long-term juvenile-detention facility—the Lloyd E. Rader Center in Sand Springs, which has 142 medium- and high-security beds.

The need for secure lockup for juveniles has overwhelmed the system. In June 1988, 98 more juveniles could have qualified for treatment at Rader if space had been available, the state Department of Human Services reported.

That same month, 44 Oklahoma judges wrote legislators and the Commission for Human Services to complain about the shortage of secure facilities.

"There is no doubt children in this state have major problems that are not being addressed," said Thomas Gillert, Tulsa County assistant district attorney. He is chairman of the District Attorney's Crimes Against Children Task Force.

"People assume that someone must be taking care of them, and that is just not happening. Why? They are not a politically powerful group."

Fred Jordan, Oklahoma's chief medical examiner, said he is appalled by the number of autopsies he performs on children who kill themselves or are murdered by their families.

"Oil and gas are not the state's major resources; our children are," Jordan said.

"We have to invest in them. It's time they came first." . . .[1]

Other articles in the "Special Report: Oklahoma's Children—A State of Neglect" deal with inadequate child-care agency resources, battered wives, court testimonies, dropouts, young parents, inadequate data, adoption problems, prevention measures, bias, fostercare programs, teen options and solutions (which require financing and volunteers).

Reconstructed Narrative

Many writers and editors believe that investigative reporting or writing is mainly telling a story.

In *Philadelphia* magazine, Stephen Fried reconstructed detail by detail the story of two teenagers' suicide leap from a quarry cliff—both what led up to it and its aftermath. Note the detail and description, the setting of the scenes, which is so important to the narrative in this excerpt from the beginning of Fried's article:

They won't do it.
   There's no path through the woods to their spot. It's pitch dark, and even with flashlights the only way to navigate is to reach out and touch the wide, black metal pipe that points the way to the cliff.

1. Mary Hargrove, "A Cry for Help: Oklahoma Failing to Cope with Children's Problems," Tulsa *Tribune*, reprint package, articles published February through April, 1989.

They don't have much with them: two sleeping bags, four packs of cigarettes, a tape recorder, a white cigar tube full of matches. And the evening's drugs, the 12 hits of LSD that remain of the 22 they bought after school that afternoon. The cliff they approach, 300 feet above the Rockhill Quarry outside of Quakertown, will be the perfect place to take the rest of the acid. The quarry is so immense and jagged and surreal that it's almost a hallucination in itself. And where they're setting up camp, no one will be wandering by to interrupt them.

Marc Landis, the gangly, long-haired pastor's son, and baby-faced Daniel Ferdock, who keeps his blond hair short because his father won't let him grow it like Marc's, finally emerge from the dark woods, amazed that five hits of acid *each* hasn't rendered them unable to feel their way through the forest. One hit is usually enough to bring a novice to his knees, and in all their LSD experience, neither Marc, who's 17 years old, nor Dan, who's 16, has ever ventured past swallowing three of the small paper squares. They are both dressed in jeans, faded denim jackets, sneakers. Marc wears a studded leather wristband. Dan had one, but he just gave it to his ex-girlfriend, in one last desperate attempt to convince her to come back to him.

They spread out their sleeping bags on the rocky ground, light up cigarettes and turn the tape machine back on. In the past they have used Dan's machine to play tapes of heavy metal music, tunes by Black Sabbath or Judas Priest or Iron Maiden. Or they would listen to one of the songs they wrote themselves, with Dan playing guitar and Marc on vocals. But tonight the tape is blank. They're here to fill it . . . with goodbyes.

They won't do it.

Before heading into the woods, before the acid had really kicked in — turning each light into a supernova, transforming sounds into screaming guitar solos — they had switched on the machine to leave last words for their parents. "Mom, Dad, you should try this stuff," Dan had softly giggled. "Remember when you said drugs weren't cool?" Then they began their goodbyes. . . .[2]

Vignettes

The Detroit *Free Press* won a Pulitzer for its coverage of the Detroit riot or rebellion of 1968. Specifically cited was an extensive article detailing the personal stories of the victims.

The Louisville *Courier-Journal* won the Pulitzer Prize in 1989 for its coverage of the tragic school bus crash that killed 27 (24 children). One of the articles told the story of each victim, with pictures. In an investigation of San Jose's status as a city with many gun fatalities, the New York *Times* told the story of eight of the 10 people killed by guns in San Jose in January 1989.

In the vignette format, a short introductory section sets forth the statistics and scope of the problem; then come the case histories or vignettes and a final word.

2. Stephen Fried, "Over the Edge," *Philadelphia*, October 1984, pp. 95–97. Copyright Stephen Fried.

Following is the introduction to the *Times'* San Jose gun article and the first of the eight case histories.[3]

From the Police Blotter: Eight Stories That End in Death

SAN JOSE, Calif. — At a time when Americans are negotiating disarmament internationally, they continue to arm themselves against one another at a frantic pace.

Each hour, about four Americans die in shootings. Each year, 33,000 die from guns; 18,000 of those deaths are suicides. Guns, which are used in 60 percent of all homicides, are now the eighth leading cause of death in the United States, well behind cancer and heart attacks, but ahead of liver disease.

There is no cure in sight. President Bush has temporarily stopped imports of semiautomatic weapons, but they are only part of the problem. Conservative estimates put the total number of firearms of all kinds in the United States at 130 million, one-third of them handguns. The National Rifle Association estimates the total at 200 million, nearly one for each American. A new gun comes off an assembly line every nine seconds.

More Americans were killed by guns in the past two years than during 16 years of hostile actions in Vietnam.

"It's incredible," said Joseph McNarama, Police Chief of San Jose, one of the cities experiencing a surge of gun murders. He wants tougher handgun control: "To drive a car we require lessons, a written test, a practical test, an eye test, a license. To buy an assault rifle we require only money. They check your credit card closer than your background."

Researchers say a major motivation for buying guns is self-protection. But 58 percent of all those arrested for murder are friends or relatives of their victims. Only 20 percent of murders occur in connection with other crimes, leading experts to suggest that, instead of offering safety, more guns in more homes simply make homicide — and injuries — more common.

As the shootings increase, the gun issue may become more a debate over public health than over constitutional rights. "A gun in the home is 18 times more likely to kill a household member than an intruder," said Dr. Garen Wintermute, who teaches family medicine at the University of California–Davis. "Twenty years from now, we'll see keeping guns in the house as just as foolish as lighting up a cigarette."

"Ten years ago, even the worst criminals needed a reason to shoot," said Police Sgt. Gregory Mills of Kansas City, Mo. "Now, a bad look can set it off."

Taken together — with details provided by scores of interviews and access to police, court and coroner records — one month's fatal shootings in one city can present an alarming pattern of killing made easy.

In 1987, San Jose had 26 murders, only 7 involving guns. Last year, 39 murders were committed, 19 of them by gun. This year, Lieut. Richard Gummow's homicide squad has already logged 25 murders, 13 by gun.

January was a month of 13 murders in San Jose, with a population of 740,000 the nation's 13th-largest city. There were 10 killings by gun. The stories here are of those 10 deaths, and the weapons that killed.

3. Andrew H. Malcolm, "From the Police Blotter: Eight Stories That End in Death," New York *Times*, April 17, 1989, p. B9. Copyright © 1989 by The New York Times Company. Reprinted by permission.

Jan. 6 — For His Own Safety: Death in a Home

Andrew H. Malcolm

Fourteen months ago, the Sacramento Police Department began issuing new rapid-fire 9-millimeter pistols to its 577 officers. It was a popular decision, the kind being made across the United States by hundreds of police departments concerned over criminals' more powerful, faster-firing weapons. The old revolvers were auctioned off, as usual with surplus city property, to a local wholesaler, who resold them to gunshops in and out of California. That is how, last Sept. 22, the blue-steel Smith & Wesson .38, serial number SK 68076, came to be lying in the lighted display case at Reed's Sporting Goods store on Alum Rock Avenue.

The shop, which also sells bicycles and Boy Scout handbooks, is a few minutes' drive from the small, aging house at 269 Chalet Drive where Carlos Oliveira lived.

Mr. Oliveira, a 24-year-old grocery store clerk, was angry: like millions of Americans every year, he had been visited by burglars, who ransacked his car. He talked, too, of concern for the safety of his 19-year-old girlfriend, Maria Barros.

Mr. Oliveira paid $195, plus tax, for the gun while the clerk completed a background form.

According to California law, the police have 15 days to check a would-be handgun buyer for drug use, felony convictions or mental instability. No police warning was received, so on Oct. 7 Mr. Oliveira proudly picked up his new gun.

When, in late December, Miss Barros began living in the same house, Mr. Oliveira kept the gun by the bed. On New Year's Eve, he showed the weapon off to friends and dramatically fired five rounds into the midnight sky. One bullet remained.

Six days later, on Friday night, the couple got into an argument over Miss Barros's fidelity. A few minutes later, she sought to make up, but Mr. Oliveira shoved her aside. "Get the hell out of here!" he yelled.

Furious, Miss Barros grabbed the gun, pointed it at the ceiling and pulled the trigger.

Click.

Then she aimed it at her own ear. "Go ahead," said Mr. Oliveira.

Instead, Miss Barros slowly turned the gun toward Mr. Oliveira and fired. The bullet entered the man's face just below his right eye and tore through the brain. . . .

First-Person Experience

Cindy Ehrlich, a San Francisco writer, won the 1989 public interest award in the American Society of Magazine Editors prestigious competition. She told about her own personal horror story with the sleeping pill Halcion. The judges said of her article, which appeared in *California*: "Cindy Ehrlich's vivid article 'Halcion Madness' started as a first-person story of her nearly deadly reaction to the country's most widely prescribed sleeping pill. Her reporting showed that her own symptoms were in fact a widespread reaction to the drug. The article focused media, government, and medical attention on Halcion's dangers, and on the manufacturer's and FDA's disregard of its side-effects. As a result of the article, the FDA is again investigating the drug's side-effects. More poignant was the outpouring of letters from readers who said, "You saved my life."

Ehrlich's article begins with her own experiences and leads into a search of medical journals and other sources for information on hazardous side-effects.[4]

Halcion Nightmare

Cindy Ehrlich

In mid-July of 1987, I was late on the rewrite of my first novel, and my mother's doctors were nagging me to put her in "supervised" housing, an idea she hated. At the same time, I had houseguests; my two-year-old daughter, Lucy, was waking me up every two hours; and my husband, Ron, was sleeping well but snoring like mad. For several nights I hardly slept. When I told this to my therapist, who happens to be an M.D., she prescribed a sleeping pill called Halcion. I had seen her once a month for seven years and she had never prescribed a drug for me, but she told me she commonly prescribed Halcion; other doctors, nurses and psychiatric-ward personnel had told her it had a "high margin of safety, no hangover and fewer problems with dependency."

A week after I began taking Halcion, I went to Los Angeles for ten days. Toward the end of the trip I began to experience bewildering emotions. Although I was sleeping only five or six hours a night (just until the pill wore off), I was buzzing with energy. The last three days of the trip, I attended a three-day screenwriting class in Westwood, and everything the instructor said struck me as profound. I cried during parts of the lectures. I believed certain comments were addressed directly to me, especially some remarks about the cowardly nature of suicide, which was

odd since I had never entertained the idea. When I said good-bye to my family in L.A. to return home, I felt deeply — for no particular reason — that this would be the last time I'd see them.

By the time I got back to San Francisco, I felt anxious and fearful. My mouth was dry, my heart pounded and I was on the verge of tears much of the time. The slightest danger, such as having to make a left turn in traffic, put me in a sweat. I called my therapist for an early appointment. Then one afternoon while I was trying to write, I heard the sound of a car crash a few blocks from our house. I felt sure Ron and Lucy were in a wreck. I jumped into my car and raced down the hill, but whatever I'd heard was so inconsequential I found no sign of it. When I told my therapist what was going on, her assessment sounded reasonable: the nearness of success, as I moved closer to seeing my novel published, was precipitating fears of loss, specifically that the people closest to me would die — all of which echoed difficulties in my childhood. She prescribed a low dose of the tranquilizer Xanax (.75 mg a day). We didn't question whether I should continue taking the sleeping pill. I was so anxious I couldn't possibly have slept without it.

Weeks went by. I got worse. Bad news disturbed me so intensely that I couldn't stand anything on TV except children's and nature shows.

Afraid that anything short of perfect fatherhood on Ron's part was going to scar Lucy's psyche, I constantly corrected his behavior toward her. When he quite naturally got mad at me, I was devastated. In August, for the first time in twenty years together, we started seeing a marriage counselor. Each night I was relieved to arrive at the hour when it was okay to take my sleeping pill and check out of hell for another few hours. I thought it was the only part of my therapy that was *working*.

I continued taking the Xanax, usually half the prescribed dose every four hours, but two hours after taking it I'd feel terrible again. It occurred to me that I was addicted to the tranquilizer, so I stopped taking it for three days. But I felt so unbearably bad I decided that if I was addicted, too bad; I had to take it. In early November I told my therapist that my emotional reactions felt disproportionate, that they felt "chemical," and we again discussed the drugs I was taking. We concluded that dependency probably wasn't a problem and that both drugs were necessary.

For the first time in my life, I thought about killing myself. Intellectually, and for my family's sake, I ruled it out, but I couldn't imagine living indefinitely the way I was feeling. I worried that, in spite of my decision not to, I might somehow kill myself anyway.

By Thanksgiving, four months into this nightmare, my sense of doom was so palpable I was convinced the world was on the brink of nuclear war or invasion from space. I sat in my therapist's office and babbled nonstop for an hour, telling her my thoughts about suicide, nuclear war, alien invasion and the meaning of bumper stickers I'd seen on the way to her office. She reassured me that eventually this would end, and prescribed an antipsychotic drug, Mellaril (10 mg). She said I should take it whenever I had "obsessive thoughts." Although I was having obsessive thoughts almost constantly, I took the Mellaril as seldom as possible, maybe once or twice a day.

During this time, I kept working compulsively on my novel because I thought finishing it would make me feel better. It didn't. Through December I cried several times a day and barely managed to do anything except care for my daughter. I had lost twenty pounds since July, going from 147 pounds to 127. At first I was pleased, but as I continued to lose weight without effort, it worried me. Right before Christmas, Ron and I bickered about whether he should play the VCR during Lucy's nap. I broke down and he said, "I can't stand this anymore." It was said in a moment of frustration, and he had no intention of deserting me, but it added to my desperation. At the end of December my therapist prescribed an antidepressant, Elavil (50 mg), which I was to take along with the Mellaril, Xanax and Halcion. It didn't help. I began to expect that I would have to be hospitalized.

Then something happened that scared me even more than my own physical or psychological state. For the six months that I had been taking drugs, I had been breastfeeding Lucy. My pediatrician once assured me that drugs like Valium "would not get through" enough to matter, and since Lucy was nearly two and a half and got most of her nourishment from table food, I wasn't too worried about the possibility. But a day or two after I began taking Elavil, I noticed that she was wobbly when she got up and asked for water constantly. (With the addition of each new drug, my own mouth had become drier and drier.) So I knew that I either had to stop taking all those drugs or wean her immediately. Something I had noticed a week earlier came back to me: when I filed for reimbursement for all my prescriptions, I had been surprised to see that it was just before the trip to Los Angeles that I started taking Halcion.

That night, I decided not to take a Halcion tablet but to take my usual dosages of Xanax, Mellaril and Elavil.

The next day I felt, if not normal, at least 75 percent better, even without sleep. I felt so well that over the next few days I eliminated the Xanax, Mellaril and Elavil, and continued to feel immensely better even though I didn't sleep *at all*
continued

continued

for eight days. I did begin to feel exhausted, and said to Ron, "What am I going to do? I can't go on without sleep and I can't take those pills." But normal sleep and normal life gradually returned.

Over the next few weeks the pain and exhaustion ebbed away. One day I stood on the same spot in my kitchen where I had thought of suicide in spite of having so much to be happy about. I looked out the window and saw fruit trees blossoming early, and felt as though I'd been given back my life.

How did it happen that my doctor and I had sat staring at each other for six months, wondering why I was going off my rocker, and neither of us had thought it might be a drug reaction?

It took me awhile to seriously ask the question and then to get angry about what had happened to me — I was just so delighted to be feeling well. But then I looked up Halcion in the *Physicians' Desk Reference* and found listed under "Adverse Reactions" many of the symptoms I had experienced — irritability, confusional states, agitation, anorexia, dry mouth and others — although never as a "syndrome" and with the distinct suggestion that they were rare, unsubstantiated and perhaps attributable to other causes. I can't say that if I had read this before taking the drug I would have refused to take it, but I might at least have been alert when those symptoms appeared. Why hadn't my doctor recognized them?

"It's such a rare reaction," my therapist said. "Every time I think of what happened to you, I feel terrible. I've prescribed Halcion a lot — a lot. . . ."

Novelist William Styron wrote in the first person in *Vanity Fair* about how he fell into deep suicidal clinical depression, a "gray drizzle of horror," as he put it, so intense that one has to experience it to believe it. The article, which tells of his struggles and how he found his way out of this disease, accompanied by a sidebar of information on agencies, won the Essays and Criticism award in the 1990 National Magazine Awards competition.

INVESTIGATIVE PUBLISHING BY STUDENTS

As complex and extensive as investigative reporting and writing can be, it need not be limited to the established professional. Students have done impressive investigative stories that have received national attention.[5] Some have even been nominated for Pulitzer Prizes. Such was the case with an investigation of sports corruption at San Francisco State. It also was the case with the investigation of the board of trustees at Ball State, Muncie, Ind., who put most of the university's investments in their own banks. Both articles appeared in campus publications.

5. See Hiley H. Ward, *Reporting in Depth* (Mountain View, Calif.: Mayfield, 1991).

A student at Mankato State University, Mankato, Minn., investigated pool regulation violations and the large number of drownings in one year at a local Holiday Inn for a campus magazine, the *Medicine Jug*. One University of California student wrote about a satanic cult, and another wrote about the admittance of teens into state mental facilities by unscrupulous doctors in an insurance scam; both articles were slated for *California*. Another article on the satanic group's leader also ran in *Newsweek* with the student's byline. A University of Washington student wrote a cover story for *Campus Voice* on the chemical dangers that students are exposed to unnecessarily in campus chemistry labs.

PUTTING THE INVESTIGATIVE ARTICLE TOGETHER

Because it does require so much research, so many interviews with sources and such careful structuring, an investigative article or series also requires a great deal of planning.

Preliminary Steps

Start by answering some preliminary questions: (1) Does an editor want an investigative article on the subject you propose? (2) Are you the one to do it — can you get the information? (3) Is it manageable — are you going to have the time to do the article? (4) Are there any legal implications?

Editors can be gun-shy — and with reason. In-depth work costs money. Readers like to be entertained and are bored, if not lost, by some investigative pieces. Legal issues — threats of lawsuits — are always a problem. And publishers, who employ the editors, sometimes prefer to keep hands off certain subjects close to home.

Bob Greene, assistant managing editor for investigations at *Newsday*, told a 1989 session of the Investigative Reporters and Editors convention that strategy to produce an investigative article should include an appraisal of the probability of success, timeliness, potential impact and whether it is good public service. At some point, he said, you hang out the "red meat" to get an editor's attention, but he also said not to get lost in the enthusiasm or fall out of touch with the editors. And not all such efforts pan out. "If it looks like it won't go, don't play it to desperation. Go to the editor quickly" and say it won't work. "You can always say you thought there was a story but never said there was."

The late Paul Williams, whose weekly newspaper, the Omaha (Neb.) *Sun*, won a Pulitzer for investigating the deceptive finances of Boys Town, said of investigative reporting strategy: "There is no magic formula, but the methods used by the experts do form a pattern, a workable plan, a roadmap along which there are certain mileposts. The mileposts represent steps along the way against which you can measure your own progress in the intellectual process." These main steps, he says, are: (1) conception, (2) feasibility study (can it be done?), (3) go/no-go decision, (4) planning and base-building, (5) original research, (6) re-evaluation, (7) go/no-go decision, (8) key interviews, (9) final evaluation, (10) final go/no-go decision and (11) writing and publication.[6]

Investigative writer Kathleen Neumeyer suggests the magazine freelancer should approach an editor "basically the same way he approaches an editor on any other kind of article — by writing a lively query letter that showcases his talent as a writer and displays the kind of piece he intends to deliver. The query for an investigative piece would indicate what research would be done and what significance the resulting article would have."

Investigative writer Samuel Greengard adds, "If necessary, you should get a guarantee (in writing) of legal support. The writer should ask for as much support — researchers, assistants, etc. — as the publication can provide. Of course, some preliminary research is necessary in order to determine there's really a story."

The Paper Trail

Investigative reporting demands patience. Much investigative reporting consists of reading documents and computer printouts. It often comes down to "following the paper trail." The gargantuan Housing and Urban Development (HUD) scandal that was investigated in 1989 and 1990 involved billions of dollars and hundreds of people. The investigation was a classic example of following the pieces of paper — memos and agency and inter-agency documents — to proof of laws being broken and patterns of corruption being set. Woodward and Bernstein helped bring down a president by following telephone records, memos and government records.

Most writers are surprised at some time by just how many records they can get. The late I. F. Stone, popular for his weekly watchdog publication, mined the *Congressional Record*, which is readily available but which few people read.

Records of any public — local, state, federal — agency and law-making body and courts for the most part are available. Private institution records are often available indirectly. For instance, institutions (including private colleges) that receive federal grants, must give an accounting to the funding agency, which in turn makes most of its dealings available.

Most states have open-record laws that guarantee access to state, county and local records, in most cases. However, those in charge of the records

6. Paul N. Williams, *Investigative Reporting and Editing* (Englewood Cliffs, N.J.: Prentice-Hall, 1978), pp. 13, 14.

aren't always amenable to following the law—or even knowledgeable about it. If you plan to do much digging around in records, know which state laws govern access to them. Pennsylvania, for instance, has a "Right to Know" law that says every person can look at and make copies of public state and local records, and the law outlines a road of appeal in the event access is denied. Some reporters carry copies of the law with them in case they are challenged. Some organizations, such as chapters of the Society of Professional Journalists, provide wallet-size cards with excerpts of the law for reporters.

On the national level, the Freedom of Information (FOI) Act says you have access to documents of every agency, department, government-controlled corporation, regulatory commission and any "other establishment" in the executive branch, including cabinet offices of the Department of State, the departments of Defense, Treasury, Interior and Justice (including the FBI). In addition you can access independent bodies such as the Federal Communications Commission, Consumer Product Safety Commission, Federal Trade Commission and government-controlled corporations such as the Postal Service. The Act calls for nine exceptions: national security information, internal agency personnel rules, information that is already clearly exempted by other laws, confidential commercial data and trade secrets, internal memos and discussions of policy, personal privacy matters, police investigations, federally regulated bank information and information on gas and oil wells.

To use the FOI act in seeking disclosure of information you send a request letter. A government booklet suggests it follow the form shown in Figure 10-1.[7]

If an agency turns you down, the government booklet suggests following the form shown in Figure 10-2 for appeal.[8]

Checking on a Person

If you want to know all you can about someone for an in-depth profile or for investigative purposes, you can mine a number of sources. Check the local city and county bureaus for death, birth, marriage, divorce records; tax assessments, bankruptcy statements, wills, criminal records, voter registration, deeds. On the state level, check with the Department of Motor Vehicles; on the national level, the Internal Revenue Service can disclose an individual company's non-profit income tax records.

---

7. "A Citizen's Guide on Using the Freedom of Information Act and the Privacy Act of 1974 to Request Government Records," Thirteenth Report of the Committee on Government Operations, 1987, Union Calendar No. 118, 100th Congress, First Session, House Report 100–199. U.S. Government Printing Office, Washington, DC 20402, p. 29.

8. "A Citizen's Guide . . . ," p. 30.

Agency Head [or Freedom of Information Act Officer]
Name of Agency
Address of Agency
City, State, Zip Code

Re: Freedom of Information Act Request.

DEAR

This is a request under the Freedom of Information Act.

I request that a copy of the following documents [or documents containing the following information] be provided to me: [identify the documents or information as specifically as possible].

In order to help to determine my status to assess fees, you should know that I am (insert a suitable description of the requester and the purpose of the request).

[Sample requester descriptions:
    a representative of the news media affiliated with the newspaper (magazine, television station, etc.), and this request is made as part of news gathering and not for a commercial use.
    affiliated with an educational or noncommercial scientific institution, and this request is made for a scholarly or scientific purpose and not for a commercial use.
    an individual seeking information for personal use and not for a commercial use.
    affiliated with a private corporation and am seeking information for use in the company's business.]

[Optional] I am willing to pay fees for this request up to a maximum of $. If you estimate that the fees will exceed this limit, please inform me first.

continued

FIGURE 10-1 Form for Freedom of Information Act request letter.

[Optional] I request a waiver of all fees for this request. Disclosure of the requested information to me is in the public interest because it is likely to contribute significantly to public understanding of the operations or activities of the government and is not primarily in my commercial interest. [Include a specific explanation.]

Thank you for your consideration of this request.

Sincerely,

Name
Address
City, State, Zip Code
Telephone number [Optional]

Agency Head or Appeal Officer
Name of Agency
Address of Agency
City, State, Zip Code

Re: Freedom of Information Act Appeal.

DEAR

This is an appeal under the Freedom of Information Act.

On (date), I requested documents under the Freedom of Information Act. My request was assigned the following identification number: . On (date), I received a response to my request in a letter signed by (name of official). I appeal the denial of my request.

continued

FIGURE 10-2   Sample appeal letter under Freedom of Information Act.

continued

[Option] The documents that were withheld must be disclosed under the FOIA because . . .

[Optional] I appeal the decision to deny my request for a waiver of fees. I believe that I am entitled to a waiver of fees. Disclosure of the documents I requested is in the public interest because the information is likely to contribute significantly to public understanding of the operations or activities of government and is not primarily in my commercial interests. (Provide details)

[Optional] I appeal the decision to require me to pay review costs for this request. I am not seeking the documents for a commercial use. (Provide details)

[Optional] I appeal the decision to require me to pay search charges for this request. I am a reporter seeking information as part of news gathering and not for commercial use.

Thank you for consideration of this appeal.

Sincerely,

Name
Address
City, State, Zip Code
Telephone Number [Optional]

The FBI makes available a chart that lists 71 types of information you can get from records and other sources when you're researching people (Table 10-1). The FBI notes, however, that the guide simply indicates "where the information can be found and does not imply that information will automatically be given to an investigation." State and federal privacy laws may say some information can only be released with the person's consent. The numbers after each category of information refer to the sources that are cataloged in the second part.[9]

9. From Guide to *Sources of Information*, prepared by the FBI's Training Division, Economic and Financial Crimes Training Unit, June 1987.

Table 10-1. FBI's List of Information Sources on Persons

Part I   *Types of Information Desired*

Type of Information	*Refer to in Part II*
1. Full Name	1, 2, 4, 5, 6, 10, 11, 16, 17, 24, 31, 34, 35, 36, 56
2. Address	1, 2, 4, 5, 6, 10, 11, 16, 17, 24, 31, 34, 35, 36, 56, 62
3. Date of Birth	2, 3, 8, 13, 24, 34, 35
4. Description	2, 3, 13, 56
5. Photograph	2, 3, 13, 22, 62
6. Occupation	6, 13, 31, 34, 35, 37, 55, 62
7. Marital Status	12, 23, 34, 55, 56
8. Prior addresses of a subject; names of persons previously living at the same address	35, 36, 62
9. Addresses, present and former, whether renting or buying; credit references; personal and business associates; names of relatives; locations of banks and finance companies	34
10. Telephone numbers and addresses; how long has the suspect had service; record of long distance phone calls; number of extensions in residence	5
11. Sources of income; expenditures; personal and business references; net worth of subject; handwriting exemplars	31
12. Information as to credit charges which have been made; what hotels are being used; where has your suspect been buying gasoline; employment and credit references	15
13. Registered owners of vehicles; legal owners of vehicles; description of vehicles; previous owners of vehicles; operators' license numbers; signatures; photographs; thumbprints; abstracts of traffic citations	56
14. Application for bonds which give personal and business references; former addresses; former places of employment	32
15. Records of stocks bought or sold; profits and losses	33
16. Recorded deeds, grants, mortgages, wills admitted to probate, notices of mechanics' liens, powers of attorney	61

continued

Table 10-1. FBI's List of Information Sources on Persons (cont'd)

Part I   *Types of Information Desired*

Type of Information	Refer to in Part II
17. Record of registration for securities offered for public sale; record of individuals and firms who have violated State or Federal regulations in securities traffic	50
18. Information concerning reputation of a business; back issues of city directories	51, 52, 62
19. Businesses' worth, associates, family, holdings and ratings	34, 55
20. Information on persons in a medical or dental practice, pharmacists, barbers, funeral directors	47
21. Names of post office box holders; return addresses on mail received at post office; mail covers	4
22. Information on forwarding addresses	4, 38
23. Marriage license applications; addresses; dates of birth; signatures	12
24. Names of the bride and groom; maiden name of bride; ages	23
25. Information on divorces, i.e., place and date of marriage; date of separation; ages of children; community property; signatures; income; places of employment	9, 62
26. Information on parents of a child, i.e., occupations; ages; mother's maiden name; name of physician	20, 24
27. Disposition of monies from an estate; value of estate; inventory of all assets of deceased	30
28. Name and description of the deceased; property found on deceased and its distribution; cause of death	25, 29, 30
29. Where death occurred; birth place; how long deceased lived in the County, State or United States; names of relatives; whether or not deceased was a veteran	25, 62
30. Civil suits—changes of name; liens; description of property involved; name of court reporter, if any, who recorded the testimony	10
31. Political party; physical disabilities which would prevent marking a ballot; name of spouse; when and where married; last place of registration to vote	6, 62

Part I *Types of Information Desired*

Type of Information	Refer to in Part II
32. Ship, boat and yacht registrations	41, 42
33. Names and addresses of owners of ships, boats or yachts	41, 42, 59
34. Ownership of aircraft	60, 65
35. Background on horse owners, jockeys, trainers and people employed at race tracks	7, 62, 66
36. Case histories of persons on welfare (usually good background information)	21
37. Student records, past and present; teachers' records, past and present	22
38. List of all County employees; occupations and rate of pay; records of all financial business for the County	26
39. Presidents and secretaries of all County medical associations; names of hospitals and sanitariums; number of rooms and beds; doctors' names by street and city; doctor's year of birth, medical school and year of graduation; office address	39
40. Bar owners' fingerprints, marital status, home addresses, employees, associates	48, 68
41. Information relative to Articles of Incorporation, giving businesses, associations, records of election returns; descriptions of seals used by various State officers; papers filed by candidates for election to State offices	43
42. Names of associates of a person involved in organized crime and which law enforcement agencies have information	27, 62
43. Transcripts of preliminary hearings; probation officers' reports; subpoenas issued in the case; names of attorneys concerned	11
44. Parole reports; inmate contacts; visitors; correspondence; work and training assignments	53
45. Copies of telegrams and money order information; possible handwriting exemplars	37
46. Record of all warrants drawn on the State Treasury; accounts of all persons indebted to the State	44
47. Legal description of property; amount of taxes paid on real and personal property; former owners of property	17

Table 10-1. FBI's List of Information Sources on Persons (cont'd)

Part I *Types of Information Desired*

Type of Information	*Refer to in Part II*
48. Amount of cost of construction; blueprints of construction; information regarding location of plumbing and wiring	19
49. Dimensions of property and taxable income of real property, and what improvements, if any, on the property	16
50. Maps of streets; locations of drains; location of utility conduits; rights of way; old names of streets	18
51. Maps having elevations, base lines; landmarks; important sites	28
52. Sources of information in foreign countries	57, 58, 75
53. Information as to anticipated travel of a person in a foreign country and vital statistics	13, 62
54. Addresses of aliens	14, 49
55. Alien information; date of entry; manner of arrival; addresses; occupation; age; physical description; marital status; children; signature; photograph	14, 49
56. A guide to newspapers and periodicals printed in the U.S. and its possessions; thumbnail description of every city, including population, County, and location with respect to the nearest large city	40
57. Information on cattle and dairies	45
58. Mining information; petroleum and gasoline; fish and game	46
59. Information on transactions in the insurance industry	54, 63, 64
60. Records of individuals and firms who have violated State and Federal regulations in commodities traffic	50, 67
61. Summary of State laws and regulations relating to distilled spirits	68
62. Regulatory commissions in United States concerning public utilities	69
63. Reports which describe duties and functions of County government offices	70
64. Record of individuals and agencies in State government	71

Part I Types of Information Desired	
Type of Information	*Refer to in Part II*
65. Record of individuals and agencies in Federal government	72
66. Record of insurance risks, agents, claimants and medical examiners	73
67. Record of scientific project in progress or being planned as well as scientists involved	74
68. Companies and individuals doing business in foreign countries	75
69. Companies making investments in less-developed countries	76
70. Credit information on prospective customers of a business entity	77
71. Elected public officials	3, 6, 62, 78

Part II Where to Find It

Sources of Information

1. Telephone directories
2. State, Department of Justice, Bureau of Identification
3. FBI
4. Post Office
5. Telephone company
6. Registrar of Voters
7. State Horse Racing Board
8. County Clerk's Office, Vital Statistics
9. County Clerk's Office, Divorce Records
10. County Clerk's Office, Civil Files
11. County Clerk's Office, Criminal Files
12. County Clerk's Office, Marriage License Applications
13. State Department, Passports Division
14. County Department of Naturalization
15. Credit card companies

continued

Table 10-1. FBI's List of Information Sources on Persons (cont'd)

Part II   *Where to Find It*

Sources of Information

16. County Assessor's Office; Title and Abstract Company
17. County Tax Collector's Office; Title and Abstract Company
18. Highway Department
19. Building Department
20. Health Department
21. Welfare Department
22. School Department
23. County Recorder's Office, Marriage License Section
24. County Recorder's Office, Birth Certificate Section
25. County Recorder's Office, Death Certificate Section
26. County Auditor's Office
27. Law Enforcement Intelligence Unit (LEIU)
28. County Surveyor's Office
29. County Coroner's Office
30. Public Administrator's Office
31. Banks and finance companies
32. Bonding companies
33. Stock brokers
34. Credit reporting agencies
35. Gas and electric companies
36. Water companies
37. Telegraph companies
38. Moving companies
39. American Medical Directory
40. Directory of Newspapers and Periodicals, N. W. Ayer & Sons, Philadelphia
41. Lloyds Register of Shipping
42. Lloyds Register of Yachts
43. Secretary of State, Corporate Division
44. State Controller

Part II   *Where to Find It*

Sources of Information

45. State Department of Agriculture
46. Department of Natural Resources
47. State Licensing Boards
48. Alcohol Beverage Control
49. Federal Immigration and Naturalization Service
50. Securities and Exchange Commission
51. Better Business Bureau
52. Chamber of Commerce
53. Department of Corrections
54. American Insurance Company
55. Dun and Bradstreet
56. Department of Motor Vehicles
57. Treasury Department, enforcement agencies
58. INTERPOL
59. Harbor Patrol
60. Airport Security
61. County Recorder's Office
62. Newspaper library or newspaper "morgue"
63. Insurance Crime Prevention Institute
64. Hooper-Holmes Bureau, Inc.
65. Federal Aviation Administration
66. Thoroughbred Racing Protection Bureau, New York, New York
67. Commodities Futures Trading Corporation, Washington, D.C.
68. Distilled Spirits Institute, New York, New York
69. Federal Power Commission, Washington, D.C.
70. National Association of Counties, Washington, D.C.
71. The National Director of State Agencies
72. U.S. Civil Service Commission, Washington, D.C.
73. American Service Bureau of the American Life Convention, Chicago, Illinois

continued

Table 10-1. FBI's List of Information Sources on Persons (cont'd)

Part II   *Where to Find It*

Sources of Information

74. The Smithsonian Institution
75. U.S. Department of Commerce, Washington, D.C.
76. Agency for International Development, Washington, D.C.
77. National Association of Credit Management, New York, New York
78. Federal Election Commission, Washington, D.C.

Helpful Investigative Organizations

Several organizations exist that will assist the investigative writer. The Reporters Committee for Freedom of the Press (800 18th St. NW, Suite 300, Washington, DC 20006; phone 202-466-6313) offers free legal advice for working journalists and attorneys (but not for basic classroom or course work questions). The Committee has an FOI center or office for answering questions on federal and state freedom of information questions. Among the guidebooks it publishes is *How to Use the Federal FOI Act.*

The Center for Investigative Reporting, Inc. (530 Howard St., Second Floor, San Francisco, CA 94105; phone 415-543-1200) develops investigative projects that its staff and interns research and write for use by major media. Among its books is *Raising Hell: A Citizen's Guide to the Fine Art of Investigation.* The center sees itself not so much as a resource but as a partner with others in projects in which it wishes to get involved.

Investigative Reporters and Editors (P.O Box 838, Columbia, MO 65205; phone 314-882-2042) has a staff that will answer questions over the phone. The IRE's annual resource book, *The IRE Book,* offers one-page summaries and case histories of selected investigative articles across the nation. IRE also publishes an index, *The Investigative Journalist's Morgue,* which lists alphabetically by topics its extensive holdings on investigative stories. Among its most widely used publications is the comprehensive *The Reporter's Handbook: An Investigator's Guide to Documents and Techniques.*

ASSIGNMENTS

1. Pick out a prominent person in the university or community and do a thorough check of that person's background. You may want to get the subject's response to the information for explanation, clarification or

correction; certainly you would need to do so if publication were planned. (One university class checked out the members of the board of trustees at the university and found one whose companies and subsidiaries were awarded a large number of university contracts; the next semester, students checked out the university president and the executive vice president. The president, who had run for political office, was not a registered voter; the vice president had a judgment against him for failing to pay a fine for a home building violation.)

2. Write an FOI request letter (following the sample in the book) to see any files the FBI might have on you.

3. Discuss consumer and environmental concerns in your area. What would make a good investigative subject for the local paper or for a national magazine? How would you go about it?

4. Develop a plan to investigate a topic for an article, from start to finish, from a hypothesis to honing the idea to approaching an editor. Set a schedule, agenda and deadlines, and form suggestions for writing and follow-up. Be able to explain how the topic is manageable.

5. Each student should prepare a report on a different local (or state or federal) agency that has offices in your community. Identify key staff (with phone numbers) and analyze what is available, the agency's procedures for providing information and the degree of assistance that can be expected from that agency.

CHAPTER 11

Columns

Not everyone can be a nationally recognized and syndicated columnist or can hold down a regular spot in a newspaper or magazine. But columns do provide additional opportunities for writing. Most publications include regular columns; and some, especially newspapers, have op-ed ("opposite editorial") pages that accept free-lance contributions.

A column is normally more personal than an article, and so most columnists write in the first person. They write about something they are emotionally involved in; and more often than not, they describe their own experiences or something tangential to them. Jim Hough, of the Lansing State (Mich.) *Journal*, has been a daily newspaper columnist for more than 25 years and has written some 8,000 columns. "Keep your emotions out of writing?" he asks. "Phooey, phooey, phooey. Nobody is made of that kind of steel. I'd hate to know how many tears have run down my face as I sat in front of my typewriter. . . . It has been impossible to prevent all those human experiences of others from getting deeply into my own life."[1]

1. Jim Hough, "Right at Home" column, "Little Alicia Destroys Journalism Myth," *Michigan County Lines*, January/February, 1987, p. 3.

A column has a distinctive character. It usually has a logo or name that remains the same for ready identification. The writer's voice comes through loud and clear. Says Jim Klobuchar, columnist for the Minneapolis *Star Tribune*: "The kind of writer who puts a personal spin on things is bound to enter into a stirring relationship with the reading public. Not that the columnist has to be likable, but at least he or she should have a well-defined character. No reader likes to sift through prose sorting out motives and mindset."[2]

A regular column — magazines might call it a "department" — is short and often tries to be easier, more focused reading. Newspaper columns run about 750 to 800 words. Don't let the brevity deceive you. Columnists must be knowledgeable — steeped in their material; some engage in heavy editing and rewriting of their material.

GENERAL INTEREST/ISSUES COLUMNS

A mainstay of a newspaper is a hard-nosed columnist who keeps on top of local issues and who goes to bat for the ordinary person.

Juan Gonzalez, columnist for the New York *Daily News*, was born in Puerto Rico and grew up in New York's East Harlem; he uses his background to relate to the "underclass" of New York. His columns dealing with poverty, the homeless, drugs, day care, health care for the poor and prisons demonstrate that some of the greatest crimes are legal.

Chuck Stone, when he was a columnist for the Philadelphia *Daily News*, where Gonzalez once worked, took on erring public institutions. (He is now teaching at the University of North Carolina.) In one column he gave the Philadelphia Parking Authority a blast from both barrels. Note his personal involvement emotionally in the issue, his simple employment of a children's analogy, his hyped rhetoric and overstatement (saying the parking authority has hurt the city more than murderers) and loaded words ("urban terrorism," etc.).[3]

Rosemary Parrillo, of the Camden-Cherry Hill (N.J.) *Courier-Post*, won first place in general-interest column writing in the 1989 competition sponsored by the National Society of Newspaper Columnists. One of her three columns in the winning entry questioned plans to build a costly aquarium in the depressed Camden area.[4]

Parrillo explains how she wrote the prize-winning column. It was "basically an enterprise effort," she says. "I wanted to know how poor people felt about $42 million being spent to build an aquarium in the nation's most economically depressed city.

2. Jim Klobuchar, "The Local Columnist," *Gannet Center Journal*, Spring 1989, p. 35.

3. Chuck Stone, "Parking Authority Quotas Killing City," Philadelphia *Daily News*, April 18, 1989, p. 7.

4. Rosemary Parrillo, "Plan Doesn't Please Aquarium Neighbors," Camden-Cherry Hill (N.J.) *Courier-Post*, Nov. 26, 1988.

"So I went to the Woolworth store in the middle of a drug-infested neighborhood and sat at the lunch counter, figuring I'd run into some folks with an opinion or two.

"I was right. Miss Mom was all I needed.

"I look at column writing as a daily conversation with the reader. Make that a thrice weekly conversation. If it was daily, I'd be dead.

"So my approach is something like: 'Hey, let me tell you about this really bizarre person I met the other day,' or 'Let's go to Camden and see if the Renaissance has arrived yet.' . . .

"Observation is the columnist's primary tool, so if you're doing a column by phone (you'd be surprised how many do this) you've just tossed away 90 percent of your content."

Anna Quindlen, New York *Times* columnist who won the Pulitzer Prize for commentary in 1992, shares the same opinion that column writing is a dialogue. "I think of a column as having a conversation with a person that it just so happens I can't see," she was quoted in the *Times* as saying in an announcement of the 1992 awards. "It's nice to know that my end of the conversation was heard."[5]

Parking Authority Quotas Killing City

Chuck Stone

One day, historians will pose a variation on the poetic inquiry, "Who Killed Cock Robin?"

Who killed Philadelphia?

Not I, said Mayor Willie Wilson Goode who became the second mayor in history to bomb his own city.

Not I, said the 389 murderers who gave Philadelphia a record third-highest increase of homicides in the nation.

Guilty! The Philadelphia Parking Authority.

PPA's ticket quotas have become a form of urban terrorism that holds Center City businesses, customers, drivers and tourists hostage.

Recently, Pearson Sporting Goods decided to leave its Center City location on Chestnut Street after 53 years.

The reason?

Parking tickets from PAVIES (Parking Authority Vultures).

Owner Jack Pearson cited the constant ticketing of customers, tractor-trailers delivering merchandise and his own delivery cars.

The PPA officials will deny they have ticket quotas, but *That which we call a rose/By any other name would smell as sweet* (Shakespeare).

And *A skunk wearing a many-splendored coat would still stink* (that's Stone).

"They're not called quotas, they're called projections," according to a ticket-writing Parking Authority officer whom I'll call PAX.

"We're not told how many tickets to write, but our supervisor will remind us, 'Don't forget

---

5. "1992 Pulitzer Prize Winners and Their Works in Journalism and the Arts," New York *Times*, April 8, 1992, p. B6. Copyright © 1992 by The New York Times. Reprinted by permission.

your projections,'" PAX said. "They talk to you in such a way that you must get them.

"Different areas have different projections." Where can PAVIES write the most tickets? "University City," PAX immediately replied. Any other area? "Society Hill. It's a gold mine."

Where else? "South Street. It's 'hot' during the day anywhere there.

"We have people who can write 1,700 to 1,800 tickets a month. They're called 'hammers.' They will even run up and write a ticket, just as the meter is expiring. They will write tickets on cars with flashing lights on. They will write tickets in hospital zones when people are delivering flowers."

PAX estimated PAVIES are paid a little over $300 a week ($15,808 a year). . . .

"'Hammers' do twice that much in a *day!*" said PAX who conceded the public holds PAVIES in low esteem.

"We have to deal with stress all the time. We get assaulted. On Saturday night, a PEO (parking enforcement officer) got beat up in Center City. They stole his car, his radio and his parking tickets. Those radios cost $1,700. He shouldn't have to pay for it."

To help PAVIES cope with stress, a stress-management teacher wrote a song which they all sang during their six-month training or probationary period.

PAX thought the song was so silly that PAX could hardly recite the words from laughing so hard.

Philadelphia Parking Authority,
From negative stress, you will find us scot-free.
We imagine, we breathe deeply, we tense, then relax.
Fail-safe against slip-ups, we cover our tracks.

"How to get rid of stress, get rid of the a------- who are running the Parking Authority," said PAX.

"But you can get your projections if you get a good area and a good shift. The biggest shift is 10:30 to 6:30.

"Four to 12, Thursday, Friday and Saturday, is a 'hot time' because people don't expect it to be enforced. We write tickets on *Sunday* in some areas!"

PAX deplored the intelligence level of some of the PEOs.

"Some of them are kind of slow. They can barely read and write.

"But if I were going to hire PEOs, I would offer two courses, one in 'Jive Talk 101' and 'How to Give Your M------------ Mother a Ticket in 10 Easy Lessons.'

"I never cursed before I came to work here," PAX lamented. "But I needed a job badly."

PAX chuckled. "We're like bloodhounds. If you park wrong, we'll *find* you."

Plan Doesn't Please Aquarium Neighbors

Rosemary Parrillo

Forty-two million dollars.

"That sure is a lot of money for fish," Miss Mom says, as she sips coffee at the lunch counter in Woolworth's on Federal Street.

See, they're putting this giant aquarium uptown along the waterfront. And it's going to cost

almost as much as it takes to run the entire City of Camden.

Miss Mom shakes her head and drags on a Kool cigarette.

"I ain't got but four dollars in my pocket. What we need is somebody to put some money
continued

continued

into these neighborhoods. That's what we need around here."

"Around here" is East Camden where the most prevalent species is the dorsal-finned drug dealer, a predatory breed that swims where it pleases and feeds off whatever happens to pass by.

Right now, it's the one giant fish that's eating Camden whole. And from what Mom says, they're doing a pretty good job on her block. She's practically a prisoner in her own home.

"I come here (to Woolworth's) every morning to get a little peace. I have breakfast and sit around so I don't have to hear all the nonsense that goes on out in the street."

Mom moved to East Camden in 1974. And in the last 14 years, she has seen the tide heading out — way out. Now she's the one who feels like a fish on dry land.

Boys' Town

"My home used to be beautiful," says Mom. "But the boys done torn it apart.

"They stand out there all day sellin' that stuff. And when the cops come, they just stick it any place they can find.

"They pull away the wood under my front window and put it in there. They bury it in my yard. They even tore the cover off my mailbox and stuck it in my front door. I come on the porch one morning and see two little bags of white stuff on the floor.

"They work the corners like they got a real job. They have shifts. I'm not kidding. They sit on my step and peel the paint off my front door. And they do nothin' but eat all day long and leave their trash all over my property.

"They already tore down my fence runnin' away from the cops all the time. It's bad.

"I'm goin' down to city hall tomorrow. I gotta find out who's gonna help me put the outside of my house back together.

"Somethin's gotta be done. An aquarium sounds nice, but I don't think it's gonna do nothin' for us.

"I think somethin's wrong with the system. I tried to get the mayor on the phone, but they wouldn't put me through. I worked for his election, but if you ask me, he's too slow. Nothin' changes."

On Broadway

I guess Mom just hasn't caught Randy on his way to Trenton. There's nothing that travels faster — and more often.

And now that he's finally reeled in the aquarium, we'll see if the Renaissance we've been hearing about (it seems since the 16th century) will finally arrive.

Meanwhile, uptown on Broadway, closer to the proposed site of the project, Sang Nam, a Korean-born businessman, thinks an aquarium isn't a totally crazy idea.

"I think is good. Will bring more business," he says with a broad smile.

You'd expect somebody like Sang to think this way. The guy owns the Fish House restaurant. OK, so all the fish here are dead. He still knows something about the critters.

"People in city like fish," he says, serving up an order of chicken wings to Joel Marsh, a marketing major at Rutgers.

Chicken wings?

"They have the best fried chicken here. I come at least twice a week for lunch," says Joel.

"We sell taco pies and cheesesteaks, too," says Sang. A Camden business owner has to be eclectic.

"Camden is good place for business. Is cheap," he says.

Sang came here from New York because he could start a business for $30,000 instead of $100,000.

"I want to move to Cherry Hill someday."

Doesn't everyone, Sang?

I don't know if any of those millions of anticipated aquarium visitors will stop by Sang's fish house on their way home.

And I don't know if Miss Mom can count on any of those admission fees getting her a new fence and a fresh coat of paint.

This is one fish story that has a long way to go before it's over.

THE SPECIALIST COLUMN

Many columns concentrate on a certain topic — food, wine, travel, behavior, lifestyles or technical know-how (such as a column on developments in computer technology).

Stephen Morrill, of Tampa, Fla., writes about maritime and shipping topics. In his column for the *Florida Shipper* (he does 26 a year), topics can range "from the extremely technical to the more general. But even the 'more general' would be pretty mysterious to a non-maritime-community reader. I'm given carte-blanche to cover the waterfront for Florida, and pretty much anywhere else I travel. Topics, therefore, can range from new technical specifications for a forty-foot shipping container, to a recent decision by a port authority — and the *real* reasons behind that decision — to a semi-travel piece on port expansion in a Central American country."

His biggest problem, he says, is "drumming up material, especially for a column about maritime trade — a topic not high on most people's summer-reading list. In fact, the biggest problem is maintaining my contacts so that I don't miss any really important stories. It's now been six years since I personally handled a ship, and even though I call people, stop by offices, and visit ships and ports frequently, it's hard to stay current on everything. You have to work at such columns. Subscribe to related magazines, attend conferences, talk, talk, talk to people."

Dr. Salvatore Didato is a New York psychologist who has done various columns on psychology, including one for the Associated Press on psychology behind the headlines. Currently, he's doing a 700-word weekly column in the form of a quiz. His "Personality Quiz" column, syndicated by News America Syndicate in Baltimore, New Orleans, Philadelphia, Dallas and St. Louis, centers on a theme. He asks questions like "How good a friend can you be?" "Would you be an effective leader?" "How much do you know about children?" "How happy are you?" "How romantic are you?" "Are you prejudice-prone?" One of his personality quizzes follows on the next page.[6]

Didato notes that he started small. It began, he says, "with a suggestion from a local paper to write a piece on the movie *The Exorcist*. From there on it built up — more articles, more papers. It was a 'pyramid' phenomenon, with old leads leading to new leads."

Specialist columns include the familiar inside-government and Washington columns, such as Jack Anderson's "Washington Merry-Go-Round," inherited from the late Drew Pearson. The political columnists follow the issues and politics of the day and depend on inside informers and investigative techniques.

The sports column is as chatty and personalized as any, usually filled with jargon and shorthand that only the initiated can understand. It is assumed that readers know what *seeded* or *hat trick* means, for instance. Yet

6. Salvatore V. Didato, "Dr. Didato's Personality Quiz," © 1986, News America Syndicate.

Can You Spot A Child Under Stress?

Salvatore V. Didato, Ph.D.

We reel under the weight of articles and books about adult stress, but not much is said about children. And with bombings in Europe, Civil War in Ireland and terrorism in the Middle East, one can only wonder how this all impacts on innocent children.

According to Dr. David Elkind, chairman of the Department of Child Study at Tufts University in Massachusetts, children today are pressured into social, psychological and political maturity too quickly and the resulting stress may have long-lasting, damaging effects. Evidence of this may be found in the fact that during that past decade the number of children seen by psychologists and psychiatrists has increased fivefold.

Have you ever considered how much stress your children, or children you know, may be enduring and how it affects them? Following is a list of stressful events each with a number at the right, 10 being the most stressful and 1 being the least stressful. The list is adapted from Dr. Elkind's latest book, "The Hurried Child." To identify how much stress a child has been under, check each item that the child you know has experienced within the past year.

1. Parent dies. 10
2. Parents separate. 6
3. Parent travels for business. 6
4. Parent fired from job. 4.5
5. Mother begins to work outside the home. 4.5
6. Mother becomes pregnant. 4
7. Family's financial condition changes. 4
8. Responsibilities at home change. 3
9. Trouble occurs with grandparents. 3
10. Family goes on vacation. 2

Scoring and Explanation

To tally the child's stress score, total the numbers given to the right of each item checked. A score of:

0 to 5.5 indicates a child with a relatively tranquil life. There is a good chance that children with this score will achieve their full potential free of personal hangups.

6 to 10 indicates that the child will have more of a tendency to develop some symptoms of stress than children who receive a lower score.

11 or more indicates a heavy stress load and a strong chance that this child may develop symptoms in physical health or in behavior.

Stress occurs when we adapt to any event in our life. Thus, it doesn't matter if the incident is a happy one or a sad one; the fact that we must make an adjustment to it produces stress. For example, it may be just as stressful for a child to be outstanding in personal achievement at school as it is to adjust to an older sibling who is put in the hospital.

Unlike most adults, children under stress usually don't express their feelings verbally. Rather, they tend to act out with behavior such as the following: bed-wetting, nail-biting, nightmares, lack of appetite, seclusiveness, aggression, inattention and stuttering. So be on the lookout for clues that your children might be experiencing too much stress. The answer may be found in their behavior.

major sports editors do advise their writers to explain at least by context just what a word means. After all, people who aren't sports fans thumb through the paper and have even been known to try to read a sports story. Inside knowledge should not be taken for granted in newspaper writing, not even in sports.

PERSONAL EXPERIENCE COLUMN

More than any other part of a newspaper or magazine, a column is fair ground for the use of personal experiences.

Sarge Sterling, an older student taking a graduate course in non-fiction writing, put his memory to work about a time long ago and produced a personal free-lance column for the Broadway *Playbill*® Magazine.[7]

A View from the Audience

Sarge Sterling

Sometimes when I try to remember the day, the picture comes back to me as a surprisingly clear-cut vision. I must have been about seven and I was going to go with my mother to the theatre — live theatre. The afternoon, as I recall, was gray and sunless and I was dressed in the new sailor suit which had been my birthday present.

I never knew how my mother got the money to take me to the theatre, even though in 1921 the prices were low. There is nothing to show that she had any kind of income. My father died when he was very young, and if he left her money, it must have been a very small sum.

I know that we went to "B.F. Keith," but I do not remember the play, although I'm sure it must have been something for a young person. Walking into the theatre my mother held my hand tightly, directed me down the aisle, where we wandered a bit until we found our seats. I do not remember an usher, perhaps because we were very early. I do not think my mother wanted me to miss the excitement of the people coming in and gossiping before the curtain went up. When we were seated, she leaned over to me and said, "Now be still, you are going to enjoy this." I can hear the words today.

The theatre was warm and snug, and on the back of each seat was a box with chocolates which you could purchase by dropping the appropriate coins in the slot. My mother noticed me looking at the box and she said gently, "You did not come here to eat chocolate, you came to see a play."

All through the performance, however, my eyes kept straying back to the chocolate, which was a very rare treat for me. Even today when I go to a theatre I see in my mind's eye that black box attached to the seat and I can almost feel my mother's firm grasp on my hand, as though to make it up to me that she could not get me the candy.

Those days are gone. The play is forgotten, but the memory of what followed is clear. When the curtain fell and we walked down the aisle, I kept looking back to the seat. Then I began to [whimper] loudly. My mother put her arms around my shoulders as she led me down toward the trolley car. I looked up at her and I saw that she too was crying. The weather was cold now, as though a wind came up from the North. When we got home my mother said she would get me some cookies. But she could not find them. I doubt if she had them. Later on she said, "Someday you will have all the chocolate you want." Then I cried again, and she snuggled me to her and I could smell the strange sweet perfume of her hair. I think I never got that close to my mother again.

In bed I cried myself to sleep. I dreamt I was going down the aisle of the theatre and that each
continued

7. Sarge Sterling, "A View From the Audience," *Playbill*®, June, 1984, p. 28. *Playbill*® is a registered trademark of Playbill Incorporated, New York City. Used by permission.

continued

box opened as though by magic, and I stuffed my mouth with the delicious creams, bars or whatever the box held. But that was a dream.

Today I cannot taste or see chocolate without envisioning my mother trying to hide her tears as we walked to the trolley. And I still feel a fleeting sadness each time I sit down to watch a play, for I now realize that the only reason my mother did not get me the candy was that she did not have the money.

Sometimes a single event—a memory—from the past can have special relevance. Patricia Volk, in her *New York Times Magazine* column, drew from her early years to make a point about children's safety.[8]

Being Safe

Patricia Volk

"I'll teach you how to protect yourself," Dad said. We were waiting in the 20th Precinct station in Manhattan to report the slashed roof of our green Studebaker convertible. I was 6. "If a man attacks you, you knee him in the private. Then you take the flat side of your hand and shove the cartilage of his nose into his brain." Dad told me this was called a rabbit punch and meant instant death. While we waited for the precinct detective, I shadow-practiced till Dad was satisfied I could kill.

That's when I learned protecting myself was up to me.

The next year, riding a packed subway with my sister, a man chatted while he tickled us someplace we knew he had no right to.

"Ma," we said getting off at 86th Street. "You know that man who kept talking to us? That man tickled us *there*."

That's when I learned not to talk to strangers on the subway.

Three years later, when my 11-year-old sister was accosted in the elevator of our building, I learned elevators can be safe provided you don't ride alone with a man you don't know.

In the eighth grade, when a boy I'd never seen before grabbed my breast between classes, I learned that couldn't happen if I carried my books in front of my chest.

When I got my own apartment, Dad gave me a book called "How to Protect Yourself on the Streets and in Your Home With an Open Letter From J. Edgar Hoover." I learned to walk in the center of the street when scared of the person behind me. I learned to tap a pencil on the mouthpiece of the phone when obscene callers called and say, "Yes, officer. It's him again." I whistled a happy tune.

In all, my wallet's been stolen 11 times, and each time I've learned something different: *not* to read at the bus stop, *not* to wear my shoulder bag slung in the back, *not* to put my handbag in the grocery cart at the supermarket, *not* to hang it on the inside of the ladies' room door at Saks, *not* to leave my briefcase in an unlocked office or beside me on the banquette at a restaurant, and *not* to think that just because you've worked with someone for 18 years, they're incapable of stealing from you. I've also learned that shoppers on escalators are sitting ducks. Twice I've turned

---

8. Patricia Volk, "Being Safe," in "Hers" column, *New York Times Magazine*, Feb. 11, 1990, p. 24.

around at Bloomingdale's to see a man's hand in my handbag.

I live in a hypervigilant way, hoping nothing bad will happen if I use what I've learned. But there's so much to learn.

My son's been mugged once and had two bikes stolen, but that was before the police told us there are certain places you're not supposed to ride in the park.

Our car's been stolen once and broken into three times. But that's because we didn't know you're not supposed to park it on the Central Park side of the street.

My husband was held up at gunpoint while walking the dog. But that was before we knew that you never walk your dog on the park side either. We're just an average New York family. Knock wood, luckier than most. We keep learning.

At Golden Acres Kosher Dude Ranch in the Catskills, the guest speaker was a karate expert who called his hands lethal weapons. He spoke of harassment on the jogging trail and how he could scare people into leaving him alone. I thought about the karate expert after learning about the Central Park jogger. Eleven months have passed since that April night. She's come farther than anyone hoped. Maybe she'll go back to work full time. Maybe she'll be able to marry and have children. We continue to talk about her, to worry and wonder. What could she have done? What could we have done?

"The truth is," I tell my husband, "I don't feel safe. I never feel safe. I haven't the vaguest idea how to protect myself."

"Stick a finger in the person's eye," he says.

"What?"

"Just stick it in." He jabs his finger into the air, hooks it, then pulls it back. "You can take a man's eye out that way."

"I could never do that," I say. "I could never stick my finger in someone's eye. Besides, my father taught me to knee them and shove their cartilage into their brains."

"Kneeing's good. But you can't shove somebody's cartilage into their brain."

So the next time Dad calls from Florida, I mention the rabbit-punch thing. "It doesn't work," I tell him. "Andy says you can't push someone's cartilage into their brain." I expect Dad to say my husband's wrong.

"Really?" he says.

"Really."

"When you come down to visit," he tells me, "I'm going to teach you how to use a stun gun."

My 13-year-old daughter asks to see where it happened in the park. It is Sunday, 3 p.m. Polly and I keep walking. We walk past four baseball fields and winding country lanes. This is a part of the park we don't know. Wooded, hilly, remote. It's like the recurrent New York dream of opening a door in your apartment and finding another room there, a room you had no idea you had. Finally, at the top of the hill, we look down and there it is.

Even during the day it is terrifying. Dense trees slide down into a ravine. The path writhes. Street lights a hundred feet away from each other. A place born for crime. We look at the faded Palm Sunday fronds, plastic flowers and plant indicators that say "Red Madness Petunias" and "Bonanza Flame Marigolds." The "Te Amo" posters and laminated Jesuses have been replaced by "Ya Gotta Have Park" and "AIDS Walk" buttons. Suddenly we are not alone. Other people have come to look too. I raise my eyes. Men are on all sides of us.

"Come," I say to Polly. As we walk I think about a Charles McGrath story called "Husbands." Unable to get along any more, the men and women live apart. I think how safe I would feel if women got, say, Manhattan and the Bronx and men got Brooklyn and Queens and people happily married 20 years or more took Staten Island. Women wouldn't have to be afraid any more, I think. I wouldn't have to memorize my children as they leave the house. Polly, 5 feet 4 in her shiny black baseball jacket, Docksiders and stressed jeans. Peter, 6 feet in his Doc Martins, rolled pants and Cushing Academy "Undefeated" Offensive Guard windbreaker. I wouldn't have to commit their clothes to memory so that, perish the thought, God forbid, spit through your fingers three times, I should have to describe how they were last seen.

continued

continued

Suddenly, out of nowhere, a man approaches. A baseball cap eclipses his eyes. He's coming straight at us. I look around. Where is everybody? He's big. Where did everybody go? I grab my daughter's hand. Her antenna is up too. I'm about to blurt "Run!" when the man says, "Hi! What are you doing here?"

It's our doorman, out for a stroll.

As we head for home, I tell my daughter, "I'm glad we came. I wanted you to see how unsafe it was. I wanted you to know that what happened to her can never happen to you. You'll always know to never go someplace so unsafe."

"Mom," she squeezes my hand. "I'm scared."

Good, I think. That's exactly what you're supposed to be.

HUMOR COLUMN

Almost all personal experience columns lend themselves to humor, but some columnists make humor primary. With an eye for human foibles — such as discoveries made when washing clothes — Erma Bombeck tickles the funny bone. Andy Rooney observes ridiculous patterns and rituals in modern life. Advertising — what is promised versus what is actually delivered — is one of his targets. Art Buchwald and Russell Baker are apt to take a current event and ask, "What if . . . what if it went this way?" The column could be an imaginary conversation between two heads of state.

Using this approach, Colin McEnroe, of the Hartford (Conn.) *Courant*, won first place in humor-column writing in the 1989 National Society of Newspaper Columnists competition. One of his winning entries was a "what if" column about Dan Quayle as a little boy.[9]

Quayle Country: The Dust Bowl of Anecdotes

Colin McEnroe

Years have passed, but I can still remember it, plain as a pea on a pile of potash.

Papa was looking out the window at the neighbor's boy, little Danny Quayle, just stand-ing out in his own back yard staring off into space the way he always did.

Papa drew back from the window and mumbled to no one in particular, "Land sakes,

9. Colin McEnroe, "Quayle Country: The Dust Bowl of Anecdotes," Hartford *Courant*, Oct. 7, 1988.

that boy doesn't have a whole lot of buckwheat in his pancake, does he?"

"Sshhhh," Mama said. "They'll hear you. The Quayles have high hopes for that little Danny."

"They can hope all they want. I always said you can't pluck peacock feathers off a drawn duck."

"I always said," Grammaw chimed in as she toted laundry up the backstairs, "a one-legged cricket can't kick a pickle barrel through a half-ton of jackstraw."

"I always said," said Uncle Gaylord, climbing down the attic stairs, "you can hook a catfish with a —"

"QUIET!" yelled Mama. "Don't you know those poor Quayles don't have any sayings? How do you think they feel hearing all your colorful sayings floating out the windows night and day? How do you think that poor little Danny feels knowing he's going to grow up with no anecdotes to shape his philosophy? I always say you can't grow corn in a —"

"MAMA!" we all yelled.

"Oh my," said Mama.

Those poor Quayles. They really were anecdote-impaired. They were saying-deprived. They had a lot of echoes in their cracker barrel. One Christmas I remember seeing Mama sneak out the back door with a basket covered by a checkered cloth.

"What you got there?" I asked.

"Ohhhh. I just made up a basket of expressions and adages and a couple of parables and homilies for the Quayles," she sighed. "It's Christmas, and we have so much, and they have so little."

We used to hear them sitting around the dining room table trying to develop a homespun philosophy.

"You can't throw . . . something down . . . some kind of hole and expect . . . something," Mr. Quayle would say.

"Carrots," Uncle Jeb Quayle would say.

"You can't throw carrots down . . . ," Gramps Quayle would try.

"Aren't carrots already down a hole?" Mrs. Quayle would ask.

"You can't take a cat out of . . . a chair if, ah . . . ," said Cousin Norbert Quayle.

"If a dog is . . . ," said Mr. Quayle.

"Carrots," said Uncle Jeb.

We just felt so bad for Danny on Wednesday night when that mean Mr. Brokaw asked him for a story or saying from his life that shaped his philosophy. We all thought, oh, Mr. Brokaw, if you only knew the kind of childhood that boy had.

I remember one time I was over at the Quayles', and somebody had put one of those needlepoint framed samplers up on the wall. It read, "Home is good."

"Gee," I said. "Don't they usually say 'Home, Sweet Home' or something?"

"Home what?" said Mrs. Quayle.

"That's terrific," said Mildred Quayle Quackenbush. "Did you make that up?"

"Get a pencil, and write that down, Mildred," Mr. Quayle said.

"I sure will, quicker than . . . something very fast," she answered.

"Home Sweet — how did that go again?"

"Is there a comma in there someplace?"

"Carrots," said Uncle Jeb.

It took me half an hour to get it all worked out for them.

"I feel sorry for little Danny," I said when I got home to my family.

"That boy is a few logs shy of a cord," Papa said.

"He's kinda all bell and no clapper, ain't he," Uncle Gaylord added.

"I don't reckon he got quite enough mercury in his thermometer," said Grammaw.

"Ssshh," Maw said.

And then, in the stillness, we heard little Danny's grandmother singing him to sleep with that song she always liked.

Be a fairly good person.
It's better than being a worse 'un.
Always look where you are going,
Especially if it was recently snowing.
And don't drink coffee when you walk downstairs
Because da da da something something.

And just as the lights went out, we heard somebody say, "Carrots."

McEnroe explains the winning Quayle column: "The family depicted there is a colorful rural, archetypal family that appears in my column from time to time. I don't know who they are, really. Sort of a cross between Thurber's looney Ohioans and the family I wish I had had. (Humorists often use their work to express veiled longings. Berke Breathed once told me the whole dandelion-spackled mise-en-scène of Bloom County was basically the place he wished he grew up in.)"

Humor techniques employed by columnists are described in the following sections.

Caricature

Political cartoons embody the meaning of caricature, often with a vengeance. Some trait or detail in a person or idea is highlighted at the expense of other characteristics. One of the most famous caricatures is the drawing of President Franklin Roosevelt with proverbial cigarette holder and cigarette jutting from his mouth. Columnists have exaggerated Harry Truman's homespun language, Dwight Eisenhower's golf game, John Kennedy's boyishness, Lyndon Johnson's Texas demeanor, Richard Nixon's personality problems, Gerald Ford's athletic prowess (or lack of it), Jimmy Carter's peanut-country upbringing, Ronald Reagan as Hollywood actor and the blandness and perceived "wimpishness" of George Bush.

Parody

The "what if" or "once upon a time" make-believe story about a real person is a form of parody. The writer imitates the style of the real subject, usually in a nonsensical manner encouraging a laugh or ridicule. Some dictionaries make parody a synonym for caricature, but parody usually takes the form of a story or tale or anecdote. Familiar storybook classics, such as *Alice in Wonderland*, *Snow White*, *Sleeping Beauty* and *Don Quixote* may be conjured up when recasting a subject's life in parody. A parody is an outrageous imitation — like many *Saturday Night Live* skits and *Mad* spreads.

Satire

Rather than just pointing out human weakness and vices, satire also holds them up for ridicule and contempt. Thomas Nast's famous cartoons showed a tiger, symbol of the corrupt Tammany Hall political entity in New York City, prepared to devour a young lady, Columbia, symbol of righteousness and liberty. After some new disclosure of Watergate cover-ups, political columnists savaged Richard Nixon in scenarios where "Tricky Dick" was the villain. Leaders of other countries, usually those not considered our allies, such as the late Ayatollah Khomeini, are the brunt of aggressive satire.

Russell Baker in a March 1992 syndicated column suggests that a reader can start an invigorating day by reading the foreign news. He ridicules news coverage by showing how the reader is bombarded with so many new, unpronounceable names that they could be names in sports or for "an old time singing sisters act."

Irony

When the intended effect of the words you use is the opposite of what they mean on the surface, the result is irony. If you describe an idea as so stupid that no one could possibly think of it, your intended effect might be to suggest that the person who did think of it is a genius. A column on the environment might compare official policy with the result. Looking at barren land, a writer might mention the "trees." Syndicated columnist Mike Royko in a February 1992 column found that he could agree with Dan Quayle—on golf.

Humorous writing depends on many techniques, including timing and the way words sound. All the literary devices—alliteration, repetition, onomatopoeia, metaphors, similes—may show up. Since every word counts—whether contributing to timing, sound or mood—some consider humorous writing to be the highest form of writing in style.

Consider rhythm and other literary techniques in this column from the Detroit *Free Press* at the beginning of a Lenten season.[10] Note the iambic meter at times (unaccented syllable followed by accented)—"I never paid too much attention to my little friend." Note alliteration: "transparent tummy," "calico cat," "humped up for hours"; simile—"like a gold knotted ribbon"; metaphor—"silvery-gold frame"; onomatopoeia—"shishy."

Last Hours of a Tiny Goldfish

Hiley H. Ward

I never paid too much attention to my little friend with the transparent tummy and gargoyle eyes, until one day he or she—I never did know which it was—took a turn for the worse.

It had had it moments of peril before. Like when Fluffy, the calico cat in our house, sat humped up for hours with its soft nose right on the water, watching. . . .

Or when the little fish flopped around in the sink while the bowl was being shined up. Or when little hands probed in the fish bowl.

And my nameless goldfish survived famine, and over-feeding by a two-year-old and by neighbors' two-year-olds, and the generations of bigger kids who fed the fish as generously as they would feed a lot of hogs.

continued

---

10. Hiley H. Ward, "Last Hours of a Tiny Goldfish," Detroit *Free Press*, Feb. 11, 1967.

continued

But now, I looked up from the ocean of junk on my desk, and I saw trouble in the goldfish bowl.

Solitary, with no cat or kid around, my finned friend looked about finished.

Once a birthday gift by a daughter, somehow the little fish had survived for 18 months.

I sprinkled in a little food—who knew how long since it had been fed.

But there it was, like a gold knotted ribbon at the bottom of the fish bowl, its silvery-gold frame barely responding to a heart beat.

A change of liquid—a firm hand to hold it . . . nothing helped.

"Shishy!" shouted my two-year-old pointing at the goldfish bowl.

"He's sick today . . . no, no, get your hands out of there . . . all right, just a little food . . ."

Later the two-year-old came back and inquired about "Shishy."

I shook my head. "He's gone . . . dead . . . I mean, sleeping. . . ."

Then, I wondered, why should I avoid giving the child a little lesson in life's reality of death. So when she came back, I said, "he's dead," then ushered her out and started her playing with something and was spared the full thunder of a child's grief.

I didn't have the heart to flush the dead little fish down the drain. For surely if I did, some kid would ask what I had done with it and it's hard to tell a lie. So I put it to rest in the garbage can, and nobody asked.

The death of a tiny, nameless goldfish on the threshold of Lent. . . .

I had long been interested in the riddle on suffering posed by the Russian Orthodox theologian, Nicholas Berdyaev: "No world order can be reconciled with unmerited-suffering," he said, "even if it be of only one creature, with one tear of a tortured child" ("Slavery and Freedom" page 86).

With the tears of a child, suffering needlessly, the justice of God does seem so far away.

But a goldfish, a nameless one, whose consciousness must be very low, also cannot escape the full span of suffering, which somehow becomes universal and not selective with its death.

The death of a man, a child, of God's own child on a cross on Good Friday—all become a little more acceptable in the universal illumination of suffering in the final, long agonies of a nameless fish.

For all creatures suffer, and there is a godliness or presence about even the tiniest of them ("Are not two sparrows sold for a farthing? And one of them shall not fall on the ground without your Father. But the very hairs of your head are all numbered"—Matt. 10:29, 30).

"God does not explain or justify the anguish of life, but takes it on himself, and tastes its full horror, and in so doing illuminates it," says Evgueny Lampert, one of Berdyaev's commentators, in Donald Attwater's "Modern Christian Revolutionaries."

Later, the two-year-old came bounding into the study, got hold of the fish food, and dumped half a box into the shallow, still, goldfish bowl. Somehow, it was fun even without the fish.

BOOK REVIEWS

"Do you read all those books?" a reviewer might be asked. Maybe, if the reviewer does only an occasional review. Authors of regular review columns must take some short cuts, but they need to do more than just skim a book. If you're going to write a review, strive to read the beginning and ending carefully and center on promising parts of the book. This will provide a fairly adequate picture of most nonfiction books. With novels you would likely read the entire book.

Reviewers like to examine the theme or main point of the book, but also want to be alert to possible news items and poignant anecdotes. Something a famous person said—discovered for the first time—might provide a lead. Other new information might be highlighted, and comparison with the author's previous work and other authors in the same genre is in order. When you're reviewing the nonfiction book, you're likely to be most interested in what the book adds to the general scope of knowledge. Deal with some specifics and not just the general tone and territory of the book.

Here's a review of an interesting and relevant book about a famous editor and reporter as it appeared in a regular book review column in *Editor & Publisher*.[11] Note that this review tries to discover some essential point or message in the book and put it in the lead. The famous, retired New York *Times* reporter and editor, James Reston, had learned something in his long career. Some of the book's anecdotes are included in the review—those that are plain entertaining and amusing and those that have special significance to the state of affairs. Several weaknesses are cited, such as the book's having too much in-house, *Times* shop talk. Then the reviewer concludes with simple, pithy advice from Reston for the reader.

Reston Relives Career; Learned Some Lessons

Hiley H. Ward

Deadline: A Memoir. James Reston. (Random House, 201 E. 50th St., New York, N.Y. 10022.) 525 pages. $25.

If there is one thing that the venerable James Reston learned in his long career as reporter and editor—50 years at the *New York Times*—is that there are many sides to a story. A lot depends on from where you see the story.

He "learned a couple of lessons" as he filed his first big story out of England for the Associated Press in the 1930s. He was told to flash the name of the winner of the Grand National Steeplechase race at Aintree outside Liverpool. He went to elaborate measures to be first, even installing a telephone at the top of the grandstand, as close to the finish line as he could get.

Two horses led the stampede nose to nose, Royal Danielli and the American horse, Battleship. Reston, the young Scotsman, kept his eye on the finish line. He recalls:

"I didn't wait for the official decision but said to the operator in Liverpool: 'Ready? Let that message go: Let me repeat it: Flash: Royal Danielli wins, repeat: Royal Danielli wins Grand National.' There was a long delay before the official announcement went up, maybe two *continued*

---

11. Hiley H. Ward, "Reston Relives Career, Learned Some Lessons," *Editor & Publisher*, Jan. 18, 1992, p. 25.

continued

minutes, which seemed to me two hours. Then the terrible signal: BATTLESHIP, it said. I think I had a heart attack, but I managed to stammer to the operator in Liverpool. 'Send another urgent message to AP in New York. Kill Flash. Battleship wins Grand National, repeat Battleship, not, repeat not, Royal Danielli.'"

He learned that day to "get it first if you can but first get it right. The other lesson was equally important. My mistake was that I was not directly facing the finish line, but saw it from an angle and therefore saw it wrong."

He comes back to vantage-point advice in the book summarizing what he has learned, after a career that included two Pulitzer prizes.

"I think," he says, "honest reporting cuts a man down to size. Out on any important story, he soon learns that truth is a scarce and slippery commodity and that there are not two sides to every problem but maybe 10, held with genuine conviction by serious people who probably know more about the facts than he does. This occasionally makes us consider that maybe sometimes we have been wrong."

Throughout the book he gives his estimate, usually offered humbly and as positive as possible, of the great figures of the century. His favorites seem to have been Dean Acheson and Adlai Stevenson. Calling Acheson perhaps the best of the 15 secretaries of state he covered, he noted that Acheson was smarter than most of those in President Truman's cabinet and stood up to Sen. Joseph McCarthy's witchhunting.

Reston feels that "Acheson made no concessions to what he called 'the attacks of the primitives,' explaining that he found it difficult to conceal his 'contempt for the contemptible.'" In his chapter on Stevenson, called "My Favorite Loser," Reston admired the failed Democratic presidential candidate for his realistic assessment of world affairs, including Stevenson's own candidacies.

There is a good bit of New York Times shop talk and some rambling on such topics as today's reporters. He tells how the CIA tried to use New York Times reporters and how he had at times put up trial balloons for President Kennedy. Reston sought Kennedy's approval on some copy, such as a column dealing with the delicate face-off with the Soviet Union over Berlin in 1961.

Reston is inspirational in latter chapters as he gives prescriptions for a new American order, including reducing "all moral posturing by congressmen and columnists as much as possible under the First Amendment."

He is not always right in his memory, for example, saying the *Philadelphia Bulletin* was one of the papers that folded in the 1950s and 1960s (it was in the 1980s).

The 82-year-old Reston seems to be enjoying his retirement: "I think it's better to take things with gratitude than for granted."

Try to give dimensions in your reviews—pros and cons on an issue, two sides of a personality. In most cases, summarize the theme of the book, usually at the outset, and conclude with a summary appraisal of that theme or a reiteration of the author's point of view, such as a quote, in this case.

FILM/THEATER REVIEWS

The bottom line in a film/drama column is to tell enough to help people make up their minds about whether they want to see the production. At the same time you can't tell so much that you give away the ending. Avoid going off on tangents that won't interest the readers of the publication you're writing for.

You might want to highlight different aspects of different productions. The effects might distinguish the production; or the acting might be exceptionable even though the plot is thin; or the production might be offensive, but still terribly funny. People have reasons for seeing bad movies or plays as well as reasons to avoid good ones, because of subject matter and other reasons. Help the reader make a decision.

Clive Barnes, critic at the New York *Post*, recommends the live performance reviewer ask questions that German poet Johann Wolfgang von Goethe wanted literary critics to ask: (1) What was the artist or author trying to do? (2) How well did he or she do it? and (3) Was it worth doing? Barnes asks a fourth question: Did I have a good time, or didn't I? Or you could ask yourself a fifth question: Did I stay awake?

Sometimes you can forget all the hype and settle down to what a movie is really saying. You can highlight the real message of a film: What is it really saying that's different from what it's advertised to be about? Here's a look at the real message in a civil rights movie, *Mississippi Burning*.[12]

Civil Rights Era Sizzles in 'Mississippi Burning'

Hiley H. Ward

Here's a movie that lives up to its title.

"Mississippi Burning" is Mississippi burning.

Old deserted churches, revived as props, are set afire at regular intervals in a rhythmic cadence as small gangs of marauding whites take out their hate on pious black congregations.

In a most graphic scene, a black child, kneeling in prayer outside a ravaged church, is beaten senseless.

Mississippi is burning in this movie in the re-creation of a historical period of confrontation over integration as teams of civil rights workers come in from the north. The fire of hate is everywhere in the white community.

It is summer 1964. The story is inspired by but not literally based on the abduction and murders of civil rights workers James Chaney, Andrew Goodman and Michael Schwerner.

Willem Dafoe, who played Jesus in "The Last Temptation of Christ," is the laid-back, Harvard-trained FBI officer, Ward, sent to head a search for the missing civil rights workers.

Their deaths begin the movie, which takes on the air of a mystery as the agents try to find the bodies.

Gene Hackman, as Anderson, a former Mississippi sheriff now with the FBI, is assigned to join Ward in the investigation.

They have their own private battle, primarily over methods. Ward, the Ivy Leaguer, goes by the book; Hackman has his own savvy way of getting information — for example, getting chummy with the wife of the deputy sheriff. The wife, Mrs. Pell (Frances McDormand) knows all about the murders through her husband. The deputy

continued

---

12. Hiley H. Ward, "Movie Review: Civil Rights Era Sizzles in 'Mississippi Burning,'" *National Christian Reporter*, Jan. 13, 1989, p. 4.

continued

sheriff, Pell, is played by the wild-eyed Brad Dourif.

All whites in "Mississippi Burning" are psychopaths except for the deputy sheriff's wife; all blacks in this movie are saintly and passive, singing and praying.

Stereotyping, the essence of melodrama, is necessary at times, and it works in this film as so great an evil is confronted.

Yet one yearns for a little bit of the gray area — more of how nice people can be racists and an underscoring that persecutors are not always certified psychos.

Despite the importance of the movie's theme and magnificent performances, especially by Hackman, the movie appears seriously flawed by trying to impose the old television cop show formula on the story.

The rivalry between the agents is a must in the police genre. But, if that seems tired and predictable, so does the formula "streetwise" solution to problems — the dispensing with law to "do it my way."

The approach of the FBI in the real case is not known. The files are sealed.

But if you believe this movie, the cracking of the case came from a series of charades geared to scare to death the suspects to secure information and confessions. Agents — some posing with KKK hoods obscuring their identities — abduct the white suspects and submit them to fear of dismemberment and lynchings.

Since so much of the last part of the movie is made up of the dirty tricks, it is sad to have the feeling concerning this basically powerful movie that the bottom line is not the pursuit of law but the righting of scores by vigilantism.

While the civil rights movement proved that unjust laws can be challenged and even broken by peaceful means, it also proved, to a degree at least, the triumph of law.

Unfortunately, the movie blesses too much the taking of law into one's own hands and the expediency of the violation of rights. The perpetrators are assumed guilty and judged guilty before trial.

Vigilantism — official FBI vigilantism — here is seen as okay.

Somehow you thought director Alan Parker and writer Chris Gerolmo had something else in mind at the start of the movie.

It's a good idea not to read about a movie until you see it. After you see it, then read what others say. That way you won't initially be influenced by someone else's opinions; on the other hand, once you've seen the movie, you can forge your own position more clearly knowing where you agree or disagree with others. Don't forget that humorous techniques, from pun to parody, work well in film and drama reviews.

HOW TO SYNDICATE

Syndication (distribution to publications by an organization or by oneself) comes about in several ways. If you have the means — staff, funds, etc.–to develop a direct mail system, you can develop your own syndication; but since columns go for $8 or $10 per publication, you need quite a distribution to make any money. Look for a syndicate organization that can include your column along with its regular distribution.

How do you get started with a syndicate? If you're an expert and you have come to the attention of a syndicate, you may be asked to write four or five sample columns; and if the columns pass muster, then you may be taken on. If you're a free-lance writer or reporter, you would be expected to publish your proposed column in a half dozen papers on your own. If the national syndicate sees that outlets want the column, it will venture to take it on for larger distribution.

Judi K-Turkel and Fran Lynn Peterson, who write a business computer column for 50 newspapers, note that they got started by lining up "six big newspapers who wanted the column and started with them, then went on to sell to other newspapers." The two have also written books on writing, including *The Magazine Writer's Handbook* and *Getting It Down: How to Put Your Ideas on Paper*.

Bard Lindeman, whose column on aging, "In Your Prime," is distributed by Tribune Media Services, notes, "I'm a career journalist— writer/editor-who saw aging as a good story—one that was not being covered."

Alice Kahn, whose column is distributed by the Los Angeles Times Syndicate, began her column, she says, when "I was approached by editors who saw my column in the alternative press."

For a list of syndicates, you can consult the annual comprehensive *Directory of Syndicated Services*, published by *Editor & Publisher*.

ASSIGNMENTS

1. Contrast a timely column with a current news story in the same subject area. Make a list of how the article and column differ.

2. Analyze a column by your favorite columnist. Highlight the "passion" or emotional points; also note any humor. Rewrite the column — taking out the subjectivity, emotion and humor.

3. Turn an article you have written into a column. Put it in first-person viewpoint, introduce feeling, humor and experience and include anecdotes. Use imagery, something you can see or envision, in nearly every sentence. Stay focused on one subject or idea.

    Sometimes the reverse happens; a column becomes the basis for an article. An editor reads a column, sees an idea—maybe a columnist is asking that something be investigated. Take a published column and create a memo suggesting to a staff how the column subject could be pursued and turned into an article.

5. Select one newspaper column and one magazine column, preferably on the same topic. Note any differences in language use, perception of audience and purpose. Are there signs that a magazine column is aimed at a more focused economic level or specialized audience?

CHAPTER 12

Genres

Although good writing techniques certainly apply to all categories of writing, some publications specialize in articles on a certain topic or category of topics — science, travel, religion, history and so on. Genre publications are aimed at a general audience interested in a particular subject. In this they differ from industry and trade magazines, which are aimed at more specific audiences. Anyone from professor to plumber to 12-year-old student might read *American Heritage*; *Packaging Digest*'s audience, on the other hand, is probably limited to packaging engineers, marketing experts and manufacturers.

WRITING ABOUT SCIENCE

Science writing allows "no room for ambiguity," says George deLucenay Leon, former editor of McGraw-Hill's electronics magazine and author of seven books. "The information should be imparted in short sentences, preferably without flourish. While humor can be used, it should be used the same way one would pet a porcupine — with extreme care."

Julie Wang, who writes about science for *New York* and *Psychology Today*, emphasizes that in science writing you need in-depth knowledge and "up-to-the-minute knowledge about what is new in the field."

One well-known newspaper science writer, Jim Detjen of the Philadelphia *Inquirer*, explains what science writing is: "My role as a science writer is translating and making it understandable. I have to talk in English, decode and spoon feed."

Just as in sports and any other specialized area, in science, jargon can get the upper hand. Words become like a secret handshake — only the initiates understand. But magazines, general and topical, exist for readers other than the experts; the writer must communicate. "I try to avoid jargon," says Benedict Leerburger, a free-lance science writer for *Connoisseur, Sky, Scenorama, Family Circle*. "I use technical phrases only if essential and then define or provide an example."

Julie Wang suggests a simple rule of thumb: "If you are writing for a professional audience (e.g., physicians), leave all common jargon intact. For a consumer audience, jargon should be eliminated or explained."

Detjen uses analogies to help make technology understood. For instance, to describe acid rain, which has a pH of 3.2 (pH is a measure of acidity and alkalinity), he says, "I'd go to a scientist and ask him to make a comparison. He said 3.2 pH has the acidity of orange juice. Now I could say that rain has the acidity of orange juice. You must relate to what people understand." In discussing scientific components of air pollution, Detjen got a health expert to say, "It's so dirty that it is twice as high as that which triggers an asthma attack. I have to compare it to something I understand."

Detjen has written many articles on nuclear subjects. Because he works in the shadow of Pennsylvania's Three Mile Island, scene of the nation's worst nuclear power accident, Detjen and other staffers have continually dealt with the "fallout" — literally and figuratively. When the accident happened in 1979, the *Inquirer* had 39 reporters on the story.

Six years later, Detjen and another writer, Susan FitzGerald, took on the complicated task of showing how tons of deadly radioactive debris still contaminated Three Mile Island, just south of Harrisburg. "We had to find a way to make it readable," he says. "We could not use a lot of jargon. We had to suck the reader into the series. We decided on a narrative style and it would tell the story of the workers, weaving in facts slowly but surely, spoon feeding the readers on the dangers of radioactivity.

"You have to be careful how much detail you use. It's better to summarize the information. Also selective decisions as to what to leave out are important."

The first article in the Detjen and FitzGerald series, "The Lethal Legacy Inside TMI," gave the background of the incident and summarized in personal terms the dangers: "TMI workers deal regularly with radioactive debris, and hundreds have been contaminated" was the blurb. Part II of the series was titled "Working with Invisible Dangers," and its blurb read, "To the cleanup workers who earn a living at TMI, radiation can be a source of fear." It concentrated on the stories of selected workers:

Part 2:
The Workers Tell Their Stories

Susan FitzGerald and Jim Detjen

The first thing James Jacobs noticed was the dust.

It was black, thick and plentiful, and before long it was clinging to his clothes.

Jacobs had been sent into the Unit 2 reactor building at Three Mile Island one day in October 1983 to pick up paint chips that had flaked off the dome. It was a routine assignment in the cleanup of TMI. But no one had told Jacobs that the area would be covered with black dust.

After finishing the job, Jacobs was checked for radiation.

A detector began to click. Then an alarm rang, registering the presence of radioactive particles on his thighs, neck and chest.

Jacobs was contaminated — or "crapped up" as workers call it. The radioactive black dust had contaminated his body.

Jacobs' experience was not unusual. TMI records show that from the cleanup's start till the end of last year, there had been 593 documented cases in which cleanup workers had been contaminated by radioactive particles on an arm, leg, chest, nose, eye or groin.

Jacobs said during an interview that he was shocked and angry about being contaminated. But he is still working at TMI.

For Jacobs and hundreds of other workers helping to clean up radioactive debris from the March 28, 1979, accident, TMI is a place to make a living.

But for many of TMI's workers, the job often entails fear. Fear of radiation. Fear of cancer. Fear of genetic defects in their children.

Yet, they say, they keep on working in the cleanup of the nation's worst commercial nuclear accident because of a more immediate fear — joblessness.

"Either you work at the island, or you might not work at all," said John Murphy, 37, a laborer. "You can't find another job in this area."

Said Sam Retherford, 41, another laborer: "The guys going in are giving part of their lives away, really." But, he added, "you need a job."

Much of the cleanup work is assigned to unskilled laborers hired through a union hall in Harrisburg, 10 miles from the crippled reactor. Although electricians, ironworkers, carpenters and other craft workers are called in for specific jobs, it is the laborers who scrub and hose away the radioactive contamination that covers the walls, floors and ceilings of the Unit 2 reactor complex.

"They're the laborers, the workers — the grunts, if you will," said James Hildebrand, director of radiological controls for GPU Nuclear Corp., the New Jersey utility that operates TMI.

Workers say one of the toughest things about involvement in the cleanup is the emotional strain. Unlike people in most other jobs, in which potential dangers easily can be seen, TMI workers deal day after day with the invisible.

When inside a radioactive area of the plant, the workers must continually monitor the radiation levels around them, which can vary greatly even within a few feet.

Even when they leave TMI at day's end, the pressures do not let up, workers say.

Laborer Jim McReynolds, 40, of Hummelstown, Pa., can recall the uncomfortable reactions of some people when they learn where he has been working.

Once McReynolds' landlady asked him whether he had brought "any" — meaning radiation — home with him. And his daughter once came home from school in tears, saying she had learned in science class that TMI was "bad."

But McReynolds said: "With the way things are today, you need a job. . . . You realize you have to make a living."

Joseph Dougherty, 28, of Elstenville, Pa., says no one seems to care what happens to laborers like him.

"On the island, laborers are as low as you can get," he said. "We are called 'drones.' The general feeling is: 'Send them in to get the dose. Use them up.'"

Even so, many of the workers find ways to deal with the pressures of working around radiation.

Rodd Feeg, 27, of Shamokin, Pa., who supervises laborers in the cleanup, said that although he was initially leery about being sent into the highly contaminated reactor building, he now approached his work as just another job. "It's no big deal," he said. "I don't mind going in there at all."

Ron Powley, 32, an electrician from Enola, Pa., who worked in the cleanup for four years, said that workers might quietly worry about radiation and cancer but that they would often cover their concerns by making wisecracks.

"It's a big joke down there. We're at lunch, sitting around playing cards, and someone says, 'In three years we'll be able to deal with three hands.' . . ."[1]

Notice how the reader is not stopped by technical terms or jargon. The writers proceed with confidence, using only scientific terms that are necessary, and which have enough familiarity to be understood, such as "particles." When introducing unfamiliar terms and jargon, such as "crapped up," they explain the words.

Part III of the series presented "TMI Critics Who Paid a Price," subtitled, "Three former TMI engineers say safety concerns were often ignored, or met with retaliation." It began with personal stories:

> For months, Richard Parks, a senior engineer at the Three Mile Island nuclear plant, had complained about safety problems in the cleanup.
>
> Then, on March 17, 1983, Parks was summoned to a meeting with Bahman Kanga, the top executive in charge of the cleanup of the damaged reactor. Kanga told Parks to keep quiet, warning him that he could be "humiliated" if he did not, federal investigators later concluded.
>
> One week after that meeting, Parks was suspended from his job.
>
> Parks was not the only senior engineer who raised fundamental questions about whether the cleanup was being run safely.
>
> Larry King, director of site operations, and Edwin Gischel, director of plant engineering, also voiced safety concerns to their superiors. Like Parks, King and Gischel each had major responsibilities in ensuring the safety of the $1 billion cleanup.

---

1. Susan FitzGerald and Jim Detjen, "Three Mile Island: Working with Invisible Dangers; Part 2: The Workers Tell Their Stories," Philadelphia *Inquirer*, Feb. 11, 1985.

Like Parks, neither King nor Gischel works at TMI anymore.

All three men have complained to investigators with the U.S. Nuclear Regulatory Commission that they lost their jobs in the cleanup as a result of their outspokenness about safety violations.

King, who worked for GPU Nuclear Corp., TMI's operator, said he was abruptly suspended and barred from further entrance to the plant in March 1983, just one day before he was scheduled to discuss his safety concerns with a TMI executive vice president.

Gischel said he was forced to transfer from GPU Nuclear to another General Public Utilities subsidiary in July 1983, amid persistent demands by corporate officials that he undergo a neuropsychological examination.

Officials with GPU Nuclear and Bechtel Power Corp., the parent company of the prime contractor in the cleanup, have told the NRC that each of the three engineers left for a valid reason. Bechtel moved Parks to another job site, they said; Gischel was transferred to a less demanding GPU job after he had suffered a stroke; and King was fired on the ground that he had a professional conflict of interest.

The NRC and the U.S. Department of Labor have concluded that Parks had been harassed and unfairly removed from his job by Bechtel officials. In a report in July, the NRC staff specifically cited the March 1983 meeting, saying Kanga threatened Parks with retaliation. Kanga, a Bechtel executive who no longer works in the cleanup, refused to talk to The Inquirer about the Parks case.

NRC investigators said that Gischel and King were improperly treated by their superiors. But the NRC staff concluded that the actions of TMI officials toward Gischel and King did not constitute harassment or retaliation. . . .[2]

When the *Inquirer* reprinted the series, it included this background:

The two reporters first began to see the broad outlines of the story during what they thought would be another routine interview. Detjen and FitzGerald met with four laborers at a union hall near TMI. Before the interview began, the workers — who were charged with the job of scrubbing and hosing away the radioactivity from the walls and floors of the reactor complex — said they feared that they would lose their jobs if they talked to reporters. They had wives and children to support, they said, and TMI was the only place around to work.

Gradually, though, the four men began to open up. They told of how it was routine for cleanup workers to be contaminated by radioactive dirt, dust and water. They said workers were not always given adequate safety gear to protect themselves from radiation. They told of how one worker had been fired for refusing to work without a respirator in a radioactive area of the plant.

Those four laborers led FitzGerald and Detjen to other workers. For months after, the reporters traveled to small towns throughout central Pennsylvania to interview TMI workers. For every worker who agreed to talk, two

2. FitzGerald and Detjen, "Three Mile Island: TMI Critics Who Paid a Price; Part 3: Allegations of Harassment," *Inquirer*, Feb. 12, 1985.

or three would not. Moreover, because nuclear workers often move from plant to plant, tracking down former TMI workers was difficult. Eventually, the reporters interviewed workers who lived in Ohio, Nebraska, Florida, California, Virginia and other states.

Scores of workers told the reporters of their experiences at TMI. The interviews were intense; with each one, the scope of the story would more vividly unfold.

Having seen the human side of this drama, Detjen and FitzGerald knew they would have to document the contamination cases through official records. But officials at Three Mile Island, as well as many federal officials, repeatedly refused to cooperate or simply refused to talk with the reporters.

Initially, officers of the U.S. Nuclear Regulatory Commission and the Departments of Labor and Energy said it would be impossible to review many of the records that the reporters were seeking. But Detjen and FitzGerald persisted with other officials, and they filed requests to see hundreds of documents under the federal Freedom of Information Act.

In December 1983, the NRC agreed to allow Detjen and FitzGerald to review cleanup records kept at the agency's office at TMI. An NRC official said he expected the reporters to spend only a few days at that office. But the reporters ended up returning day after day for several months. They read through tens of thousands of pages of documents — most of them never before made public.

The records confirmed what the workers had been saying. Scores of cases in which workers had been needlessly exposed to radiation were documented in detail. And though the reporters were never given access to complete radiation-exposure files, the records they saw showed 593 skin-contamination instances from the cleanup's start through the end of 1984.

The reporters also interviewed scientists and health experts from Georgia, California, Colorado, Virginia and Japan. By the time they completed their research, they had interviewed more than 225 workers, scientists, federal and state regulators, TMI cleanup managers and other experts. . . .[3]

Magazines that deal largely with science appear to be getting less stuffy. *Psychology Today*, once the reserve of the latest developments in psychological studies, has softened. Says Julia Kagan, new editor of *Psychology Today* after its purchase by *American Health*: "Now it's psychology with a small 'p,' since the magazine no longer belongs to a psychology organization and does not need to report everything of interest to a neuro-scientist." She says the magazine now can deal with subjects like "Left-handed people ride motorcycles better" as psychological trivia; first-person columns, such as someone describing personal recovery from a stroke; new developments — "we can look at how this piece of research helps people live"; articles like "Spiritual Healing in the Suburbs"; book reviews; "interactive software" ("readers are computer literate. We are extremely interested in computers, concerning management and

3. "Behind the Scenes: How This Series Was Written," *Inquirer* reprint of series, "Three Mile Island: Accident Without an End," no date.

learning"); sports — the effect of a color on opponents, "fascinating and funny."

Regarding resources that can help a science writer, George deLucenay Leon says: "I would regard an up-to-date science dictionary and one with biographies of scientists as something every science writer should have. Publications such as *Science Digest* should also be part of the writer's library. Several popular publications can keep the science writer abreast of current advancements." And for an easy general understanding, don't forget to take a look at the books, some of them very specialized, prepared for elementary and high school students, often found in the children's section of a library.

Julie Wang finds the National Institutes of Health in Bethesda, Md., "very helpful," but "contact early, as information may take two to three weeks to come." The NIH comprises 13 institutes, each dealing with a specific disorder or malady. Wang also says the Scientists' Institute for Public Information (SIPI) in New York has access to leading researchers and institutions.

If you have a desk computer and a modem, Benedict Leerburger suggests "saving weeks of work" by directly accessing Magazine Index, DIALOG and Knowledge Index.

WRITING ABOUT TRAVEL

Travel writing is one of the more inviting kinds of free-lance endeavors. A new experience, a new environment, a new adventure looms. Why not write about it?

Travel articles do offer an opportunity to break into print, but they are not as easily written as you might think. Most travel publications operate under rigid guidelines and taboos.

Many students believe they have just the right idea for a magazine article: "my last summer vacation!" Sometimes the student has a pliable angle, such as how to keep from being robbed on the beaches of Europe. Perhaps the would-be writer could get by with a how-to based on past experience. But with travel pieces, it's hard to recover the flavor of the place from a distance. You need to be working on your story and taking notes from the outset. So, rule number one: don't suddenly decide after the fact that you're going to write a travel article. Prepare for it, plan it and — while you're at your destination — work every angle, from the scene to the people to an issue. You have to know before you go somewhere that you're going to be doing an article.

"A good writer can write a travel piece the first time out. But it's not easy," says Christopher Hunt, executive editor of *Travel & Leisure* in an article in *Writer's Digest*. "Writers who come to us thinking it is get a rude awakening. To write a description that's vivid and sounds fresh is hard. It's as hard as any kind of writing you do. You have to approach it with the same kind of seriousness and integrity." He says the best travel writing has "a personal passion on the part of the author." He tries to find out what travelers like, what makes them excited. "More than anything else we try to find out what their enthusiasms are. I ask them if there is some place they really want to go back to or a place that they are really dying to see. We try to work with that enthusiasm."[4]

Margaret S. Simmons, features editor, *Condé Nast Traveler*, in a companion article in the same issue of *Writer's Digest*, says she wants the travel writer to bring all of his or her experience to the articles. Her writers have a "personal relationship" with what they see. She cites an article about the Silk Route in China. "The author of the China Silk Route piece happens to be a very accomplished pianist," she says. "His ear is fabulous, and you hear it in the article. So conveying a sense of place involves not just sight, for instance, but hearing. All the senses are engaged. But that power is absent in lesser writers whose perceptions are clouded by clichés."[5]

When Harold Evans was editor-in-chief of *Condé Nast Traveler*, he told a seminar of magazine writing professors: "I like some original authority; for example, 'I am an archeologist. I'm going on a dig.'"

Writing Travel for Magazines

Because they come out less frequently than newspapers, travel magazines use much less free-lance material. The staff editors write many of the articles themselves and spend much time reworking those they don't. A newspaper normally has just one person in charge of a travel section, with perhaps an office assistant, and the editorial process is less extensive.

Magazine editors suggest you pay more attention to what is near home, rather than looking to far misty shores.

Big pieces are generally assigned to staff or established writers, says Pamela Fiori, editorial director and executive vice president of American Express Publishing Corp. about American Express's *Travel & Leisure*. "But we have regional sections—six of them—and there is a crying need in the east and west editions for local material.

"Start with what you know and care about and where your interests lie. Yes, the back yard. You can expand (to wider areas) as you go along. If you wrote and said you were from Los Angeles and were going to Indonesia, I'd say I'd prefer the ideas from LA. I have a whole staff who wants to go to Indonesia."

She says you have to keep the audience in mind. For *Travel & Leisure*, it's an "upscale readership, but by the same token, it is pretty mainstream." While some magazines talk to "an audience on the fringe and about offbeat

4. Christopher Hunt, "It Isn't Easy: Advice from *Travel & Leisure*'s Executive Editor," *Writer's Digest*, June 1989, p. 25.

5. Margaret S. Simmons, "Record What You See: Advice from *Condé Nast Traveler*'s Features Editor," *Writer's Digest*, June 1989, p. 24.

places, our readers want to know the best restaurants in Paris. They're not celebrity hounds or interested in the restaurant of the minute. They travel for experience, not status." The readers of *Travel & Leisure*, she says, include "intensive business travelers, those in their 40s and incredibly well traveled. They just don't want to go off and sleep on the floor. What unites them is a passion for travel."

Not reported enough is the environment, says Harold Evans, recent past editor of *Condé Nast Traveler* who is now president and publisher of Random House Adult Trade Books. "What, for example, is being done to save a ruin? What should you do with a ruin to restore it?" he asked when he was still editor. At *Condé Nast Traveler*, he paved the way in investigative travel writing. The magazine may cite the hardship rather than the pleasure of a place. "If you have a chest condition, you need to know if the air is clean." The magazine rates locales on air quality. Evans explained before he took his new job: "If we do not offer the truth and guidance, what do we offer? Not only do we have truth in news reports, we take a stand, an editorial voice." Some recent topics in *Condé Nast Traveler*: "Asia's Overcrowded Routes — How Bad Are They?" "The Yellowstone Fires: The Serious Questions for Our Parks," "Aging Jets: Who Has the Oldest (and Youngest) Planes?" and "The Lowdown on Medical Advice for Travelers."

Travel & Leisure emphasizes service to the reader. Says Fiori: "We are more apt in the travel and money section to tell which automated cash machines are the best, how to decipher an airline ticket; safety in airlines; how to get collision damage waivers on car rentals. We do not try to scare the jesus out of the reader."

Airline publications and ground transportation passenger magazines such as *Amtrak Express* offer opportunities for writers. Others include *Adventure Magazine* (camping), *Away* (auto travel), *Diversion* (travel for physicians), *The Connoisseur* (arts and travel), *Camperways* (vehicle camping), *Caribbean Travel and Life*, *Chevy Outdoors*, *National Geographic Traveler*, *Journal of Christian Camping*, *New England Getaways*, *Travel-Holiday* and *Traveling Times*. *Endless Vacation* is a general purpose magazine for vacation travelers. The magazine's guidelines, provided by associate editor Laurie Borman, say "it is not for business travelers or armchair travelers. *Endless Vacation* shows readers where to go and what to do on vacation and, perhaps most important, why." The brochure has specific advice "before you write your query":

1. The editors strongly suggest that you read the magazine thoroughly to get an understanding of our style and approach. Reading the magazine may also prevent you from querying us on a topic that has recently been covered.

2. Because our readers are doers, not dreamers, your article should cover destinations they can visit and activities in which they can participate. Unusual experiences should be woven into that context.

3. Articles must have a narrow focus but not be so limited as to have parochial appeal. An article on the resurgence of a city is good; an article on a common event or festival in a city usually is not.

4. Articles should provide a fast read, packed with anecdotes, examples and ministories. Many, many publications are competing for our readers' time. Brevity, clarity and conciseness should be hallmarks of your article.

5. Audience (based on 1986 demographic study by Simmons Market Research Bureau, Inc.):

- Sex: 62.3 percent male; 37.7 percent female
- Median age: 44.6
- College graduates: 46.5 percent
- Married: 85.7 percent
- Income: $48,000 median; $63,000 mean
- 98 percent own a timeshare condominium (although the number of subscribers who do not own a timeshare condominium is rising)
- Most important activities while on vacation (in descending order): leisure time, visiting local tourist attractions, dining, shopping, swimming, sports activities, cultural activities, entertaining.

Prolific travel writer Nino Lo Bello, based in Vienna, says he looks out for the "offbeat ideas. I look for the odd-ball locations — anything not mentioned in the guidebooks." He noted that a "Believe-it-or-not" Sunday comic mentioned a town in France called "Y." He made a point to go there and write about it. He picks up information on the spot. One time, arriving in Pisa, Italy, he asked directions to the famous Leaning Tower of Pisa. A traffic officer in Pisa said, "Which one?" Was there more than one? Lo Bello was told there were three, and off he galloped to write about one of the unknown leaning towers in Pisa.

A young free-lance travel writer in New York, Alice Garrard, pursued a long-time fascination — people who trample grapes. Through contacts she arranged to take part in the processing of grapes in a French village and sold the resulting article to newspapers and magazines, among them the Boston *Globe* and the magazine *Scanorama*. Entertaining and informational, she made you feel as if you were there as she also described the process.[6]

I Picked Grapes in the Médoc

Alice Garrard

I became fascinated with the French grape harvest, or *vendanges*, long before I knew much about French wines. For years I nurtured fantasies of chateau doors being flung open to adventuresome wayfarers who arrived eager to work for meager wages, companionship and good wine.

Last fall I became a grape harvester in the Médoc, in the township of Pauillac, at a lovely

continued

---

6. Alice Garrard, "I Picked Grapes in the Médoc," *Scanorama*, September 1984, pp. 111–115.

continued

chateau with the lyrical name Pontet-Canet. The property director, 37-year-old Alfred Tesseron, agreed to let me pick grapes after much cajoling by a French friend who has known the Tesseron family all her life. It was a greenhorn grape picker's dream come true.

The Médoc, late in September, was engulfed in golden Indian summer days.

I had expected the other pickers at Pontet-Canet to be French peasants or Spanish migrant workers who flood into France this time of year. It was with great surprise that I watched two buses heave into the chateau's courtyard and deposit 90 tired, hungry people, all of whom I could understand when they opened their mouths. It was English all right, but with a cadence and charm lacking in my own: British.

Alfred Tesseron had contracted their help through an organization in England, called Vacation Work, and instead of *bonjour* or *hola* I was saying *hello* to James, Elaine and four score others from England, Kim and a few others from Scotland, Paul from Wales, Chris and Roberta ("call me Bert") from Northern Ireland, Michael and Jason from Bermuda and Carl from South Africa.

My co-workers were young: being female and over 30, I was doubly in the minority as there were only 20 women, including four from the only French family that picked but lived and ate separately from us.

Likes Meeting People

Fred Ayers, perhaps the oldest and most experienced picker, was over 60, and this was his fourth harvest. "I find this kind of work good exercise for the hand I broke playing cricket," is how he explains his continued participation in work that is back-breaking. "And I like meeting people."

On the morning of our first day of picking, Alfred Tesseron divided us into two groups of 40 pickers and 8 porters, whose job it would be to transport the grapes we'd plucked to waiting wagons. One group headed off to one side of the expansive vineyard — at almost 70 hectares (170 acres), Pontet-Canet is the largest of the classified growths. The overseer and the vineyard manager, Pierre Geffier, was a jaunty, compact man with a weather-creased face continually shaded by an English-schoolboy cap. Geffier has lived and worked in the Médoc all his life; Pontet-Canet has employed his services for the past 15 years. "Every year Monsieur Geffier threatens to retire," says Tesseron, "but I hope he never does."

Never Stops Learning

My group, baskets in hand, took off behind the chateau, where most of the vast estate lies and from where a worker can straighten up to unkink weary muscles and gaze at the still peaceful surroundings, the neat white manor house and the orderly gray outbuildings with the appropriately claret-colored shutters. Keeping us in tow was Hughes Combes, Geffier's assistant and a newcomer to Pontet-Canet. He had started his career in wine-making in a roundabout way, after completing five years' study toward a law degree. His change of heart sent his family, none of whom had ever worked in wine production, into shock and him back to school for another couple of years. "I love my work," he says. "You never stop learning in this job."

Combes assigned each of us a number, 1 through 40, and we lined up row by row to pick. As we worked, Combes strode constantly among the rows, his sheepdog, Bill, close at his heels, checking our pace and sending those who had finished a row to help someone else.

Occasionally some good-natured grape warfare broke out, but rarely did he chastise. "I don't want to see grapes in the air," he'd say.

It took about an hour-and-a-half to finish one set of 40 rows, but seldom did we have time to relish the accomplishment. Combes, anticipating that the end was in sight, was already moving ahead in his lanky gait, propelling us forward to the next verdant strip. *"Allez, allez!* Number One," he'd call, and our scruffy band would pick itself up from the side of the road, where we had fallen like war-wounded, and move on.

Blood and Blisters

I had always heard that grape picking was hard work, but nothing had prepared me for just how rigorous and dirty it really is. The lower back pain, the twinges and swelling in knee joints, the cramps in the tops of the thighs, hands that are dirt-coated, blistered, stained and bleeding, and the insidious bone-tiredness at the end of the day are in sharp juxtaposition to the elegance of the product.

To pick grapes successfully, one must arrange oneself to reach the clusters on both sides of a row while avoiding collecting leaves or dropping grapes in the dirt — a Tesseron imperative. The fruit is pruned to hang low to the ground to enhance its sweetness, but this creates numerous problems for pickers, who accomplish their goal in a variety of ways: squatting bent-kneed was a popular method; leaning completely over the vine, as if in a ballet position, another; the third and dirtiest approach was to sit cross-legged on the ground and sidle down the row, crablike. A combination of techniques usually worked best.

Pickers do not pick at all; they clip. A pair of small snippers is essential to separate the bunches of grapes from their tenacious stems. Most workers wore gloves to avoid snipping their hands and to stay cleaner, but most ended up cutting off the tips of their gloves and nicking their hands anyway. The mixture of dust on the vines, sandy soil, sticky juice from punctured or smashed grapes, and the dew on the vines in the mornings ensured that everyone walked around with purplish hands etched with black creases that defied the heartiest scrubbings.

After three or four days of picking, the worst of the aches and pains subsided; the hard part of the job then became finding ways to pass the time. The porters adopted the habit of whistling in unison — a practice that undermined their popularity after four or five hours of it nonstop — or fiddling with what they called "mind occupiers," a couple of smooth stones, a chestnut dangling from a string, or even one of the small frogs that makes the vineyard its home.

Each porter carried a container the size of a bushel basket strapped to his back. When full, it weighed almost 50 kilos. They dumped their bounty into half a dozen large oak barrels with a quick flick of one shoulder that sent the grapes tumbling with a muted drumroll. When the barrels were filled to overflowing, they were hauled by tractor to the press house to be destemmed and slightly pressed for the fermentation process.

"You begin to take joy in little things," says Sue Masterson of Great Yarmouth, England, "like finding a gap in your row or no queue for the loo." My special treat was happening upon a small cluster of grapes dangling from a tendril near the top of a vine. I'd pop the tight little sphere into my mouth for a quick drink, and although the grapes were too bitter to be truly tasty, that was soon forgotten in the heat of the Médoc sun.

Thank God for lunch. The two-hour respite between the morning's grueling four hours and the four that were still to come was welcome. The doors to the dining hall were flung open and we sat down at long tables covered with red and white tablecloths on which lay tin utensils, long loaves of French bread, and 50 cheery green bottles, half of them filled with water and half with wine — not the prestigious chateau-bottled variety but a lowly substitute made by a local cooperative. Twice as many wine-filled bottles would greet us at the evening meal, one for every two people to share.

Four women who lived on the property worked 12 to 14 hours a day to feed 130 workers. Lunch and dinner fare was basic and hearty — no gourmet cuisine this. It included beef, chicken, fish, potatoes, peas, tomatoes, fruit for dessert, and the addition of soup for dinner. Breakfast, typically French but not very energizing, consisted of coffee (served in the customary cereal-size bowls), bread and a very sweet jam. We drank wine, water, and coffee out of the same glass tumblers. By the end of our stay at Pontet-Canet, most people claimed they would be happy if they never saw a loaf of French bread or a grape again.

Most afternoons Alfred Tesseron, perhaps clad in an alligator-pattern shirt, slacks and dusty

continued

continued

loafers, arrived on his Honda XL500 to survey the troops. Pontet-Canet is the only one of the three chateaus he manages (all of them owned by his father) not harvested by machine. "Machines don't complain about the food or the hours," he says, "and there are no buildings or bed to be maintained." Yet he prefers the atmosphere at the chateau when the seasonal workers arrive. "With the machine it's just work," he says, "but with people here, the place is alive, it's human."

During the harvest Tesseron allows no visitors to the chateau, which, like most Médoc properties, is open to the public for tours, tastings and sales, and he turns off the answering machine in his office. The atmosphere during this brief but intense period is a cross between that of a cloister and a summer camp, the stillness and organized activity as apparent as the dust. Pickers who came to Pontet-Canet felt the isolation intensely. Most embraced it. This was, after all, a temporary endeavor. I never heard the sound of a radio or television or telephone during my stay, and the occasional bleep of someone's electronic watch in the vineyard never failed to startle me.

In the evenings many pickers spirited into town, a half hour's walk away, even when they were exhausted. On Saturday nights they made a special effort to go out, just because it was Saturday. There were a few local bars and a tiny movie theater. By the time we got off work and had had dinner, the local swimming pool was closed. The full-time employees at the chateau, most of whom worked four to six hours a day longer than the pickers, never went home to bed.

After 16 days with no time off, the pickers were beginning to break under the strain and the monotony, and one of the harvesting machines put in a day's and night's work to help bring the harvest to a close at Pontet-Canet.

There is an urgency and an economic necessity to gather the grapes as soon as possible once they are ripe (Merlot matures first, followed by the Cabernets). Even if it had rained — it never really did, the best sign for an excellent 1983 vin-

tage — we would have gone into the vineyard in boots and raincoats to harvest. Sunlight keeps the sugar level of the grapes high, and this contributes to a longer lasting, higher quality wine. As we picked that last day, the air was filled with the insistent drone of the machine, signaling not only the close of the year's harvest, but of an era. We were becoming an anachronism as we worked, part of a tradition that will die out as surely as stomping on the grapes did with the advent of machine presses.

My guess is that more and more of the Médoc will be harvested by machine in the next three to five years. The flat terrain and the thick-skinned red grapes lend themselves to machines. Hand harvesting costs nearly 10,000 francs, or about $1,280 for a bit more than a half hectare (1-1/2 acres), while a machine costs only 3,600 francs, about $462, to rent. A machine can harvest more than half a hectare in just three hours and could pay for itself in three or four years. Hand harvesting at Pontet-Canet has a couple of years of grace left while Alfred Tesseron and vineyard directors like him throughout the Médoc determine whether the fruit that is machine-harvested, and the wine produced from it, is as high in quality as grapes that are carefully hand-picked.

While the machine is becoming economically feasible for chateau owners, picking hardly seems so for laborers. At Pontet-Canet, pickers earned the equivalent of $2.79 an hour for their first 39 hours in the field; 25% overtime for the next 8 hours; after that, and each Sunday, they were paid 50% in overtime. They paid their employer about $7 out of their wages every day for food and lodging (little more than a cot in a shared room, with five showers and three toilets used by everyone); and they had already paid the agency in England about $175 for their insurance and the mandatory one-way bus trip from London.

The experience, less than lucrative, seems laughable when you consider that wine-producing is a multi-million-dollar business. Chateau Pontet-Canet wine sells for about $15 a bottle, and a million and a half bottles lie aging in its cellars.

On day sixteen of the picking, Hughes Combes said "You've picked the last grape."

The end was anticlimactic; we simply picked up our baskets—no hurling them aloft and cheering—and walked slowly back to our modest dwellings as we had done so many times before. The women in the kitchen put together three large bouquets and we paraded to the chateau to present them to the owner, Guy Tesseron, as well as to Alfred and his stepmother, who were at the door waiting for us. They were having lunch with Pierre Cardin that day; we ate in our dining hall but drank sparkling wine instead of our usual red.

Garrard's article was accompanied by two sidebars—one describing customs and history of the Médoc region and the other listing information and addresses for those interested in grape picking in France.

Writing Travel for Newspapers

What are editors of travel sections in newspapers looking for?

- "We want regional material." — Catherine Watson, travel editor, Minneapolis *Star Tribune*.

- "We particularly like pieces involving activities (climbing Mt. Fuji, walking the Milford Track) rather than sightseeing." — Joan Boer, Alameda Newspapers Group.

- "Destination pieces, 1,500 words max." — Mary Botter, Denver *Post*.

- "Useful information, less essay, more nuts and bolts." — Joan H. Smith, travel editor, Bangor (Me.) *Daily News*.

Travel editors say one of their biggest problems is "getting art appropriate to the story" and in particular "getting good color art."

Watson of the *Star Tribune* says one of her biggest problems is finding "good, quotable, honest sources—most difficult in foreign countries that don't, as a cultural rule, trust journalists. To overcome it, I work real hard and tie my stomach up in knots, and keep trying till I find good people who'll talk." The three most common mistakes writers make, she says, are, "They don't contact me. They just send unrequested manuscripts. Secondly they write general pap, instead of detail-packed, specifically focused controlled articles. Third, they treat the rest of the world as 'natives'—seldom quoting residents of a destination, or, if they do, using only first names, 'Juan' and 'Maria.' It means they don't respect their sources." Alfred S. Borcover, travel editor of the Chicago *Tribune*, complains that "they don't know how to write or spell."

Among bits of advice for the travel writer, Watson says: "Read. Work. Think. Don't expect to get a good piece out of a vacation." Denver *Post*'s Botter: "Rite tite!" Alameda Group's Boer: "Put people in the story. Lyrical descriptions go just so far." Bangor *News'* Smith: "Learn what a reader wants first: 'What's in it for me' is today's reader's battle cry."

Travel writers don't agree on which point of view works best:

- "I like first person if it has quotes, and I find that third person works best for most writers. I hate second person stories." — Boer

- "It depends on the content. I prefer second — avoids the ego in viewpoint many writers slip into with first, and avoids the god-like tones of third." — Watson

- "Second or third, unless first person is absolutely necessary. Too many insignificant 'I's.'" — Borcover

- "I prefer third, but all that depends on the writing. Unpretentious first can be fine." — Botter

Travel Writing Aids

Government offices, tourist agencies and the embassies and consulates of the country to be visited can be called upon for information and procedures for making contacts for a project or area you wish to feature.

The *Travel Writer's Handbook*, published by Writer's Digest Books, offers, as its blurb says, "Everything you need to know to write and sell your travel experiences." It takes up query procedures, getting pictures, "what to look for while you're traveling," questions of freebies and tax deductions and a section on "The Twelve Most Popular Types of Travel Articles." *Writer's Market* has a section on travel magazine listings, although several of the larger publications and carrier publications decline to be listed.

Travel Publishing News is an eight-page quarterly reviewing new travel books and magazine articles (Winterbourne Press, 1407 Gilman St., Berkeley, CA 94707). *Publishers Weekly* devotes an issue to travel books in February.

Travel writer Robert Scott Milne in New York puts out a monthly *Travelwriter Marketletter*. This typically points out travel article ideas, resorts and other centers offering invitations to travel writers. The publication also includes a generous mix of new travel market developments (*Travelwriter Marketletter*, Room 1723, Plaza Hotel, New York, NY 10019).

WRITING ABOUT HISTORY

Byron Dobell, retired editor of *American Heritage*, commented in a speech to the American Society of Magazine Editors that, of all the editorial positions he had held (including stints as an editor at *Esquire* and *Time*), being editor of a history magazine had to be the most interesting. His point was simple: While most magazines do the familiar topical stories others are doing — AIDS, day care, latchkey children, child abuse, the homeless, racial and ethnic violence, political and celebrity profiles — a history magazine can use topics that no one else is thinking about. You can always find something fresh in history.

In an interview before his retirement in 1990, Dobell expanded on his views. Take any article, he said. "Most have read it before — it's another one on AIDS. Name the subject. It's the same damn article. The great thing about history is that it's not in the news; it's not just another incremental story. It's eye opening."

History writing is similar to reporting, he says. "Since the bulk of a reporting story is history, history is reporting. But there are a couple of differences. If you go back more than a generation, everybody is dead. You can't call them up!" But, he adds, there are documents. "An advantage, though, in history writing is that most of the facts are no longer secret and people are no longer worried for their jobs." The historian can get more of the story.

"You can do a story on anything that happened 15 years ago and come up with a great story," says Dobell. "I advise anyone who wants to break into the big time to go back seven years or so, in *Time* magazine, for instance, and pick two or three stories and go back on them." You can put together a sound investigative story if you collect all the documentation for an old story; consider the stories that came out in 1991 about the 1980 Inauguration Day release of American hostages in Iran. "In a breaking news story, you have a first perception; one year later, a hypothesis; 20 years later, you really get close to what actually happened."

Dobell called attention to the life and claims of celebrated military historian S.L.A. Marshall, who claimed in *Men Against Fire* that no more than one-fifth of any given body of American infantry in combat ever fired their weapons at the enemy. Fredric Smoler, writing for *American Heritage* ("The Secret of the Soldiers Who Didn't Shoot," March 1989), disputed this. Using documents, Marshall's notes and writings, and interviews with those who knew Marshall and other researchers, Smoler concluded that Marshall wasn't telling the truth about his own military record nor could he have done the research that led to the oft-quoted conclusion about the firing ratio of Americans in battle. A report on the revisionist *American Heritage* article made the front page of the New York *Times*.

Regarding probing into the past, Dobell advises, "Never avoid the obvious. Present it in a new way. There is always room for new biographies of Lincoln and Washington.

"Be immersed in some aspect of a great man's life," and you can spot some of the stories and ideas that contradict common opinion. "There are no bad ideas, only undeveloped ideas. Every subject is good in any area of American life."

When it comes to history writing, Dobell suggests, "Pure academics may be stuck with minutia; journalists are too cosmic and full of air. As in all good writing, we look for a mixture of the specific and the general. Know when to put in the flour and the raisins.

"A good article should not merely convey gee whiz, but it should not be boring. Tell how people lived and thought in a voice that is not lecturing or condescending or jokey."

History writing is storytelling, says Dobell. "Historian Francis Parkman was a great adventure teller. He used anecdotes; it was human history. There is nothing more interesting to humans than human history. Academicians often forget this — if they ever knew it to begin with."

The kind of lead — or angle — that works, he says, is to say in so many words "here's what the conventional wisdom says, but now I'll tell you what really happened." A good history article has "a strong element of detection; it can be a wonderful detective story."

Dobell described *American Heritage*'s audience: "The intelligent grown-up who is not an expert — the general educated reader."

History magazines include *American History Illustrated, Blue & Gray* (Civil War era), *Old Mill News, Old West, Timeline* (published by Ohio Historical Society), *True West, Preservation News* (National Trust for Historic Preservation) and *Christian History. Smithsonian*, museum magazines, regional journals, *National Geographic* and indeed most other magazines also use history articles on occasion.

Media history can provide topics, such as the article on Polly Pry, a colorful reporter at the turn of the century, in the *Smithsonian*, January 1991.

Media History Digest, which includes university students and Pulitzer Prize–winning historians among its writers, also looks for the popular subject. Its articles center on people — unsung heroes (such as who really invented radio and TV?), overlooked personalities (such as Joseph Pulitzer's suicidal brother, Albert, who also ran a New York newspaper, the *Journal*) and unknown stories about the famous (such as the plans of the ailing Franklin Delano Roosevelt to start a national newspaper). The magazine, published by *Editor & Publisher*, has had its share of special issues on themes such as the Constitution, the West, Native Americans, religion, science fiction, war and peace, humor and cartoons, Lincoln, personalities such as Joseph Pulitzer and Horace Greeley, sports.

University students who are given an assignment for *Media History Digest* must put their articles through one rewrite, not a bad idea for any writer. Students get the following guidelines to help bring their history articles into publishable shape:

FORMAT
1. Start in the middle of the page; use margins; number pages. Double-space all.

2. Use special indent for all quotes over one sentence.

3. Keep paragraphs reasonably short—not over eight lines.

4. Eight or 10 pages—good length. Those who are writing 25 to 30 pages, try to get the length back to 15 pages.

ADDENDA

1. Full set of footnotes (author, title, publisher, year, page, etc.).

2. Bibliography.

3. A page with some ideas for illustrations—mention any good quality pics, cartoons you came across and how to find them.

4. Paragraph about yourself and where you can be reached in the future.

WRITING THE ARTICLE AND STYLE

1. On first page or near top (lead) have an establishing paragraph that summarizes in a sentence or two what the article is about. This will be your *focus*. All the rest of the article must develop and relate to your establishing paragraph.

2. Use anecdotes. Don't just give us an encyclopedic chronology. Select the most interesting and significant points—present them in scenes and story/dramatic fashion.

3. Write pictorially. Let us *see* and live (or re-live) what you are talking about.

4. Don't assume any prior knowledge of reader on the subject.

5. ID's of people in your article: Full names on first reference; it is also important to know who the person is (vocation, basic background tags).

6. Explain briefly any and all terms, strange titles, etc.

7. *Sources*: Touch base with, if not exhaust, the realm of possible sources. Must have some evidence of using primary sources. Ideally, most of article would reflect primary sources (original newspapers, diaries, records, etc.) *Do not* rely on just four or five secondary books. If you do any interviewing, don't settle for inane bland quotes from anybody. Interviews are best limited to descendants of the subject, others who knew the person or acclaimed historians.

8. Verify (double-check) all names, exactness of excerpts.

Here's one *Media History Digest* article on a lesser-known U.S. president and the press—part of a series. Note the descriptions of people, explanation of terms and use of primary sources, namely, the newspapers of the time (not too difficult in this case, for William Henry Harrison's tenure as president covered only one month).[7]

7. Hiley H. Ward, "'President-for-a-Month': William Henry Harrison and the Press," *Media History Digest*, Spring/Summer 1988, pp. 38–45.

'President-for-a-Month' William Henry Harrison and the Press

Hiley H. Ward

To get elected in 1840, a candidate had to be bigger than life. He still had to run in the image of the great hero, Andrew Jackson, the victor of the War of 1812 and a man identified with the rigor and strength of the frontier.

The new candidate had to be an astute politician with a knack for knowing when to lunge forth or when to lay back and let the people come to him. He would ride in on a wave of discontent, just as Jackson capitalized on the discontent with the unpopular John Quincy Adams, who held the press at bay and was totally unconcerned with image making.

The new President elected in 1840 would also likely be one who countered the aristocratic, high-handed image of Jackson's handpicked successor, Democrat Martin Van Buren, who had won in 1836. Van Buren's administration was cursed largely by an economic panic started in 1837.

The winning candidate—a Democrat or a member of the catchall new party, the Whigs—had to be a myth, a product of imagination and more. On the heels of economic austerity and the paucity of entertainment on the plains and in the cities, the new man had to be entertaining. He would also need a good press.

The man to fit the bill was perfectly at hand. Aging General William Henry Harrison, largely retired at his farm in North Bend, Ohio, 16 miles west of Cincinnati, had spent much of his life on the frontier, was a war hero, made friends easily, was identified with the fresh new party, the Whigs, and was free of the accumulated baggage of Jackson and Van Buren.

Harrison came from a rich Virginia family. His father, Benjamin Harrison V, was a signer of the Declaration of Independence. The young Harrison studied medicine with the distinguished Benjamin Rush but soon opted for the glamour of the military, using his connections to be appointed as an officer. He served under General Anthony Wayne in the famous battle of Fallen Timbers in 1794 at Maumee, Ohio against an Indian confederacy. Then Harrison led troops victoriously against Indians at Tippecanoe Creek near Lafayette, Ind., in 1811. During the War of 1812, he crushed once and for all Tecumseh's Indian confederation at the Battle of the Thames (October 5, 1813) in Ontario—a victory over a sizable force of British troops and Indians.

Harrison had a considerable career in government, first administrator of the Northwest Territory and then as governor of the newly created Indian Territory for over 10 years. He served in the Ohio Senate and the U.S. Senate, where John Quincy Adams said he showed "a lively and active but shallow mind." (Adams *Memoirs*, May 6, 1838 entry)

As the first U.S. minister to Colombia, under President Jackson, Harrison even had foreign experience, but his taking sides—criticizing the Colombian liberator Simon Bolivar for despotic leanings—prompted his recall. Along with other Whigs he had already tested the waters as a Presidential candidate against Van Buren in 1836.

Now he waited, like the Roman Cincinnatus at his plow, ready to be summoned to lead his nation from suppression. He was now merely a clerk of the Court of Common Pleas in Hamilton County as he enjoyed the good life in the magnificent mansion built around a four-room cabin he had bought from his father-in-law after leaving the military in 1796. (For Harrison's life story, see Dorothy Goebel, *William Henry Harrison: A Political Biography*, Indiana Historical Collections, Vol. XIV, and Freeman Cleaver, *Old Tippecanoe*).

There were still the battles and skirmishes to be fought figuratively with the hordes of editors cultivated by the media-conscious Jackson, who through his spoils system had rewarded editors in virtually all the states. Jackson's devotee Francis Blair was still at the key *Washington Globe*, and Jackson's closest aide, Amos Kendall, was editor of the *Extra Globe* and before the inaugural in 1841, had launched the 16-page fortnightly *Kendall's Expositor*. Blair and Kendall together captained Democratic forces to re-elect Van Buren.

Harrison had the influential Thurlow Weed and his powerful Whig-bent organ, the *Albany* (N.Y.) *Journal*, but most of all the laid-back Harrison had a youthful, ambitious moon-faced newcomer, Horace Greeley. Fresh out of the print-shop, Greeley, the future founder and editor of the *New York Tribune*, listened to Weed and Weed's ally, Gov. William H. Seward of New York, and launched *The Log Cabin*, a full-size weekly paper devoted unashamedly to fostering the Presidential bid of Gen. Harrison in 1840. *The Log Cabin*, dedicating its space to debunking at length any rumor or criticism belittling the general, recounted with splendid woodcuts and detailed narrative the military crusades against the Indians by the general, and even curiously included songs—words with music—praising the general.

Some 15 songs were printed during the campaign by *The Log Cabin*. Most notable perhaps is the one dedicated to the familiar political slogan about the general and his running mate, "Tippecanoe and Tyler, too."

What has caused this great
commotion, motion, motion,
Our Country through!
It is the Ball a rolling on,
For Tippecanoe and Tyler too—
Tippecanoe and Tyler too,
And with them we'll beat little Van,
Van, Van is a used up man,
And with them we'll beat little Van.

And there are 15 more stanzas, all printed by Greeley:

So the marching of mighty waters,
waters, waters,
On it will go,
And of course will clear the way
For Tippecanoe, etc., etc.

John Tyler, a less pleasant man, was a Southerner brought on to give balance to the ticket. Curiously, Van Buren's vice president, Richard Johnson, was a rugged, woodsy war hero whose five scars from bullet wounds and a shattered hand made Harrison look as if he had only been to Sunday school picnics. Johnson, while serving under Harrison, was credited (though incorrectly) with killing the Indian war chief Tecumseh. Johnson, nicknamed "Rumpsey Dumpsey," was conspicuous by his style. He wore bright red vests, and he was a thunderous orator. He once lived with a young black woman.

While some critics called Harrison the "Petticoat General," General Jackson weighed in simply saying that Harrison never had the qualities befitting a commander of an army. (See *The Log-Cabin Campaign*, Robert Gray Gunderson, citing various newspapers, among them the *Richmond Enquirer* and the *Logansport* [Ind.] *Herald*.)

Greeley, in Vol. 1, No. 1, May 2, 1840, starts his *Log Cabin* off with the concern for setting the record straight, with high emotion, curiously never to be rewarded when Harrison is elected. (William Hale, *Horace Greeley*). Says Greeley:

Of the many malignant and wilful calumnies with which Faction has attempted to sully the fair fame of a brave defender of his country, this is the vilest. At the close of the last Presidential Contest, when everything had been raked up and blazoned that an unscrupulous Party and Press could discover or invent in disparagement of General Harrison's character and services— how much of it has survived the canvass? How much could any man who voted against Gen. Harrison in 1836 remember of all that had been vomited forth against him through the preceding year? Barely

continued

continued

vague aspersions of his military capacity and services, such as have been set afloat by ignorance, rashness, and envy, against every wise and prudent commander from Fabius to Washington. . . .

Harrison also got help from a little-known plainsman, Abraham Lincoln. At 31, Lincoln himself, running for the Illinois House of Representatives, stomped the state for the "Log Cabin" candidate. In one encounter, Lincoln, suspecting the Democrat opponent in his debate of being as vain and pompous as Van Buren, reached over and tore open the Democrat's coat, showing beneath it ruffled silk and velvet vest and a gold watch and chain. Lincoln went on to joke about his own days growing up in buckskin. (Carl Sandburg, *Prairie Years*, I, 236)

Harrison's supporters not only knew how to capitalize on the foibles of an opponent, but also how to turn around a nasty comment into a cheerful slogan on the general's behalf.

When Harrison began to emerge as a possibility over perennial Whig candidate Henry Clay for the nomination, Clay's followers wondered aloud how could they get rid of Harrison. Jokingly, a reporter, John de Ziska of the *Baltimore Republican*, Dec. 11, 1839, suggested that the way was to "give him a barrel of hard cider, and settle a pension of two thousand a year on him, and my word for it, he will sit the remainder of his days in his log cabin by the side of a 'sea coal' fire, and study moral philosophy."

A month later the article was remembered when two Harrison men, a banker and a Harrisburg, Pa., editor met to create some symbols for the Harrison campaign. One of them suggested that "passion and prejudice, properly aroused and directed, would do about as well as principle and reason in a party contest." (Gunderson) They decided that the aristocratic-born Harrison would be a "log-cabin" candidate. They drew up a campaign picture of a log cabin which had a coonskin nailed to the wall and nearby were a woodpile and a cider barrel. Log cabins were raised across the country as Harrison headquarters; hard cider flowed at picnics and other occasions, courtesy of the followers of "Old Tip," or "Old Tipler," as some critics now began to call him.

Because of his age—67 in 1840, and his delicate personality, "Old Tip" was also often called "Granny" by his critics. Van Buren, too, picked up a nickname by his followers. "O.K." for Old Kinderhook, in reference to his New York hometown. However, Whig editors, Van's critics, switched this to "K.O.," "Kicked Out."

The Whig strategy was to avoid taking stands on any issue, for to do so would have fractionated the party. Some even characterized "Tip" as a Whig and his running mate "Ty" as a Democrat. The Whig Party from 1836 on was, as Historian Thomas Bailey puts it in his *American Pageant*, "a hodgepodge of malcontents—'an organized incompatibility.'" Their guiding star, he said, was opportunism. "Under the same political roof were gathered all kinds of Whigs; protectionists and free-traders, Southern nullifiers and Northern nationalists, rich Southern planters and poor Northern farmers." Slavery was looming as a big issue, and Harrison generally walked down the middle.

Harrison, once elected, did not enjoy a honeymoon with the press in his brief tenure of service in the month before his death in office, April 4, at 68.

His inaugural speech, while praised by some and worshipped by Greeley, was also savaged and mocked by others.

Kendall, tongue in cheek, made Harrison out to be a giddy old "granny" whose inaugural substance could be boiled down to some simple statements. . . .

In New York, the *Herald* gave it a few good marks but for the most part found it "trash":

. . . The address is one of the most unevenly composed and written documents that ever came from the brain or pen of a public functionary. Parts of it are most excellent, and other parts of it are most trashy. The best parts of it contain some of the soundest and purest doctrines that were ever conceived; but they are very,

very hard to live up to. Many other parts are unworthy of the tyro at college or his first attempt at composition.

... There is too much said about nothing.... There is too much twaddle; all the points could have been given in a dozen lines.

The nonsense about "an exclusive metallic currency" is a crotchet of his own brain; a sort of shuttlecock which he stuck up and knocked down for amusement three times in a paragraph. The remarks about the District of Columbia are miserably written; the sentences are involved, complicated, and tortuous; they may be contrived to mean anything or nothing. The balderdash about Oliver Cromwell, Caesar, and Bolivar, will elevate the president in the eyes of no one. He does not understand the character of either. ...

In that month of March—in the first month and the only month of the Harrison Presidency—the newspapers began to hint of the President's illness. Most brushed if off with a paragraph each day. The *National Intelligencer* said:

April 1—We learn from the physicians attending the President that, at eight o'clock last evening, there was a slight improvement in his condition.

April 2—We learned two additional physicians were called yesterday to consult upon the President's case, and we have pleasure in announcing that in their opinion there is evident improvement in his situation.

April 3—Saturday—We are informed by the attending physicians that there is no material change in the condition of the President since Thursday evening.

The *New York Herald* identified fatigue as a contributing factor as the generous-spirited President sought to oblige all who came seeking appointment to office. Said the *Herald*, April 1:

The President has been very much indisposed for the last few days; he was taken on Saturday last with an attack of the bilious pleurisy now prevalent, and has been confined to his bed ever since. The bell at the front door of the White House was muffled this morning to prevent any noise from the coarseless ring of office seekers. ...

The President began to sink fast on Saturday and at 12:30 a.m. on the Sunday, the fourth, he passed away. His last words: "Sir, I wish you to understand the principles of the Government. I wish them carried out. I ask nothing more."

Most editors expressed sorrow over his death, running black borders on page two where national news was normally carried. In New York, William Cullen Bryant (*New York Post*) was alone in his contempt for the President, even in death. Bryant mused that he was sorry about Harrison's death "only because he did not live long enough to prove his incapacity for the office of the President."

Over at *The Log Cabin*, Greeley wrote about the "painful tidings" from his heart but used the occasion to wonder about the future with the new president, John Tyler—"He has not that tried and proved popularity and strength with the people—his armor has not been tested against the storm of vindictive hostility...."

Greeley also took the occasion to turn philosophical:

The toils, the anxiety, the importunities, the pomp and ceremony of exalted station in one brief week are exchanged for the perfect, enduring rest and solitude of the narrow "house appointed for all the living." How solemn is the thought! how impressive the lesson!

... one month ago who dreamed that he stood on the brink of the grave!

"Leaves have their time to fall,
And flowers to wither at the Northwind's breath,
And stars to set—but all,
Thou hast *all* seasons for thine own, O Death."

When thinking about history articles, consider the anniversaries of people and events in history. Look a year or two ahead to allow for research, writing and placing of the article. You can get ideas of anniversaries — centennials, bicentennials, etc. — from various books, among them *The Book of Days*, which tells what happened of importance each day of the year, and *The New York Public Library Book of Chronologies*, which gives the key dates in many categories, from philosophy to sports. For example, journalism itself celebrates significant anniversaries: 1990 marked the 300th anniversary of the first newspaper in America (Benjamin Harris's *Publick Occurrences*); 1991 was the 250th anniversary of the first magazine in America (Andrew Bradford's *American Magazine*) and the 150th anniversary of Horace Greeley's founding of the New York *Tribune* — all of which were celebrated in journals. 1991 was also the 50th anniversary of the American entry into World War II. The year 1992 saw the much-celebrated 500th anniversary of Columbus's arrival in America; the 75th anniversaries of the United States' entering World War I and the espionage laws that restricted freedom and brought heavy censorship; and the 20th anniversary of the Watergate break-in and the ensuing scandal that brought down President Nixon two years later. In addition to looking through dates singled out in calendars and chronology books, look through old newspapers from 25, 50, 75 and 100 years ago for ideas.

WRITING ABOUT RELIGION

The stereotypical view of the religious magazine is that it's preachy, with a moral tucked into every line — offering a narrow approach to reality and insisting on compliance with its view of spirituality and ancient codes of conduct.

Although religious magazines may offer more constraints than some other types do, by and large they are open to the same subjects that other magazines feed on. Thus, you can read in religious magazines about sex, abuse, incest, AIDS, lifestyles, nuclear development, racial and ethnic strife, the arts, the environment. In some of the magazines, in fact, you would have to press hard to find clues that they are religious.

These magazines range from liberal to moderate, conservative and ultraconservative. In general, the more conservative, the more narrow the outlook. The differences are gauged by the degree of adherence to various doctrines. The "liberal" magazine and reader pay less heed to prescribed formulas and creeds of belief. Moderates hold to tradition but not necessarily to literal interpretations. Evangelicals represent those Protestants who ascribe to and follow Scripture closely. In recent years, however, evangelicals have shown a vigorous capacity for dealing with issues of social justice. The brightly evangelical *Christianity Today* hardly misses a beat in following what is going on in the world.

Fundamentalists represent the most conservative of today's Protestant classifications, but even this far right end of the spectrum has seen some movement. Once generally opposed to going to movies, fundamentalist opposition to modernism mellowed with the advent of TV. The *Fundamentalist Journal* deals with many different subjects. A recent issue reprinted the story of a former slave-ship captain turned abolitionist, "The Amazing Grace of John Newton," by Alex Haley, originally published in *Reader's Digest*.

A religious magazine reflects the interests of its audience. Viewpoints may reflect the stated positions of the governing body of the sponsoring denomination or group (in official church publications) or positions of a clustering of subscribers (in the independent publications). The evangelical and fundamentalist publications are more likely to cite Scripture. Roman Catholic publications may reflect papal encyclicals; Jewish publications will reflect concerns of respective rabbinical councils and movements.

A religious publication is likely to support traditional family values of monogamy and fidelity, while at the same time discussing the life of the single parent and alternate lifestyles. The conservative publication *The Plain Truth*, of the Worldwide Church of God, freely quotes the Old and New Testament to urge perseverance in its article on "The Single Parent" in the July 1989 issue.

All religious magazines oppose drug use and substance abuse and most would include taboos against any recommended or sanctioned use of tobacco and alcohol. Obscenity and swearing and—to a large extent—slang are taboo. "The sexual lifestyle revolution is probably the subject we would be most leery of," says John A. Lovelace, managing editor of the *United Methodist Reporter*, largest-circulation religious newspaper in the world. The Methodists are composed of liberal and conservative factions, but are vocally liberal nationally on social issues. Other mainline denominations, such as Presbyterians, American [Northern] Baptists, United Church of Christ and Episcopalians, reflect positions on social issues similar to those of the Methodists. (Secular publications using religious subjects sometimes reflect the orientation of editors, some of whom may check material with Protestant, Catholic and Jewish advisers.)

Subtle taboos play a role. Van Varner, editor of *Guideposts* (with the 12th-highest circulation of any magazine in the nation and developed by the noted "positive thinking" minister, Norman Vincent Peale), steers the magazine away from political figures and "no-win controversies" such as abortion. "Hot issues like abortion get into endless controversy," says Varner. "If you use political figures, it colors all you say." He acknowledged the risk in publishing anything on any living celebrity, because someone who is a hero one day might fall the next. But politicians are a guaranteed risk. "If you take on a politician you lose 50 percent at the outset," assuming that people are evenly divided between political parties.

"I think of us as a general interest magazine with religion," says Varner. "The moment you say religion, it closes off the reader, and people don't realize that we can write about anything. Some things come to us overtly religious. We seldom can use an article by a clergy person. You have to concentrate on story," not preaching.

"It's very difficult to write for us. The article must be true; it must be a story, strong narrative; it must be something helpful to the reader that he or she can take away; it must be short and concise; there must be reader identification. We use fiction techniques. That is exactly what we do."

Even some of the most serious of religious publications get messages across through people stories. The *National Catholic Reporter*, well edited but about as serious as a publication can get with its concern over church and world issues, will take the people route when possible. Says NCR editor Thomas C. Fox: "We deal with the moral issues facing Catholics and other Christians but often like to write about these issues through the lives of people."

An example of religious writing about an issue through the life of a person is Marvin Olasky's profile of Illinois Congressman Henry Hyde in the evangelical *Christianity Today*. Olasky, a Texas journalism professor who specializes on writing on anti-abortion topics, sets the scene with a description of Hyde's world. He leads into an overview of Hyde's beliefs which foreshadows Hyde's specific views on abortion. Olasky repeats and dwells on the anti-abortion stand. Although not a particularly objective article and one-sided, it nevertheless does have some good technique. He sets the scene graphically. The reader is led from the larger to the particular and so isn't hit over the head right away with the message. Olasky saves some of the less interesting background facts for later in the article.[8]

A Gadfly in the House

Marvin Olasky

The walls of U.S. Representative Henry Hyde's outer office sport all the trappings of democracy and reveal much about this 67-year-old veteran of conservative politics. Visiting constituents can look to their left in Room 2262 of the Rayburn Building just south of the Capitol and see a giant map of the Illinois Sixth Congressional District, which extends from Chicago's O'Hare Airport south and westward past Wheaton College. They can stare ahead at two gargantuan blowups of thank-you notes to Hyde from kindergarten classes to which he sent flags. They can look to the right and see a large photograph of the Capitol, with the words of Alexander Hamilton, "Here, Sir, the people govern."

It is not clear, however, whether Hamilton said those words proudly or sarcastically. (He was not overly fond of what "the people" tended to decide.) A look at Henry Hyde's inner office also suggests most ambivalence than first meets the eye. His two Illinois-obligatory busts of Abraham Lincoln are outnumbered by three statuettes of Don Quixote, whose impossible dreams were not of, by, and for the people. Standard photos of Hyde handshakes with smiling Presidents are overshadowed by a large portrait

8. Marvin Olasky, "A Gadfly in the House," *Christianity Today*, March 9, 1992, pp. 30, 32.

of a weary George Washington at Valley Forge: "His force of character kept 11,000 men together during a terrible winter," Hyde says.

The inner office also displays photos of Douglas MacArthur, and of Oliver North testifying at the Iran-Contra hearings. Hyde was a determined defender of Ronald Reagan at the hearings, and his office walls have many photos of "the best" President of recent decades. Hyde's office also has room for the two bulldog bookends of twentieth-century British politics, Winston Churchill and Margaret Thatcher, and a portrait of Thomas More, the sixteenth-century English lord chancellor. Catholic attorneys such as Hyde often hang a print of that great Holbein painting because More is considered the patron saint of lawyers; but Hyde has a bust of More as well: "He gave his life for a principle."

A congressman, Hyde says, "has to decide to *be* somebody or *do* something," and the former is, unfortunately, far more prevalent. "Congress is a following institution, a poll-taking, weathervane kind of enterprise. You will not see an awful lot of profiles in courage," he says.

That might not be so terrible if American society were in such good shape that courage could be a luxury. But, as Hyde notes, "the overturning of the spirituality that undergirded society, and the ascendance of secularism, of materialism, of the denial of spiritual values, seems to be the regnant philosophy today in America."

Hyde is known as an antiabortion crusader, but he generally fights society's ruling ethos not just on one issue but across the board. The leaders of media and academia, he says, "admire and implement the Enlightenment ethic, the notion that [theological] revelation has nothing to teach us. In their view, the obstacles to a good society are simply ignorance. 'If only we could educate everybody,' they cry, 'not only would racism, sexism, and crime disappear, but we'd have a wonderful life—Utopia itself!' Ask them about sin, and they reply, 'Sin? There's no such thing. *Society* is the cause of evil and crime.' Somehow, it appears, society has 'failed' the rapist, the dope dealer, the mugger, the murderer. Society's to blame, not the individual responsible for his choices."

There have been three great styles of twentieth-century American oratory—northern Irish, southern white, and black evangelical—and all three are disappearing under the pressure of media mavens who teach public figures to speak in clipped sound bites. Hyde's rolling cadences represent an unapologetic throwback to a better class of rhetoric. For example, while lots of conservative politicians like to mention the references to God in the Pledge of Allegiance and on the back of a penny, only Hyde issues the challenge: "A nation 'under God' means a nation under God's judgment, constantly reminded by our smallest coin that the true measure of ourselves comes from beyond ourselves."

Hyde's office walls display photographs of Pope John Paul II and Mother Teresa, but he also has words of praise for Jerry Falwell and Pat Robertson and sentences of scorn for those who decry the Religious Right: "There *is* a repressive fundamentalism extant in our country today, but it's not of the religious variety. It is the secular fundamentalism that the courts, the ACLU, People for the American Way, and many of our law schools are teaching."

Hyde is relaxed as he rocks softly in his office chair, but there is an edge to his voice as he talks about colleagues who roll over under media pressure: "People want to do what's right, but unfortunately they would rather be *perceived* as doing right than as actually doing what's right. I think they are torn, and perception wins out, because the adoration of the secular press is heady."

Hyde rolls in his right hand a long cigar as he discusses the job of a member of Congress: "You are supposed to be better informed than the average constituent who gets his information from a paragraph or two in the newspaper, or a sound bite on the television at night. You can make people aware of the truth."

Hyde is perhaps best known for his constant enunciation of one unpopular stand—that human life begins at conception. He became a pro-life advocate in 1969 while serving in the Illinois House of Representatives, and during his first term in Congress introduced the Hyde Amendment

continued

continued

which, since 1976, has prohibited the use of federal funds to pay for abortion. Yet, with over 90 percent of media leaders favoring abortion, Hyde acknowledges that many politicians are retreating from antiabortion positions. He is irritated by so-called seamless-garment rating systems that link abortion to other "life issues," such as the death penalty and nuclear deterrence. They are just a "way of protecting the Kennedys and the Moynihans," he says. He also does not care for the merging of birth-control and abortion concerns found among some Catholics and fundamentalists: "Abortion is killing an innocent human life. The other is preventing conception of a human life, which I think is morally wrong, but there is a vast distinction."

Hyde is concerned about future leadership for the prolife cause. He was once square-jawed and lean, but years on the rubber-chicken and chocolate-mousse circuit have softened the lines. He senses a similar aging taking place in the prolife movement. The future of abortion, he argues, is tied to development of a new generation of prolife leaders: "Mario Cuomo says, 'There is no consensus,' but it's the job of political leaders to help form a consensus."

Hyde does not seem optimistic as he runs through a list of younger politicians who might have been prolife leaders but flip-flopped instead: "Thirty pieces of silver don't seem to me to be worth it." Hyde added, "I say this as one ready to condemn myself. I in the last election endorsed some prochoice people," including Illinois's new conservative, Baptist governor, "but the more I think about it, the less comfortable I am with my decision."

Nevertheless, Hyde still hopes for the conversion of even those who are legalistically prochoice: "You've got to believe in redemption, you've got to believe in Saul of Tarsus, you have to believe that people will change their minds." Good teaching in churches is vital, he believes: "We need prophets and emissaries of transcendence, rather than people who compromise with the world." A major problem, however, remains "the quality of clergy emerging out of the sixties and seventies."

In Catholic churches, Hyde complains, "You have bishops lobbying for female priests and homosexuals. You have a Catholic press that is a great occasion of sin, a way to lose your soul." Many of the church's clergymen and even some cardinals, Hyde says angrily, "lack moral energy," and "the big Catholic colleges are a great place to lose your faith; you send your kid to Notre Dame, and he comes out an agnostic at best."

After graduating from a Catholic high school in 1942, Hyde went on to receive B.S. and J.D. degrees from Georgetown University and Loyola University School of Law; in those days, he emerged from schooling with a strong faith and a strong body. Now Hyde walks the floor of Congress with burly grace, but almost a half-century ago, during the last half of a 1943 NCAA playoff game, Hyde at 6'3" and 180 pounds ran the floor of a basketball court well enough to hold DePaul great George Mikan to one point.

Hyde has similarly outplayed top-rated liberal politicians year after year, so that even Cokie Roberts of Left-leaning National Public Radio grudgingly admits, "Hyde is one of the smartest men that ever walked."

Nevertheless, the task gets harder each year, and he comments, "You can show the truth to people, you can rub their face in it, but if their will isn't ready to accept it, they're not going to accept it." . . .

Sample Guidelines

It's especially important in this more restrictive field to be acquainted with the guidelines of a particular religious publication before you write your query letter. Know which publications concentrate on stories about people, current events, popular issues; know which ones concentrate on discussion, opinion, serious news.

A religious magazine's guidelines for features may be similar to these guidelines provided by *The Lutheran*, which serves the newly formed Evangelical Lutheran Church in America, the result of a merger of several major Lutheran denominations:

> *The Lutheran* GUIDELINES FOR FEATURE ARTICLES
> *The Lutheran* is the magazine of the Evangelical Lutheran Church in America, and is published 18 times each year. About half of its contents are articles up to 2000 words in length intended to be of helpful interest to average lay members of the denomination. Most of these articles fall into one of four categories:
>
> 1. **Church-at-work.** Stories describing the unique aspects of a specific church unit's program, such as a local congregation, an institution, or a churchwide agency. Of specific interest would be elements in the story that might be helpful elsewhere.
>
> 2. **Profile.** Stories about individuals whose accomplishments reflect commitment to the Christian faith.
>
> 3. **Reflection.** Articles that explore important issues related to Christian belief and that encourage readers to think about human values. These articles may deal with theological, sociological, philosophical or historical matters. They must be written simply enough to be intelligible to the average reader and should offer specific insights into the subject.
>
> 4. **Personal experience.** Articles in which the writer describes real-life encounters with adversity, family problems, the frustrations and opportunities of every-day living. The relevance of the Christian faith in dealing with these matters must be clearly indicated.
>
> In general, writers should seek to convey information rather than express personal opinion, though the writer's own personality should be reflected in the article's style. A query may save time, but all manuscripts received are given careful consideration. We try to reply to submissions within a month, but occasionally a manuscript may require more time for evaluation. Payment is upon acceptance, and is from $100 to $400. If important for the design of the article, photographs should accompany the manuscript.

Most Common "Sins" of Religion Writers

What do editors of religious magazines consider the most common mistakes or "sins"?

- "Not studying their writers' market guides enough to notice that we are a newspaper, not a 'magazine'; not targeting their submissions to us but seeming to 'shoot an arrow into the air' and letting it fall somewhere." — John A. Lovelace, managing editor, *United Methodist Reporter*.

- "Preachiness, wordiness, simplistic answers." — Terry Muck, executive editor, *Christianity Today*.
- "They write too many words; they write too many words; they write too many words." — Richard H. Schmidt, managing editor, *The Episcopalian*.
- "Lack of focus; not well researched; lack of impact (does it make a difference in real life?)" — Kenneth J. Holland, editor, *Signs of the Times*.
- "Failure to query before you write; not writing deftly; writing over 800 words without permission." — Thomas C. Fox, editor, *National Catholic Reporter*.
- "Either sentimentally pious or ignorant of the theological context; unable to indicate *why* readers should care about the issue at hand — what is it that was revealed in an event or meeting that tells us something fresh about our theological situation or the forces shaping religious life today. In other words, they lack an authentic voice or perspective of their own that renders their accounting interesting; tackling a perennial theological or moral question in an over simple way, seemingly unaware of the prior literature (including that in our magazine)." — David Helm, managing editor, *Christian Century*.

A useful book is the *Yearbook of American and Canadian Churches*. A publication of the National Council of Churches (475 Riverside Drive, New York, NY 10115), the annual lists periodicals published by religious groups in the United States and Canada along with pertinent information and contacts for each group.

A directory of religious publications and their needs is provided in *The Religious Writers Marketplace* by William Gentz and Elaine Wright Colvin (Running Press, 125 South St., Philadelphia, PA 19103).

WRITING FOR CHILDREN

When you consider writing for children, you have to consider age subdivisions as well as the variety of subject areas. Topics like science, sports, famous people — biggies for adults — also interest children.

Classifications within the category of "children" include preschool, primary (the first three grades), junior (ages 9, 10, 11), intermediate (12 to 14), high school (teens) or young adult. Or the age divisions can be made in more general terms — pre-adolescent, adolescent, preteen, teen, young adult.

Age differentiation isn't as clear-cut as it once was. Today's elementary school youngster knows about computers, science and history and is introduced to the classics. In fact, if the enjoyment level is sufficient, you can treat kids much as you treat adults.

Nevertheless, each level demands appropriate subject matter and approach. Boy-girl relationships differ from age to age, of course; and so do hobbies, music, TV preferences, "jobs" (chores vs. careers) and relationship to parents (who also get older and change even as kids do).

Girls' and Boys' Magazines

Gender gaps persist; boys' magazines and girls' magazines exist independently of each other, just as men's and women's magazines do. But the gender gap is blurring. *Sports Illustrated for Kids* features boys and girls on the covers. One summer cover, for instance, had a boy and a girl jumping into a swimming pool with Olympic swimming medalist Janet Evans. Says Ann S. Moore, publisher of *Sports Illustrated for Kids* (published by *Sports Illustrated*): "We have a dual audience — two-thirds boys, one-third girls. What's a girl article? We have an article on a woman coach of a boys' high school basketball team. The word *tomboy* doesn't exist any more, for people feel it is normal for little girls to be as active as boys."

A long-time dictum in the genre says to slant to boys. The idea is that if you're in doubt about your audience's gender, write for boys, because "girls will read anything, but boys won't." Some writers and editors, however, will challenge this assumption.

It is true, though, just as with adult magazines, that more youth magazines are aimed at girls. Think of all the women's magazines in comparison with the handful exclusively for men. Girls and young women read *Seventeen*, *Teenage*, *YM* (Young & Modern, originally *Young Miss*), *Sassy*. Bright and slick, *YM* remains true to more traditional fare. "*Sassy* made a big mistake assuming young teens are a lot hipper than they are," says Elizabeth Crow, president of Gruner + Jahr which publishes *YM*. "*Sassy* takes the teen at 15, 16 and has the point of view they reign supreme. We now avoid the 15-year-old. They are powerless in our society. Everyone has the dumb 15-year-old inside them." *YM*, she says, slants to the 16- and 17-year-olds. "They are more interesting and accessible as adults."

The competition among teen-age girls' magazines and the trends they represent are captured by Boston *Globe* writer Andy Dabilis:

> . . . Whatever happened to tips on how to do your hair and the Clearasil ads?
>
> For years, you've been able to find *those* in Seventeen, the aging but still reigning queen of the teen scene. Or (No. 2) Teen, the Los Angeles-based fanzine. Or even Young Miss, which, following a $10-million facelift, changed its name to YM and began chasing older teen readers.
>
> But now there's Sassy.
>
> Filled with rampaging teen talk and provocatively posed photos, the brash, two-year-old magazine is waging war against its more conservative sisters for a share of the lucrative 13-to-19-year-old market: 11.7 million girls who spend more than $30 billion a year, much of it on clothes and makeup they see in magazines.
>
> That young audience, says YM editor Bonnie Hurowitz-Fuller, has "discretionary income. And," she adds with a smile, "they have time to go shopping."

The magazine battles are mostly taking place in New York, where Seventeen, on top as it has been for 47 years, and YM are produced several blocks from each other on prestigious Third Avenue, their editors trying to discern trends and hitting the fashion spots on Seventh Avenue. The magazines' offices are filled with dresses, Day-Glo backpacks, jeans with chains, and models and editors scurrying back and forth.

Across town, in gritty Times Square, in a ninth-floor office called "the Pink Cave," are the bad girls of the teen mags, the funky and bohemian staff of Sassy, writing about more than just fashion and beauty. If Seventeen flirts and YM teases, Sassy goes all the way.

Life hasn't been easy for Sassy. Financially shaky, the magazine is under attack not only from the competition, but also from parents shocked by a style that, they say, shows a dark side of the vulnerable adolescent years. They criticize the pouty, Lolita-like sensuality of the models. . . .

Sassy's executive editor, Mary Kaye Schilling, 30, who came from YM, says the staff hasn't been daunted by criticism — including a protest from the Moral Majority about sexually graphic material, which led several major advertisers to pull out. "We go for kids a little beyond the pale who are interesting," she says. "We're always pushing the edge. We don't ever want to be boring."

Boring it's not.

In its second-anniversary edition in March, Sassy offered "Prom Dresses That Aren't Disgusting" and lured readers with "My Parents Put Me in a Mental Ward." Seventeen, meanwhile, had articles about feminism and teenage alcoholism, and promised "Our Biggest Prom Issue Ever."

Sassy was started by Australia's Fairfax Publications and was patterned on the successful Dolly in that country.

"Their staff is fabulous, but they can't come in from Australia saying 'We'll take over,'" says Seventeen editor Midge T. Richardson, a powerful figure in the magazine industry.

"I'm not editing for the young person, and we never have, not for 47 years, and we're getting them," says Richardson. It is Seventeen, she says, that is in high-school libraries, that gets 5,000 letters a month, that can bring 7,000 girls out to a Houston fashion show.

Seventeen, with 1.7 million readers, is still far ahead of Teen, with 1.1 million; YM, with almost 1 million, and Sassy, with about 500,000. Schilling is confident circulation will surge because, she says, Sassy has a link with teen readers. "We talk like they talk," she says.

But YM's publisher, Alex Mironovich, 37, says Sassy will burn out: "They were being a little too aggressive with their market. They have an attitude." Mironovich pulls out a copy of an article from a Sassy first edition that graphically depicts a teenage girl with her hands on a boy's crotch.

Sassy staff writer Karen Catchpole says the magazine simply captures the natural wildness of the teen years.

Mark Clements, whose New York firm has analyzed magazines for 30 years, says teen girls usually buy only one title. With projections of a 15 percent increase in the teen female population in the 1990s, he says, the magazines are responding with striking new looks and more sophisticated approaches.

"Seventeen had gone along for years with a traditional teenager vein," says Clements. "But the YMs and the Sassys are getting more experimental, because you are dealing with a market which likes these experimental things. . . ."[9]

What do boys read? *Boys' Life* reigns almost alone, although some Sunday school publications serve boys only, such as the Southern Baptist *Pioneer*, for boys 12 to 14. "Boys," says Crow, "they are all over the lot. Their needs are satisfied by comics, car magazines, records, tape decks, but much of that is in *Rolling Stone*." *Mad* magazine is also popular with boys.

Special Interests

Most publications for young people are based on an interest. This parallels the development of the specialized adult magazine. Sports is represented by the already-mentioned *Sports Illustrated for Kids*; *Cobblestone* is history for kids; *Cricket*, and its new younger counterpart, *Ladybug*, with the same publisher, are literary; *Junior Scholastic* and the new *News for Kids* consider current events: *Spark* for ages 3 to 11 has craft projects and creative skills activities. Science publications for children include *Owl* and its younger version, *Chickadee*, both very slick magazines published by the Young Naturalist Foundation; *Odyssey*, which centers on astronomy and space travel; and, of course, *National Geographic World*, a child of *National Geographic*, and *Ranger Rick*, published by the National Wildlife Federation. Time Warner Inc. and music producer Quincey Jones were set to launch a new youth music magazine, *Volume*, in September 1992.

An Indianapolis-based health organization, Children's Better Health Institute, has managed to corner a large part of the juvenile periodical field. The organization publishes *Jack and Jill* (once a junior flagship of the Curtis Publishing Company, which put out the *Saturday Evening Post*), *Turtle Magazine for Preschool Kids*, *Humpty Dumpty's Magazine*, *Children's Playmate Magazine*, *Child Life* and *Children's Digest*. Of course, health care and good eating habits are primary topics in these publications.

The religious publications for children have cut back — merger of denominations and severe budget cuts have left behind dozens of publications, particularly the weekly colorful story papers: *Teens*, *Young People*, *Classmate* and others. Magazines such as *Alive* and *Youth* have fallen victim. But there is still a formidable outlet in the youth religious press. For example, consider *Bread*, *Campus Life*, *Christian Adventurer*, *Guide*, *In Touch*, *Keynoter*, *Straight*, *TQ* (Teen Quest), *Youth Update*, *Action*, *Clubhouse*, *Discoveries*, *The Friend*, *Junior Trails*, *Noah's Ark: A Newspaper for Jewish Children*, *Our Little Friend*, *Pockets*, *R-A-D-A-R*, *Venture*, *Wee Wisdom*, *Shofar*, *Touch* and *With*.

9. Andy Dabilis, "The Bad Girl of Teen Magazines," reprinted from Boston *Globe* in the Philadelphia *Inquirer*, April 14, 1990, p. 1-D.

Growth in Children's Publishing

The growing field of youth publishing has been a surprise to media commentators. The myth that kids are glued to TV at the expense of print apparently doesn't hold up. *Time* expressed amazement in the spring of 1989 when it cited a report by the Educational Press Association of America that said the number of children's publications had nearly doubled from 85 to 160 in the preceding two years. Some 40 million kids (and adults?) read these publications, the magazine said. *Time*'s explanation for the phenomenon lay with the increase in baby boomers, now adults concerned with growing illiteracy and the decline of the schools. About half of the children's publications are teaching aids for schools — *Junior Scholastic, Calliope, Weekly Reader, Science Weekly*, for instance.

Stephanie Loer, children's book editor for the Boston *Globe*, explains the increase in an article in *Publishers Weekly*. "The children's magazine market has changed recently," she says, "because the product itself has changed. Magazines are glossy, colorful, evocative, decked out in contemporary wraps — and are enjoying boom times." She quotes Donald Stoll, executive producer of Ed Press, which prints an annotated list of current children's magazines, as saying, "Behind the resurgence in the popularity of magazines is that they offer an opportunity to children to explore their world in bite-sized chunks."[10]

Advertising, long missing in this genre, accounts for some of the increase. *Time* quotes *Sports Illustrated* publisher Donald Barr as noting that children between nine and 12 spend $5 billion annually and influence parents' spending of $40 billion more. Some publications, *Time* observed, such as *Alf* and *Mickey Mouse*, published by Welsh Publishing in New York, "are little more than promotions surrounded by ads for sugar-coated breakfast cereals and video games."[11] Disney has its *Disney Adventures* for ages 7 to 14, with 375,000 monthly circulation, launched in 1990.

Taboos

Children's publications have always had to deal with a hierarchy of taboos. Universal taboos include support for use of alcohol, tobacco and drugs. However, problems associated with using such substances are topics for discussion in children's magazines.

Social taboos for children's publications change. Some years back, an editorial director — a former editor of *Boys' Life*, working at a religious publishing house — would not let the editor of the religious weekly for juniors, *Sunday Pix*, show white and black basketball players receiving an award to-

10. Stephanie Loer, "A New Leaf in Magazines for Children," *Publishers Weekly*, Feb. 24, 1992, p. 20. The article was adapted from the Boston *Globe*.

11. "Tapping the Kiddie Market: In spite of video-age competition, children's magazines boom," *Time*, April 24, 1989, p. 64.

gether. Now the reverse is more apt to occur; publications show mixed racial and ethnic groups as a matter of course.

Not so long ago most articles and stories (and TV) seemed to think all people lived in the suburbs with back yards and barbecues. Today there's a greater emphasis on urban and apartment living. Something you have to remember: Parents buy the publications. Some publications appeal more to the parents' biases; others appeal to the parents' idealism — what Johnny and Jane *should* do.

What Do Children Want?

A bottom line, nevertheless, is still "what do the children want?" Parents buy publications to please the kids or to try to do so. Aunts and uncles give subscriptions, and they want the gifts to be entertaining and enjoyable as well as educational.

Isaac Bashevis Singer, Nobel Prize winner for literature, wrote many stories for children's publications such as *Cricket*. Although he wrote mostly fiction, his views on writing for children are applicable to nonfiction as well. When he won the National Book Award in 1970, he explained why he wrote for children:

> There are five hundred reasons why I began to write for children, but to save time, I will mention only ten of them.
> Number one: Children read books, not reviews. They don't give a hoot about the critics.
> Number two: They don't read to find their identity.
> Number three: They don't read to free themselves of guilt, to quench the thirst for rebellion, or to get rid of alienation.
> Number four: They have no use for psychology.
> Number five: They detest sociology.
> Number six: They don't try to understand Kafka or *Finnegans Wake*.
> Number seven: They still believe in God, the family, angels, devils and witches.
> Number eight: They love interesting stories, not commentary, guides, or footnotes.
> Number nine: When a book is boring, they yawn openly without any shame or fear of authority.
> Number ten: They don't expect their beloved writer to redeem humanity. Young as they are, they know that it is not in their power. Only adults have such childish delusions.

Singer reread the reasons at the Nobel Prize banquet in Stockholm in 1978. Commenting on Singer's "reasons," Mark Bernheim in the *Christian Century* mused:

> We need not lament the absence of the other "490 reasons," for it is doubtful that they could add anything beyond the principles put forth here: the writer's conviction that much of what passes for critical or interpretive profundity is bunk — with which children have no patience.

Singer also clings to the past — to the strengths that he absorbed as a child from his own upbringing — as a means of providing stability in an uncertain and disturbing world.[12]

Bernheim quotes an interview with Singer in the *New York Times Book Review* section:

> Our children, God bless them, don't read to discover their identity, as so many wiser adults pretend to do. Young as they are, fresh from the egg, they know exactly who they are, and where they belong. . . . With an instinct no fashion-making can destroy, the child has become the guardian of those moral and religious values which the adults have rejected in the name of an ill-conceived notion of social progress. Our children refuse to mock or subvert family life. Daddy and mommy, grandma and grandpa, brother and sister, remain for them serious and stable institutions.[13]

Children like to *think*, believe it or not. Perhaps that explains the use of puzzles, riddles and mysteries in many publications for the young. Donald Sobol has shown that kids will buy books that make them think — witness his *Encyclopedia Brown* collections of mystery stories for children, selling over 11 million copies.

You can make a mystery out of anything, even Scripture. The following minute mystery from *Kidbits* makes a new point about an old story:[14]

The Bethlehem Beggar

Hiley H. Ward

Now when Jesus was born in Bethlehem of Judaea in the days of Herod the king, behold, there came wise men from the east. . . . They fell down, and worshipped him . . . and opened their gifts. . . . Warned of God in a dream that they should not return to Herod, they departed . . . another way. — The Gospel of Matthew

Jedidiah lay on top of the roof of the two story clay dwelling and watched the crowds gather in Bethlehem.

It was tax collecting time and all kinds of interesting people filled the city. There were couples and families on donkeys, iron-clad Roman soldiers, taxmen, old and young, various tough culprits, and beggars. Jedidiah tried to think out stories for each one.

His eyes fell particularly to one tall, straight-back beggar who seemed so different from the rest. His long beard was unkept, his clothes were shreds, and his only possession was a ragged bundle like a cushion upon which he sat. The old beggar just held out his hand and received a few morsels or coins, but he never shouted like the other beggars, "Food for the poor."

---

12. Mark Bernheim, "Writing for Children: Singer's '500 Reasons,'" *Christian Century*, Nov. 18, 1981, p. 1189.

13. Quoted in Bernheim, p. 1189.

14. Hiley H. Ward, "The Bethlehem Beggar," *Kidbits*, December 1981, pp. 16–18.

Night after night the beggar gathered his little bundle and settled down in a corner of an alley street, and Jedidiah's eyes would follow him. Sometimes the old man just spent the night at the gate where he begged.

Other visitors interested Jedidiah, too, particularly three well-to-do men — wise looking nobility carrying expensive boxes on their animals and accompanied by their own guards in turbans that showed they were from far-away lands. They certainly weren't here to pay Judaean taxes, but why, Jedidiah wondered.

One night Jedidiah stayed out on the roof. It was a night much different from others. There was a glare among the stars and the night seemed to sing with some kind of mystery.

The next day Jedidiah watched the crowds again. He moved among them, heard stories of a strange birth of a future king, saw the nervousness of the Roman soldiers.

Then Jedidiah saw the three magnificent men leaving, their burdens seemed less, the ornate boxes gone. They were in a hurry and had the look of concern or fear.

Back on the rooftop Jedidiah studied all the people. The crowds were continually changing. But gone also was the one person that he had gotten used to seeing. Gone was the old beggar.

Jedidiah wondered.

He figured out a story about the old man. Jedidiah knew why he was gone.

How would you write the ending to this story?

Bethlehem Mystery Answer

The Scriptures do not speak of only three wise men, although tradition later introduced the idea of three. Perhaps there were four — maybe an old man — fearful, too, of Herod and bringing his gift of gold or expensive perfumes wrapped in a ragged bundle and pretending to be a beggar. Was the old man making sure he would go undetected and be able to give the gift to the Christmas child?

Children love humor. Younger children, in particular, less burdened with the concerns of adolescence and approaching adulthood, are ready, it seems, to dimple and giggle over anything funny. Along with articles on the origins of ghosts and "How to Haunt," an October "haunted house" issue of *Kidbits* included a page of humor, "Mr. and Mrs. Ghost Go to Dinner," with some "horrible riddles":[15]

Mr. and Mrs. Ghost Go to Dinner

Hiley H. Ward

Mr. and Mrs. Ghost stood before the mirror primming for dinner.

"Wasn't it awfully nice of the Smiths to ask us to dinner, Mortimer?"

"It certainly was, Elvira. In this big house, we seldom bump into them. It is nice to visit with the people whose house you haunt."

continued

---

15. Hiley H. Ward, "Mr. and Mrs. Ghost Go to Dinner," *Kidbits*, October 1981, p. 7.

continued

"Oh, dear, I really haven't a thing to wear," said Elvira.

"Try just basic white," said her husband.

The ghostly couple joined the Smiths in the dining room.

"Oh, goodie. We're eating by candlelight! How heavenly!" said Elvira.

"The table looks just out of this world!" declared Mortimer. "And look, dear, they're having finger sandwiches. My favorite!"

"You know, Mrs. Smith, we haven't been to dinner since the time Mortimer was the after-dinner spooker at the Bat Club."

Mortimer laughed: "That's the time I told them to avoid a daily plan of exorcise, unless they want to be a shadow of their former selves."

"Believe me, he left his audience screaming," crowed Elvira. "It was enough to raise the dead."

"People have to think ahead," said Mortimer. "We all have to have a ghoul in life."

The dinner went on smoothly, like a breeze.

"Oh, the dessert!" said Mortimer. "Devil's food, isn't it?"

Horrible Riddles

How does a ghost cry?
Boo hoo

What did the little ghost have for dessert?
Ice scream

What do you call the first flea on the vampire?
First up to bat

What do you say of a cemetery worker who misplaced a tombstone?
It's a grave mistake

How does it rain in Ghosttown?
In sheets

What kind of sport do English ghosts who ride horses like best?
Fox haunt

What Do Children's Magazines Want?

Perhaps the most successful of the children's publications is *Highlights for Children*. What child hasn't read it while waiting to see a doctor or dentist? Going strong since its start in 1946 by Garry and Caroline Myers — he was 61 and she, 59 — in a few rooms of an automobile showroom in the small town of Honesdale, Pa., the 8½ × 11 monthly leads the field with over 2 million circulation.

In an interview with the Philadelphia *Inquirer*, marking the magazine's 40th anniversary, editor Kent Brown, Jr. (grandson of the founders) said that the philosophy of the magazine has remained the same: "'Fun With a Purpose' is a good way to talk about it, because we believe learning doesn't have to be dull. It can be fun. It can be purposeful."

Highlights doesn't accept advertising. "The founders didn't believe in it, because you're just introducing another problem into the home — 'Mother, buy me this, Father, get me that.'"

From the beginning the magazine has carried this dedication on its inside front cover: "This book of wholesome fun is dedicated to helping children grow — in basic skills and knowledge — in creativeness — in ability to think and reason — in sensitivity to others — in high ideals — and worthy ways of living — for children are the world's most important people."

According to Brown, *Highlights* seeks to avoid competition with text-books by putting the emphasis on anecdotes and the inspirational point. The hardship of Christopher Columbus's voyage is emphasized — not the historical background, which can be left to the textbooks.[16]

Highlights breaks the mold, too, in its concept of language. While other juvenile publications worry about reading levels, *Highlights* allows a big word to be slipped in once in a while — as long as it's explained in some way — so that the youngster builds a vocabulary. Since the magazine is aimed at children from 2 to 12, the stories and articles must be not only readable but also listenable — the kind that can be read to the preschooler.

Sample Guidelines

The *Highlights* guidelines for nonfiction follow:

HIGHLIGHTS FOR CHILDREN is published monthly (except bimonthly July-August) for children from 2 to 12. Circulation is over 2,000,000. Sold by subscription only.

Factual Features   We are always looking for gifted writers, especially engineers, scientists, historians, artists, musicians, etc., who, having a rich background in their respective fields, can interpret to children useful, interesting, verifiable facts. References or sources of information must be included with submission. Photos or art reference material is helpful when we evaluate such submissions.

Also, we want authors who write from firsthand experience and can interpret well the ways of life, especially of children, in other countries; who show appreciation of cultural differences; and who don't leave the impression that our ways always are the best — in short, writers who can help foster world brotherhood.

Biographies stressing the early lives of individuals who have made significant contributions through their own efforts are particularly welcome.

For science and other factual articles within 900 words, we pay $75 and up.

Parties   We want original party plans for children, giving clever ideas and themes clearly described in 300 to 800 words, including drawings or samples of items to be illustrated. $50 and up.

Crafts   We want fresh, novel, tested ideas, with clear directions. We require a well-made sample to be submitted with each craft idea. Projects must require only salvage materials or inexpensive, easy-to-obtain materials. The wider the age range, the better; especially desirable are crafts easy enough for

continued

16. David Singleton, "Celebrating a 40-year Run: Children's Magazine Has Seen Little Change," Philadelphia *Inquirer*, March 20, 1986, p. 19-BN.

continued

primary grades or preschoolers. We are particularly interested in ideas for projects that result in the creation of attractive, useful gift items and interesting toys and games.

Finger Plays/Action Plays   Should have lots of action. Must be easy for a very young child to grasp and for parents to dramatize, step-by-step, with hands, fingers, and body movements. Should not be too wordy. $25 and up.

General Information   We don't pay persons 15 or under for contributions.

No inquiries needed. We buy all rights, including copyright, and do not consider material previously published.

All material is paid for on acceptance.

Be sure to enclose with the manuscript a self-addressed, stamped envelope for its possible return.

Most of the children's magazines are very agreeable about sending guideline sheets and sample issues. *Boys' Life* will send guidelines but is stingy with its sample issues. A self-addressed, stamped 9 × 12 envelope is required to get a *Boys' Life* sample copy. Its guidelines:

AREAS FOR FREELANCE WRITERS
- Nonfiction articles, columns and special features (how-tos).
- Fiction (short stories).
- Cartoon scripts (fiction and nonfiction).

For original material, we buy first rights only. Copyright returned to author 90 days after publication. Exception: We buy all rights to comics. Payment on acceptance.

Articles   Length: 750–2500 words. Payment: $500 and up. Each issue contains at least one full-length piece about a Scout activity—mountain climbing, canoeing, hiking, bike touring, camping, etc. Depending on season, we also use athlete profiles (adults and children), how-tos (fishing, camping, money-making, game playing), history, humor, hobbies, etc.

Special Features   Up to 700 words. $200 and up. Hobby how-tos such as wood carving, model building, painting, and crafts. Descriptive writing that's clear and simple is a must; step-by-step photos or sketches helpful. An occasional how-to crosses over to a full-length article—i.e., building a robot, a model train layout, using remote-controlled cars.

Columns   400–750 words. $250. Each issue uses seven columns, on average. A partial category list: Science, Outdoors, Health, Cars, Bicycling, Electronics, Sports, Fishing, Entertainment. See actual issues for others.

Fiction   750–2500 words. $750 and up. All short stories feature a boy or boys. Humor, mysteries, science fiction, adventure.

Comic Pages One-page scripts, $150. Large format comic strip (not newspaper style). Script must describe page layout, action, characters, dialogue. Best writing has maximum action, minimum words. Three types of comics:

- **Monthly.** "Pee Wee Harris" about Boy Scouts. "The Tracy Twins," about Cub Scouts. "The Pedro Patrol," nonfiction Boy Scout program activities.
- **Serial.** Usually science fiction. Boy protagonist. Runs consecutively for 12–15 months.
- **Nonfiction features.** Half- or full-page cartoon. Titles include (but are not limited to) "Dinosaur Hall of Fame," "Space Adventures."

A Final Note No set of guidelines can substitute for careful reading of as many back issues as possible. *Boys' Life* can be found in the children's section of most libraries.

BOYS' LIFE FACTS

- Published monthly since 1911 by the Boy Scouts of America.
- Readers are mostly boys 8 to 18.
- Sold by subscription only.
- Total readership: 6.5 million.
- Editorial content covers practically every interest of all boys.

Cobblestone, "the history magazine for young people," offers the most precise guidelines. It will give you not only the basic requirements (features — 800–1,200 words; activities, from crafts to recipes — 1,000 words) but will give you the theme planned for each month for several years in advance. The themes for each month in a recent year, for instance, included: "great debates, the Hudson River School, Alexander Hamilton, Chicago, Civil War — Reconstruction, Transcendentalism in America, the automobile, the South as perceived by its artists, American Revolution — British loyalists living here, Albert Einstein, the Amish and Theater."

The Gannett tabloid for kids, *Pennywhistle Press*, with 2.9 million circulation, uses mostly Gannett-generated material and has room for little contributed material, a brief statement by the editors says.

The annual *Children's Writer's & Illustrator's Market* book, published by Writer's Digest Books, offers lists of juvenile and youth publications and their needs, plus additional information on agents, contests and awards.

A national directory, *Magazines for Children*, listing 125 publications, was published in 1990 by the Educational Press Association with the International Reading Association (P.O. Box 8139, Newark, Del. 19714).

ASSIGNMENTS

1. This chapter hasn't discussed every genre that exists. Make a list of all the other areas that might qualify as a genre (a genre being identified as an

area for which special magazines exist). Identify what appears unique for each genre.

2. Select one genre in which you would like to write. Make a brief directory of resources for that genre.

3. Select five genres and make a list—perhaps in the form of a chart—comparing the taboos for each.

4. The class can draw up a list of basic interview questions and then divide up to interview local writers in the various genres. Compare the way the different writers answer the same questions.

5. Prepare a report showing the differences between a science article (or an article from another genre, such as religion) in a general magazine and in a specialized magazine.

6. Invite a specialized beat reporter from the local newspaper to speak to the class and ask how he or she prepared for his or her job.

7. Some professors and counselors advise would-be reporters to develop a specialty that might figure in a specialized job opportunity some day. Discuss what your specialty could be and why.

CHAPTER 13

Business and Trade Publications

A magazine or tabloid "newspaper" that serves a particular business, profession or industry is a trade journal. A "horizontal" trade publication — such as a magazine for salespeople — cuts across various industries, businesses and professions to serve everyone who falls into an inclusive category. A "vertical" trade publication serves just one specific audience (such as nurses or carpet manufacturers).

In fact, the word *trade* is giving way to the term *specialized*. According to Phyllis L. Reed, director of the Business Press Educational Foundation's Student Intern Program, in New York: "'Trade' conveys the sense it is an advertising tool, and the trade press is constantly struggling against this kind of view." And she asks, just how do you separate business from trade? Every trade magazine discussion seems somehow to turn upon the subject of business. "I think that what we struggle with is that the word *business* gets used regardless what we talk about." She says her group is now using the term *specialized business press* instead of talking about business and/or trade press. Nevertheless, the term *trade press* is still in general use.

Aspiring journalists should not overlook the trade press. With smaller circulations and staffs and with special needs, these publications offer opportunities for publication — with less competition. Yet articles for these journals can be very demanding on the writer who needs to have expertise or to be able to handle information from experts in sometimes very technical areas.

Business Publication Rates and Data, Part I, published by Standard Rate and Data Services, lists 4,118 business and trade publications. The volume describes the publication's audience and what it offers and includes names of the publication's staff. Donald McAllister, Jr., vice chair of the Business Press Educational Foundation and chair of Geyer-McAllister Publications, reports that the business and trade publications serve more than 70 million readers and harness 2 million advertising pages each year.

While each trade or specialized business publication will have its own particular audience in mind, some topics cut across the board, even among vertical or very specialized magazines. A writer can take one idea and rework it in several different magazines. Lisa Napell, writing on trade publications in *Writer's Digest,* discussed how the "cross over" process works:

> All trade magazines stretch the particular envelopes of their specific industry. Retail trades do stories on the hiring and firing of employees that could be used (in theory) by any industry. Medical magazines do stories on practice management that could be extrapolated into general client building pieces for another profession. It's in the murky area of extrapolation that freelancers tend to lose their focus.
>
> Regardless of their broad-based applicability, these cross-over stories must still be geared specifically to the target magazine's particular industry. A store security feature for a restaurant magazine will need to focus on aspects of security that a similar article for a retail store magazine wouldn't. Editors want quotes from people in their industry who have had success with whatever you are teaching. They want references their audiences can relate to.
>
> Take, for example, the window display how-to I did for *Eyecare Business.* In it I interviewed several visual artists who had designed windows for large department stores my editors had heard of. They talked about the specific props an optometrist could use to display eyeglasses effectively. Much of the text gave examples and explained the essentials of design, color and scale, as they related to eyewear.
>
> After it was published, I realized I could sell the idea to other retail magazines. I queried the magazines listed under retail trades in *Writer's Market* (WD Books). Some half dozen retailers' magazines, covering children's clothing to hardware, responded positively. All sent sample copies for me to read before I began work.
>
> After reading the back issues for major style differences, I called the experts from my eyeglass story and took them through the piece again. Together we changed the examples to fit each industry and adjusted the design theory lessons to the scale of the objects being displayed.
>
> This approach worked because I was able to make each editor feel that the article he received was written specifically for his magazine, even though

most editors knew I'd done this story before (in fact, many had seen the original clip as an example of how long the story would run and how it would read).

Crossover stories don't work when writers think they can do exactly the same story for several different markets, or when they mistakenly believe that general, all-purpose examples and quotes from unknown outsiders are okay. . . .[1]

HOW WRITING FOR TRADE IS DIFFERENT

While all writing should be interesting, the trade or specialized business publication may want you to get to the point and deliver information more quickly. As Ralph R. Schulz, senior vice president–editorial for McGraw-Hill, Inc., told a specialized business publications class at Pace University in New York:

> The specialized business editor has an easier time of it because he or she knows with great exactness what the reader is interested in, where the general magazine editor has got each week to try to tantalize and to seduce the reader into reading. It's all up for grabs every issue. Now, the editor of the specialized business publication has it a lot tougher than the editor of the general publication because he or she has to deliver good, hard information. You can't get away with romance or mood music.
>
> People read these specialized business publications for only one reason, and that is to get useful information, information that will be useful to them in making business decisions or making decisions about their own careers. That's the only reason people read business publications. If anybody settles down with a good trade magazine for a good read, you've got to suspect. I'm not suggesting that they read poorly. By no means; there's a craft to writing business copy, and a lot of it is very good writing. But it's not the kind of writing intended to give you emotional satisfaction. It's the kind of writing intended to convey useful information. The specialized publication editor has got to deliver useful information, because, if he doesn't, the reader quickly becomes disenchanted. And business people today don't have an awful lot of spare time. They're not going to stay with you, they're not going to read you unless you have something to say, something that's useful to them. So the specialized business editor has got to deliver.

Says J. P. Donlon, editor, *Chief Executive*: "Our readers are shrewd, market wise and well informed. A specific approach should be taken that doesn't waste their time." A news angle is important, more so than in general feature and magazine writing. Perhaps a convention or an exhibit is coming up; a new product is about to be launched or has been launched; a political or economic development demands a response. And another difference, according to Ken

---

1. Lisa Napell, "Wanted: Trade Writers," *Writers Digest*, January 1991, p. 48.

Anderberg, editor of *Business Atlanta*, is that the specialized business magazine will be "more localized and more detailed."

Curb the Jargon

One misconception that students have when they approach a trade or business journal is that they can use a lot of technical and obscure language that
the insiders know. But this approach is only for the lazy. Although many of
these magazines are technical and full of industry jargon, their editors do not
necessarily prefer it that way and spend much time deleting jargon and making the meaning precise and relevant. One editor of a computer magazine
summed up his approach: "We allow some words that have become very
common and are generally understood by our readers, but explain everything
else." When a student "expert" writes on a technical subject and insists on
using excessive technical language, one professor asks the student to submit
two drafts — one using the technical language, the second translating it to the
general reader. Invariably the draft with the simplest, most direct language is
a better draft — even for the expert audience.

Some editors solve the jargon "fog" problem in part by asking that the
articles be personalized. Says Marianne D. Mattera, editor of *RN*, a nursing
journal: "Don't use jargon, do use conversational, easy-to-read language."

In one of his presentations, Douglas Mueller, who conducts seminars
and counsels publications and companies on ways to be understood, discusses
how an editor must be a diplomat when he encounters jargon and stilted
language. This excerpt also appeared in *Editors Only*, a newsletter for professional and trade publications.

> Guest authors can be a challenge to any magazine editor. They bring new
> ideas from specialized areas, and their viewpoints add authority. What's
> more, they may ask little or no fee for their contribution — a boon to a tight
> publication budget.
>
> The problem is that the guest author may be an expert in his field — yet
> decidedly NON-expert as a writer. And he (or she) may be highly sensitive
> about your attempts to rewrite the article, especially if you're not paying a fee.
>
> You can meet this challenge by using a combination of diplomacy and
> editing skill. Diplomacy will help you reassure the writer that his contribu-
> tion is of value both to your magazine and to him as a professional — but that
> his ideas can reach a much wider audience if the piece is edited to be more
> readable. Skill as an editor enables you to let his message come through un-
> changed, and with no apparent change in style. The acid test is when he reads
> your draft. If you've done well, he'll say, "You hardly made any changes!"
>
> Here's part of a story about a low rate loan program at a small bank in the
> Midwest, printed in a banking journal. The author is a bank officer.
>
> "Of course the primary objective of the low-interest rate loan program
> was to stimulate the local economy, as the program itself would have an ad-
> verse effect on the short-term profitability of the bank. It was hoped that the
> influx of additional money would improve the economic climate as well as the

psychological outlook of consumers and business people alike. It was also agreed that the loan proceeds must be kept locally to have the most benefit."

That passage would be hard reading for college graduates. The article itself, which describes an innovative public relations program by the bank, is hard going even for the most determined reader.

If I were the editor, I would use that information, but with great care. When I showed my re-draft, I'd point out the value of getting the author's personal viewpoint into the article:

"The main goal of the low-interest rate loan program was to stimulate our local economy. We knew the program itself would have an adverse effect on short-term bank profits. Yet we hoped the influx of new money would improve not only the economy, but also the psychological outlook of consumers and business people. We also agreed that the loan proceeds should be spent in town."

The original has a Fog Index of 16; the rewrite, 10. Based on the educational attainment of U.S. adults, the rewrite could be read easily by *five times as many people* as the original. Isn't it worth the trouble to edit the article to make such a gain?

GUIDELINES FOR WRITING FOR SPECIALIZED BUSINESS PUBLICATIONS

Editors of specialized business publications offer the following rules of advice:

- Stanley H. Slom, senior editor, *Accounting Today*: "(1) Do your homework; (2) know the market about which you're writing; (3) know the readers and what they want; (4) be aware of artwork. . . . send pictures; (5) keep the stories fairly short."

- Ken Anderberg, editor, *Business Atlanta*: "(1) Know the magazine's industry; (2) know the magazine's audience; (3) tailor your idea to each media; (4) narrow your focus, and then narrow again; (5) use anecdotes and illustrations."

- R. O. Gray, editor, *Nation's Business*: "(1) Determine information needs of audience; (2) develop expertise in specific areas of those needs; (3) use case histories of real people as much as possible; (4) don't preach, give personal opinions; (5) write clearly—organize and make sure copy flows."

- Marianne D. Mattera, editor, *RN*: "(1) Include only material that your audience needs to help them do their jobs better; (2) come right to the point, telling reader in the lead why he or she needs to know this; (3) don't use jargon, do use conversational, easy-to-read language."

- J. P. Donlon, editor, *Chief Executive*: "Rule 1—*Read* the goddam publication you intend to write for. Rules 2–5: See Rule 1."

Consider guidelines for *RN* Magazine, typical of many trade magazines:[2]

RN GUIDE FOR CONTRIBUTORS

The vast majority of our 285,000 subscribers are registered nurses, and most articles accepted for publication are written by RNs. Very few of our authors are professional writers. It's more important for contributors to have useful nursing knowledge than to have writing experience. If you want to submit an article, here's what you need to know:

Editorial Content   Articles published in *RN* keep nurses up to date on practical, clinical, and professional developments, with heavy emphasis on information that can be applied immediately in everyday nursing practice. Subjects include nursing management in medical, surgical, and all specialty nursing areas, patient assessment, drugs, and any and all approaches designed to promote improved patient care.

References and Citations   All articles should be thoroughly researched. If you quote from other publications, enclose the quoted material in quotation marks and reference it. Also cite references for statistics, research findings, and information paraphrased from other publications. You should also include a complete reference list, alphabetized by author's surnames. Citations and reference lists should follow APA style.

Style   The writing style in *RN* is simple and direct—colloquial rather than formal. Clinical terminology is welcome; pompous phrases are not. Use a narrative approach where possible. Give examples from your clinical experience to illustrate specific points. Include anecdotes, quotes from patients, and case histories. Discuss clinical techniques thoroughly, precisely, and in maximum detail.

Format   Manuscripts should be typewritten, double-spaced, on one side of 8½ × 11 paper; handwritten submissions will not be considered. Aim for five to 10 typewritten pages. On the first page, type your name, address, home and business telephone numbers, place of employment, current license number, state of licensure, and social security number. Number all pages. Enclose a copy of your resume or curriculum vitae. Send us the original of your manuscript and one copy. Photos, sketches, and diagrams are a most important adjunct to text, and we give manuscripts illustrated in this manner special attention. Enclose a stamped, self-addressed envelope if you want material we do not accept returned. Usual time to evaluate a submission is six to eight weeks.

Editing   All manuscripts that we accept are subject to editing. Such editing may involve nothing more than putting the material into conversational language, or it can entail heavy condensing and extensive restructuring. In every instance, we take pains to preserve the author's ideas. You'll see a prepublication draft of your article before it gets into print.

Payment   We pay $75 to $250 for the typical article — the honorarium depends on the subject matter and the amount of editing that we think will be required.

Copyright   We usually buy all rights, but we're willing to discuss other copyright arrangements. Published articles may be reprinted only with our written permission.

We strongly recommend that any nurse who wishes to write for *RN* study an issue of the magazine first. We also encourage query letters about our interest in a particular subject. Send queries and manuscripts to Acquisitions Editor, *RN*, Five Paragon Drive, Montvale, NJ 07645.

THE BEST SPECIALIZED BUSINESS ARTICLES

Editors have their ideas for the "best" examples of articles in their specialized magazines.

- "We like the *Wall Street Journal* approach to features," said Stanley H. Slom of *Accounting Today*. "Narrative lead, a paragraph up high as to why the story is being written at this time, the broad picture and then back to the subject of the narrative lead."

- J. P. Donlon, *Chief Executive*, cited an article "Greenbusters" by Ron Bailey in the July/August 1990 issue. The reasons: "(1) It counters conventional pop thinking prevalent in most journals; (2) identifies a danger to readers [of] which they may not be aware; (3) offers a remedy to deal with potential threat."

- Mike Espinole, managing editor, *HOC*: "Partners in Business, Partners in Love," Melinda Cory, January 1990 — "well researched; supporting sidebars provided; strong topic."

- R. D. Gray, editor, *Nation's Business*: "A New Energy Crisis?" by Donald C. Bacon, February 1990 — "This article alerted readers to a problem that was serious but not generally recognized at time of writing. Events have validated this early warning."

- Scott Melnick, associate editor, *Building Design & Construction*: "One of the best stories I've written for the magazine was on Hurricane Alicia and what the industry could have done and can do in the future to minimize damage from wind storms. We were the first publication to point our editorial finger at roof gravel as the major culprit in building damage and I'm proud of the impact (no pun intended) we had on roofing regulations in Houston. Stories of that type appear in BD&C's news section and I'm willing to compare the quality of our news section with that of any consumer magazine's. We are the publication of record for our industry and our figures on everything from the volume of reconstruction activity to the cost of construction are accepted as gospel."

- Ken Anderberg, *Business Atlanta*: "Paper Tiger" by Shelley A. Lee, June 1990 — "Detail, anecdotes, analysis."

Note the chatty, informal, anecdotal way "Paper Tiger," a story about a paper mill takeover began.

It was over.

"Lot of telephone calls that weekend. Marshall came up Saturday, I think. It was a very long weekend. Some holiday, yeah, President's Day. Long weekend, we decided it would be a good time to deal. We approached them and they weren't interested in talking. Gave them a written offer. I was talking to Marty Lipton, you know, our people with theirs. They said it wasn't high enough. We tried to figure out other alternatives. We had lots more discussion. We finally agreed on a price. I think it was Sunday, or maybe Monday morning — $65.75. I told Marty we wouldn't pay any more than that — they wanted $66, we said no. We finally agreed we wouldn't let a quarter stand in the way. Back and forth, working on the contracts. Board meeting Monday night. Then we stayed up through the night negotiating the contracts. Finally got them all signed early Tuesday morning. That was it."

No champagne, no celebration.

"Champagne? Right. We're gonna have a party. No, we didn't own the company yet. Just had a deal. We all shook hands. I think we had orange juice and muffins. But I'm not really sure. We were there all night, it's hard to remember. It was a great deal."

For Stephen Volk and his team of 75 or so legal minds at Shearman & Sterling in New York, orange juice and muffins at that moment of exhaustion and satisfaction were about the best they could do. Sometimes it's the small gestures that count.

A day or two later, in a small forest town 500 miles away and after the world was notified of the victor and his spoils, a couple of paper makers at Georgia-Pacific's (G-P) Woodland, Maine, operation made their own small gesture. They sent a condolence card, a message of sympathy, to their brethren in Millinocket, mills owned by Great Northern Nekoosa (GNN) that now would pass to G-P. It was, says a union representative dryly, "just a 'welcome to the fold' greeting."

Such were, and continue to be, the widely disparate reactions to the largest acquisition in the history of the forest-products industry. This $3.8 billion shotgun wedding between two very proud companies came after a noisy and bruising battle that included charges and countercharges of lying, board irresponsibility, willful neglect, mismanagement, attempted union-busting and gross misconduct. It sucked into its daily drama — played out largely in the press — the Federal Trade Commission, several state courts, influential institutional investors, a large contingent of superstar Wall Street advisers, the AFL-CIO, environmental groups, 19 banks representing an international Who's Who of lenders, and Maine's governor, attorney general and the entire State House.

This cast of characters included the biggest names in deal-making. . . .[3]

3. Shelley A. Lee, "Paper Tiger: An Exclusive Inside Look at Georgia-Pacific's 'Unfriendly' Takeover of Great Northern Nekoosa," *Business Atlanta*, June 1990, pp. 45, 46.

How They Did It

For her article, "Illumination: Casting Light on Carpet Sales," for *Carpet Retailing*, Fall/Winter 1988–1989, Polly Guerin turned to familiar ground and augmented her own knowledge with outside sources. She summarizes her approach to the article, which highlighted the problem of proper lighting in carpet sales rooms.

> With my expertise on the subject of color and light, a topic which I have lectured on, the idea lit up a spark of creativity for a story on how important the correct source of light is in carpet retailers' showrooms or stores.
>
> The main thrust of the story focuses on how light in the showroom or retail store may be one source, say on the warm side, while the customer's home lighting might be on the cool side. Two different light sources will make the colors in a carpet appear lighter or darker, warmer or cooler. This kind of problem can cause customers to be dissatisfied with the color of the carpet when it is installed in their home, as they perceived it as another tint or shade in the store.
>
> In order to confirm the information I contacted the Lighting Research Institute and obtained background information to substantiate my story, and included a quote from a director fulfilling the method described. I also obtained diagrams on lighting to augment the story.

Guerin is an adjunct assistant professor at the Fashion Institute of Technology, New York. The beginning of her article follows.[4]

Illumination: Casting Light on Carpet Sales

Polly Guerin

Customers Reaction to Color

How a customer reacts to carpet colors has a great deal to do with how they perceive the color based on the kind of lighting source used by the carpet retailer on the selling floor. Most people notice the color first and are drawn to a carpet that is pleasing to their eye. Usually colors under cool or warm artificial lighting in stores appear one way, but under full-spectrum natural light they seem quite different. Even the most elegant furnishings, particularly carpet, a major purchase, need adequate lighting to emphasize their full beauty. For example, ordinary light bulbs used in home fixtures wash out colors and throw a yellowish hue upon the room. Lighting units in the carpet retailer's store likewise may similarly affect colors in a dull and depressing way. As a result, what the customer sees is not always what they get, on delivery of the carpet.

Richard L. Vincent, director of development and programs, at the Lighting Research Institute says, "Our eyes perceive color and receive signals from the wavelength of light and depending

continued

---

4. Polly Guerin, "Illumination: Casting Light on Carpet Sales," *Carpet Retailing*, Fall/Winter, 1988–89, pp. 4, 5.

continued

upon the light source, whether it be cool fluorescent or warm incandescent, each lamp produces its own unique spectrum. The light from these sources varies in spectral distribution and color rendition, and the lamps differ in efficiency." He further explains that incandescent bulbs, by far the most popular in most homes, emit a visible light in the yellow and red wavelengths, and many people perceive this as warm and soft. Fluorescent lamps, on the other hand, produce a cool effect and focus more on the blue tones. Most significant about incandescent and fluorescent is that the ability to distinguish colors is affected by the spectrum of the light source.

Customer Assurance

However, the best assurance that customers are buying the color they want is to show the carpeting under a light source which closely imitates natural light. Ideally it would be best to show carpets in the natural setting of outdoor sunlight, but this is obviously not feasible in the retail carpet showroom. New technology, however, has introduced improved sources of light that closely imitate daylight, yet many consumers are not aware that these bulbs are available for domestic use.

Therefore, it is important that the carpet retailer do a little probing with the customer and discuss the kind of room to be carpeted and the kind of artificial lighting the home owner uses.

Questions to Ask

Is the room sunny or shaded? How big a room? Are there any partitions? How many windows? How much artificial light is needed for the room? What kind of light does the customer presently use? Do they feel satisfied with the lighting results? If the room is generally flooded with full-spectrum natural light, cool green or blue carpeting will make the room seem more inviting and relaxing.

A shaded room, on the other hand, can be enlivened and given an appearance of warmth by the use of yellow, orange or red tones in the carpet design. . . .

In a university magazine writing class, Rosalie M. Doherty took a rather familiar subject, credit unions, and turned it into a sale to *Entrepreneurial Woman*, September 1990. Notice how she uses a variety of sources but does not let them interfere with the fast informational flow of the article.[5]

Management Smarts: A Perk That Works

Rosalie Doherty Matthews

A no-cost, minimal-effort employee benefit package is yours for the asking. It's nothing new, but its potential is often overlooked, undiscovered or misunderstood. It's a credit union for your employees.

A credit union is valuable regardless of company size. It is often the only benefit program a small company can afford to offer. A larger company, on the other hand, may offer a credit union to enhance its comprehensive benefit program.

---

5. Rosalie M. Doherty, "Management Smarts: A Perk That Works," *Entrepreneurial Woman*, September 1990, pp. 12–14.

"[Employers] who don't know about credit unions are really missing out," says Cecile Wilson, co-owner of Viplex Corp., a Melbourne, Florida, company that manufactures acrylic products for the marine industry. Wilson's company has been affiliated with Space Coast Credit Union since 1985, when she had 17 employees. She now has approximately 100 workers, and the credit union still plays an important role in employee relations. "A credit union helps you develop loyalty among your people, because they know you care about them," she explains.

Wilson, a former credit union president, speaks from experience. "Credit unions help people in ways [banks] don't," she says. "Unfortunately, a lot of employers don't even know they are available."

According to the *1989 Member Survey* by the Credit Union National Association (CUNA), only 39 percent of members and 8 percent of nonmembers said they were "very familiar" with the services credit unions offer. This means almost two-thirds of all members aren't enjoying the full potential of their credit union's services.

The significance of credit unions in the financial sector, however, should not be understated. As of April 1990, there were 15,000 credit unions in the United States, with 60.9 million members. About 80 percent of credit unions are affiliated with employers.

What Credit Unions Offer

There's one significant difference between a credit union and standard company-provided benefits: The credit union, rather than your company, provides the services and assumes the expenses.

The following are services frequently offered by credit unions:

1. **Payroll deductions.** Payroll deductions allow employees to save by automatically deducting funds from each paycheck and depositing them in a credit union account. The credit union distributes the deductions to different accounts or for loan payments — whatever the employee wishes.

2. **IRAs.** Employees can contribute to credit union Individual Retirement Accounts (IRAs) through payroll deductions. They can also make larger, immediate investments in IRA certificates for specific rates and terms.

3. **Savings Certificates.** Yields through credit unions are sometimes higher than yields at banks or savings and loans.

4. **Personal Loans.** These are unsecured loans that offer employees an alternative to seeking salary advances or company loans.

5. **Lines of Credit.** As the employee makes payments on these unsecured, revolving loans, the available funds are replenished and can be borrowed again.

6. **Life Savings Insurance.** This protection is based on the amount of savings a member has on deposit. At no direct cost to members, this service matches their savings accounts at death up to a certain amount — usually $2,000.

7. **Loan Protection Insurance.** This coverage ensures a member's loan will be paid back (within certain limits) in the event of death or disability.

8. **Auto Loans.** In conjunction with used rental car dealers, credit unions may offer members reduced rates and complete financing. Standard auto loans are also available.

9. **Sharedraft (Checking) Accounts.** This is the best value in checking. There are no fees and no minimum balance requirements.

10. **Club Accounts.** Employees can use savings accounts with restricted access and save for special purposes like Christmas.

11. **Share and Certificate Secured Loans.** Employees who need cash can have their accounts or certificates "frozen" while their funds continue to earn interest. They can then obtain loans for an equal amount at just a few percentage points above the rate they are earning on their savings.

continued

continued

How It Works

Credit unions are owned and directed by members; each member has one vote in determining who may serve on the board of directors. Members who serve on the board are volunteers and receive no monetary compensation. The members/directors set service and rate policies.

"The ownership structure is dramatically different," says Rick Sheridan, director of customer service for the CUNA Service Group. "The fact that you're a member with a vote—you don't find that situation in other financial institutions."

Unlike banks, credit unions are generally not-for-profit, cooperative institutions with no outside investors or stockholders. After expenses are paid and reserves set aside, all earnings go back to the members, who typically benefit from higher interest rates on accounts and certificates, lower loan rates and lower minimum balance requirements.

In addition, credit unions are as safe as, if not safer than, most banks. They are chartered and regulated by either a state regulatory agency or an agency of the United States government. Federal credit unions are supervised by the National Credit Union Administration (NCUA), which oversees the National Credit Union Share Insurance Fund (NCUSIF), and insures each member's account up to $100,000.

You can rest assured, therefore, that you are not liable for any debts your employees incur with the credit union. "When a member gets a loan, it's a contract between the member and the credit union," explains Sandy Lemmon, director of the division of insurance for the NCUA, Region II.

Getting Started

Clearly, offering a credit union is not only inexpensive and easy, but also essentially risk-free.

The question, then, is finding the right credit union for your employees.

Start by contacting your state's credit union league, a trade association that can direct you to local credit unions. For a list of state leagues, write to the Public Relations Department, Credit Union National Association, P.O. Box 431, Madison, WI 53701, or call (800) 356-9655, ext. 4045. For the *NCUA Directory*, a national listing of credit unions, send a check or money order for $12 to the NCUA, Administrative Office, 1776 G Street, N.W., Washington, DC 20456.

Interview key people at several credit unions. Learn how they operate, communicate with their sponsor groups and respond to their members' needs.

Next, obtain references from organizations the credit unions already serve. Determine how the credit unions rate as service providers.

Examine the accessibility of each credit union. Is the credit union conveniently located? Does it provide automated teller services for easy access?

Compare the services available. Do you want a large credit union to be your employees' primary financial institution, or would you prefer a smaller, more intimate credit union?

When making your decision, Sheridan says, consider the end users—your employees. "Try to match the products and services at the credit union to their needs," he advises.

Credit unions are a well-kept secret. Employers who discover that secret can offer a range of services to attract and keep employees. It's a mutually beneficial arrangement that strengthens the relationship between you and your employees. "At the credit union, you're not just a number, you're a member," Cecile Wilson says. "You own it. That's what I want to pass on to my employees. Even in multi-million-dollar credit unions, the caring is still there."

Doherty explains how she did the article:

The key to selling my article was the topic. I knew something the reader didn't. I knew how a company owner or manager could offer an employee benefit package at no cost and with little effort.

I decided what type of reader would be interested in my topic — an entrepreneur, a self-starter who couldn't afford to provide employees with a lot of the usual perks. I queried magazines for small business owners and got an excellent response. About five editors said they would review my article on speculation.

I drafted the article in a "how-to" format, using a tightly structured outline with numbered steps. I explained the benefits of a credit union, and how to select and affiliate with one.

The manuscripts were returned, but I kept trying. In February, the managing editor of *Entrepreneurial Woman*, a magazine for women business owners, agreed to consider my article. She told me to include quotes from experts as well as women business owners who offer credit union services to their employees. Because *Entrepreneurial Woman* is a national magazine, she stressed the quotes should come from women in different parts of the country.

I tailored my original article to fit these requests. The format, however, was lacking. The editor wanted prose with smooth transitions, not an outline with numbered steps. She also wanted more quotes.

I rewrote the article. Unfortunately, I wrote too much. I used too many quotes, including several quotes from a man. The editor reminded me this was a magazine for and about women. The readers had to relate to the article. The person featured in the article had to be female.

I wrote a third draft, eliminating the male perspective entirely and focusing on the female. The editor was satisfied. I received a copy of my first published article and a check for $400 in the mail.

I also learned an important lesson: know the magazine you are writing for. Study it. Use its style. Know its readers, their interests, their demographics. Write an article that will fill their needs and appeal to their interests. There is no other way to get published.

Joe Mullich writes for trade and business magazines, in addition to *Reader's Digest*, *Ladies' Home Journal* and *Cosmopolitan*. He wrote about chickens for *Food Business*, Sept. 24, 1990.[6]

Meet The Upscale Chicken: He's Lean, Trendy — And Profitable!

Joe Mullich

In this health-conscious age, it's not surprising that Americans are eating so much chicken. Per capita consumption is expected to reach 72.6 pounds in 1990, compared with 65.2 pounds in 1988, according to the U.S. Department of Agriculture.

continued

---

6. Joe Mullich, "Meet the Upscale Chicken: He's Lean, Trendy — and Profitable!" *Food Business*, Sept. 24, 1990.

continued

What's surprising is the *kind* of chicken that's being gobbled up: Consumers—starved for time, but hungry for taste and nutrition—are paying a premium to processors who debone, portion and marinate chickens for them. Retailers are stocking up on chicken concoctions that would fit right in at a swank French bistro, like Chicken Cordon Bleu and Chicken Kiev.

Still think of chicken as a cheap meal to make between sirloins? Sure, it can be. But certain products like boneless, skinless chicken are relatively expensive not only for chicken, but for anything in the meat case.

In short, the once lowly chicken has gone upscale.

"That's where you're going to make your money," said Jack Dunn, vice president of marketing for retail for Tyson Foods, the Springdale, Ark.-based company that was the first to recognize that "the more you do to chicken, the more you enhance its value."

Approximately 30 percent of the $16 billion chicken market is now value-added, estimates the National Broiler Council. That's up from 10 percent in 1980 and a mere 5 percent in 1970 when "there was a thing called 'chicken fatigue,'" said Bill Roenigk, director of economic research for the National Broiler Council. "There was some indication that the man of the household only wanted chicken once a week, and you served chicken more to stretch the budget."

Now, as Jack Pederson of Pederson's Fryer Farms in Tacoma, Wash., puts it: "My wife can serve chicken seven days a week and it tastes different every day."

By introducing such pricey products as Chicken Cordon Bleu and Teriyaki Chicken Jerky, Pederson's has seen sales leap 250 percent over the past five years to $60 million.

The upscale chicken was hatched in an unlikely place: fast-food eateries. After chicken nuggets and patties were introduced to restaurants in the mid-1980s, consumers began to clamor for similar dishes they could serve at home. Processors, aware of the higher margins of the value-added products, were happy to oblige.

"Value-added products put processors in a more steady market position because they're less sensitive to meat cycles and to consumers who are only looking for price," said Roenigk.

Companies are also trying to change consumers' ideas about where and when to eat chicken. Pederson's, for example, is now test-marketing a breakfast chicken sausage, which the company says has 57 percent less fat than comparable beef or pork breakfast meats. "We found that a lot of consumers weren't able to eat meat in the morning because they were cutting back on fat and cholesterol," said Alison Clayton, the firm's director of marketing.

Pederson's is also trying to bring chicken to the afternoon. This fall, Pederson's will launch "Chicken Snack Sticks," which the company describes as "like a chicken pepperoni." The product won first place among snack foods in a recent competition put on by the Northwest Meat Processors Association.

Value-added chicken is being fortified by more attention to marketing as well. On British television, actor Dudley Moore can be seen hawking chicken, according to the *Wall Street Journal*. In the Northwestern United States, Pederson's has begun an intense demonstration program for which it designed more than 100 chicken recipes. The company also opened a toll-free line. "It's been a big success," said Clayton. "We get everything from questions on how to thaw chickens to how to cook them—a lot of the new generation doesn't know."

Tyson's, which processes some 28 million chickens a week and has roughly a quarter of total chicken sales, is looking for untapped markets like latchkey kids. Tyson's recently introduced Looney Tunes Meals, a microwave line that includes chicken products. In the first 90 days since their debut in March, the meals—which retail for $2.29 to $2.59—were ahead of forecast, selling their millionth case. "We're probably going to come out with a Looney Tunes breakfast," said Dunn.

With all this clucking, what *are* the limits to where, when and how much chicken can be sold? Pederson, whose family has been in the chicken game for more than four decades, said he can't think of any limits.

"Unlike other proteins, chicken is almost a neutral flavor," said Dunn. "The wonderful thing about chicken is that it will take on the characteristic of the spice or whatever you cook it with. Beef and pork do not have that range of adaptability."

And unlike meats like pork, chicken producers say their fowl food doesn't seem to have any cultural barriers. Chicken leg meat is now being shipped to the perestroika-opened Soviet Union (conveniently helping to balance out the overriding demand for breast meat in this country). Japan has worked out a deal with Tyson to ship chicken to Mexico, where it will be made into shish kabob products, according to Roenigk.

The next large chicken trend on the horizon: ground chicken. All the major chicken companies are expected to bring out ground chicken to supermarkets nationwide by year's end. Initially, at least, companies are expected to position ground chicken with a simple list of ingredients to take the place of ground beef in such products as tacos and meatballs in spaghetti. Probable first customers: those who now favor ground turkey.

"We expect ground chicken to really take hold," said Roenigk. "I won't predict that McDonald's will add chicken patties to the menu right now, but I wouldn't be surprised if one of the major chains offers a chicken hamburger as an alternative in the next couple of years."

And that, as they say, ain't chicken-feed.

Mullich tells the story behind the "Upscale Chicken:"

Joan Holleran, a talented assistant editor at *Food Business* magazine, noticed that chicken producers were coming out with increasing upscale and value-added products, such as chicken cordon bleu. She asked me to look into the trend of the upscale chicken and write a 600-word article for her magazine. To me, this is the perfect example of a straightforward trade magazine article that a competent business journalist should be able to report and write in a few hours.

Here are the steps I took:

- Joan sent me a letter specifying the assignment, including length, deadline, and the amount allotted for my expenses and my payment. Any writer working on a free-lance basis should request and receive an assignment letter of this nature, especially for articles that will involve a significant amount of work and time.

- With her letter, Joan enclosed some articles about the chicken industry the magazine had run in the past, and she also sent contact names and phone numbers for leading chicken producers. Obviously, this gave me a big head start.

- I ran a computer search for newspaper and magazine articles about the subject. Most of the larger public libraries, and certainly most university libraries, have databases indexing newspaper or magazine articles (and some have databases solely for articles about business subjects). In addition, many libraries have bound indexes, by year, for business periodicals and for the *Wall Street Journal*. The reference librarian can tell you what resources the library can make available to you (often at no cost). A literature search should be the first step for any kind of assignment.

- I began to make phone calls to set up interviews. I wanted to talk to representatives of one large chicken company, one small company, and one economist who could give me an overview of the upscale chicken trend. For this article, I did all the interviews by phone. This is because the article was a short one and my expenses and payment for the article did not justify spending time to travel on assignments. In general, well-prepared phone interviews are more concise and expeditious than in-person interviews, though in-person interviews are usually desirable if you are trying to coax delicate information from a source or capture the personality of your interview subject.

- Upon reading the articles I found through my computer search, I discovered a reference to an economist at the National Broiler Council, a poultry industry trade group. Trade groups are usually good places to start acquiring information on a specific business subject, though of course you must keep in mind that the groups are advocates for their industry. The trade group economist turned out to be extremely helpful, giving me an overview of the chicken scene and its history. He also told me about a small company in the state of Washington that was on the cutting edge of producing "upscale chickens."

- I called the Washington company and spoke to its president. He sent me some literature on the company and samples of his products. Normally, I will not accept products from companies, or I will return the products after the story is completed, but in this case I felt sampling the products would enable me to write a better story.

- After I received the material, I called and set up an interview with the company president and his marketing director. I conducted the interview by phone.

- From the list Joan gave me, I selected a representative from Tyson Foods, which I knew from my literature search to be the nation's largest chicken producer. I called to set up an interview and later conducted it by phone.

- I called a representative from the U.S. Dept. of Agriculture, also on Joan's list, and got figures on chicken consumption.

- I wrote a 600-word story and sent it to Joan.

- Joan called me back shortly. She and the other editors liked the story so much they wanted me to add a few hundred words to it so the magazine could use it as a cover piece. We negotiated compensation for the additional work. I went back to my notes. Instead of merely tacking information onto the existing story, I rewrote the article, fleshing out the existing framework with material I couldn't squeeze into the previous 600-word structure. Because the story was in my computer, I was able to complete the revised story in less than an hour.

- The story ran as a cover piece, with a nifty illustration, on Sept. 24, 1990.

Obviously, I could have done a great deal more work on this piece. For example, I could have spoken to other chicken companies, competitors (such as a beef industry group) and to analysts who follow the larger, publicly held companies. (You can find analysts by calling the research department of bro-

kerage firms in New York, or other large cities, and asking if they have someone who tracks the company you are interested in. Or you can call the public
relations or investor relations departments of public companies and ask them
to send you any analysts' reports about the company they have on file.)

In this case, though, I felt that the steps I took would produce sufficient
information for me to write a story meeting the needs of the magazine and (a
point that far too many free-lance writers fail to take into consideration) allow
me to earn a satisfactory per-hour return for my work.

Although the specialized business article may seem to be one of the easier articles to write, if the author is an expert in the area, Mullich and others in
this chapter demonstrate there may be more involved in these articles than
others. You not only need to be the expert or be able to present expertise in
the subject, but you also need to search out data and other authorities and
keep abreast of all developments in the area. Also you have to be a bit of a
translator or editor as you avoid jargon and make technical subjects readable,
using techniques other articles also require.

ASSIGNMENTS

1. In the business room of a library, study three specialized business/trade
   publications. What do they have in common in style, content, overall
   policy? How do they differ?

2. Study one particular trade publication by looking through a year's issues.
   Draft guidelines for the publication on the basis of what has been published in the past year.

3. Interview an editor of a specialized business/trade magazine in your area
   on the wants and needs of the publication and the background of the
   editor.

4. Write a page on your "specialty" or — if you don't have a specialty — a
   page on how to become an expert or at least knowledgeable in a selected
   area. Who are the experts to consult? What are the books and publications to consult? Conclude with a suggestion for an article in the area of
   "expertise."

5. Examine 10 articles that could be brought to class or put on reserve in
   the library representing 10 different trade publications. Prepare a report
   on which are the best and worst — rank them — using advice and guidelines of editors in this chapter.

6. The same topic areas work for many magazines. Compare one subject as
   treated in four publications: a newspaper feature, a genre magazine (such
   as children or travel), a general magazine (such as *Playboy* or *Ladies Home
   Journal*) and a specialized trade publication. For example, consider a
   travel topic, such as protection from terrorists. What does a newspaper
   travel section tell would-be tourists? What does a travel magazine, which

is more national than local, say? What does a general magazine which may be more interested in a demographic grouping (men, women, young or old) say? What does the specialized business/trade publication, such as *Travel Weekly*, serving the corporate business traveler, say on the subject?

7. Take a subject and compare how that subject would be handled by a dozen different publications. Collate the information in class into one master chart.

8. Some specialized business/trade publications are becoming more in-depth in their approaches. Report on an in-depth, investigative article found in a specialized business/trade publication.

9. Design a proposed new trade magazine, with simulated cover. What would be an exciting line up in a proposed table of contents for the first issue?

10. Make a list of jargon words that need translation in selected publications. Which publications have a more readable style and why?

CHAPTER 14

But Is It Ethical?

When the answer to what's right or what's wrong seems obscured by dense fog, you can always ask yourself: What's the best action for all involved? What's best for humanity at large? You can certainly apply the golden rule to individual cases: Do unto others as you would have others do unto you. The trouble is that what works between two individuals might not be best for humanity. Keep in mind as well Immanuel Kant's "categorical imperative": "Act only according to a maxim by which you can at the same time will that it shall become a general law." Or: "Act as if the maxim of your action were to become through your will a general natural law."

Acting by some categorical imperative, however, doesn't guarantee that you will do the right thing. What you consider to be right may not be what others consider right. Human history resounds with the horrible stories of what happens when those who believe they act on a higher initiative condemn and censor others. The Inquisition and the Protestant Reformation abound with excesses—with heretics on both sides being drowned, quartered and burned at the stake, oftentimes over a slight disagreement in definitions and wordings. Hitler claimed to be following a "higher" sense of good when he initiated policies of racial purity and waged wars of destruction and extermination. When extreme Muslim sectarians called for Salman Rushdie's death because they felt his book *The Satanic Verses* was blasphemous, they applied their own interpretation of right to a world that mostly disagreed with them.

Some say "Let your conscience be your guide," but perhaps that is too whimsical. Why not let your conscience, informed by one or several of the world's great traditions (in philosophy or religion) and tempered by a golden rule or a categorical imperative, be your guide?

ETHICAL CODES

You can establish your own code of ethics. Keep track of the questions that bother you. Pretend that you're the boss at the newspaper or magazine. As situations arise, what would you do? What would you tell someone else who asked you for direction in each case? Begin by checking company policies if you're working on a newspaper or magazine. You also can start with the opinions of others you respect and with published codes.

Beware, however, of putting too much store in a code. It's like endowing a major religion or cult with excessive power. Just whose code is it? A code can reflect the preferences of a class, a racial majority or even a dominant religion or tradition.

Codes may leave too many possibilities out or be inadequate under special circumstances. Consider the commandment "Thou shalt not kill." The Old Testament is filled with bloody accounts in which the Deity sent troops off to battle. Most faiths embody the concept of a just war, although some preach total pacifism. Many accept the concept of a just killing; in fact, German theologian Dietrich Bonhoeffer and others engaged in a plot to kill Hitler in order to end the slaughter of millions. Bonhoeffer paid with his life.

Among the writers' codes journalism students and journalists might encounter is that of the Society of Professional Journalists (Figure 14-1).

For free-lance writers the code of the American Society of Journalists and Authors is as concerned with legal protection as with ethical conduct (Figure 14-2).[1]

THE REAL WORLD:
WHAT DO YOU DO WHEN . . . ?

Read the codes and learn what you can from them. You'll need all the help you can get when you have to make specific decisions. Some of the questions you will have to answer as a feature or magazine writer follow. In fact, you will likely have to answer them all.

1. From the *1992 Directory*, American Society of Journalists and Authors, pp. 86–88.

Society of Professional Journalists

CODE OF ETHICS

SOCIETY of Professional Journalists, believes the duty of journalists is to serve the truth.

We BELIEVE the agencies of mass communication are carriers of public discussion and information, acting on their Constitutional mandate and freedom to learn and report the facts.

We BELIEVE in public enlightenment as the forerunner of justice, and in our Constitutional role to seek the truth as part of the public's right to know the truth.

We BELIEVE those responsibilities carry obligations that require journalists to perform with intelligence, objectivity, accuracy, and fairness.

To these ends, we declare acceptance of the standards of practice here set forth:

I. RESPONSIBILITY:

The public's right to know of events of public importance and interest is the overriding mission of the mass media. The purpose of distributing news and enlightened opinion is to serve the general welfare. Journalists who use their professional status as representatives of the public for selfish or other unworthy motives violate a high trust.

II. FREEDOM OF THE PRESS:

Freedom of the press is to be guarded as an inalienable right of people in a free society. It carries with it the freedom and the responsibility to discuss, question, and challenge actions and utterances of our government and of our public and private institutions. Journalists uphold the right to speak unpopular opinions and the privilege to agree with the majority.

III. ETHICS:

Journalists must be free of obligation to any interest other than the public's right to know the truth.

1. Gifts, favors, free travel, special treatment or privileges can compromise the integrity of journalists and their employers. Nothing of value should be accepted.

2. Secondary employment, political involvement, holding public office, and service in community organizations should be avoided if it compromises the integrity of journalists and their employers. Journalists and their employers should conduct their personal lives in a manner that protects them from conflict of interest, real or apparent. Their responsibilities to the public are paramount. That is the nature of their profession.

3. So-called news communications from private sources should not be published or broadcast without substantiation of their claims to news values.

4. Journalists will seek news that serves the public interest, despite the obstacles. They will make constant efforts to assure that the public's business is conducted in public and that public records are open to public inspection.

5. Journalists acknowledge the newsman's ethic of protecting confidential sources of information.

6. Plagiarism is dishonest and unacceptable.

continued

Figure 14-1. The Code of Ethics of the Society of Professional Journalists. Revised, 1987.

Society of Professional Journalists

CODE OF ETHICS (cont.)

IV. ACCURACY AND OBJECTIVITY:

Good faith with the public is the foundation of all worthy journalism.

1. Truth is our ultimate goal.

2. Objectivity in reporting the news is another goal that serves as the mark of an experienced professional. It is a standard of performance toward which we strive. We honor those who achieve it.

3. There is no excuse for inaccuracies or lack of thoroughness.

4. Newspaper headlines should be fully warranted by the contents of the articles they accompany. Photographs and telecasts should give an accurate picture of an event and not highlight an incident out of context.

5. Sound practice makes clear distinction between news reports and expressions of opinion. News reports should be free of opinion or bias and represent all sides of an issue.

6. Partisanship in editorial comment that knowingly departs from the truth violates the spirit of American journalism.

7. Journalists recognize their responsibility for offering informed analysis, comment, and editorial opinion on public events and issues. They accept the obligation to present such material by individuals whose competence, experience, and judgment qualify them for it.

8. Special articles or presentations devoted to advocacy or the writer's own conclusions and interpretations should be labeled as such.

V. FAIR PLAY:

Journalists at all times will show respect for the dignity, privacy, rights, and well-being of people encountered in the course of gathering and presenting the news.

1. The news media should not communicate unofficial charges affecting reputation or moral character without giving the accused a chance to reply.

2. The news media must guard against invading a person's right to privacy.

3. The media should not pander to morbid curiosity about details of vice and crime.

4. It is the duty of news media to make prompt and complete correction of their errors.

5. Journalists should be accountable to the public for their reports and the public should be encouraged to voice its grievances against the media. Open dialogue with our readers, viewers, and listeners should be fostered.

VI. MUTUAL TRUST:

Adherence to this code is intended to preserve and strengthen the bond of mutual trust and respect between American journalists and the American people.

The Society shall — by programs of education and other means — encourage individual journalists to adhere to these tenets, and shall encourage journalistic publications and broadcasters to recognize their responsibility to frame codes of ethics in concert with their employees to serve as guidelines in furthering these goals.

American Society of Journalists and Authors

Code of Ethics and Fair Practices

Preamble

Over the years, an unwritten code governing editor-writer relationships has arisen. The American Society of Journalists and Authors has compiled the major principles and practices of that code that are generally recognized as fair and equitable.

The ASJA has also established a Committee on Editor-Writer Relations to investigate and mediate disagreements brought before it, either by members or by editors. In its activity this committee shall rely on the following guidelines:

1. Truthfulness, Accuracy, Editing

The writer shall at all times perform professionally and to the best of his or her ability, assuming primary responsibility for truth and accuracy. No writer shall deliberately write into an article a dishonest, distorted or inaccurate statement.

Editors may correct or delete copy for purposes of style, grammar, conciseness or arrangement, but may not change the intent or sense without the writer's permission.

2. Sources

A writer shall be prepared to support all statements made in his or her manuscripts, if requested. It is understood, however, that the publisher shall respect any and all promises of confidentiality made by the writer in obtaining information.

3. Ideas and Proposals

An idea shall be defined not as a subject alone but as a subject combined with an approach.

A proposal of an idea ("query") by a professional writer shall receive a personal response within three weeks. If such a communication is in writing, it is properly viewed and treated as business correspondence, with no return postage or other materials required for reply.

A writer shall be considered to have a proprietary right to an idea suggested to an editor.

4. Acceptance of an Assignment

A request from an editor that the writer proceed with an idea, however worded and whether oral or written, shall be considered an assignment. (The word "assignment" here is understood to mean a definite order for an article.) It shall be the obligation of the writer to proceed as rapidly as possible toward the completion of an assignment, to meet a deadline mutually agreed upon, and not to agree to unreasonable deadlines.

5. Conflict of Interest

The writer shall reveal to the editor, before acceptance of an assignment, any actual or potential conflict of interest, including but not limited to any financial interest in any product, firm, or commercial venture relating to the subject of the article.

6. Report on Assignment

If in the course of research or during the writing of the article, the writer concludes that the assignment will not result in a satisfactory article, he or she shall be obliged to so inform the editor.

7. Withdrawal

Should a disagreement arise between the editor and writer as to the merit or handling of an assignment, the editor may remove the writer on payment of mutually satisfactory compensation for the effort already [expended], or the writer may withdraw without compensation and, if the idea for the assignment originated with the writer, may take the idea elsewhere without penalty. *continued*

Figure 14-2 The Code of Ethics of the American Society of Journalists and Authors.

American Society of Journalists and Authors

Code of Ethics and Fair Practices (cont.)

8. Agreements

The practice of written confirmation of all agreements between editors and writers is strongly recommended, and such confirmation may originate with the editor, the writer, or an agent. Such a memorandum of confirmation should list all aspects of the assignment including subject, approach, length, special instructions, payments, deadline, and guarantee (if any). Failing prompt contradictory response to such a memorandum, both parties are entitled to assume that the terms set forth therein are binding.

All terms and conditions should be agreed upon at the time of assignment, with no changes permitted except by written agreement signed by both parties.

9. Rewriting

No writer's work shall be rewritten without his or her advance consent. If an editor requests a writer to rewrite a manuscript, the writer shall be obliged to do so but shall alternatively be entitled to withdraw the manuscript and offer it elsewhere.

10. Bylines

Lacking any stipulation to the contrary, a byline is the author's unquestioned right. All advertisements of the article should also carry the author's name. If an author's byline is omitted from a published article, no matter what the cause or reason, the publisher shall be liable to compensate the author financially for the omission.

11. Updating

If delay in publication necessitates extensive updating of an article, such updating shall be done by the author, to whom additional compensation shall be paid.

12. Reversion of Rights

A writer is not paid by money alone. Part of the writer's compensation is the intangible value of timely publication. Consequently, reasonable and good-faith efforts should be made to schedule an article within six months and publish it within twelve months. In the event that circumstances prevent such timely publication, the writer should be informed within twelve months as to the publication's continued interest in the article and plans to publish it. If publication is unlikely, the manuscript and all rights therein shall revert to the author without penalty or cost to the author.

13. Payment for Assignments

An assignment presumes an obligation upon the publisher to pay for the writer's work upon satisfactory completion of the assignment, according to the agreed terms. Should a manuscript that has been accepted, orally or in writing, by a publisher or any representative or employee of the publisher, later be deemed unacceptable, the publisher shall nevertheless be obliged to pay the writer in full according to the agreed terms.

If an editor withdraws or terminates an assignment, due to no fault of the writer, after work has begun but prior to completion of a manuscript, the writer is entitled to compensation for work already put in; such compensation shall be negotiated between editor and author and shall be commensurate with the amount of work already completed. If a completed assignment is not acceptable, due to no fault of the writer, the writer is nevertheless entitled to payment; such payment, in common practice, has varied from half the agreed-upon price to the full amount of that price.

American Society of Journalists and Authors

Code of Ethics and Fair Practices (cont.)

14. Time of Payments
The writer is entitled to full payment for an accepted article within 30 days of delivery. No article payment, or any portion thereof, shall ever be subject to publication or to scheduling for publication.

15. Expenses
Unless otherwise stipulated by the editor at the time of an assignment, a writer shall assume that normal, out-of-pocket expenses will be reimbursed by the publisher. Any extraordinary expenses anticipated by the writer shall be discussed with the editor prior to incurring them.

16. Insurance
A magazine that gives a writer an assignment involving any extraordinary hazard shall insure the writer against death or disability during the course of travel or the hazard or, failing that, shall honor the cost of such temporary insurance as an expense account item.

17. Loss of Personal Belongings
If, as a result of circumstances or events directly connected with a perilous assignment and due to no fault of the writer, a writer suffers loss of personal belongings or professional equipment or incurs bodily injury, the publisher shall compensate the writer in full.

18. Copyright, Additional Rights
It shall be understood, unless otherwise stipulated in writing, that sale of an article manuscript entitles the purchaser to first North American publication rights only, and that all other rights are retained by the author. Under no circumstances shall an independent writer be required to sign a so-called "all rights transferred" or "work made for hire" agreement as a condition of assignment, of payment, or of publication.

19. Reprints
All revenues from reprints shall revert to the author exclusively, and it is incumbent upon a publication to refer all requests for reprint to the author. The author has a right to charge for such reprints and must request that the original publication be credited.

20. Agents
An agent may not represent editors or publishers. In the absence of any agreement to the contrary, a writer shall not be obliged to pay an agent a fee on work negotiated, accomplished and paid for without the assistance of the agent. An agent should not charge a client a separate fee covering "legal" review of a contract for a book or other project.

21. TV and Radio Promotion
The writer is entitled to be paid for personal participation in TV or radio programs promoting periodicals in which the writer's work appears.

22. Indemnity
No writer should be obliged to indemnify any magazine or book publisher against any claim, actions, or proceedings arising from an article or book.

23. Proofs
The editor shall submit edited proofs of the author's work to the author for approval, sufficiently in advance of publication that any errors may be brought to the editor's attention. If for any reason a publication is unable to so deliver or transmit proofs to the author, the author is entitled to review the proofs in the publication's office.

Should I Take "Freebies"? You know what freebies are: anything offered free to a writer or editor. While these gifts are given under the pretext of friendship or good will, their real purpose is to gain mentions or space — in other words, free advertising.

Some newspapers won't let reporters accept even a cup of coffee; others allow a meal or drinks from a source ("anything you can eat at one sitting"). The consensus of opinion nowadays is that the organization the reporter is representing picks up the tab. A starving free-lancer, with expenses largely out of pocket (unless expenses are spelled out in contracts), might not worry so much about who pays a food tab. The development of sources is important for reporters and free-lancers and whoever pays (and it could vary) is immaterial to many. A good compromise, especially when the writer isn't backed up by an unlimited expense account, is to suggest at the beginning that each party bears his or her own expense.

The case of freebies becomes more complicated when it comes to free transportation; the money involved is much greater. It is hard for an editor or writer to turn down a junket sponsored just for the press to some part of the world. Usually the airline or tourist company expects at least a mention. Or the subject speaks for itself, as when Israel sponsored a tour for news media to accompany 1,000 persons from the Northeast to Israel. If you go on the trip, you can't help but mention the country and thus contribute to free advertising.

Some editors don't have problems with accepting free world travel. In fact, the history of media is full of free travel grabbers. Over 100 years ago, the National Newspaper Association was launched when editors took free trips. When a group of them met in New Orleans during an international exposition, they proceeded to organize, and the organization exists today.

Some newspapers won't use free-lance travel writers who admit to taking free travel. The travel editor of one of the leading newspapers in the South, who did not want to be quoted by name, says, "We prefer not to use material writers get from free trips, so that just about takes us out of the [free-lance] market." One newsmagazine fired its managing editor for taking a freebie with the Unification Church (the "Moonies"), which has sponsored many free tours for media personnel and scholars.

Edgar North, the famed writer on China, never took any expense money from the People's Republic of China. He stood on the platform with Mao Tse-tung and took part in many high-level sessions in China. North had many critics. Can you imagine how much more difficult it would have been if he had taken expense money? A seemingly innocent freebie would have come back to haunt him, and in his case would likely have destroyed his illustrious career.

Can I Do "Outside" Work? And how much can I trade on or use the name of my company or publisher to further outside interests? The term *outside interests* refers to assignments, appearances on or hosting radio-TV shows, consulting. Since the media cover all aspects of society, it's hard to think of any gainful activity that might not be a conflict of interest. Some journalists would argue that you should not be involved in politics, even religion—at least to the extent of sitting on committees. Check carefully with the rules of the establishment you work for, and check with your superiors. Get any concessions or exceptions to general policy in writing. If, for instance, you want to serve on your local school board, get your management's OK in writing. Your current boss might move on, and the successor might charge you with conflict of interest. An official memo that says otherwise would help your position.

Should you use the office stationery to solicit writing assignments? Again, what are the rules? In the absence of a rule, it's your call. Certainly a newspaper or magazine letterhead will help to convince an outside editor that you should be able to deliver the free-lance piece. Your boss might argue you're wasting company products (stationery) or that the company does not want to be associated with your private projects. On the other hand, some publishing firms like to encourage outside writing projects as creative and mind-expanding and don't object to the use of company stationery to make contacts.

A related issue is the use of office time for outside projects. Much *Time* and *Newsweek* coverage depends on news persons on the job feeding material into the regional news bureaus and national desks while they are on the job for other organizations across the country. In many instances, management tolerates staffers' stringing for national media—as long as their own newspaper or magazine gets a story first and the effort does not interfere with regular deadlines and procurement. Whatever the ethics of the matter may be in these instances, the general practice, one suspects, is: Don't ask; if there are rules, follow them.

Can I Ever Tell a Little Untruth?   If you tell even a small untruth, you are a liar. And liars seldom tell one lie. Lying not only can get you in trouble, but it can also destroy your character. Does anybody really like or trust a known liar? It's always amazing how glibly students handle the little lie. In one case, a young lady had made an appointment to interview somebody during class time, but then decided it was important to be in class! "I just told him I was sick and I could see him some other time," she said. But "he" was a very busy vice president of the university, who called the prof and gently admonished him because journalism students were using up too much of his time. Nobody wants to hire or use a writer who will lie at any whim.

In general, some institutions, even religious ones, justify a lie in a life-threatening situation. For instance, an old man has just died. His widow is in the hospital on the brink of death. A word about the death of her spouse would likely kill her. The humane course of action would be to tell the woman her husband is still alive, or at least to delay telling her that he is dead. Journalistic ethics has its counterparts, theoretically at least, to this classical situation. You can construe situations where one could lie to save a life or lives, but such exceptions are rare. If you are entertaining the possibility of exceptions, consult with a supervising editor.

Can I Misrepresent Myself?   People like to know to whom they are talking; be up front with them. If you were being interviewed, you would want to know to whom you were talking. Some possible reasons for exceptions emerge: (1) Situations where you simply don't identify yourself unless asked. Group scenes, public forums and even riots are not places where you just stand up and say "Hi, I'm a reporter!" Sometimes a low profile works better, but you don't misrepresent yourself when asked. (2) "Participatory" arrangements. Newspapers and magazines have produced important investigations by going under cover.

When the Chicago *Sun-Times* rented a Chicago bar and its reporters served as waiters and bartenders so that they could overhear extortion attempts, this was misrepresentation. It was not lying in a strict sense, because the patrons didn't ask the bar workers if they were reporters. Examples of prize-winning participatory journalism in recent years include penetration of Nazi groups, the Ku Klux Klan, doctors' offices where illegal drugs were distributed (a Chicago *Tribune* reporter got a job as a secretary to a doctor in order to get a story).

At the ethics workshop preceding the 1989 annual convention of the Investigative Reporters and Editors, Inc., Ralph D. Barney, of Brigham Young University, summarized "pragmatic guidelines for justifying deception":

> If the particular circumstances of a proposed deceit do not pass all three, deceptive tactics in the pursuit of information may not be morally justifiable:
>
> 1. *Information sought must be of overriding public importance.* A strong case would need to be present that the public NEEDED to know, as opposed to the providing of [information] that is merely interesting.
>
> 2. *There must be no reasonable likelihood that comparably accurate and reliable information could be obtained as efficiently through conventional investigative techniques.* When "past experience, common sense, and hard work . . . first demonstrate there is no other way to get the story, when conventional reportorial techniques just will not yield the necessary information," this justification may become valid.
>
> 3. *Deception contemplated must not place innocent people at serious risk.* Posing as a fireman to investigate the Fire Department would put other firemen and others at risk if the reporter were called upon to act as a fireman.
>
> *Caveat:* If the three-part test is applied and the deception accomplished, readers/viewers should be told exactly what the methods of investigation were and exactly why deception was used.[2]

2. Ralph D. Barney, "Pragmatic Guidelines for Justifying Deception," prepared for Investigative Reporters and Editors Ethics Workshop, adapted from Lou Hodges' "Undercover, Masquerading, Surreptitious Taping," in *Journal of Mass Media Ethics*, Fall 1988.

Should I Make My Connections Entirely Clear? Suppose a student tells a subject he or she is writing something for a writing class and it might appear in print; but the full truth would be: "I'm doing this for an advanced or graduate investigative reporting class, and the Philadelphia *Daily News* is interested in printing it." Nothing is really untrue about what the student initially said. Although technically truthful, the reporter is living on the edge of full disclosure.

One Philadelphia *Inquirer* police reporter, following up on a police activity, would tell the person at the other end of the telephone line: "Hello, I'm calling from the Police Administration Press Office," but somehow seemed to mumble the last two words, and those he called would assume that somebody in the police authority was calling.

Some journalists would argue that mumbling or using body language to purposely communicate the wrong information or the wrong impression is lying; others would put the responsibility on the listener. Most journalists would take a dim view of anyone who regularly practiced deception, even if it were through muttering.

How Enterprising Can I Be in "Generating" a Story? An editor says, "You can't create the story," but the editor also says: "You have to be entertaining." Obviously, you cannot go around making up stories from whole cloth. If you do, your career will be jeopardized. Howard Kohn, a prize-winning reporter at the Detroit *Free Press*, made up a story about being kidnapped at gunpoint; later he confessed it wasn't true and left the paper. Janet Cooke of the Washington *Post* led off her story on youth drug addiction with the case of an 8-year-old addict. She did not say the child was fictional or a composite. She had to return the Pulitzer Prize when the truth was discovered, and she left the paper.

Consider the expectation that reporters be enterprising. That means coming up with innovative ideas for stories, as well as keeping alert to spot ideas. But coming up with an idea may in effect be "creating" it. Many topical stories (economical, social, political issues; self-help articles) and most investigative articles (following a paper trail of corruption) are "created" articles, but based on fact.

Should I Withhold Information from an Article That Might Hurt Somebody or Cause a Death? A decision to publish or not to publish can be a life or death matter. A judge in Seattle, Gary Little, committed suicide in the summer of 1988 after the Seattle *Post-Intelligencer* ran a report detailing allegations that the King County Superior Court judge had sexual relations with a number of boys. If the paper had known the judge would shoot himself, should it have run the story? In a more celebrated case, the Dallas *Times-Herald* ran a story detailing the alleged double-agent spying activities of Norman Rees, who had been an oil company engineer. Just before the paper went to press with the allegations that Rees had spied for both the Soviet Union and the FBI, he told the paper he would kill himself if the story appeared — he did.

The *Times-Herald* issued a statement following the suicide: "From time to time newspapers receive threats about stories from people attempting to protect their identities. In our judgment, if a story is newsworthy and supported by the facts, it is our policy to publish it. In this instance it was decided that the story could not be suppressed, even in the face of Mr. Rees's threats." Newspapers and magazines do suppress stories, such as articles that might stir a race riot or endanger a hostage. It is hard to set a general rule for such decisions, but they should be consistent (if the caller were Larry Flynt or Mother Teresa, would that make a difference?) and conform to the highest humanitarian motives.

Can I Break an Embargo on a Press Release and Use it Ahead of Time?
The press release, once in a person's hand, is a kind of contract, not a legal one but functional. Because you want to play fair, you don't break the release date. Once you break a release date, the source will likely dry up.

There are ways you can get around the embargo. At a convention, for instance, if you don't go to press room pigeonholes where embargoed documents are distributed at crucial moments, you can get your own materials from delegates and various authorities and informers. That's the importance of good beat reporters. They know where to get the information without going to standard public relation releases.

Some journalists also feel an embargo can be broken if it persistently favors the competition — for example, releasing information at 9 a.m. when morning papers are "dead." This practice used to be a problem but with the death of so many afternoon papers and the switch to deadlines for morning papers — actually the afternoon and evening before — the item can now be released in favor of a morning paper. The problem is the instantaneous use by broadcasting media. But they too can be limited to a time compatible with morning newspapers, since broadcasting is a 24-hour-a-day medium.

If the FBI or CIA Wants Something from Me, Should I Oblige?   Again, an exception to a rule is possible. Normally you don't share information, but if a manhunt is on for a mass killer and you know where that person is, cooperation is in order.

The FBI and CIA have a history of trying to tap news sources, even posing as newspersons. The intentions of national law-enforcement agencies or even local ones aren't always entirely honorable. You don't know how the information will be used. You can't lie to such federal agencies; that's a crime. But you have no obligation to "work" for them in any capacity. It might come back to haunt you. Spies may be intriguing in fiction, but not in our midst.

Should I Tell People I Am Taping Them?   As we have seen in Chapter 5, in most states, but not all, it is legal to tape record without getting consent. Some people prefer that a reporter tape the interview or the proceedings in order to be sure the reporter has it right. Others feel the tape recorder is too intimidating and might record too much. According to a study by the Associated Press Managing Editors association in 1984, editors were sharply divided. Some felt that taping was a tool of the trade and it would be irrelevant to a subject whether the reporter was taking notes or taping or both. Others felt it was sneaky not to tell a person he or she was being taped. Others offered compromises: Generally tell the person; then, if exceptions are to be made, consult first with the editor.

The use of tape recorders is so pervasive today that an enlightened subject should assume one is being used. In face-to-face encounters, the use of a tape recorder can be obvious. If you're taping over the phone, consult state law and management. Magazine editors do not seem to get involved in the taping debate, but source sheets often submitted with articles can identify for the editor how you obtained the information.

Should I Ever Pay for Information?   The answer for a reporter is "no," although it does happen. In effect, a news person buying a source a free meal or drinks is providing material benefit or compensation. Newspapers shrink from buying information directly, but TV and magazines are more likely to engage in "paycheck journalism." It's "paycheck journalism" when magazines or TV networks sign news subjects to exclusive contracts, as *Life* did with the original Mercury astronauts. Only *Life* had access to the stories of the pioneering astronauts as they prepared for their journeys. And all media seem to have little trouble in paying for an on-the-spot news photograph.

The free-lance writer is likely to pay for some material. All writers and reporters must pay research fees and charges at libraries and agencies. Free-lancers might use an assistant or even hire experts to write some portions of a book, with attribution.

Would It Be Ethical for Me to Ghostwrite Something?   Ghostwriting, of course, is writing something for somebody and putting that person's name on it instead of yours. Writing students are sometimes asked to ghostwrite a term paper and out of enthusiasm for writing might do so. Professors have been known to get graduate students to do most or all the work, then take most if not all of the credit in the published article. Don't cheat; don't be a part of a dishonest arrangement.

Yet ghostwriting — particularly with books or speech writing — is a legitimate approach. Other people write most of a president's speeches. In writing other people's material, especially books and articles, try to get some recognition (such as the "as told to" designation).

Should I Send Out Simultaneous Submissions?   When it comes to sending more than one copy of an article at once, the answer is a strong no. Submit one copy at a time, but contact the editor after a month or two if there has been no reply. The question of submitting simultaneous article queries was discussed earlier.

When it comes to nonfiction books, authors, agents and most publishers have little problem with multiple submissions of queries and proposals. Book publishers can sit for years on a proposal. If you give a proposal to publishers one by one, it may take a lifetime for the proposal to make the rounds.

How About Using an Author's Published Writings as a Part of an Interview? Sometimes authors being interviewed will say, "Take something from my book and include it if you want." Some newspaper reporters working against a deadline might say to a busy interview subject or a largely inaccessible subject, "Can I take a few quotes out of your newest book and say you said it to me?" A writer who does so should always indicate, however, that the quotes come from a book. Maybe someone reading the article has also read the book.

Beware, too, that what someone said in a book might not be true today. It's always best to indicate in some way the place and source of your information.

Should I Reveal How Old Some of My Research and Material Is? Nobody is interested in old information. That's a problem with using books and periodicals for research. The survey quoted might be 10 or 20 years old. Some writers might be tempted to gloss over the date and say "in a recent survey . . ." with some kind of update from a more recent survey or quote from an authority.

A source sheet with the article can give an editor the dates and other reference notes on the material. This is useful for the fact checkers that most major magazines employ. Editors appreciate the courtesy and it also assures them you're not trying to hide behind camouflaged facts. In addition, a source sheet makes you more conscious of the need to be up to date.

Can I Put Quotes Around a Summary of a Person's Remarks? A summary doesn't have the flavor of a person's own speech. Your subject won't recognize your representation and will probably feel uncomfortable with words put into her or his mouth. Paraphrase without quotes if you're summarizing remarks. Save the quotes for the clever, interesting, entertaining utterances. But a caution: don't fragment remarks. When you do quote them, generally let people speak in full sentences. Fragmented quotes can be misunderstood and manipulated.

Should you edit or clean up the direct quotes? It depends. Most human speech needs some smoothing out or light editing when it is used in print. The "uh huhs" and "and so forths" can come out. Don Fry, associate director of the Poynter Institute for Media Studies in St. Petersburg, Fla., demonstrates how to clean up quotes in a conference document he distributes. In his handout at a panel he was moderating at the 1989 Investigative Reporters and Editors conference, he contrasted "actual" speech with the ways the speech would be used in various media. He took a transcript of his phone interview with *Newsday* columnist Murray Kempton and showed what could be done to it in print:

MAKING HUMAN SPEECH SOUND REAL

1. Murray Kempton Telephone Interview 3-27-85 Verbatim Transcript:

> FRY: I don't think you're too pleasant in these pieces in front of me, like the, the one about the woman who burned up while the cops ate their breakfast, you know. I mean. . . .
>
> KEMPTON: Well, I mean, you know. . . .
>
> FRY: That one's sharp.
>
> KEMPTON: Well, well, I'll put it this way, if you're gonna get mad, get, feel mad and then write.
>
> FRY: Yeah?
>
> KEMPTON: Don't sit down and work yourself up into a lather, I mean you really have to care, you know, I mean. . . .
>
> FRY: Yeah?
>
> KEMPTON: In other words, an awful, I think one of the mistakes of a lot, that, well I speak now of the mistakes of my own youth, I used to manufacture rage a lot. . . .
>
> FRY: Oh?
>
> KEMPTON: And then, yeah, and I think there's a certain tendency, among some guys, that I've noticed, and I think that it is to make the mistake that I made in my youth, and their youth, and I think that, the point is, that there's, there's, there's enough to make you mad, uh, but just be sure that the thing that makes you mad, my, this is, I'm saying this to myself and not to them, the thing that makes you mad genuinely makes you mad.
>
> FRY: Yes?
>
> KEMPTON: I mean, don't whip yourself up into [pause] a fancy prancy, because then, then you're, you're an actor, and there's the truth of the matter is that you won't be on the stage very long.
>
> FRY: You know, uh. . . .

2. Edited for *Best Newspaper Writing 1985* Conversation:

> FRY: I don't find you too pleasant in some of the prize pieces, particularly the one about the woman who burned to death while the cops ate breakfast.
>
> KEMPTON: If you're going to get mad, feel mad and then write; don't sit down and work yourself up into a lather. You really have to care. I used to manufacture rage a lot, but now there's enough to make you mad. You don't whip yourself up into a "fancy prancy," because then you're an actor, and you won't be on the stage very long.

3. "Everything between the quotation marks is verbatim":

> KEMPTON: ". . . if you're go[ing to] get mad [about alleged outrageous police behavior], . . . feel mad and then write [your column]. . . . Don't sit down and work yourself up into a lather. . . . You really have to care. . . . I used to manufacture rage a lot, . . . [but now] there's enough [alleged outrageous behavior] to make you mad. . . . You . . . don't whip yourself up into a fancy prancy, because then . . . you're an actor, and . . . you won't be on the stage very long. . . ."

4a. Edited for Newspaper Quotation (Hard News):

Kempton admits he formerly faked anger in his columns, but now he finds enough outrage in the world. He warns against overstimulation. "Don't whip yourself up into a 'fancy prancy,' because then you're an actor," he said.

4b. Edited for Newspaper Quoting (Features):

Murray confesses to tricking up anger in his earlier stuff, but lately people have supplied all the outrages any journalist needs. "I mean, don't whip yourself up into — a fancy prancy," he cautions wistfully, "because then you're an actor, and you won't be on the stage very long."

5. Edited for Fiction Treatment:

Don leaned toward Murray, his voice probing. "I don't think you're too pleasant in these pieces, like the one about the woman who burned up while the cops ate their Danish."

Murray twisted in his chair. "Look, Don, if you're gonna get mad, feel mad and then write. You really have to care, you know. I used to manufacture rage a lot. . . ."

Don gaped, unbelieving, but Murray continued, "Yeah, I did, but now there's enough to make you mad, and you have to be sure that the thing that makes you mad really makes you mad."

Murray lowered his eyes, clearly distressed, groping. "I mean, don't whip yourself up into — " (He flapped his hands like a cornered bird) " — into a, a, fancy prancy, because then, then you're an actor, and the truth is —, you won't be on the stage very long."

The younger man sank his head, all his illusions wrecked.

6. *USA Today* style:

Rage Easier for Journalists

Advises against fancy prancy

by Don Fry

Poynter Institute

Journalists had to "manufacture rage a lot" in the past, but things have got a lot better, a prominent columnist says.

Murray Kempton, prize-winning *Newsday* essayist, is pleased that nowadays "there's enough to make you mad."

Kempton advises:

• "Feel mad, then write."

• "Ensure the thing that makes you mad genuinely makes you mad."

• "Really care."

When Should I Show Copy to a Subject?   The answer is "rarely." Newspaper reporters do not show or read back copy because (1) time is too short and (2) the story is likely to be "lost" or killed by somebody with an objection to it. Most interview subjects have their own ideas about how the article should appear and might try to impose them on you.

Newspaper reporters, however, might telephone a source or a subject to check a paragraph or a particular quote or fact, but that's not the same as showing an article to the subject for final review.

Magazines generally follow the same pattern as newspapers, but some magazines will show a highly technical article to a subject. Some prominent magazines, such as *Guideposts*, will allow the subject to see the edited article. Says *Guideposts'* Van Varner: "We get written releases (from the subject) with signed approval. Nothing goes in that is not reviewed, because the topics are intimate matters. We lose some? Yes. They might say it is not exactly what they want." *Guideposts* deals with the positive, but private, side of the individual and has a special interest in getting the nuances right.

The important thing is that when you deliver an article to an editor you feel it is right.

Can I Doctor or Change Something in a Photograph?   For a long time, there has been a kind a naturalism to media photography. The developer might enhance the lighting and mood, but otherwise generally leaves the photo alone. In former days newspaper artists were airbrush happy—they would airbrush or paint out backgrounds (such as the weird drapery behind a speaker at a podium).

Lately, concern has been expressed over whether pictures should be doctored. It is somewhat of a nonsensical debate, for pictures have always had some doctoring—such as cropping off parts (done to nearly all pictures) or outlining a picture by dropping out the background. Pictures can be enhanced when a second color is added or when they are shot twice as a duotone.

New electronic devices are allowing newspaper artists to zap out various trivia—in effect to airbrush out an object. For some reason, when a Diet Coke can was cut out of a picture by Pulitzer Prize–winning photographer Ron Olshwanger in the St. Louis *Post-Dispatch* in March 1989, a lot of people got excited, while some oldtimers wagged their heads and asked what's new about this?

Then came a real picture altering. *TV Guide* put an artist's rendering of a photograph of Oprah Winfrey on its cover—but look again: the head was Winfrey's, and the body was borrowed from an 11-year-old picture of actress-dancer Ann-Margret. If *TV Guide*, newly captained by Rupert Murdoch's organization, did this for obvious humor, then it would make sense. If it was standard procedure, and the picture was meant to look real, then most journalists would have trouble with that particular "doctoring."

Pictures are supposed to reflect a real world, so most editors and photographers are not happy with "doctoring" procedures. Whether a missing Coke can or a bodyless Oprah constitute nefarious deceit and treacherous phoniness may depend on your ideas of reality, art and esthetics and even humor.

Can I Pad Expenses for an Article When Someone Else Is Paying? It's always best to be honest and, in many cases, even a little conservative. You may want to work for the publication again. Generally, if you have a per diem allowance or can guess what the publication would allot, you can juggle within that amount. If you skip lunch, as some reporters do when they pursue a story, then you might eat (and drink) more at night. The important thing is to be honest about what you spend and report. Respect the money of the funding organization. Use of receipts keeps most journalists honest.

Can I Stretch My Achievements and Experience in My Letters to Editors or in a Résumé? Some students think if they spend an internship with a publication or if they are a "stringer" or part-time correspondent, they can list themselves as a staff reporter on their credits and résumés. Some people consider themselves co-authors of a book if they are mentioned in it. Just look at their résumés. It says so.

A good rule of thumb: Would those in charge of the publication you claim association with accept your appraisal of your standing or title? Would it stand up? Again, it pays to be totally honest.

If you have stretched your credits a little and someone checks, you may look more foolish than employable. If you're not sure of an honor — for example, if you're a member of a staff that won a prize, did you also win the prize? Get the interpretation in writing from the managing editor. If you're challenged about your claim 20 or 30 years down the road, you'll have it in writing. Keep everything you claim about yourself verifiable.

PLAGIARISM

Just as burglars and robbers steal material goods, plagiarists steal words, ideas, parts of articles and even the whole thing sometimes. Many editors admit to having had plagiarized material published in their magazines. The editor of one science publication tells about a writer who plagiarized from a Washington *Post* story. The writer used the last paragraph of a *Post* story as her lead and then picked up four quotes from the *Post* article. Yes, plagiarism exists, says Ronald P. Kriss, executive editor of *Time*. "As a young writer at *Time*," he recalls, "I realized a file from a correspondent had been lifted directly from a report in a newspaper. I had read the newspaper clip in the course of gathering information for my story." Says Rebecca Greer, articles editor, *Woman's Day*: "We once published an article in which the author had plagiarized anecdotes. The original author saw the article and recognized the source."

In the summer of 1991, the Fort Worth (Tex.) *Star-Telegram* fired columnist Katie Sherrod for running a column that her editor insisted had "substantial similarity" to a Washington *Post* article.[3] In January 1992, the *Star-*

---

3. Steve Polilli, "Fired for Plagiarism," *Editor & Publisher*, Aug. 17, 1991, p. 15.

Telegram reported it dealt with two more cases of alleged plagiarism. A political writer resigned after he was accused of using quotes from a TV program and another newspaper without attribution. And an editorial writer was suspended for one week after writing an unsigned editorial that borrowed a part of a New York *Times* opinion article without attribution.[4] The dean of Boston University's journalism school resigned in 1991 following a report in the Boston *Globe* that showed that he had plagiarized in a commencement speech. Analyzing a tape of Dean H. Joachim Maitre's commencement speech to the College of Communication, the paper cited 15 passages nearly identical to parts of an article written by PBS film critic, Michael Medved, in the scholarly journal *Imprimis* and reprinted in *Reader's Digest*. "My folly and carelessness are indisputable and indefensible," Maitre said in his resignation letter.[5] Some journalism students plagiarize — perhaps the person sitting next to you does.

Plagiarism is a sign of an amoral, if not perverse personality. No thinking person should descend to plagiarism. Plagiarists — who almost always get caught — have to live with guilt all their lives.

Professors have learned not to be too trusting. And with good reason. Researcher Michael Moffatt, an anthropologist at Rutgers University, discovered that nearly half of the students he surveyed at the university said that they cheated occasionally and that 33 percent said they cheated regularly.[6]

Even though professors may not say much about plagiarism and the "wages of sin," they may prove more canny and prosecutorial than you would imagine. The best students are not above their scrutiny. Consider the case of a graduate journalism student at Temple University. He was a graduate assistant; his tuition was paid and he received a stipend toward his expenses, plus — in this case — several scholarships. The professor of the graduate nonfiction writing class in which the student was enrolled suspected early on that the student's work might be the result of plagiarism. When the student turned in a how-to article on repairing bicycles, the article seemed compact, technical and polished. The professor sent the article to a friend, an editor of a bicycle magazine. The editor said the article was likely copied from a bicycle repair manual or brochure.

The professor intended to follow through by checking nearby bicycle shops in case one of the stores had a manual that corresponded to the "manualese" bicycle article. And other articles by the student seemed even more phony, such as the student's profile interview article on the new editorial

4. Steve Polilli, "More Plagiarism Incidents Plague Texas Daily," *Editor & Publisher*, Jan. 18, 1992, p. 11.

5. "J-School Dean Resigns in Plagiarism Controversy," *Editor & Publisher*, July 20, 1991, p. 11. See also James Fox, "Cover Story: Rash of Cases Raises Questions — Some Test the Line Between Borrowing and Stealing," *USA Today*, pp. 1B, 2B.

6. "The Urge to Cheat," *On Campus*, February 1991, p. 2.

director of Condé Nast in New York. The professor, who happened also to have an office in New York, went uptown one day and, with the help of the editorial director's secretary, found the original article that had been pilfered. The article on the editorial director was taken from a rather obscure publication, *Marketing & Media Decisions*. The student article and the *Decisions* article by another writer were the same, except that the "clever" student borrowed a few names from an adjoining article and sprinkled them into the original article. The student lost his financial support, received an F in the course and was dismissed from the university.

How about stealing ideas? Beginning journalists always ask the question: Will the editor steal my idea and give an assignment to somebody else? Yes, but usually not knowingly; most editors insist they are conscionable and do not pilfer ideas. The problem is that ideas are not necessarily unique. For every idea you have, you could find 1,000 persons out there with the same idea. As you'll see in Chapter 15, ideas cannot be copyrighted.

Experienced writers learn to keep their ideas to themselves and communicate the idea only to the editor with whom they want to work. Almost every writer feels an idea has been stolen or borrowed at one time or another. Successful writers have many ideas, and they "lose" a few in the process and over the course of time. Remember: it's always possible that a publication that declines to use your idea, and eventually uses the idea with another writer, may indeed have had the same idea submitted from someone else.

How about stealing a phrase or figure of speech? A Chicago columnist was disciplined by his editors for lifting phrases from another publication. But what if a phrase is appropriated inadvertently? Terry McDonell, editor-in-chief, *Esquire*, makes it a point to say that it's not possible for a seasoned writer to assimilate more of another writer's words than he realizes. A careful and disciplined writer, and particularly one who has developed a personal, individual style, should not have this problem. One way to avoid accidentally picking up someone else's phrasing is not to read a report or column or review on the subject you're writing about until after you have thought through what you want to write. Such an approach preserves spontaneity and freshness. If you tend to be unduly influenced by a great writer whom you have read a lot, Lois Wilde, associate editor of *Sports Afield*, suggests: "Reread your article with your favorite author in mind and ask: are these my words?"

Truth and originality have their own satisfying rewards, but it may take some will power and effort to achieve them.

ASSIGNMENTS

1. Take an article and discuss possible ethical problems that might have risen in the development of the article.
2. Write down an ethical dilemma, particularly as it relates to the media. Then discuss in class.

3. Prepare a several-page report on a famous reporter or writer. What ethical dilemmas did this person have? How were the problems handled or how should they have been handled?

4. Monitor one of the TV shows that are referred to as "trash journalism." What are some of the ethical problems involved?

5. Review the beliefs of a philosopher; choose one, and determine how it would apply to media ethics.

6. Which are the three most difficult ethical decisions to make in journalism? Discuss in class.

7. Design an ethics questionnaire that reporters, writers, editors and photographers might use.

8. Bring in speakers from the Christian-Judaic-Islamic-Humanist traditions and ask them how they would answer some of the ethical questions and dilemmas journalists face.

CHAPTER 15

Matters of Law

Many laws, from tax laws to postal laws, relate in some way to writers and the publishing business. As a writer, you will have a special interest in laws of libel, privacy and copyright.

LIBEL

Libel is a published form of defamation—attacking one's reputation. "Actually, the old distinction between libel as written defamation and slander as oral no longer holds true," says Douglas S. Campbell, author of *The Supreme Court and the Mass Media: Selected Cases, Summaries, and Analyses.* "The distinction now is between libel, which is considered longer lasting and more widespread, and slander, which is more ephemeral and local. With the advent of broadcasting, spoken defamation can last longer (tape recordings) and reach more people over the airwaves than can an article in a small weekly newspaper for example. Thus, nearly all instances of defamation in the media today (print *and* broadcast) are libel." But, Campbell adds, "the old distinctions still hold for libel by an individual. If, for example, a physician were to defame a colleague, then he still would be charged with libel if he did it in a letter, but with slander if he did it at a committee meeting."

Libelous statements have four characteristics: They are not true, they harm a person's reputation, they inflict damage and they have been communicated to a third party or more. "You cannot ruin, or even threaten, a person's reputation, until a third party learns of your defamatory words," says Campbell, who is chair of the Department of English, Journalism and Philosophy at Lock Haven (Pa.) University. "Speaking only to the person you defame may be impolite or even nasty, but it is not libelous."

Defenses against libel include:

- *What is regarded as fair comment*, such as editorials and reviews, although the waters have not been clear in this area since a U.S. Supreme Court judgment in 1990 against an Ohio sports columnist. The Court distinguished between a statement of opinion that has the effect of fact and so can be proven false and one that is merely "loose, figurative or hyperbolic language."

- *Right of reply and retraction.* A quick retraction sometimes serves to soften the damaging effect of a published statement on one's reputation, but yet may not be enough to avoid a suit.

- *Special privilege.* Statements by public officials and politicians made in a legislative body or legal proceeding or appearing in most public records constitute *absolute privilege*. A public official in the line of her or his official duty in privileged chambers cannot be convicted of libel. In addition to this absolute privilege there is *qualified privilege*, referring to a reporter or editor's use of privileged material. A reporter in most cases would not be held accountable if the statements and material were deemed privileged to begin with and if the published account were accurate and fair.

  Yet defining what is privileged is not always predictable. In 1989 the U.S. Supreme Court let stand the conviction of the Pittsburgh *Post-Gazette* on libel for publishing a defamatory statement taken from a deposition that was a part of an official pretrial proceeding.

- *The truth.* The best defense against charges of libel is to have the facts right and be able to prove them correct. However, truth should not be confused with accuracy. One may report accurately, but the information may prove false. And beware of innuendo. If the facts are right, but are worded in such a way that by implication the person is put in a light that would damage her or his reputation, the matter is actionable. In a $6 million ruling against the Philadelphia *Inquirer* in 1990, a judge said the paper's inferences and the way paragraphs were placed in a story made the plaintiff look dishonest.

- *Consent.* Someone allows or gives permission for publication of material about her or him, knowing the risk of possible defamation exists. Consent may be explicit, implied or merely apparent from the person's words or actions.

A false statement alone is generally not enough to secure a judgment of libel in cases involving public figures. In these cases there must be malicious intent. However, as Campbell points out, "malice (or actual malice) in libel has a special meaning. It does *not* mean ill will. It means *knowingly* disseminating a falsehood or not caring about the truth. It is not so much malicious intent that makes a false statement libelous as it is the existence of a fault. That is, some sort of fault must be shown. The level of fault is higher for public persons than for private persons. For private persons the level is set by the states, but it can be no lower than negligence. For public persons, the level is actual malice: knowledge that the statement is false or reckless disregard of the truth."

The presence of "malice" as a basis for determining libel in regard to a public figure was underscored in *New York Times v. Sullivan* in 1964. In that case, civil rights leaders had taken an ad in the *Times* opposing a group of Alabama officials, including Montgomery Police Commissioner L. B. Sullivan. Sullivan sued, arguing that some of the information was not correct. He won in the courts initially but eventually lost before the U.S. Supreme Court.

The majority opinion said:

> The constitutional guarantees (the First and Fourteenth Amendments) require, we think, a federal rule that prohibits a public official from recovering damages for a defamatory falsehood relating to his official conduct unless he proves that the statement was made with "actual malice" — that is, with knowledge that it was false or with reckless disregard of whether it was false or not.

Private persons in many states have cause for action if the published information is merely false, on the grounds of negligence. But what is a private or public figure? Having a moment in the limelight does not make someone a public figure. In reporting a messy divorce proceeding between Russell A. Firestone, Jr., tire maker heir, and his wife, Mary Alice, *Time* reported that the divorce trial had produced testimony of adultery on both sides. The judge found a "lack of domestication," not adultery. In Florida (there are no national libel laws) where the case was originally tried, negligence was enough to establish libel in regard to a private person. The U.S. Supreme Court agreed in *Time v. Firestone* that Mrs. Firestone was not a public person. Even though she held press conferences and subscribed to a clipping service, the Court found she did not "thrust herself to the forefront of any particular public controversy" and therefore was not a public figure.

Not checking out allegations thoroughly or not balancing the information can lead to a libel suit. The U.S. Supreme Court in 1989 upheld a jury verdict against the Hamilton (Ohio) *Journal News*. The paper had printed a story saying that Daniel Connaughton, a candidate for Municipal Court judge, had been accused by a grand jury witness of offering to bribe her in exchange for testimony that the court, headed by the judge's opponent, was guilty of corruption. The ruling found that the paper, by purposely avoiding an investigation, did not pursue the truth and showed malice—a sure test for libel. The decision said the paper should have contacted other sources and listened to an available tape of the alleged incident. The Supreme Court said the jury was justified in finding the paper's action "a deliberate effort to avoid the truth."

As a writer you also have to be careful what you say in memos and letters. The Alton (Ill.) *Telegraph* was sued over a memo that never was published— and still lost. Two reporters at the paper had written a memo setting out their suspicions that a local builder was receiving "loans" from the Mafia. The "tip" was never substantiated, but the memo found its way to federal bank regulators in Chicago. The regulators forced the local savings and loan association to cut off the builder's credit. The builder blamed the failure of his business on the memo. The suit was settled out of court for $1.4 million in 1982.

Corporations can be libeled. In August 1989, a Florida jury awarded the GTE Corporation $100 million in damages, ruling that the company had been libeled by Home Shopping Network Inc. Home Shopping had accused the telecommunications company of providing inferior telephone equipment that caused Home Shopping, a shop-by-television retailer, to lose calls and $500 million in profits. GTE had countersued Home Shopping for libel, charging that Home Shopping was masking its own inadequacies. At the time the judgment in favor of GTE was the largest in history.

You're not safe from libel because a story has been printed before. It's possible that a subject could have tolerated the first and second publication of the libel, but then decided your repetition of it was the straw that broke the camel's back.

PRIVACY

The laws on invasion of privacy are complex and still evolving. Only about one-fifth of the states have invasion-of-privacy laws. Yet the right to privacy is enunciated in most states through common law; its authority derives from customs and practices, plus decisions and decrees of courts, or "case law." (A federal law protects private records.)

You might be invading privacy when you do something as innocuous as printing items from back files of the newspaper in a "years ago" column. A laundromat owner posted the picture of a convicted burglar in Alexandria, La.; he hoped to discourage other intruders by showing that a burglar had been caught. The convicted burglar sued and won on the grounds of invasion of privacy.

Four kinds of invasion of privacy have been enunciated by law and court decisions:

- Intrusion into a person's seclusion or solitude or into his or her private life. Examples: trespassing or taping without permission; pursuing someone and taking photographs at times that person considers private.
- Putting a person in a false light before the public. Example: taking a photograph of a fire at a homosexual bar and publishing it with a caption that makes the onlookers seem to be patrons of the bar.
- "Appropriation" of a person's name or likeness for someone else's advantage. Examples: filming a performance and putting it on TV without permission for commercial gain; printing personal documents without permission to further a cause or event. Some papers have been challenged for using someone's photo to illustrate an article: A well-dressed black man appeared on the cover of a magazine section in a newspaper illustrating the new upward mobility of minorities—the man did not know the picture was going to be used and objected to it. Another paper faced a suit over using a crowded street scene to illustrate a feature on riots. One person who showed up as a face in the crowd was unhappy to be linked to the idea of rioting. Yet, says Campbell, "While persons may file suit over a photo taken when they appeared in public, it would be very difficult indeed for them to win such a case. The simple fact of their voluntary appearance in public strongly argues against their claim that they do not want their photo in the paper. The photo would have to contain a truly offensive revelation in order for a suit to have some possibility of success."
- Disclosing publicly embarrassing private facts about a person. A former Marine was an instant hero when he lunged at Sara Jane Moore, would-be assassin of President Ford. But when a columnist in the San Francisco *Chronicle* implied that the man was gay and frequented well-known gay bars, the White House then appeared to snub the man. The hero, Oliver Sipple, sued the *Chronicle* for unduly playing up his private life. Sipple lost on the grounds that he had not hidden his sexual preference before.

Journalists, and particularly photographers, use release forms for parties to sign when it's possible that the use of the material or picture would be challenged at a later time. Photographs tend to show up in many places and are used in many ways; some photographers want a model release signed before they take a picture.

Figure 15-1 is a model release used by an author/photographer for a young people's book on world religions. The use of the words "in connection with a book" allows some extended use of the photograph(s), such as on book jackets or promotion of the book, if needed.

Figure 15-2 is a model release form distributed by magazine lawyer Slade R. Metcalf at a workshop of the American Society of Magazine Editors. And Figure 15-3 is a more formal model release form.

MODEL RELEASE

I, the undersigned, being the parent or guardian of

_____ hereby irrevocably consent

to and authorize the use and reproduction of

photographs of _____ taken this

day by _____, or of any additional

photographs, taken for the purpose of use in

connection with a book on world religions for

young people to be published by _____ .

_____
(Signature of parent or guardian)

Witnessed by: _____
                        (Signature of witness)

Date _____

FIGURE 15-1   Model release provided by a book author/photographer.

Date: _____

I understand that _____ wants to take my photograph or draw my likeness for publication in one of _____'s magazines. I hereby give my consent for such use and for use in any other publication chosen by _____. I understand that I will not receive any money for such use, and the satisfaction of having my picture in a magazine will be sufficient. I also give my consent to _____ to use my photograph or likeness as it appears in the magazine to promote and advertise _____. I realize that I cannot withdraw my consent after I sign this form.

Name: _____
(Please Print)

Signature: _____

Address: _____

_____

Telephone Number: _____

I am the parent or legal guardian of the individual named above (if he or she is under the age of eighteen), and I hereby sign this consent form on behalf of such individual in accordance with the statements above.

Name: _____
(Please Print)

Signature: _____

Address: _____

_____

Telephone Number: _____

FIGURE 15-2 Sample model release for a magazine.

THE STAR

Consent for Publication of
Photograph

NON-PROFESSIONAL

Place _____

Date _____

To be Used When Person is Not
of Legal Age

We, being the parents or legal
guardian of the minor named
on this release, hereby approve
this agreement and waive all
rights we may have as to the
subject matter of this release.

For valuable consideration I
hereby give my consent to
News Group Publications, Inc.
and to anyone else whom News
Group Publications, Inc. may
authorize to photograph me
and to use any photographs of
me, at any time in the future,
with or without my name, for
any editorial, promotion,
advertising, trade or other
purpose whatever, except for
testimonial and endorsement
of product advertisements.

Date _____

Signed _____

Signed _____

Witness _____

Signed _____

Address _____

City _____

Witness _____

Telephone _____

FIGURE 15-3   Formal consent form used by a newspaper.

COPYRIGHT

Writers worry about having their ideas or work stolen—that is, used by someone else, with someone else's name on it. Ideas and topics and titles cannot be copyrighted; but, of course, the actual project can. If you're afraid your ideas are going to be stolen, don't offer them.

Most editors are conscientious. If an editor likes your idea and feels it's fairly original with you but doesn't think you're the one to write the article, the editor might offer you compensation for the idea but assign it to somebody else. This usually hits the would-be author like a lead balloon, but some writers do let their ideas go for a fee.

Actually, the editor has no obligation to you for your undeveloped idea. A few publications send out disclaimers when an idea is suggested to them, saying that the magazine is in no way responsible for the idea, that it did not solicit the idea or manuscript and retains the freedom to come up with ideas and develop them on its own.

What You Cannot Copyright

The U.S. Copyright Office spells out "what is not protected by copyright":

- Works that have *not* been fixed in a tangible form of expression. For example: choreographic works that have not been notated or recorded, or improvisational speeches or performances that have not been written or recorded.

- Titles, names, short phrases, and slogans; familiar symbols or designs; mere variations of typographic ornamentation, lettering, or coloring; mere listings of ingredients or contents.

- Ideas, procedures, methods, systems, processes, concepts, principles, discoveries, or devices, as distinguished from a description, explanation, or illustration.

- Works consisting *entirely* of information that is common property and containing no original authorship. For example: standard calendars, height and weight charts, tape measures and rules, and lists or tables taken from public documents or other common sources.

Is a Copyright Line Necessary on a Manuscript?

Under the old Copyright Act of 1909, publication was the means of obtaining statutory copyright. But under the Copyright Act of 1976, which went into effect in January 1978, publication is not necessary to guarantee copyright status for a manuscript. The work is automatically copyrighted from the moment of creation.

Contrary to popular opinion, you don't need a copyright line on your manuscript. You've seen them: © 1992 John Smith. "The copyright notice is not required on unpublished works," says the Copyright Office, but adds, "to avoid an inadvertent publication without notice, however, it may be advisable for the author or other owner of the copyright to affix notices, or statement such as *Unpublished Work* © John Doe, to any copies or phonorecords which leave his or her control." Such lines do serve as a reminder to publishers of the copyright and establish the time of creation. For your work is not merely automatically copyrighted, but is in fact copyrighted from the time of creation.

You can establish the time of creation by registering a work right away with the U.S. Copyright Office (send a copy of the work with $10 and form TX to the Library of Congress, Washington, DC 20669). Or you can establish time of creation from copies of query letters sent to editors. Or you can send a copy of the manuscript to yourself by registered mail. However, few writers bother with these measures.

Registration, the Office argues, has value in establishing a legal record necessary in a case of litigation. Registration of the copyright is necessary before an author can sue for infringement. Registration within five years of first publication sets the legal ground for copyright validity. If the registration comes after the infringement, the author can sue only for actual damages, the loss of income or other tangible remuneration. If the copyright is registered within three months of publication, the author can sue for statutory damages (which allows a punitive award) and for recovery of attorney fees.

Unless you have transferred rights, the work is copyrighted for the length of your life, plus 50 years.

Respecting Copyrights of Others

If you quote from the copyrighted writings of others, you may need permission — depending on what you are quoting, how much and sometimes in what context. Sometimes you will have to pay a fee. Normally you contact the publisher to secure permission to quote. Most publishers have staff members who handle permission requests. But since the publisher may have bought only first publication rights, you could be referred to the author, the author's lawyer or an estate for permission to reprint. Magazines and newspapers usually designate a key editor, such as a managing editor, to handle the requests. Most requests are granted for editorial use, but may be denied for use in advertising. To find the permissions editor of a book publisher, consult the *Literary Market Place* directory.

Generally reviewers of books in newspapers and magazines can use a brief quote without contacting the publisher. Some indicate on the book release how many words are allowed and encourage excerpting.

You have to be very careful in quoting from songs and poems. Since they are very short, if you're going to quote even a few words, you need to make contact with the holder of the copyright.

You might think you can lift things from a newspaper. But newspapers, like magazines, are copyrighted in their entirety. A copyright notice up front applies to all contents.

The concept of "fair use" in the Copyright Act of 1976 is purposefully vague, allowing interpretations according to circumstances. The exact number of words you can quote fairly without securing permission is not spelled out. Some believe you can quote up to 200 words; others say the practice allows 250 or 300 words to be quoted without permission from a book, perhaps more from a book published by a university press. Some publishers want more excerpted than others. Viking Penguin Inc. allowed its normal 300-word limit to be waived for Salman Rushdie's controversial *The Satanic Verses*. So that the reader could understand the controversial part of the book, Viking distributed two passages totaling 750 words.

"Fair use" was an issue in 1985 with the publication of former president Gerald Ford's memoirs. The contract said that Harper & Row, the publisher, and *Reader's Digest* controlled the first rights of use of the book. At publication time, the publisher sold rights to *Time* to excerpt 7,500 words from a section dealing with Ford's pardon of Richard Nixon. But two weeks before the *Time* issue was to come out, *The Nation* printed excerpts from a copy. *Time* canceled its contract with Harper and refused to pay the rest of the money owed. Harper sued *The Nation*, and the judge ruled that *The Nation*'s 300 words of verbatim use from the 200,000-word book (a part of a 2,250-word article) was a key section and not fair use, thus an infringement of copyright. *The Nation* argued it was, printing news, but the court declared that purloining a manuscript violated the spirit of acting in good faith — necessary, it said, to fair use.

The Copyright Act (Section 107) says of fair use:

> ... the fair use of a copyrighted work, including such use by reproduction in copies or phonorecords or by any other means specified by that section, for purposes such as criticism, comment, news reporting, teaching (including multiple copies for classroom use), scholarship, or research, is not an infringement of copyright. In determining whether the use made of a work in any particular case is a fair use the factors to be considered shall include —

1. The purpose and character of the use, including whether such use is of a commercial nature or is for nonprofit educational purposes;
2. the nature of the copyrighted work;
3. the amount and substantiality of the portion used in relation to the copyrighted work as a whole; and
4. the effect of the use upon the potential market for or value of the copyrighted work.

Permission Forms

Most publishers, particularly book publishers, provide forms to use in seeking permission to quote. The forms vary. You should state the reprint rights you want, usually to quote in the world market. Some publishers want assurances that no liability will attach to the reprint. You usually state the approximate number of words to be quoted, giving the beginning few words and the final few words of each selection. You include a form of credit line, although publishers will change the line to suit their own preference.

Figures 15-4, 15-5, and 15-6 are samples of three different permission request approaches.

Kinds of Rights

When you sell an article, you have the option of selling these rights:

First Serial Rights   Don't be misled by the word *serial*. It's a library term for *periodicals*. First serial rights refer to first use by a periodical. A publication buying such rights will assume it is the first to publish the article.

First North American Rights   A publication has the right to publish the article first in North America, namely in the United States and Canada.

One Time Rights   The publication has the right to publish the article once. This differs from first serial rights in that it may not be the first publishing of the article.

Second Serial Rights   The publication has a right to reprint an article or book chapter already published.

Foreign Serial Rights   A writer selling North American first serial rights can cut his or her deal with sales to foreign markets.

Simultaneous Rights   Two different publications, normally not in competition, can use the material simultaneously. For example, a writer could sell an article to the Methodists and the Presbyterians at the same time — readers would not be subscribing to both publications. But you should always indicate if you are giving simultaneous rights.

Syndication Rights   A book, for instance, might be made available to one or more publications prior to its release. (If the additional publishing comes after official book publication, that would be providing second serial reprint rights.)

All Rights   This is just what it says; the author relinquishes all rights. "All rights" usually means the contract has a "work for hire" clause, an idea strongly opposed by writers' organizations. In "work for hire" you are treated as a staffer — as if you wrote the piece on the job the way a newspaper reporter or magazine staffer would — and you have no further claim to the work.

A U.S. Supreme Court decision in 1989 said that unless hired writers are actually employees, they retain the right to copyright their work. The case dealt with James Earl Reid, who had prepared a sculpture for the Community for Creative Non-Violence. But when CCNV sought to take the work of art on tour, Reid claimed the copyright and challenged CCNV's ownership.

SELECTION REQUESTED

AUTHOR: _____

Newspaper/Magazine: _____

Publisher and date of publication: _____

Title/Headline: _____

Beginning _____ Ending _____

Beginning _____ Ending _____

Beginning _____ Ending _____

Approximate number of words _____

Credit to be given _____

_____

Name _____ Date _____

I (we) hereby grant permission to _____

to reproduce the material described above in _____

_____.

If you are an individual copyright owner, please include your Social Security number to ensure prompt payment.

Social Security Number _____

Reply to:

FIGURE 15-4   Sample permission request.

To:

REQUEST FOR PERMISSION TO REPRINT MATERIAL

I am preparing a college textbook entitled _____
to be published in _____ and I would like to include
the material specified on the reverse of this form.

May I have permission to include the material in my book and in
future revisions and editions thereof for distribution:

        (   ) in U.S. and Canada

        (   ) throughout the world in all languages.

These rights in no way restrict republication of your material in
any other form by you or others authorized by you. If you do not
control these rights in their entirety, would you please let me know
where else to write?

Full credit will be given as follows, subject to your approval:

Thank you for your cooperation.

Date: _____ Author: _____
                    Please return form to:

continued

FIGURE 15-5   Sample permission request form used by a book publisher.

continued

Material requested:

(Give name of author, title of publication, name of publisher, date of publication, page numbers, and opening and closing words of excerpts.)

I (We) give permission for the use of the material requested above.

                                      _____

                                      _____

Date: _____

The court unanimously ruled that work for hire is not determined by how much control over the project a contract gives the employer, but whether the person is an actual employee of the firm in the normal sense of the word is used. The decision was widely heralded by writers' groups.

A bill was prepared by Sen. Thad Cochran (R.-Miss.) that called for any work-for-hire contracts to be signed before a work begins and for the agreement to have no binding stay on author/artist's future work. The bill would also define *employee* as a formal, salaried staff member.

When rights are not spelled out and an "oral agreement" in essence prevails, the custom, according to Slade R. Metcalf, a lawyer for magazine publishers, is for all parties to assume that first North American rights are being offered.

Box 8118
University Station
Grand Forks, ND 58202

April 17, 1989

Media History Digest
c/o Editor and Publisher
Permissions Office
11 W. 19th St.
New York, NY 10011

Dear Media History Digest:

In my forthcoming textbook, <u>The Media of Mass Communication</u>, a
paperback to be priced about $25 and scheduled for publication by
Allyn and Bacon in 1991, I would like to include a few words from
your Spring-Summer 1988 issue article, "Horrendous PR Crises" by
Lael M. Moynihan:

Page 21: Hygrade's PR effort . . . consumer appreciation for its
products.

May I have your permission to include this material in my forthcoming book and in all future editions and revisions thereof, including nonexclusive world rights in all languages? These rights
will in no way restrict republication of your material in any other
form by you or others authorized by you.

Should you not control these rights in their entirety, would you tell
me who does.

continued

FIGURE 15-6   Permission request letter sent to a periodical.

---

continued

A release form is provided and a copy of this letter is enclosed for your files. Your consideration is appreciated.

Sincerely,

John H. Vivian
Visiting Faculty

JV/sh

I (We) grant the permission requested on the terms stated in this letter. This is the credit line to be used:

Date: _____   By: _____

Social Security _____   _____

                                      _____

Besides "work for hire" clauses, artists/writers' groups are concerned with "indemnification" clauses that try to switch the liability in any libel suit to the writer. Such groups also campaign for "moral rights," the right of artists/writers to be involved in how their work is handled. Novel writers and script writers in particular like to see that the movie made from their work properly reflects it. Writers do not want to see their work "mangled" or substantially changed by editors. Moral rights are set forth in the Berne Copyright Convention Treaty, which the United States finally joined in 1988. Efforts are under way in the United States to legislate principles of the Berne Treaty.

While writers generally favor moral rights, which would give them greater say in the end product of their work, magazine editors live in fear that authors could gain the right to say even how pictures are cropped or how their name is used on a cover or in a promotion ad for their work. Publication lawyer Metcalf, a member of the firm of Squadron, Ellenoff, Plesent & Lehrer, says an application of the principles of moral rights in the United States by law would be "devastating" for magazines.

CONTRACTS

Magazines — particularly larger ones — issue contracts to writers when an article is accepted for publication. The contract spells out the relationship with the writer, matters of performance compliance, liability and the nature of the rights the author is selling.

Lawyer Metcalf distributed the sample contract shown in Figure 15-7 at an "Update on Legal Problems for Editors" seminar sponsored by the American Society of Magazine Editors. The American Society of Journalists and Authors has drawn up a suggested letter of agreement, originating with the writer, to be used when a publication does not issue written confirmation of an assignment (Figure 15-8).

AGENTS

New writers often wonder if they need an agent. The answer is no. For one thing, agents don't normally take on new writers. Agents are business-oriented and want an instant return for their investment of time and energy. While many successful writers use agents for their books, few agents will try to market a magazine article except as a favor to a writer already in their stable. And why should they? Most agents receive 10 percent of the gross return on a book or article. If you sell an article for $800, the agent would get $80. Most agents feel this low amount of return is hardly worth the effort.

Beware of an agent who charges for reading your manuscript. If your intention is to get some feedback and instruction, then it's OK. Know what you're getting. Expect results from an agent. An agent's real job is to deliver your work to appropriate publishers and to negotiate an agreement for publication.

Most magazine editors would prefer to deal directly with the writer, for it is the writer who is doing the assignment and not the agent. When it comes to books and their greater complexity in development and marketing, many publishers prefer to work with agents.

Some of the services agents provide are available from others. Consider the agent who told the writer he wanted 15 percent of the income and then said to the author, "You go ahead and sell it (the book). You know more about the subject. I'll help write the contract and publicize it." If that's the case, maybe the services of an attorney who can write the contract and of a publicist would be more useful than those of an agent.

Again, you're not going to get an agent for magazine publication unless you're successful. If you're successful, you have to decide if you need an agent.

Date:

To:

This will confirm the Agreement between you as author
("Author")   and
(the "Company") as publisher concerning an article (the "Article")
to be written by Author for publication in   magazine.

(1) Title or the Description of the Article is:

(2) Author grants to the Company the following rights in the
    Article:

    (a) exclusive first North American publication rights;

    (b) for a period of time from the date set forth below until ten
        (10) days after the on-sale date of the issue of
                            in which the Article appears, the option to
        acquire exclusive, first, one-time United Kingdom and ex-
        clusive, first, one-time Australian periodical rights in the
        Article; and

    (c) the exclusive right to authorize syndication of the Article
        in all print media throughout the world for a period of time
        from ten (10) days after the on-sale date of the issue of
                            in which the Article appears until three
        (3) months after the off-sale date of the issue.

(3) In consideration of the foregoing and other representations
    and warranties of the Author hereinafter set forth, the Com-
    pany will pay the Author the following amounts:

    (a) upon acceptance of the Article for publication in
                        magazine $_____;

    (b) upon sale of one-time United Kingdom or one-time Austra-
        lian periodical rights, 60% of the sale price not to exceed
        10% of the original purchase price;

    (c) upon sale of any other syndication rights, one-half of the
        net proceeds received by the Company; and

FIGURE 15-7   Sample of contract between magazine and writer.

(d) if a decision is made not to publish the Article, a "kill fee" of $_____.

(4) Author represents that nothing in the Article will be libelous or obscene or infringe the copyright, or violate the right of privacy or right of publicity or any other right of any person, firm or corporation. Author further represents that he or she is the sole author of the Article, and that the Article has not been previously published in any form.

(5) Author agrees that the Company has the right to edit, abridge, or augment the Article and that publication of the Article will be solely at the discretion of the Company. Author further agrees to cooperate fully with the editorial staff of magazine.

(6) Author agrees that the Company shall have the right to use the Author's name, biography, and likeness in connection with the publication and promotion of both the Article and magazine.

(7) Author agrees to write and submit the Article to the Company no later than _____.

(8) If this Agreement is executed by an agent on Author's behalf, that agent warrants that he or she has full authority from Author to grant the rights and to make the representations set forth above.

Very truly yours,

By: _____

Position: _____

CONFIRMED AND AGREED:

_____

Social Security No.: _____

Date: _____

Suggested Letter of Agreement

originating with the writer (to be used when publication
does not issue written confirmation of assignment)

DATE

EDITOR'S NAME AND TITLE
PUBLICATION
ADDRESS

Dear EDITOR'S NAME:

This will confirm our agreement that I will research and write
an article of approximately NUMBER words on the subject of BRIEF
DESCRIPTION, in accord with our discussion of DATE.

The deadline for delivery of this article to you is DATE.

It is understood that my fee for this article shall be $ AMOUNT,
with one-third payable in advance and the remainder upon acceptance.[1] I will be responsible for up to two revisions.

PUBLICATION shall be entitled to first North American publications rights in the article.[2]

It is further understood that you shall reimburse me for routine
expenses incurred in the researching and writing of the article, including long-distance telephone calls, and that extraordinary expenses, should any such be anticipated, will be discussed with you
before they are incurred.[3]

It is also agreed that you will submit proofs of the article for my
examination, sufficiently in advance of publication to permit correction of errors.

FIGURE 15-8 Sample contract initiated by author.

This letter is intended to cover the main points of our agreement. Should any disagreement arise on these or other matters, we agree to rely upon the guidelines set forth in the Code of Ethics and Fair Practices of the American Society of Journalists and Authors. Should any controversy persist, such controversy shall be submitted to arbitration before the American Arbitration Association in accordance with its rules, and judgment confirming the arbitrator's award may be entered in any court of competent jurisdiction.

Please confirm our mutual understanding by signing the copy of this agreement and returning it to me.

> Sincerely,
>
> (signed)
>
> WRITER'S NAME

PUBLICATION

by _____
  NAME AND TITLE

Date _____

NOTES

[1] If the publication absolutely refuses to pay the advance, you may want to substitute the following wording: "If this assignment does not work out, a sum of one-third the agreed-upon fee shall be paid to me."

[2] If discussion included sale of other rights, this clause should specify basic fee for first North American rights, additional fees and express rights each covers, and total amount.

[3] Any other conditions agreed upon, such as inclusion of travel expenses or a maximum dollar amount for which the writer will be compensated, should also be specified.

ASSIGNMENTS

1. Check the media law books and report on one of the noted media libel cases — among them, *Curtis Publishing v. Butts, Time v. Pape, Rosenbloom v. Metromedia, Gertz v. Welch, Herbert v. Lando, Hutchinson v. Proxmire, Wolston v. Reader's Digest, Burnett v. National Enquirer, Philadelphia Newspapers v. Hepps, Flynt v. Falwell, Sharon v. Time, Westmoreland v. CBS.*

2. Examine articles in a supermarket tabloid. How does the publication escape charges of invasion of privacy? How close does it come?

3. Research recent reports on libel cases, using media magazines and media sections of the newsmagazines. Where is libel law heading? Be ready to discuss in class.

4. Make a list of the "10 Easiest Ways to Commit Libel" based in part on actual libel convictions.

5. Should the present copyright law be changed? Examine — with pros and cons — several areas of concern based on this chapter. Be prepared to debate in class.

6. Role-play ethical/legal situations in a mock trial. Have witnesses take different sides. A transcript of a media trial could serve as a working "script."

7. Watch and report on a media ethics/law movie. Perhaps a video can be rented and shown in class. Some possibilities: *Absence of Malice, A Flash of Green, Perfect, And Nothing But the Truth, Not for Publication, Under Fire, The Year of Living Dangerously, The Mean Season, Fletch, The Killing Fields.* Some older ones: *It Happened One Night, Five Star Final, While the City Sleeps, The Front Page, Mr. Deeds Goes to Town, Libeled Lady.*

8. Create a class ethical/legal media code. Involve a student newspaper editor, and suggest the code could be advisory for campus journalists as well.

9. Make a "crisis" list of "do's" and "don'ts" for each crisis situation you can think of. Include a list of "gray" situations, in which various responses exist, depending on circumstances.

10. Secure copyright registration applications (form TX) from the U.S. Copyright Office at the Library of Congress. Fill out a form for one of your articles. Follow through, and send one in for registration.

Postscript

After you've produced a successful piece and seen it published, it's so easy to forget about it. But a newspaper or magazine article can have an extended life, even reincarnation into a different world. Consider reselling and recycling.

RESELLING

Your article may have more life in terms of distribution than you realize. Recall from Chapter 15 that you normally are selling first North American rights. But you also can sell simultaneous rights and reach a number of markets at once or sell foreign rights and reach non–North American markets.

Consider the international markets. Prolific writer Paulette Cooper, author of six books and 500 magazine articles, points out that 50 nations have 50,000 magazines that are potential markets. "You can sell more than once in one nation," she adds. For example, in one country you can sell to an English-language publication, then to a foreign-language publication — the translation will be done for you, she says.

Cooper has advice for the writer sending a manuscript to find its way to a foreign market: "Keep English simple and short; avoid American slang; be sure to include international mail coupons (for possible return of the manuscript)."

Among sources for foreign publications are the *Writer's & Artist's Year-book* and the *Markets Abroad* newsletter, published by Michael Sedge (2460 Lexington Dr., Owosso, MI 48867 — $25).

RECYCLING

Recycling is different from reselling. You take your basic material and turn it into a new article for other outlets.

You can, for instance, write about a newly reported disease just beginning to get attention. Consider how Lyme disease gained notice at the beginning of the 1990s. You could identify the top 10 states with such a disease, then target each state for an article. Cooper did just that. For publication in nine of the states, she pointed out that each state respectively was among the top 10 with the problem; for the top one, she started her article with the fact that the particular state was number one in cases of the disease.

She also gleaned articles from statistics about stress. She wrote articles for newspapers in 25 least-stressed states, as well as articles in states that headed the list as most-stressed. In each case, she called an assistant managing editor, "someone not as busy as the managing editor but one above a city editor." On each article she typed "exclusive to your area" and a copyright line that granted first serial rights. The material is essentially the same, but a different lead is on each. In some cases, in recycling, an anecdote may be brought up from the ending or from the middle to be expanded in the lead for another audience.

CONSIDER A BOOK

Expanding an article into a book is not as difficult as it sounds. Take an article you have published and turn it into a book. The article becomes a chapter or at least the basis on which the book is written.

If you aspire to write a book, don't start by writing it in its entirety. As with article writing, you first write a query. In fact, many publishers, among them Doubleday, will not even open and read unsolicited manuscripts. Apparently so many manuscripts come in — most, if not all, of an inferior, self-serving quality — that it is more cost-effective just to return them than to hire extra assistant editors to read and discuss them.

Book publishers, as we have noted in Chapter 14, will "sit" on a proposal for an ungodly length of time, especially if they are only mildly interested. If it's a trade book idea for distribution in bookstores, a year may pass before a publishing house comes to a decision; technical and textbook publishers can sit on an idea three or four years. In fact, as their editors change, some even forget they have your proposal. Big publishers are no better than small. They are all slow. So if you're sending a book proposal, and it takes each publisher a year or so to decide, you won't be able to get the proposal or manuscript to many houses. You could be tied up a lifetime waiting to hear.

So, when proposing a book, send multiple queries. When they have a hot subject, agents hold an "auction"; that is, they call in a number of publishers to bid on a proposal or manuscript, and then the book goes to the highest bidder. The individual writer working independently can also seek an answer from many houses.

What do you send in a book query? It can vary. Certainly one of the best ways is to prepublish something in your topical area in a magazine or newspaper. The article should be well written and well researched and establish you as a voice of authority in the subject area. Send the article along with an outline (proposed table of contents) and a synopsis (a paragraph description of each of the proposed chapters).

Book agreements are negotiated in many ways by the author or by the author via agent. With more experienced writers, they may be discussed over several lunches, with the would-be author asked perhaps only to give a one-page letter of intent. Then a contract and advance follow.

You should never agree to write sample chapters for a proposed nonfiction book, unless it's out of desperation. A theory prevails that a publisher who wants sample chapters may not be serious. If an editor likes the idea, he or she can proceed on the basis of an outline or proposal. With fiction and humor books, where style is so important, it is normal to present two chapters or the first fifty pages.

Writing several book chapters on speculation can be a tremendous amount of work. Such preliminary chapters will never be as good as the finished product (in which you would have completed your research), so you are offering inferior material. Most publishers just want to know if you can research, write well and deliver a satisfactory manuscript. A magazine piece on the subject or — in other cases — selected clippings of your work can indicate to a publisher the quality of work he or she might expect.

In approaching a book publisher you need to answer several basic questions: why you are the one to do the book — your credentials — and why the publisher should want to publish the book. Yet beware, a good publisher will know if the idea is hot and won't want to be lectured. Sometimes, however, an author can expand the horizon of possible interest and marketability.

Readers of a textbook on nonfiction writing aren't expected to jump immediately into the deep waters of book writing. But a student can, with a little luck perhaps, approach, negotiate and make a deal with a major publishing house. It's been done.

Don't let good ideas die with the brief life of a newspaper or magazine piece. Remember, the idea might be resold and recycled, even turned into a book.

APPENDIX

Getting Jobs in Newspaper Feature Sections and Magazines

How do you become a feature writer/editor for a newspaper or a magazine?

For newspapers, the route is fairly simple. You start at a small publication, a neighborhood paper or weekly; and then as time goes on, you move up to larger papers with greater responsibilities and opportunities. To gain that first newspaper job, you'll need some clippings — from working on the college paper, internships, covering sports or meetings part time for a paper. Such part-timers are known as stringers (from the day when novices would string their clippings together or put them in a scrapbook to show prospective editors).

Armed with samples of your published writing and possessing determination and enthusiasm, you can cross the threshold of a larger newspaper. But you'll need good language skills. Most editors today are inclined to give the applicant a grammar and writing test, screening out immediately those who don't have requisite language and spelling skills.

If you aspire to write in a specialized or beat area, become an expert in that subject. A science editor would likely have majored in science; a business or finance editor, in business. Film critics often have a master's in film; religion writers, seminary degrees and/or demonstrated interest in religion; sportswriters, participation in sports; travel writers often have some facility in one or several foreign languages. But again, the newspaper feature writer — general or specialized — normally comes up through the ranks. You get your first job, move on once or several times, all the time demonstrating (oftentimes through winning awards) that you have a facility for writing features, in general and/or in specialized areas.

MAGAZINES ARE DIFFERENT

Getting a magazine job can be more complex. Fewer magazines are published, and they are published less often than a daily paper; the magazine staffs are smaller. Magazines also make more use of free-lance writers.

Yet what works for getting a job in newspapers — clippings, internships, meeting people — works for magazine employment, too. In fact, many magazine writers and editors came by their jobs by way of newspapers. They worked on student papers, did stringing, engaged in internships, worked on weeklies and proceeded to move up — and out — into the magazine field.

Entry-level positions, nevertheless, do exist, even for those right out of college. It's a kind of apprenticeship syndrome, based on the willingness of the newcomer to do the menial jobs. Something similar used to exist in newspapers. Copy boys — later called clerks — would do the errands — change ribbons, get coffee for the reporters, distribute copy to proper pigeonholes. Neal Shine, publisher of the Detroit *Free Press*, and various Pulitzer Prize winners have come up that way. Much of that system has gone by the way, as newspapers place more emphasis on professional development — and prior experience. But magazines do on occasion acquire staff through menial entry-level positions, although editors would likely argue that this would be very rare.

Being a good typist and being willing to come in at a secretarial level has been the route taken by some. An editor of a popular science magazine said that he was the best typist on the staff. A former managing editor of *Travel & Leisure* commented a few years back: "It's sad to see recent graduates come to New York City and spend 2½ years looking for a job and never learn to type" (or keyboard) with speed. A junior editor of a national travel magazine, who had come to the staff as a secretary six weeks earlier, received an assignment that took her to China for two weeks. A switchboard operator at *Travel Weekly* was promoted to an editorial position.

And then there's the mailroom. "See that young man," said Don Sider, a vice president of *Time*, at lunch one day. He pointed out a young man from the magazine's mailroom who had come in the door of the restaurant. Sider pointed him out as a promising young man for whom there would be a future.

Many of the editors in New York are where they are today because they got a "foot in the door."

A *Ms.* editor noted that the magazine hired young people to answer phones and to do some research. Requirement: some demonstrated research ability, such as an impressive term paper, and "an ability to answer the phone without intimidating anybody."

Fact checking—used by most large magazines—can be an entry-level position, although you can get pigeon-holed. These staffers verify facts from an article by talking to experts or checking with books, specialized publications or databases. The checkers will mark each fact checked with a checkmark or color dot, the markings indicating that the fact has been checked and whether it was checked with a publication or person.

Josh Gillette went to *Spy* magazine in New York right out of college as a fact checker and editorial assistant. It was a six-month internship, at only $50 a week, but it was a foot in the door and he has a job there now. On the way to *Spy*, the 22-year-old native of Randolph, Mass., was opinion editor of his high school paper in Milton, Mass., and served in various editorial positions, including editor-in-chief, of the *Spectator*, the student paper at Columbia University, from which he graduated with a major in history. In his summers he was a stringer for the Dedham (Mass.) *Transcript* and an intern for the Quincy (Mass.) *Ledger* and the Boston *Globe*. "I always wanted to work for *Spy*," he said. He met the publisher, Tom Phillips, when he interviewed Phillips for a profile feature for the *Spectator*. Gillette also gained the attention of *Spy*'s editors when he wrote a critical letter to *Spy* saying that one piece *Spy* had recently used was a rehash of a piece two years earlier. He also attended a public forum sponsored by *Spy* and met some more editors. "I also wrote to the editors posing story ideas," and one of his letters was published as a letter to the editor in *Spy*. His internship included errand running (photocopying), fact checking, researching (finding quotes from grown-up stars who were behaving like children for an article on pampered stars; also uncovering strange and weird sex experiments for an article on sex research) and reporting and writing a half-dozen bylined articles. He is now an assistant to one of the editors.

Leslie Whitaker, reporter-researcher at *Time*, took a rather circuitous route to get there. She majored in English at Bryn Mawr College and worked her junior year on the *Wharton* (business) *Quarterly* at the University of Pennsylvania. Upon graduation, she worked for *Operations Research Journal*, an academic publication—"I didn't understand a word of it." After nine months she went to the *Wharton* magazine as assistant editor for two years, then to a new daily paper in Austin, Tex. When it folded in six weeks, she became an assistant director of publications—newsletter and brochures—for the Texas Historical Commission. She free-lanced on political subjects for the liberal biweekly, the Texas *Observer*. After a few years, she felt she didn't have enough actual reporting experience for newspaper work and spent nine months at the Graduate School of Journalism at Columbia University. She wrote letters and received offers at *Money* and *Time*. She started part time at *Time* and free-lanced for the *International Herald Tribune* in Paris. During her first four months at *Time*, she was in the business section and then spent four months with the New York bureau. Her work now in effect (although her title doesn't reflect it) is assistant editor of the Press section in *Time*.

Your clippings — especially if they are of a high quality — are essential passports to employment. But even with them you'll need strategies — and some luck.

HOW EDITORS GOT THEIR JOBS

It is instructive to take a look at how some seasoned editors in the business got their jobs.

Elizabeth Crow is president of the international firm, Gruner + Jahr USA/Publishing which produces *YM* and other magazines. She is a past editor-in-chief of *Parents*.

She came to New York after graduating from Mills College, Oakland, Calif., where she majored in English and American studies. She dropped in on a media employment agency that came up with a couple of entry-level openings — one was with an architecture magazine; the other, which she took, was with the *New Yorker* in the advertising department. She stayed a year, then went to graduate school for a year at Brown University. "Then I did a scientific study of the field of magazines." She tailored letters to 40 publications and included her résumé. She had a few bites and took a fact-checking job in the editorial library of *New York*. She even had to check facts in cartoons. But, she adds, "I was as willing to write as to Xerox. I was willing to do anything. Fortunately it was a city room atmosphere. You could throw a pencil and stab an artist or aim to another." She was noticed and got a chance at some writing. She moved on to other publications, including *Baby Talk* and *Parents*: "I presume moving around a bit makes some sense," she says. She moved on eventually to Gruner + Jahr and was prepared to leave for another position when Gruner + Jahr offered her the presidency. "I had done a lot of little things and they had the 'mistaken' idea that I was a generalist," she joked.

Money's Richard Eisenberg, a graduate of Northwestern University, studied the magazines. "It doesn't hurt to get your name out," he said. He looked at mastheads of magazines. "I talked to people who were low enough to talk to me; I would ask them who I should be talking to." He came in the door of *Money* as a fact checker.

Mike Sivvy at *Money* earned an M.A. in classical languages, Greek and Latin, and landed a job with the *Quarterly Review* of the Federal Reserve Board. "They figured with my training in Latin gerunds I could construct sentences." Eventually he sent out 150 letters with résumés and clips (15 said no, three expressed interest). He landed at the *Financial World*. "I did a cover story and I got a phone call from Mr. Loeb" (Marshall Loeb of the related publication, *Fortune*), and he ended up at *Money*. "I honestly think the biggest problem is communicating to people you are there."

Carolyn Kitch, senior associate editor for articles at *Good Housekeeping*, is a graduate of Boston College where she won an internship sponsored by the American Society of Magazine Editors. That internship is an entry into the magazine world for many (see list at end of this appendix).

Sylvia Barsotti, senior editor, *Family Circle*, recalls, "After college, I enrolled in New York University's Summer Magazine Publishing Workshop. I interviewed with a few magazine publishing companies after the course, but no definite offers were given. After some traveling, I sent résumés out and was called in by the New York Times Co. (whom I had met in the summer). Although there were no editorial openings, there was one in the production department. I took it and switched into editorial 18 months later."

Mike Schwanz, associate editor at *Sports Afield*, worked for a trade association upon graduation from Northwestern, then *Outdoor Life*, then *Sports Afield*.

Ned Zemen, a major in English, worked on the University of Michigan daily and then spent an internship in the Detroit bureau of *Newsweek*. He then went to Columbia University, where he took all of the magazine classes. One of his former professors had been at *Newsweek*. During an internship at the Detroit bureau of *Newsweek*, he said, "I kept pulling on jackets and convinced them to bring me back as a researcher. I got along with an editor in national affairs and a job opened up there. It takes persistence." Jerrold Footlick, senior editor, commented about Ned that "he played well on a team."

John Stoltenberg, managing editor, *Lear's*: "I began reading proofs at a law firm on the lobster shift through a temporary agency. Through an ad in the New York *Times*, I got a job as proofreader at *Esquire*."

Caitlin Meehan, publicity coordinator, *Seventeen*: "I sent my résumé, was interviewed and followed up. Some of it is timing—if there is a position available."

Ripley Hotch, deputy editor, *Nation's Business*: "I started as copy editor for a medium-sized newspaper."

Gay Bryant, editor-in-chief, *Mirabella*: "Through a friend of a friend (informal word of mouth still is most common way in). Began in England, checking "Where to Buy" information for $45 a week salary."

Gary A. Soucie, executive editor, *Audubon*: "When I left Friends of the Earth (where I was executive director) in 1971, my first free-lance assignment was *Audubon*. Then I became a field editor. In January 1979, I joined the editorial staff."

James Lloyd Greenfield, recent past editor of the *New York Times Magazine*, had a long background in foreign affairs and as a foreign correspondent. Upon graduating from Harvard, he became a correspondent for *Time* in Korea and Japan, bureau chief for *Time* in New Delhi and *Time* deputy bureau chief in London. Then he was chief diplomatic correspondent for Time-Life in Washington. He served as deputy assistant, then assistant secretary of state for public affairs. Along the way he was also assistant vice president for international affairs at Continental Airlines in Los Angeles, then vice president of Westinghouse Broadcasting in New York. His 20 years at the New York *Times* also includes eight as foreign editor.

Barbara H. Penland, editorial operations director at Whittle Communications, Knoxville, Tenn., tells how some of the editors of the company (which publishes several dozen magazines) got their jobs:

"Editor A: High school work on local paper and magazine; free-lance writing; internships in PR and at a national magazine; entered competitions; during senior year called an editor at the magazine for advice on getting a job and landed a full-time position.

"Editor B: Graduated with a degree in Spanish. Got a job at a research firm. Moved to a newspaper, then to a magazine.

"Editor C: Ran the college's humor magazine, which led to an ASME (American Society of Magazine Editors) internship, which led to a job as fact checker."

Diane Salvatore, senior editor, *Redbook*: "I started as an intern at the *Soho News*, a weekly newspaper (in New York City) that folded within nine months of my arrival. I had arranged the internship myself and was not paid. After the summer, they hired me — but only after I told them I had an offer at a trade magazine. They matched that salary, which was breathtakingly low. I was a reporter/researcher. After it folded, I was unemployed for a few months, and spent that time sending my résumé all over town. And visiting personnel departments. And combing the ads.

"I was hired as an editorial assistant at *Metropolitan Home*. After three months, I got a call back from Hearst (with whom I had also met while I was unemployed). They now had an opening with *Cosmopolitan* as an editorial assistant, so I jumped at it. I was there 2½ years, and spent the last 1½ of it looking for a job one notch up the masthead. It was the hardest search of my career. Finally, I landed a job at *Ladies' Home Journal* as an associate editor and worked very, very hard. After that, the moves got easier. I went next to *Glamour*, and then to *Redbook* as articles editor, running a staff. Then I was promoted to a department head and now report directly to the editor in chief."

ADVICE FROM EDITORS

Several editors, who were asked "what advice would you have for the new university graduate who wants to work in the editorial department of a magazine," offered their views:

- Diane Salvatore, senior editor, *Redbook*: "Be realistic, even humble. Unless you have some extra special selling point (i.e., you had a successful career as a free-lance writer for consumer publications while you were at school) chances are excellent that you will start out as an editorial assistant. That means 85 percent of your time will be spent typing and doing administrative work (and I will make little distinction between someone with a BA or an MA, if both are in journalism). But all the editors I know started this way. You must try to take on — through your own initiative — any editorial work you can, to get the attention of your boss. Don't wait to be asked. For example, if you see that a story needs a caption — write one and let me see it. If it's good, I may ask you to write the next one, and it may become part of your job. If it's not good, I'll tell you why and you'll have learned something.

"Or if you're opening my mail and see a newsworthy press release or report, ask if you can read it thoroughly and write up some story ideas based on it. All this will make my life easier — and serve to make you more valuable. But you'll be expected to have the administrative work always in tip top shape all the while.

"And bear in mind that you might have to move to another magazine in order to be promoted to 'assistant or associate editor.' Sometimes it's just hard for your first editor to see her assistant as anything but. But doing this extra editorial work gives you something important to talk about on your job interviews."

- Barbara H. Penland, Whittle Communications: "Hone your writing skills before leaving college. It's impossible to learn to write in a professional setting. The employer's expectations require excellent writing immediately. Before graduating, be sure to read the best magazines — *Atlanta*, *Harper's*, *New Yorker*, *Esquire*, *Texas Monthly*, etc. Be sure you know what really good journalism is. Bring experience to the prospective employer — internships, free-lance writing experience, contacts made during previous experiences, possibly jobs in related fields."

- Norman Bleichman, managing editor, *World Monitor*: "Write a lot; read a lot. Identify good writing and try to exemplify it. Gain world experience, firsthand, if possible — not from TV."

- Gay Bryant, editor-in-chief, *Mirabella*: "Have persistence; use contacts; show you know the magazine; you are literate and versatile; be prepared for low money."

- Caitlin Meehan, *Seventeen*: "Keep a portfolio of all your writing. Send your résumé to every magazine, follow up. Be persistent, but polite."

- John Stoltenberg, managing editor, *Lear's*: "Send a smart typo-free cover letter and résumé to top editors. Enclose a clip of your best writing sample. Say what you've done and what you're eager to do. Be prepared for long hours, low pay, some drudge work."

- Sylvia Barsotti, senior editor, *Family Circle*: "Scan the market and select publications you'd like to work for. Accept any job the company offers. If you're good, you'll be noticed and be able to move into the position you want."

When it comes to trade and specialized business publications, the Magazine Publishers Association in its *Guide to Business Careers in Magazine Publishing* sums up "Finding a Job in Magazine Publishing":

> A college degree is a definite plus when it comes to finding a job in the magazine business. But exact qualifications will vary from magazine to magazine and from job to job. Most publishers will look for a broad educational background in their entry level candidates, with courses in advertising, communications, business and economics being most desirable. Knowledge of computers and new technological advancements in communications will become more and more important as magazines move more toward electronic editing and telecommunications.
>
> It is essential that you are able to communicate effectively, both orally and on paper. One way to demonstrate this ability is through your resume and interview. Remember, competition will be keen, so present yourself as creatively and professionally as possible to get the edge.
>
> More than likely, potential employers will lean toward the individual who knows something about magazines. So learn as much as you can. The most obvious first step would be to read a wide variety of magazines yourself, comparing editorial styles and advertising direction. Library books are also a good source of basic information. . . . Keep up with current developments in the field by reading advertising trade magazines and advertising, marketing and media columns in major newspapers like the *New York Times*, *The Chicago Tribune* and *The Wall Street Journal*.
>
> Most important, talk to people in the business about what they do. Find out what areas of magazine publishing interest you most, then focus your job search on these areas.[1]

Editors also answered the question "What are several mistakes young people make in seeking a career in magazines?"

- Norman Bleichman, *World Monitor*: "They believe that only journalism/creative writing courses are needed. That's only half. *What* do you write about? Familiarity with as much of the world (culture, literature, politics, economics) as possible broadens a writer's facts, context, references, etc."

- Sylvia Barsotti, *Family Circle*: "I think many are leary of starting at the bottom—and most do not want to perform clerical duties. Unfortunately, you have to pay your dues if you want to become an editor—and it is a terrific way to learn the ropes."

- John Stoltenberg, *Lear's*: "Spelling and copy-editing mistakes in cover letters."

- Caitlin Meehan, *Seventeen*: "Don't keep at it enough—they give up."

---

1. "Guide to Business Careers in Magazine Publishing, Magazine Publishers Association, Education Committee, Adolph Auerbacher, chair, New York, n.d.

- Ripley Hotch, *Nation's Business*: "Not knowing anything about the magazines they apply to. Not having a body of knowledge about a subject (as opposed to technique). Not being able to think freshly or originally."
- Gay Bryant, *Mirabella*: "Wanting to write — most magazine jobs do not include writing."
- Gary A. Soucie, *Audubon:* "Unrealistic aspirations; unclear goals."
- Barbara H. Penland, Whittle: "Complaining about heavy editing instead of learning from it. Being impatient with the unglamorous jobs that everyone must do. Thinking that PR and journalism are similar. (We don't hire PR graduates.) Applying for jobs with no writing experience and no experience in reading good magazines (demonstrates ability and interests). Naïveté about entry-level jobs in magazines. Few such positions allow novice editors to write full-length features, for example. They do require excellent research, writing, grammar and interviewing skills, and a tremendous amount of energy, creative thinking and initiative."
- Diane Salvatore, *Redbook*: "They expect too much too soon. They don't want to do unglamorous work for 2 to 3 years. This is a test of perseverance. Also, anyone truly obsessive about details and willing to work like a dog will have an edge."

INTERNSHIPS

Many magazines will take one or several college interns for the summer or longer. *Spy* has as many as 20 interns. Of course, many other magazines do not use interns, at least on a regular basis.

Students looking forward to a magazine career can also take advantage of other publishing internships. Newspapers use interns in the summer months. Apply early; most newspaper internships for the ensuing summer want applications as early as the previous November. Consider some of the newspaper organizations and centers. One center using a number of interns internationally is the Center for Investigative Reporting, 530 Howard St., Second Floor, San Francisco, CA 94105.

Publishing internships with book companies are also available. Simon & Schuster offers a summer internship "to work directly with publishing professionals — editors, publishers, artists, designers, publicists, sales and marketing executives." Applications by Feb. 1 to Anne M. Cripps, Corporate Communications, Simon & Schuster, 1230 Avenue of the Americas, 17th Floor, New York, NY 10020.

Three major magazine internship programs are:

- Magazine Internship Program, American Society of Magazine Editors. Deadline, Dec. 15. "The program is for editorially oriented students, with emphasis on the tasks of editing magazines and business publications. . . . Applicants must finish their junior year in May or June and be heading for a full senior year that fall." Marlene Kahan, executive director, ASME, 575 Lexington Ave., New York, NY 10022.

- Student Intern Program for the Specialized Business Press, Business Press Educational Foundation. Deadline Nov. 30. "Most interns are juniors with majors in journalism, English, business or technical writing. Many have dual majors or areas of specialization." Phyllis Reed, Business Press Educational Foundation, Suite 400, 675 Third Ave., New York, NY 10017-5704.

- Whittle Communications Editorial Internships. Deadlines, March 1 (for summer), June 9 (for fall), Oct. 6 (for winter), Dec. 8 (for spring). "Interns write articles of varying lengths for publication. They also conduct research and help develop story ideas. . . . Applicants should have some experience in writing news or feature stories and should possess research skills." Kathey Gentry, Edit Internships, Whittle Communications, 505 Market St., Knoxville, Tenn. 37902.

Index